THIRD EDITION

Understanding and Using Microcomputers

THIRD EDITION

Understanding and Using Microcomputers

Steven M. Zimmerman
College of Business and Management Studies
University of South Alabama

Leo M. Conrad
Imagineering Concepts, Inc.
Mobile, Alabama

West Publishing Company
St. Paul   New York   Los Angeles   San Francisco

Printed in the United States of America

98 97 96 95 94 93 92 91   8 7 6 5 4 3 2 1 0

Library of Congress Cataloging-in-Publication Data

Zimmerman, Steven M.
  Understanding and using microcomputers / Steven M. Zimmerman, Leo
M. Conrad. -- 3rd ed.
    p. cm. -- (The Microcomputing series)
  Includes bibliographical references.
  ISBN 0-314-76172-1
  1. Business--Data processing. 2. Microcomputers--Programming.
I. Conrad, Leo M. II. Title. III. Series.
HF5548.2.Z58 1991
650′ .0285′416--dc20   90-39182
                                                 CIP

Copy editor: *Mary Berry, Naples Editing Services*
Text design: *John Edeen*
Compositor: *Carlisle Communications*
Artwork: *Rolin Graphics*
Index: *Jo-Anne Naples, Naples Editing Services*

Registered Trademarks

Ability is a trademark of Xanaro Technologies, Inc.; Allways, Lotus Freelance, Lotus Freelance Plus, Lotus Manuscript, Lotus 1-2-3, and Symphony are trademarks of Lotus Development Corporation; Amiga and PET computer are trademarks of Commodore Business Machines, Inc.; Animator, AutoCad, and AutoSketch are trademarks of AutoDesk, Inc.; Apple I, Apple II, Apple IIc, Apple IIe, Apple III, Apple DOS, Apple HyperCard, Apple Macintosh, Apple Macintosh DOS, Apple Macintosh Plus, and Hyper-Pad are trademarks of Apple Computer, Inc.; Atlas*Graphics, Stat-Graphics, and GB Stat are trademarks of Strategic Locations Planning, Inc.; Compaq i486, Compaq LTE, Compaq Portable II, and Compaq Portable III are trademarks of Compaq Computer Corporation; CompuServe and CompuServe Information Services are trademarks of H & R Block Company; ComputerEyes is a trademark of Digital Vision, Inc.; CP/M is a copyright of Digital Research Corporation; dBASE III Plus, dBASE IV, and Map-Master are trademarks of Ashton-Tate; DEC Rainbow is a trademark of Digital Equipment Corporation; DeskMate, EasyNet, and Laplink III are trademarks of Traveling Software; DESQview is a trademark of Quarterdeck Office Systems; Dow Jones News/Retrieval Service is a trademark of Dow Jones & Company; Electric Pencil is copyrighted by Michael Schrayer; Ethernet and Xerox 8010 Star are trademarks of Xerox Corporation; Excel, Microsoft BASIC, Microsoft Chart, Microsoft Windows, Microsoft Windows-Paint, Microsoft Word, Microsoft Works, MS-DOS, Multiplan, PC DOS, and Xenix are trademarks of Microsoft Corporation; ExpressCalc is a trademark of Express Ware; Fancy-Fonts is a trademark of Softcraft, Inc.; Financial Action Service Terminal (F.A.S.T.) is a trademark of Dean Witter Company; FONTASTIC is a trademark of IHS Systems; Frieze, Publisher's Paintbrush, and Publisher's Type Foundry are trademarks of ZSoft; Gem is a trademark of Digital Research Inc.; Graph-in-the Box and Graph-in-the-Box Analytic are trademarks of New England Software, Inc.; Harvard Graphics, pfs:Graph, and pfs:Professional Write are trademarks of Software Publishing Corporation; HiJaak and InSet are trademarks of Inset Systems; Home-Base

(continued on page 436)

To our students

Contents in Brief

PART IV

Microcomputer Software and Hardware Selection   355

APPENDIXES

Appendixes   381

Glossary   403

Index   427

Contents

PART I

Microcomputer Foundations   1

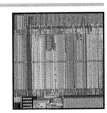

CHAPTER 1

Microcomputers   2

PART II

Microcomputer Applications   91

CHAPTER 4

Word Processing   92

CHAPTER 5

Spreadsheet Programs   **126**

CHAPTER 6

Data-driven Graphics   **178**

PART III

Microcomputer Communication and Integration

CHAPTER 10

Communication and Local Area Networks   296

CHAPTER 11

Operations and Data File Integration   336

Publisher's Note

This book is part of THE MICROCOMPUTING SERIES. This series was started in 1985 and quickly grew to provide the most comprehensive series of textbooks dealing with microcomputer applications software. We intend to continue the high standards of our earlier books as we expand the number of software topics and provide a flexible set of instructional materials. This unique series currently includes five different types of books:

1. *Understanding and Using Microcomputers, Third Edition* is a general concepts book that teaches basic hardware and software philosophy and applications. This provides the student with a general overview of microcomputer fundamentals including history, social issues, and a synopsis of the software and hardware applications.

2. A series of hands-on laboratory tutorials are entitled *Understanding and Using . . .*; they are software specific and cover a wide range of individual packages. These manuals, written at an introductory level, are both self-paced tutorials and complete reference guides. A complete list of series titles can be found on the following pages.

3. Several larger volumes combining DOS with three applications software packages are available in different combinations. These texts are titled *Understanding and Using Application Software.* They condense components of the individual lab manuals and add conceptual coverage for courses that require both software tutorials and microcomputer concepts in a single volume.

4. *Essentials of Application Software* workbooks, new in 1991, serve as introductory tutorials, combining three applications software packages with DOS. These books focus on the software and omit coverage of more general microcomputing concepts. This series will provide skill development for classes that use a separate text for general concepts and issues.

5. A series of advanced-level, hands-on lab manuals provide a strong project/systems orientation. These are titled *Developing and Using. . . .*

THE MICROCOMPUTING SERIES has been successful in providing you with a full range of applications books to suit your individual needs. We remain committed to excellence in offering the widest variety of current software packages. In addition, we are committed to producing microcomputing texts that provide you both the coverage you desire and also the level and format most appropriate for your students. The Acquisitions Editor of the series is Rick Leyh of West Publishing; the Consulting Editor is Steve Ross of Western Washington University. We are continually planning for future volumes in this series. Please send us your comments and suggestions.

We now offer these books in THE MICROCOMPUTING SERIES:

General Concepts

Understanding and Using Microcomputers, Third Edition by Steven M. Zimmerman and Leo M. Conrad

Operating Systems

Understanding and Using MS-DOS/PC DOS: The First Steps, 2nd Edition by Laura B. Ruff and Mary K. Weitzer

Understanding and Using MS-DOS/PC DOS: A Complete Guide by Cody T. Copeland and Jonathan P. Bacon

Understanding and Using MS-DOS/PC DOS: Hard Disk Edition by Cody T. Copeland and Jonathan P. Bacon

Understanding and Using MS-DOS/PC DOS 4.0 by Jonathan P. Bacon

Programming Languages

Understanding and Using MICROSOFT BASIC/IBM-PC BASIC by Mary L. Howard

Word Processors

Understanding and Using Displaywrite 4 by Patsy H. Lund and Barbara A. Hayden

Understanding and Using Microsoft Word by Jonathan P. Bacon

Understanding and Using Microsoft Word 5.0 by Jonathan P. Bacon

Understanding and Using Multimate by Mary K. Weitzer and Laura B. Ruff

Understanding and Using PC-Write by Victor P. Maiorana

Understanding and Using PFS:WRITE by Mary K. Weitzer and Laura B. Ruff

Understanding and Using WordPerfect by Patsy H. Lund, Barbara A. Hayden, and Sharon S. Larsen

Understanding and Using WordPerfect 4.2 by Patsy H. Lund and Barbara A. Hayden

Understanding and Using WordPerfect 5.0 by Patsy H. Lund

Understanding and Using WordPerfect 5.1 by Cody T. Copeland
and Jonathan P. Bacon

Understanding and Using WordStar by Steven C. Ross

Understanding and Using WordStar 4.0 by Patsy H. Lund and Barbara A. Hayden

Spreadsheet Packages

Understanding and Using Lotus 1-2-3 by Steven C. Ross

Understanding and Using Lotus 1-2-3 Release 2 by Steven C. Ross

Understanding and Using Lotus 1-2-3 Release 2.2 by Steven C. Ross

Understanding and Using Lotus 1-2-3 Release 3 by Steven C. Ross

Understanding and Using SuperCalc 3 by Steven C. Ross and Judy
A. Reinders

Understanding and Using SuperCalc 4 by Judy A. Reinders and
Steven C. Ross

Understanding and Using VP-Planner Plus by Steven C. Ross

Database Packages

Understanding and Using dBASE III (Including dBASE II) by Steven
C. Ross

Understanding and Using dBASE III PLUS, 2nd Edition by Steven C.
Ross

Understanding and Using dBASE IV by Steven C. Ross

Understanding and Using PFS:FILE/REPORT by Laura B. Ruff and
Mary K. Weitzer

Understanding and Using R:Base 5000 (Including R:Base System V)
by Karen L. Watterson

Integrated Software

Understanding and Using AppleWorks (Including AppleWorks 2.0) by
Frank Short

Understanding and Using Educate-Ability by Victor P. Maiorana and
Arthur A. Strunk

Understanding and Using FRAMEWORK by Karen L. Watterson

Understanding and Using Microsoft Works on the Macintosh by Gary
Bitter

Understanding and Using Microsoft Works on the IBM PC by Gary
Bitter

Developing and Using Office Applications with AppleWorks by M. S.
Varnon

Understanding and Using PFS:First Choice by Seth A. Hock

Understanding and Using Symphony by Enzo Allegretti

Combined Books

Understanding and Using Application Software, Volume 1: DOS, WordStar 4.0, Lotus 1-2-3 Release 2, dBASE III PLUS by Steven C. Ross, Patsy H. Lund, Barbara A. Hayden

Understanding and Using Application Software, Volume 2: DOS, WordPerfect 4.2, Lotus 1-2-3 Release 2, dBASE III PLUS by Steven C. Ross, Patsy H. Lund, Barbara A. Hayden

Understanding and Using Application Software, Volume 3: DOS, WordPerfect 4.2, VP-Planner Plus, dBASE III PLUS by Steven C. Ross and Patsy H. Lund

Understanding and Using Application Software, Volume 4: DOS, WordPerfect 5.0, Lotus 1-2-3 Release 2, dBASE IV by Patsy H. Lund, Jonathan P. Bacon, and Steven C. Ross

Understanding and Using Application Software, Volume 5: DOS, WordPerfect 5.0/5.1, Lotus 1-2-3 Release 2.2, dBASE III PLUS by Steven C. Ross, Jonathan P. Bacon, and Cody T. Copeland

Understanding and Using Share-Ware Application Software: DOS, PC-Write, ExpressCalc, and PC-File by Victor P. Maiorana

Introductory Tutorials

Essentials of Application Software, Volume 1: DOS, WordPerfect 5.0/5.1, Lotus 1-2-3 Release 2.2, dBASE III PLUS by Steven C. Ross, Jonathan P. Bacon, and Cody T. Copeland

Advanced Books

Developing and Using Decision Support Applications by Steven C. Ross, Richard J. Penlesky, and Lloyd D. Doney

Developing and Using Microcomputer Business Systems by Kathryn W. Huff

Preface

In 1986, when *Understanding and Using Microcomputers* was first published, the microcomputer revolution was beginning. The microcomputing course was taking form and included coverage of hardware, operating systems, word processing, spreadsheets, and database topics.

The second edition, published in 1988, required tremendous updating due to the many changes in software and hardware. The capability of microcomputers to communicate with central computers and with one another over cable or telephone lines had expanded rapidly. Local area networks grew from dream to reality, and protocols for improving the communications became common. Programs were developed to handle data-driven and image-driven graphics. The field continued to change at an incredibly rapid pace.

The third edition of *Understanding and Using Microcomputers* is built on the foundation of these two prior editions and continues to reflect the rapid changes occurring in student needs, in microcomputer hardware and software capabilities, and in the microcomputing courses themselves. Some of the hardware and software innovations discussed in this edition include the growth of hardware speed, support equipment (such as scanners), desktop publishing, communications, and software that integrates graphics with text on quality printers. In addition, three appendixes have been added for those programs that include material on decision support systems, artificial intelligence, and BASIC.

Although the capabilities of microcomputers have grown so that more than an introductory course is required to understand them all, the student must still learn the basics of word processing, spreadsheets, and databases. This book is intended to help microcomputer users learn these basics about microcomputing rather than to train them in the use of specific application programs. Through a systematic approach, our readers will learn about the concepts of word processing, spreadsheets, data-driven and image-driven graphics, databases, desktop publishing, communications, and integrated programs. The first three chapters of this text provide a general overview, a detailed look at micrcomputer hardware, and an examination of the disk operating system (DOS). Once past these foundation chapters, the reader will be able to learn about the concepts and uses of a variety of software applications.

This textbook is neither software nor machine specific, and a variety of products are used as illustrations. Generally, the more popular hardware and software have been selected to show the various aspects of microcomputers; any mention of specific manufacturers is meant to elucidate key concepts.

Flexibility of Organization

Understanding and Using Microcomputers, third edition, is designed to afford flexibility of topical order so that material can be used out of sequence without disrupting the flow. For example, the word processing, spreadsheet, and database chapters are all independent. However, the nature of some topics—such as desktop publishing—requires foundations in both word processing and graphics.

Part I: Microcomputer Foundations includes the three foundation chapters, which cover an overview of microcomputers and how they fit into our society, the hardware of microcomputers, and the disk operating system. This section also includes an introduction to the problem of computer viruses and the social issues associated with using computers. We recommend that the foundation chapters be covered first by all students.

Part II: Microcomputer Applications includes a series of software chapters covering word processing, spreadsheets, data-driven graphics, databases, image-driven graphics, and desktop publishing. With the exception of desktop publishing, which integrates word processing and graphics, the chapters in this section can be presented in any order.

Part III: Microcomputer Communication and Integration includes a chapter on communications and a chapter on integrated programs. It is easier for the student to understand these chapters if a number of the chapters in Part II are studied first.

Part IV: Microcomputer Software and Hardware Selection consists of a single, final chapter. It is not necessary to cover all of the text before studying this chapter, but we recommend that a foundation of word processing, spreadsheets, and database be studied before beginning this section.

Appendixes on decision support systems (DDS), artificial intelligence (AI), and BASIC have been provided as optional material. These can be covered at any point, although the basics of microcomputing should be learned first.

Changes in This Edition

Many new developments in both hardware and software have occurred since the printing of the second edition of *Understanding and Using Microcomputers.* Advances in hardware and hardware speed, graphics techniques, desktop publishing, and other areas have come about due to user demands and increased microcomputer capabilities. This text attempts to cover the latest progress within these spheres. Specific changes in this edition include the following:

Color. This edition introduces color to assist the student in learning basic concepts. Color is used pedagogically to add interest and readability to important material and to illustrate key concepts and learning aids. This has the added benefit of showing how the use of color affects and emphasizes a presentation, which is important in computer graphics and desktop publishing.

Desktop Publishing. Due to great strides in desktop publishing, the third edition covers this topic in a full chapter. The manner in which computers control printer font selection and the number of fonts available have changed since the second edition of this text. At the time the second edition was published, few printers had a fraction of their current capability to create a variety of font sizes and styles. In addition, word processors and desktop publishing programs can now display a page that closely matches the output generated on a printer. The page preview capabilities of word processors are also examined in the third edition.

Graphics. The popularity of desktop publishing has increased with the use of the Apple Macintosh and has forced a general improvement in the hardware and software that create and display graphics. In the first and second editions, graphics was contained in a single chapter. In this third edition, there are three chapters that examine the use of graphics, with one on data-driven graphics, one on image-driven graphics, and one on desktop publishing. Furthermore, the text integrates graphics created by the software covered in the text to develop illustrations; users can see some of the potential for graphics with these examples.

Software Releases. The application software discussed in this edition was selected from the most popular programs. Many of the features covered in the basic chapters did not exist at the time of the second edition. For example, the capability to integrate graphics and text was just being developed when the second edition was created. Every attempt has been made to make this text current as of 1991; however, the field of software changes rapidly, and today's software may become quickly outdated with the advent of tomorrow's new releases.

Decision Support Systems. An appendix on DSS provides an overview of this rapidly expanding area of computer-assisted management decision making. Examples and comparison tables of some of the programs in accounting, statistics, and management science are included, such as SPSS, MINITAB, StatGraphics, and STORM.

Artificial Intelligence. An appendix on AI discusses computer operations resembling human intelligence. Examples and illustrations of how to use an expert system are provided, as well as the utilization of the VP-Expert program.

BASIC. An appendix was created to help the user learn to use BASIC programs. Discussion of how to review BASIC files on a disk and the importance of looking for READ.ME files are in this appendix, together with other general topics.

Proven Pedagogy

Among the pedagogy used in the third edition are Micros in Action, key terms (defined in both the text and the margins), structured review questions, discussion and application questions, and laboratory assignments.

Micros in Action

Micros in Action are boxed sections that introduce real examples of how concepts are used in practice. They provide a context for discussing and understanding microcomputing topics and applications and are meant to stimulate and enhance class discussion and student learning.

Margin Definitions

Learning about microcomputers begins with an understanding of the language used to describe the component parts of microcomputing. Thus, important terms are boldfaced and defined where first introduced, and the definition of each key term is presented in the margin to reinforce student comprehension. All key terms are also listed at the end of each chapter and in the Glossary.

Review Questions

Review questions help focus the user's attention on the important aspects of each chapter. Twenty short-answer essay questions per chapter will reinforce the student's learning the major topics discussed.

Discussion and Application Questions

Discussion and application questions force the reader to go beyond the textbook to look for microcomputer applications in school or in the workplace. Readers are asked to look for information about microcomputers in local retail stores, newspapers, and magazines.

Laboratory Assignments

For courses that emphasize hands-on use of application software, we have included multiple laboratory exercises at the end of each chapter. These serve as brief tutorials, and their objective is to provide the user with a large variety of problems from which to choose. The number of activities depends upon the subject of the chapter; most exercises are designated as appropriate for accounting, economics, algebra, and general business, as well as general word processing and database.

Supplements

This third edition includes a number of support products that can be obtained to supplement the textbook. They include an instructor's manual; a test bank; transparency masters; a computer test generator (Westest); and *Essentials of Application Software, Volume 1*, an application software text containing coverage of DOS, WordPerfect 5.0 and 5.1, Lotus 1-2-3 (Release 2.2), and dBASE III PLUS software packages, an accompanying instructor's manual, and a data disk.

Instructor's Manual

The instructor's manual, prepared by Steven M. Zimmerman in association with Richard Daughenbaugh of the University of South Alabama has been expanded for the third edition. It contains additional problems, suggestions on course organization, integrated cases, and answers to the text exercises.

Test Bank

The test bank contains over one thousand multiple-choice, fill-in, and true-false questions prepared specifically for this edition. The test bank is available upon request on Westest, a PC-based test generator.

Transparency Masters

A set of transparency masters of key figures and concepts summarizing important topics as discussed in the text is provided for classroom use.

Software Applications Manual

Essentials of Application Software, Volume 1, a software applications manual for use with operating systems (DOS), word processing (WordPerfect 5.0 and 5.1), spreadsheets (Lotus 1-2-3 [Release 2.2]), and database (dBASE III PLUS), is written by Steven C. Ross, Jonathan P. Bacon, and Cody T. Copeland. This workbook provides complete introductory tutorials on the above software packages without discussion of microcomputing concepts. It is appropriate for classes emphasizing hands-on skills development and is available with or without educational versions of WordPerfect 4.2, VP-Planner Plus, and dBASE III PLUS. Its features include a great number of guided activities and exercises. An instructor's manual and student data disk accompany the application software text.

Acknowledgments

We would like to thank the following reviewers for their helpful comments during our revision of this text:

Eric Bloom
Bentley College

S. Mahesh
University of New Orleans

John E. Castek
University of Wisconsin—LaCrosse

Hugh McHenry
Memphis State University

William Nelson Coxe, Jr.
Louisiana State University

George P. Novotny
Ferris State College

Nikunj Dalal
Texas Tech University

Helen O'Brien
Pima Community College

Donna Elsdon
California State University,
Bakersfield

Len Proctor
University of Saskatchewan

Charles Evans
University of Mississippi

Chuck Riden
Arizona State University

Catherine Holloway
Tidewater Community College

Jeff O. Smith
University of Texas at Arlington

Thomas C. Irby
University of North Texas

Sandra Stalker
North Shore Community College

Robert Larsen
Texas State Technical Institute

Hamilton Stirling
University of South Florida

Many individuals helped in the effort to create this book. Among those helping were an outstanding team of educators who reviewed drafts of the manuscript for previous editions. We thank them for their time, their ideas and their commitment. They are: Bev Bilshausen, College of Dupage; Lloyd Brooks, Memphis State University; Carol Clark, St. Louis Community

College-Florissant Valley; David Cooper, University of Connecticut; Ilene Dlugoss, Cuyahoga Community College; Ben Guild, Wright State University; Don Lyndahl, Milwaukee Area Technical College; Robert Nau, Tulane University; Gregory Parsons, University of South Maine; Floyd Ploeger, Southwestern Texas State University; Tim Robinson, Ramapo College; Arthur Strunk, Queensborough Community College; Jack VanLuik, Mt. Hood Community College; Karen Watterson, Shoreline Community College; Jack Gilman, Florida International University; Russell Hari, Chemeketa Community College; R. Wayne Headrick, Texas A & M University; Cynthia Kachik, Santa Fe Community College; Jeanette Muzio, University of Florida; Norman McNeal, Sauk Valley College; Paul Saunders, Royal Business School; Ralph Shafer, George Washington University; Jimmy K. Tang, San Diego Community College; George Upchurch, Carson-Newman College; Karla Vogel, University of New Hampshire-Manchester; Michael R. Williams, Kirkwood Community College; George Bright, University of Houston; Elaine Daly, Oakton Community College; Cynthia J. Kachik, Sante Fe Community College; Norman McNeal, Sauk Valley College; Chris Moyer, Wright State University; Michael R. Williams, Kirkwood Community College.

The "Micros in Action" feature would not have been possible without: Carol A. Zimmerman of Commercial Investor Services, Inc.; Bart Johnson of Scott Paper Company; Aubrey Diehl of Schneider Fleming Insurance; Jean King of Jean King and Associates; John Hanley of Burnett-Wilson Inc., General Contractors; Frank Knippenberg of Dean Witter Reynolds; Robert Moore of Gleem Paint Center; Andres Aviles, Paul Reeves, and Stanley M. Zimmerman of International Software Consultants; and Bryan Nearn of Flautt and Mann Properties, Inc.

We would also like to thank our editors at West Publishing Company, Rick Leyh, Jessica Evans, and Susan Smart, for their help and guidance throughout the project. Many thanks to West Publishing production personnel Mary Garvey Verrill and Lori A. Zurn for a beautiful job on the text and cover respectively. A special note of appreciation goes to Mary Berry and Carol Zimmerman for their extra efforts, and to computer screen models Arthur, Nicole, and Samantha.

In addition, we would like to thank all of the manufacturers of the software mentioned throughout the text. This text would not have been possible without their help. We would like to acknowledge the makers of the software packages WordPerfect and InSet in particular. The manuscript was prepared using WordPerfect for word processing and InSet for graphics integration.

We are very interested to hear about your experience with *Understanding and Using Microcomputers*, third edition. If you have comments or suggestions, please write to the following address:

Steven M. Zimmerman
College of Business and Management Studies
University of South Alabama
Mobile, AL 36688

Steven M. Zimmerman
Leo M. Conrad

PART I

Microcomputer Foundations

CHAPTER 1

Microcomputers

Goals

Upon completion of this chapter, you will be able to do the following:

- Understand how the microcomputer is used.

- Define a microcomputer from several points of view.

- Discuss the history of computers and microcomputers.

- Identify some of the social, moral, and legal issues involved with using microcomputers.

Outline

Getting Started

Mary LeNissa, a transfer student, found herself wandering into the campus bookstore on a dreary day. She had just come from the registrar's office, where she had received her class assignments for the next quarter. Once inside, Mary examined her class schedule and reviewed the posted book list. On her schedule was a computer literacy course.

Her parents had promised to help her purchase a computer when she needed one. Mary decided to do a little shopping. She walked over to the area where a number of computers were displayed. She walked around and listened to several students talking about their computer needs. The more she listened, the more confused she became.

Mary next checked the bulletin boards to see if any used computers were available. There were a few computers for sale. The advertisements and comments she was overhearing created more confusion in her mind. She decided to wait until class before making a computer purchase decision.

After attending a few lectures, she found there were two important considerations to make in her decision:

- Identify the programs she would use.
- Identify which computers other students were using so she could exchange files.

Mary's computer literacy course required her to use some application programs. Included in these programs were student versions of WordPerfect (a word processing program), VP-Planner (a spreadsheet program), and dBASE III Plus (a database program). She found out that if she selected business as a major, these programs would be used over and over again. If she selected education or engineering as a major, these programs she needed would run on an Apple Macintosh. She decided to wait until she selected her major before purchasing a computer.

The microcomputer is a recent arrival on the computer scene. This chapter describes the uses and parts of the microcomputer, as well as outlines the history of computers and microcomputers. It also examines historical and future trends of software developed for microcomputers, because accomplishing objectives depends on software. Along with the rapid changes and increases in capabilities that have occurred in microcomputers, a number of business, legal, moral, and social issues have developed. This chapter examines these issues as well.

In this chapter we also start building a microcomputer vocabulary. We define many terms. Some of the definitions are simplified for introductory purposes and are enhanced later in the text.

The microcomputer is an important tool when combined with programs, because it can be used to increase personal and business produc-

Program
A set of instructions telling the computer how to perform a task.

Software
Programs.

tivity and to facilitate information processing. A **program** is a set of instructions telling the computer how to perform a task. The Micros in Action "Getting Started" illustrates how programs are important when selecting a computer. Combined with **software,** the microcomputer is often credited with being "powerful," meaning it has many capabilities to accomplish a variety of objectives.

Application programs are programs designed to perform a specific task, such as producing professional documents (word processing programs); making analyses (electronic spreadsheet programs); maintaining lists of customers, clients, and inventories (database programs); producing presentations (business graphics programs); communicating with other computers (communication and networking); integrating or combining several of these tasks (integrated programs); and performing specialized functions, such as accounting (specialized application programs). There are three levels of application programs:

General application programs: word processors, spreadsheets, graphics, and communications.
Specialized application programs: general ledgers, tax forms, analysis, inventory control, and quality control.
Custom application programs: programs created by a programmer for a specific purpose in a specific organization.

Operating system
The program that directs the flow of data and instructions among the parts of the microcomputer, the user, and the application program; often called the disk operating system (DOS or OS).

The microcomputer is a valuable productivity tool, because programs called **operating systems** have been developed to make the microcomputer easy for the user to control. The operating system is the controller, similar to a police officer directing traffic flow. The operating system directs the flow of data and instructions among the parts of the microcomputer, the user, and application programs (see Figure 1–1). The microcomputer as a personal computer is used by individuals to increase personal productivity in solving problems, as well as a productivity tool.

The user of a large central computer system is expected to have some knowledge of how the computer works, how to use the operating system, and sometimes how to program the computer. The microcomputer user expects the microcomputer and its programs to be designed to solve problems. The microcomputer and its programs and **documentation** are expected to be user friendly. Documentation is the narrative supplied with programs to help users operate the software. User friendly means that the software and documentation is easy for a target user group to use. If a user is not a part of the target user group, the program and documentation may not be user friendly.

Documentation
Narrative supplied with programs to help the user operate the software.

Microcomputer Functions

The microcomputer combined with software is a tool to enhance productivity by aiding in problem solving and making selected tasks easier. There are several general classifications of programs available for microcomputer software that are particularly valuable to the user: word processing;

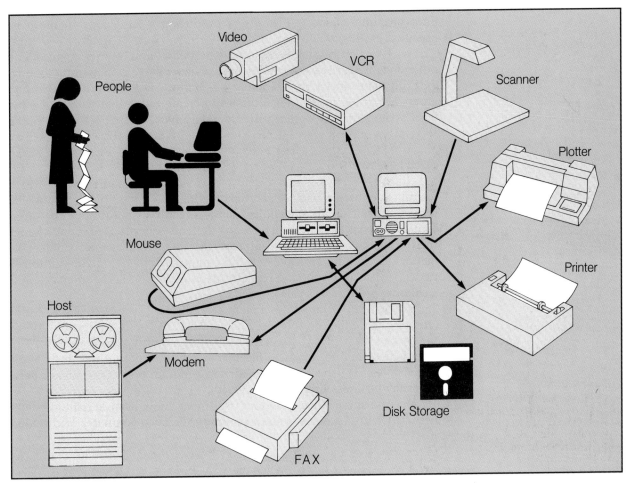

Figure 1–1
The Operating System Directs the Flow of Data and Instructions

spreadsheets; data-driven graphics; file and database management; image-driven graphics; decision support tools; communication with other computers; local area networks; and combinations of the above. Most of these types of software are reviewed in this text. It is a list of what we believe is important for you to learn about microcomputers.

Word Processing

A **word processing program** produces good-looking documents more quickly and accurately than a typewriter. Its capabilities include creating, editing, and formatting text; saving and retrieving text files; and printing text files.

     Creating text is the entering of characters (usually through the keyboard), and editing is making changes in the text entered. Formatting is the organizing of text for display and printing. Saving is recording the text for future use. Retrieving is the reading of a computer file from the disk

Word processing program
A program to aid an individual in creating/editing/formatting, saving/retrieving, and printing of text.

into computer memory. Printing is producing a hard copy in the form specified by the edited material.

Word processing is the production of letters, reports, memos, and other documents. It also includes the use of spelling, grammar, footnoting, indexing, and document assembly capabilities. Document assembly programs are often used in legal offices to create individual wills and other legal documents from prerecorded paragraphs.

Spreadsheets

Spreadsheet program
A program that helps users enter/edit, save/retrieve, calculate, and present results of numerical operations.

Spreadsheet programs are used for entering and editing data, saving and retrieving, calculating (formulas), and presenting data under the direct control of the end user, which means the end user may enter and change the formulas without the aid of a programmer. In a manner similar to a manual accounting spreadsheet, the computer screen is divided into columns (vertical division) and rows (horizontal division). The intersection of a column and a row is called a cell.

Figure 1–2 illustrates a manual accounting spreadsheet for posting (entering the data into the spreadsheet). Figure 1–3 is the form found on the back of the report you receive from your monthly bank statement. This form is designed to help you balance your checkbook. It is a good application of a spreadsheet. The spreadsheet program helps the end user solve everyday business problems and tasks.

The spreadsheet program user must know how to solve the business problem but needs only a minimum of microcomputer knowledge.

Figure 1–2
A Manual Accounting Spreadsheet

(a)   General Journal   Page 1

Date 19XX		Description	Post. Ref.	Debit	Credit
	1	CASH	11	15000	
		OWNERS EQUITY, STACEY CAPITAL	31		15000
		STACEY CONTRIBUTED FUNDS TO THE			
		BUSINESS			
	2	TRUCK	15	4000	
		CASH	11		4000
	2	EQUIPMENT	17	1800	
		CASH	11		1000
		ACCOUNT PAYABLE	21		800
		EQUIPMENT FOR BUS $ 1000 DOWN			
		BALANCE DUE IN 30 DAYS			

IMPORTANT Please examine this statement immediately. We will assume that the balances it shows are correct unless you notify us of any disagreement within 60 days

BALANCING YOUR CHECKING AND SAVINGS ACCOUNT

Before you start, please be sure you enter ***In your checkbook or savings register*** any interest earned, automatic transactions or bank charges includig those shown on this statement.

A. Enter deposits not shown on this statement.

date of deposit	amount

Total A

B. Enter all checks, withdrawals and bank charges not shown on this statement

outstanding check number	amount

Total B

Follow instructions below to compare transactions recorded on your statement with those in your checkbook.

NEW BALANCE shown on other side

PLUS Total A ______

EQUALS ______

MINUS Total B ______

EQUALS your current checkbook balance ______

Figure 1–3
Checkbook Balancing Form

Any problem that can be solved with pencil, paper, and calculator can be solved using a spreadsheet program.

Data-driven Graphics

Data-driven graphics programs help individuals create charts such as area, bar, high-low, line, and xy charts, often referred to as business charts. Business charts are explained in detail in Chapter 6. Data-driven programs are available to create normal charts and maps and to integrate images of all types for data presentations (Figure 1–4). These programs are often used to make presentations to customers or supervisors more interesting and clear than lists, words, or tables would be. The data from spreadsheet or database programs can be used to prepare graphics presentations without the need to re-enter the data.

Data-driven graphics program
A program to create/edit/format area, bar, high-low, line, and similar types of graphs; to save/retrieve data; and to print results on a printer or plotter.

File and Database Management

File and database management programs help users create/edit (update), save/retrieve, and sort and organize data. Data are facts that have been collected, organized, and saved. A **database** is a collection of data saved in a microcomputer that is used for a variety of purposes. File and database management programs help turn data into information (data organized into a useful form). The entering/editing, saving/retrieving, sorting/orga-

Database
A collection of data saved in a microcomputer that is used for a variety of purposes.

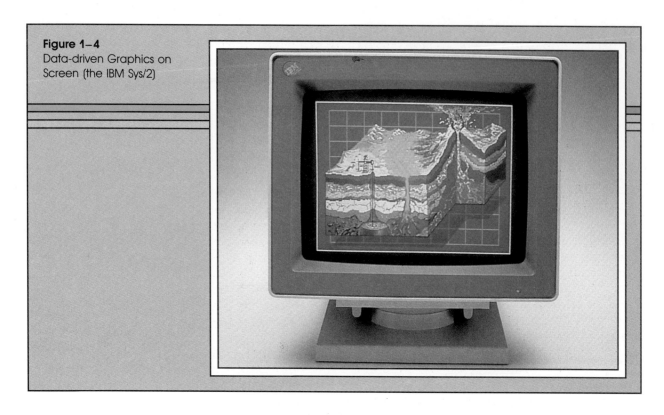

Figure 1–4
Data-driven Graphics on Screen (the IBM Sys/2)

File management program
A program to create/edit (update), save/retrieve, process data saved in a single file, and print reports.

Database management program
A program to create/edit (update), input format/datastructure/ data/ output format, process data saved in one or more files, save/retrieve data saved in one or more files, and print reports.

Programming language
A language used by programmers to create/edit and save/retrieve instructions tocomputers.

nizing, and using of saved data should be controlled by managerial guidelines so that the objectives of the end user can be accomplished.

File management programs are often limited to helping users create/edit (update), save/retrieve, process (search, organize, and so on), and print reports using a single data file. **Database management programs** create/edit (update), input format/data structure/data/output format, process data saved in one or more data files, save/retrieve data in one or more files, create/edit/save/retrieve report formats, and print reports. Database management programs may include complete application programs with an objective such as an inventory system, or they may include **programming languages** in which many different applications can be created. A programming language can be used by programmers to create/edit and save/retrieve instructions to computers. Often database management programs handle a number of data files. The objective, the skills available, the cost of the programs, and the microcomputer available determine which option is better.

Databases include customer mailing lists, inventory lists, employee records, student records and grades, credit information, medical records, pharmaceutical records, research reports, social security data, and so on. Microcomputers with the addition of database programs can be used to manage and maintain many organizational databases.

Hypertext is the nonsequential linkage of ideas in a database. It involves the presentation, linkage, and filtering of data. Hypertext concepts are used in Apple's HyperCard to make it easy for users to perform information management tasks. These programs have routines for the creation of customized reports and data organization. Figure 1–5 illustrates an Apple Macintosh using a program that integrates text with graphics.

Image-driven Graphics

Image-driven graphics programs help users create/edit, save/retrieve, and print images. These programs can be used for free-hand drawing (presentation) or engineering/scientific graphics.

Image-driven graphics programs can combine art and photography (on the screen) with data for sales and other presentations. The graphics capabilities of the microcomputer include the handling of television pictures and their combination with microcomputer output. Marketing managers are interested in these capabilities for their potential in advertising. Figures 1–6 and 1–7 are examples of the scanning capabilities available in microcomputers to enter images into image-driven graphics programs. A **scan** uses a device for sensing printed material (text and graphics) or images and entering them into a computer system.

Engineering/scientific graphics include computer-aided design (CAD), computer-aided engineering (CAE), and computer-aided design and drafting (CADD), among other similar applications. Figure 1–8 is an example of engineering graphics in use. Other image-driven graphics programs include animation and the creation of custom letters.

Image-driven graphics program
A program that helps the user create/edit, save/retrieve, and print images.

Scan
The use of a device for sensing printed material (text and graphics) or images and entering them into a computer system.

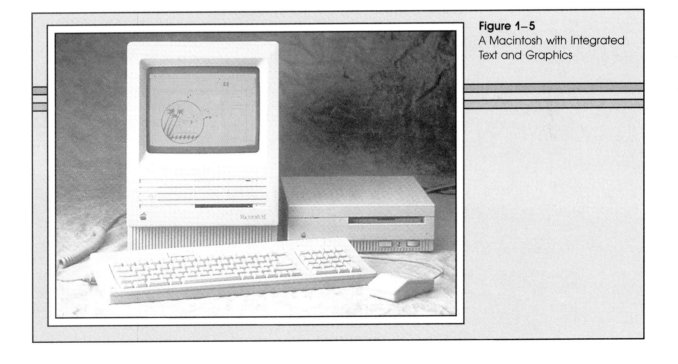

Figure 1–5
A Macintosh with Integrated Text and Graphics

Figure 1–6

Scanning a Photo Using a
Hewlett-Packard ScanJet

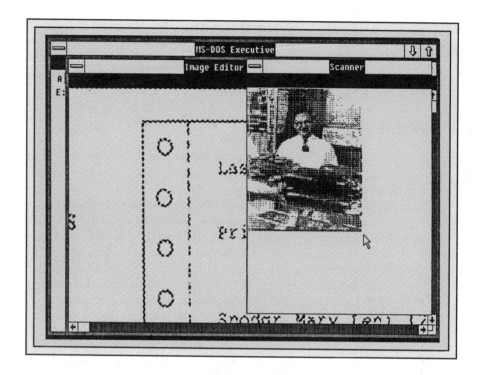

Communication

Communication software
Programs that allow users to use
computers to communicate with
each other, including the transfer of
files.

Communication software, with the addition of communication hardware, are programs that make it possible for microcomputers to communicate with most other computers. The microcomputer can act as a dumb terminal (one that can communicate only under the control of an operator using the keyboard) or as a smart terminal (one that can transfer files between two computers). The capability to communicate requires a modem (a device to connect the computer to a telephone) or a null-modem (a device that makes the computer behave as if it were connected to a telephone). Cables and software complete the communication needs.

Desktop Publishing

Desktop publishing software
Programs that help users
create/edit/transfer, format/integrate
text and graphics, save/retrieve,
and print/typeset output on a
quality output device.

Desktop publishing software are programs that help users create/edit/ transfer, format/integrate text and graphics, save/retrieve, and print/typeset output on a quality output device. As shown in the Micros in Action "Majoring in Journalism," a number of computer systems will perform desktop publishing. Text and graphics can be created and edited in a desktop publishing program, but it is usually easier to transfer them via a file from a word

Figure 1–7
Results of the Photo Scan

processor or graphics program than to create them in a desk top publishing program. Aldus PageMaker is an example of desktop publishing software.

Integrated Programs

Integrated programs combine the features of one or more general programs. Integrated programs often combine word processing, spreadsheet, data-driven graphics, database, communication, and (in a few cases) image-driven graphics program capabilities.

Integrated program
A program that combines the capabilities of two or more general or specific application programs.

Figure 1–8
Engineering Graphics with
the Hewlett-Packard Integral
PC

Majoring in Journalism

Near the end of the term, Mary decided to select journalism as her major. She visited the journalism department and examined the computer equipment being used. She asked about the programs used and the systems being used by advanced students.

She found out that both the department and individuals used either IBM PC compatibles or Apple Macintoshes. Some of the Apple Macintoshes had disk drives that read disks created by the IBM compatibles.

Because she had a choice, Mary decided to comparison shop for a small, low-price laptop. She selected her system based on her needs.

Decision Support Tools

The management teams of most organizations use many programs either directly or indirectly for decision making. When programs help management make decisions, they are called decision support tools. Among the decision support tools available to management are specialized application programs, artificial intelligence programs, and decision support system programs.

Specialized Application Programs

Specialized application programs help those who need to solve a specific problem. Examples include statistical, accounting, inventory, payroll, real estate evaluation, or project management programs, as well as others. Figure 1–9 shows a profit-and-loss statement produced by an application program on a microcomputer and printer.

A common approach to creating special programs is to design them for a vertical market—a narrow market limited to a specific user area. Examples of vertical markets are accountants; medical doctors; veterinarians; and building contractors.

Decision Support System Programs

An integrated management information and planning system is a decision support system (DSS). Decision support system programs provide management with the ability to query its computer systems for information in a variety of ways, to analyze information, to integrate information from a number of application programs, and to predict the impact of decisions before they are made.

The programmer who creates a decision support system uses AI and computer behavioral, financial, economic, statistical, and mathematical models, among other tools. The DSS is the integrated set of tools that helps management make better decisions. See Chapter 7 and Appendix A for additional discussion.

Artificial Intelligence Programs

Intelligence is the ability to learn, to understand, and to deal with new situations. Intelligence is associated with human beings. Artificial intelligence (AI) is the art and science of making computers behave in a manner resembling intelligent human behavior. Artificial intelligence is used to create programs for end users. The end user is often not aware of the use of AI in the program.

Figure 1–9
Profit-and-Loss Statement

```
                        January 3, 1987

                 West Brook Real Estate
                    4151 Bay Lane Road
                  Mobile,Alabama 36605

        P r o f i t   and   L o s s   S t a t e m e n t

Revenue
Number Account      Current Period        Year to date
                    Amount      Percent   Amount      Percent
                    ----------------------------------------------
6010 Rent Inc       1,760.00    32        4,810.00    28
6020 Evaluation         0.00     0        4,116.39    24
6025 Mgt Serv.      2,701.75    49        2,701.75    16
6030 Capital          571.98    10        2,262.50    13
6040 Interest         364.37     7        1,708.19    10
6050 Consultant         0.00     0        1,000.00     6
6900 Misc. Co         124.00     2          496.00     3
                    -----------           ------------
                    $5,522.10             $17,094.83
                    ===========           ============


Expenses

Number Account      Current Period        Year to date
                    Amount      Percent   Amount      Percent
                    ----------------------------------------------
9100 Maintena         837.47    27        2,139.95    16
9200 Supplies          68.48     2        2,530.32    18
9300 Deprecia       1,286.37    42        5,145.48    37
9400 Interest         577.52    19        2,336.62    17
9500 Operatio         134.90     4          141.06     1
9501 Advertiz           0.00     0           36.30     0
9510 Utilitie           0.00     0          150.00     1
9520 Insuranc           0.00     0          117.17     1
9530 Taxes Re           0.00     0          435.95     3
9532 Other Ta           0.00     0            0.00     0
9540 Professi         133.40     4          240.73     2
9550 Travel (           0.00     0            0.00     0
9560 Local Au          52.70     2          246.33     2
9570 Medical            0.00     0          239.67     2
                    -----------           ------------
                    $3,090.84             $13,759.58
                    ===========           ============

Profit              $2,431.26             $3,335.25
```

One application of AI is the design and development of expert
systems. An expert system contains the decision-making rules of experts
that have been captured and saved in a computer. Expert systems can be
developed for a situation where a database exists, the decisions are based
on the facts saved in the database, and the decision process is relatively
simple. See Chapter 7 and Appendix B for additional discussion.

Microcomputer Costs

The cost of a microcomputer includes its purchase price, maintenance costs, and operational costs. These costs vary depending upon the location of the purchaser, the time in the life cycle of a microcomputer when it is purchased, the source from which it is purchased, the support included in the purchase price, and whether the purchase is in cash or on credit.

The user who purchases a microcomputer when the model is first introduced to the market might expect to pay full list price. After the initial sales period, the price usually drops, and some discounting is available.

Many users pay less than $2,000 for "full-featured" microcomputer systems. Few units, except ones with "extra capabilities," sell for more. Figure 1–10 shows a typical microcomputer system. A full-featured system includes most of the accessories available, a printer, and memory capacities equal to the standard of the time. Figure 1–11 illustrates a full-featured system. Extra capabilities are state-of-the-art developments that are being introduced. The extra capability feature of one year is often a standard feature the next year. Figure 1–12 shows an example of a system with an extra capability: electronic mail.

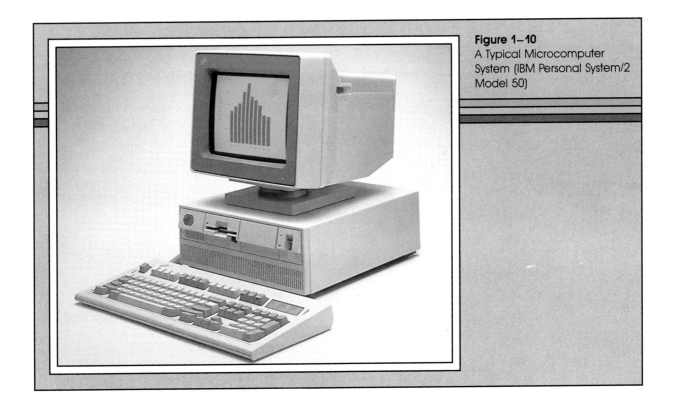

Figure 1–10
A Typical Microcomputer System (IBM Personal System/2 Model 50)

Figure 1–11
A Full-Featured System (Hewlett-Packard's Touchscreen II)

Figure 1–12
Electronic Mail (Hewlett-Packard NewWave Office)

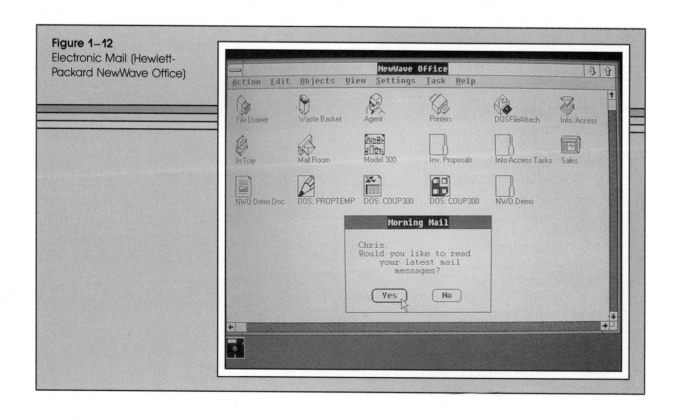

The purchase price is not the only cost consideration for micro-computers. Maintenance contracts are also available at extra cost. Most microcomputer systems are reliable and have minimal maintenance costs. However, business users may want to protect themselves with maintenance contracts that cover repairs on **hardware** (the part of a microcomputer you can see and feel). These annual contracts cost between 10 and 20 percent of the purchase price and are available from local computer dealers. Most problems may be avoided with periodic cleaning and careful use.

The cost of operating a microcomputer system also includes salaries, ribbons, and paper. The benefits obtained in terms of increased productivity mean that the cost of operating a microcomputer can be expected to be less than the cost of performing the same functions some other way. Chapter 12 will discuss business evaluation methods called breakeven and payback analysis. These techniques compare the cost of two alternate methods of doing a task and can aid you in determining which is best for your needs.

Hardware
The part of a microcomputer you can see and feel.

Microcomputer Parts

Microcomputer hardware consists of the following:

The system case, which contains, as a minimum, a microprocessor central processing unit (CPU), cards with circuits to control data storage devices, circuits to communicate with external devices, and chips containing the computer's internal memory random access memory (RAM) and read-only memory (ROM).

Input devices that connect the user to the computer, such as a keyboard, voice recognition device, bar code reader, and so on.

Output devices that show the user what the computer has done or is doing, such as a cathode ray tube (CRT), screen, monitor, telephone modem, printer, and plotter.

On-line data storage devices, such as a floppy disk drive, hard disk drive (fixed or removable), and tape recorder (tape backup units).

Inside the System Case

The core of the microcomputer is the microprocessor, an integrated circuit on a silicon chip that is the central processing unit (CPU). The CPU includes the arithmetic, logic, control, and memory units. Usually, the capabilities of microcomputers are contained on cards or boards with special circuits, such as ones that control data storage devices or that communicate with devices such as monitors and printers. The hardware that supports the CPU includes the memory of the microcomputer, read-only memory (ROM) and random access memory (RAM). ROM is memory with instructions (programs) needed when operating the microcomputer. The user cannot write data into ROM. RAM is memory used for data and program storage by the user. The user can write and read data in RAM.

Input Devices

The primary method of input from a human to a microcomputer is through a keyboard. Keyboards have many designs, but most are similar to that of a typewriter (Figure 1–13).

Output Devices

The primary method of output from a microcomputer to humans is cathode ray tube (CRT), also called a screen, monitor, or video display tube (VDT). The CRT looks like a television set. Input and output devices are often called **I/O**.

I/O device
Input and output device or method.

On-Line Data Storage

On-line data storage devices save (record) computer data and programs, but they are not electronically an internal part of the computer. On-line storage devices are sometimes referred to as secondary storage devices. In

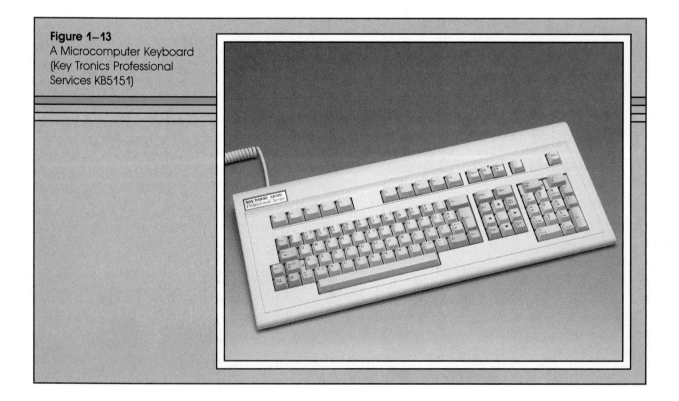

Figure 1–13
A Microcomputer Keyboard (Key Tronics Professional Services KB5151)

many microcomputers, these devices are mounted in the same case as the other parts, but they are electronically connected through special controller boards only. The methods of recording computer information include removable disk drives, hard disk drives, and large-format magnetic tape. Figure 1–14 shows a computer system with removable disk drives and a hard disk.

Microcomputer Sizes

The wide variety of sizes, shapes, capabilities, and designs among microcomputers makes it easy for the user to find a system that fits a particular need. A microcomputer can be one of four sizes: a desktop, a transportable, a laptop, or a pocket computer.

Desktop Microcomputers

A **desktop microcomputer** fits on a desk and requires an external power source (Figure 1–15). It may be a full-featured unit having all the parts usually found in a microcomputer at any given time. Desktop units may have large monitors and external on-line storage devices, as well as other

Desktop microcomputer
A microcomputer that has the greatest capabilities and most expansion room of any microcomputer. A desktop requires a part of a desk for its work.

Figure 1–14
COMPAQ System Pro with Removable Disk Drives and a Hard Disk

Figure 1–15
A Desktop Microcomputer
(COMPAQ DeskPro 486/25)

Peripheral
A device such as a printer, bar code reader, or modem connected to a microcomputer to give it special capabilities.

peripherals. Peripherals are devices such as printers, bar code readers, or modems connected to microcomputers to give them special capabilities.

Desktop microcomputers have the greatest capabilities of any microcomputers. They have the most internal room to expand to satisfy many needs by using add-on boards or cards containing additional circuits.

Transportable Microcomputers

Transportable microcomputer
A portable microcomputer that is packaged with most of the features of a desktop, including a monitor, and requires electrical power connection.

The **transportable microcomputer** is similar to the desktop microcomputer in its capabilities. The transportable is a self-contained package (Figure 1–16). Its parts generally include a monitor, both floppy and hard disk drives, a keyboard, and a microprocessor, including external connections for a printer and communications. Some units include printers, whereas others include built-in modems for communication over telephone lines. The transportable requires electrical power connection to operate.

Users who travel can use the transportable to give sales and educational presentations, because it often can be connected to external monitors for group viewing of the contents of the screen. Transportables are also desirable for users who want a microcomputer that takes up less room (that is, has a smaller footprint on the desk).

Figure 1–16
A Transportable Microcomputer
(COMPAQ Transportable)

Laptop Microcomputers

Laptop microcomputers (Figure 1–17) have small keyboards but offer all the necessary operations, including the usual special keys for program control. Laptops are enjoying a surge in popularity among travelers, who use them in airports and on some airplanes. Outside salespeople find it convenient to use laptops for direct sales support when making calls.

Laptop microcomputer
A computer that fits easily on a lap or inside a briefcase and offers full functions, including a hard disk drive, with its own power supply (battery). Most laptop microcomputers have AC adapters that can run the unit and that can be used to recharge the battery.

Figure 1–17
A Laptop Computer at Work, the COMPAQ LTE

Pocket Computers

The smaller the computer, the more specialized it tends to be. The **pocket computer,** which fits in a pocket, has the most limited memory and capabilities, and it tends to be a calculation and data storage device only. Some pocket computers have expanded memory and are useful in many business applications where physical size is critical.

Historical Development of Computers, Systems, and Software

The history of microcomputers can be divided into several phases, as shown in Figure 1–18:

> Phase 1, premicroprocessor: Before the development of the Intel 4004 chip, the groundwork for the microcomputer was laid.
>
> Phase 2, hardware and operating system development: Computer clubs and the creation of basic hardware led to the creation and development of microcomputer hardware and the operating system.
>
> Phase 3, software development: Commercial programs needed by the business user were developed.
>
> Phase 4, professional use: The microcomputer could be used by individuals without computer training or background.
>
> Phase 5, connectivity: The microcomputer was used as part of a system.
>
> Phase 6, power tools: The number and quality of tools for management decision making and personal productivity is growing.

Phase 1 included the development of computer and electronic theory and the manufacturing capabilities to produce smaller computers. The development of the Intel 4004 microprocessor delineates the end of this phase.

Phase 2, hardware and operating system development, covers the period when computer clubs and hobbyists, called hackers, were responsible for the creation and design of microcomputer hardware and the operating systems needed to make the microcomputers work. Michael Shrayer developed Electric Pencil in 1976 for the Altair and later adapted it for the Radio Shack Model I microcomputer and other microcomputers. Electric Pencil was the first word processor available for microcomputers. Word processing resulted in a big increase in the use of microcomputers, because it was so much easier, quicker, and less expensive than typing.

Phase 3, software development, includes the development of general, specialized, and custom application programs. The software hobbyists first developed programs for their own use. Many of these programs became the first commercial programs. Programs were generally produced only for selected microcomputers. The rule "Find the software, then pur-

Figure 1-18
The History of Microcomputers

Phase 1, premicroprocessor: Before the development of the Intel 4004 chip, the groundwork for the microcomputer was laid.

Before 1880	The abacus. The abacus was an early device for increasing the speed and accuracy of calculation.
1800–1850	Charles Babbage designed the analytical engine.
1851–1900	Allan Marquand created the electric logic machine. Herman Hollerith made the tabulating/sorting machine.
1901–1925	The Computing-Tabulating-Recording Company became International Business Machines (IBM).
1926–1940	Benjamin Burack made the first electric logic machine. John V. Atanasoff and Clifford Berry used vacuum tubes as switching units; Iowa State College, in Ames, Iowa, developed the "ABC," or Atanasoff-Berry Computer (the first electronic computer).
1941–1950	John Mauchley and J. Presper Eckert, Jr., proposed an electronic analyzer to develop ballistic tables for the U.S. Army. Mauchley, Eckert, and John Von Neumann built ENIAC, the first all-electronic digital computer. The transistor was developed at Bell Laboratories. The Mark I computer (Automatic Sequence Controlled Computer) was built by Dr. Howard Aiken at Harvard University under an IBM grant. The stored-program concept was developed.
1951–1955	UNIVAC 1 was the first commercial computer to become operational. IBM planned production of 50 model 650 computers; over 1,000 were sold. FORTRAN (FORmula TRANslator) computer language was developed.
1956–1960	COBOL (COmmon Business Oriented Language) computer language was developed under the leadership of Grace Hopper.
1961–1965	President John F. Kennedy dreamed of space flight and created the National Aeronautics and Space Administration (NASA). BASIC (Beginner's All-purpose Symbolic Instruction Code) was developed in 1964 at Dartmouth College by John Kemeny and Thomas Kurtz under a National Science Foundation grant. Operating systems were developed.

Phase 2, hardware and operating system development: Computer clubs and the creation of basic hardware led to the creation and development of microcomputer hardware and the operating system.

1966–1970	Intel received a commission to produce integrated circuits (ICs) for calculators. Intel built the 4004 microprocessor with Ted Hoff, Stan Mazer, Robert Noyce, and Federico Faggin as the project team.
1971	Intel developed the 8008 microprocessor.
1972	Gary Kildall wrote PL/1, the first programming language for Intel's 4004.
1974	Intel 8080 was developed. A microcomputer disk operating system, Control/ Program Microcomputer (CP/M), was developed by John Torode and Gary Kildall.

1975	The MITS Altair—the first microcomputer in kit form, based on the 8080 microprocessor—went on sale. Bill Gates developed MicroSoft BASIC for Altair. Many computer clubs started across the United States. Dick Heiser opened The Computer Store, the first retail computer store, in Los Angeles.
1976	IMSAI started shipping its first computers. The World Altair Computer Conference (the first microcomputer conference) was held. Stephen Wozniak demonstrated the Apple I. CP/M went on sale. Michael Shrayer developed Electric Pencil, the first word processor for microcomputers.

Phase 3, software development: Commercial programs needed by the business user were developed.

1977	Computerland opened its first franchise in Morristown, New Jersey. Apple introduced the Apple II. Commodore introduced the PET computer. Tandy-Radio Shack introduced the TRS-80 Model I microcomputer.
1978	Apple added disk drives.
1979	Tandy introduced the TRS-80 Model II. MicroPro released the word processing program WordStar. VisiCalc, the first electronic spreadsheet, was produced by Personal Software. Source—national database for electronic mail and other information services—was started. CompuServe opened its computer for information services, electronic mail, and so on for microcomputer users.
1980	Hewlett-Packard released the HP-85. MicroSoft developed PC DOS, the operating system for the IBM PC. Dow Jones News/Retrieval Service was opened to Apple computer users. The first local area networks (LANs) became available.

Phase 4, professional use: The microcomputer could be used by individuals without computer training or background.

1981	Osborne Computer Corporation introduced Osborne 1 with packaged software. Xerox released the 8010 Star using a graphical interface and 820 computers. IBM introduced the IBM PC personal computer.
1982	Apple III was introduced.
1983	IBM introduced PCJr. Osborne Computer filed for reorganization. DEC introduced the Rainbow personal computer. Apple introduced the Macintosh.
1984	IBM PC AT was introduced. AT&T entered the microcomputer market after divestiture. Laser printers were introduced for microcomputers.
1985	IBM PC Jr. production was discontinued. AT&T introduced the UNIX-PC, a multi-using, multi-tasking personal computer with network capability. Many firms introduced LANs. Methods were developed to increase the amount of internal memory using special hardware and software systems.

Figure 1-18
The History of Microcomputers, continued

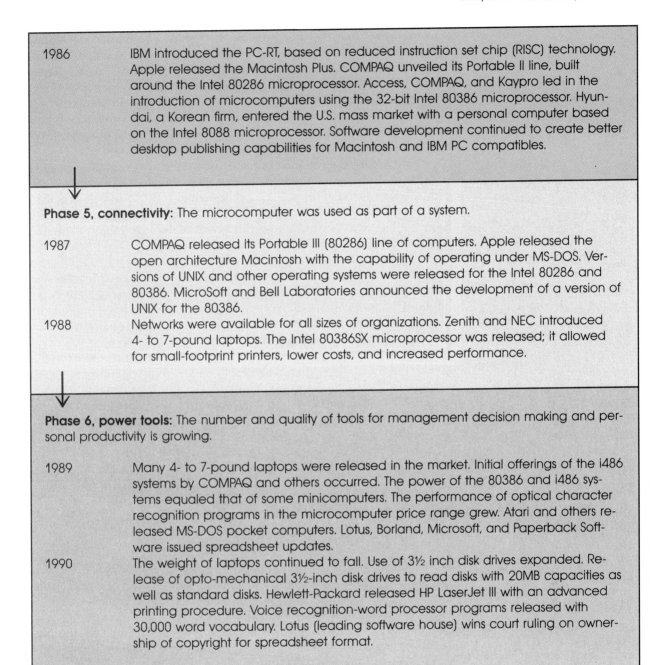

1986	IBM introduced the PC-RT, based on reduced instruction set chip (RISC) technology. Apple released the Macintosh Plus. COMPAQ unveiled its Portable II line, built around the Intel 80286 microprocessor. Access, COMPAQ, and Kaypro led in the introduction of microcomputers using the 32-bit Intel 80386 microprocessor. Hyundai, a Korean firm, entered the U.S. mass market with a personal computer based on the Intel 8088 microprocessor. Software development continued to create better desktop publishing capabilities for Macintosh and IBM PC compatibles.

Phase 5, connectivity: The microcomputer was used as part of a system.

1987	COMPAQ released its Portable III (80286) line of computers. Apple released the open architecture Macintosh with the capability of operating under MS-DOS. Versions of UNIX and other operating systems were released for the Intel 80286 and 80386. MicroSoft and Bell Laboratories announced the development of a version of UNIX for the 80386.
1988	Networks were available for all sizes of organizations. Zenith and NEC introduced 4- to 7-pound laptops. The Intel 80386SX microprocessor was released; it allowed for small-footprint printers, lower costs, and increased performance.

Phase 6, power tools: The number and quality of tools for management decision making and personal productivity is growing.

1989	Many 4- to 7-pound laptops were released in the market. Initial offerings of the i486 systems by COMPAQ and others occurred. The power of the 80386 and i486 systems equaled that of some minicomputers. The performance of optical character recognition programs in the microcomputer price range grew. Atari and others released MS-DOS pocket computers. Lotus, Borland, Microsoft, and Paperback Software issued spreadsheet updates.
1990	The weight of laptops continued to fall. Use of 3½ inch disk drives expanded. Release of opto-mechanical 3½-inch disk drives to read disks with 20MB capacities as well as standard disks. Hewlett-Packard released HP LaserJet III with an advanced printing procedure. Voice recognition-word processor programs released with 30,000 word vocabulary. Lotus (leading software house) wins court ruling on ownership of copyright for spreadsheet format.

Figure 1-18
The History of Microcomputers, continued

chase the hardware" had to be followed carefully. Among the first programs to become commercially available in the late 1970s were accounting programs such as general ledger, accounts payable, and accounts receivable. Payroll programs came later. VisiCalc was the first electronic spreadsheet program to be developed (1979). Its existence created a market for microcomputers that had not previously existed. The market developed because VisiCalc could be used by the business user to solve selected business problems more efficiently than any other method available. There are many different brands of spreadsheet programs, such as SuperCalc, Multiplan, Quattro, Excel, and Lotus 1–2–3. They are all similar to the original VisiCalc. The capabilities of newer versions of spreadsheet programs have expanded to include graphics, communications, database functions, and others.

In Phase 4, the end user came to dominate microcomputer use. The hardware and operating system concepts were developed in Phase 2; the basic software—word processing, spreadsheet, and database programs—were created in Phase 3. The introduction of microcomputers sold with programs, like the Osborne 1, and the introduction of the IBM PC in 1981 marked the beginning of Phase 4. You are part of it.

Phase 5 saw the integration of the operations of all computer facilities in an organization. Microcomputers were connected to minicomputers and mainframe computers as workstations. Programs were being written that look, feel, and work the same on all sizes of equipment, from microcomputers to mainframes. Data were being transferred up and down between computers of different sizes.

Phase 6 is the power growth state. Microcomputer hardware is faster, bigger, and less expensive than in earlier phases. Software developers use the power to develop specialized programs for desktop publishing, graphic animation, statistical analysis, and more. The microcomputer replaces many minicomputers and mainframe computers.

The Hierarchy of Hardware, Operating Systems, and Software

Hierarchy
Classification or grading of a group or set from a high to low rank or precedence.

Hardware is the foundation upon which operating systems are developed. An operating system is the program that makes the parts of a microcomputer work as a system. After operating systems became available, utilities and programming languages were developed. Application programs were then developed more easily on the hardware—operating system foundation. An overview of the **hierarchy** of hardware and software is shown in Figure 1–19.

Disk Operating Systems

The disk operating system (DOS) is the program used to make all the parts (hardware and software) of the microcomputer work together. While hardware was being developed, disk operating systems underwent concurrent

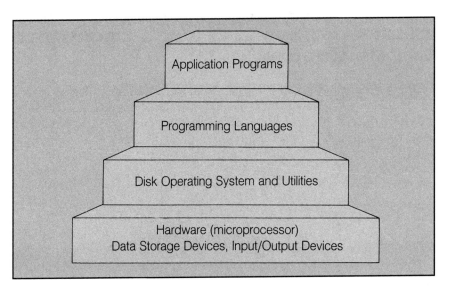

Figure 1–19
Hierarchy of Hardware,
Operating System, and
Software

development. Computer users, usually through programs, send instructions to the disk operating system, which then directs the hardware on how to carry out the given instructions. The disk operating system is what makes the computer hardware, printer, monitor, keyboard, disk drives, tape recorder, and software work together as a system. Each part of the microcomputer system must react with split-second timing to accomplish different tasks. A good operating system makes the task of getting useful results from a microcomputer look easy.

The more popular operating systems found in microcomputers include the following:

> Apple-DOS, the Apple Disk Operating System used on Apple computers.
> Apple-Macintosh DOS, the Apple Disk Operating System used on the Apple Macintosh.
> MS-DOS/PC DOS, the Microsoft Disk Operating System/Personal Computer Disk Operating System used on the IBM PC, XT, AT, and compatibles.
> OS/2, the operating System 2 for multiuser operation on the IBM Personal System/2 microcomputers (models 50 and above) and compatibles.
> UNIX, the multiuser operating system developed by Bell Laboratories. Versions of UNIX include Venix and Xenix.

Some formerly popular systems, such as CP/M and TRS-DOS, are being phased out as the hardware they control ages and is retired.

A family of microcomputers is defined by the operating system used. Application programs created to work on one member of a microcomputer family will often operate on most microcomputers using the same operating system.

Computer Languages

Computer language bridges the gap between machine and human languages. A machine language is a formal system of signs and symbols, including rules for their use, that conveys instructions to a computer. Humans speak English, French, and other similar languages. Microcomputers speak with on and off switches, a binary number language. Computer languages are often classified as low-level languages (computer languages near machine language) or high-level languages (computer languages near English). An assembly language is close to machine language and may be easily converted using a special program called an assembler.

Computer languages have been developed to fit different user needs. To program (give instructions to) a microcomputer, a computer language is used. The objective in designing a computer language is to create a limited language that human beings can relate to and that a computer can understand so that a set of machine language instructions can be generated.

One of the more popular microcomputer languages is BASIC (Beginner's All-purpose Symbolic Instruction Code). The original version was developed at Dartmouth College by John Kemeny and Thomas Kurtz as a teaching language. The version of BASIC on today's microcomputers has many capabilities beyond the original language. BASIC's popularity can be traced to its relative ease of learning and its added capabilities.

Standards defining the acceptable statements in BASIC and other languages are maintained by the American National Standards Institute (ANSI). The standard is not complete because of the rapid change in hardware, capabilities, and software in the microcomputer industry. There are many "dialects" of BASIC, and they vary greatly.

Instructions written in a computer language can be converted to machine language using a compiler or an interpreter. A compiler is a translator program that takes the near-English **code** (use of symbols or numbers to represent letters, numbers, and so on) and translates it into a set of machine language codes all at one time and saves it as a program. If there are any **syntax** errors, such as misspelled words, the compiler will not be able to complete its task. (Syntax is the manner in which a code must be put together for the computer to understand.) Thus, all syntax errors must be eliminated at this step.

An interpreter is a program that translates a line of near-English code into machine language, executes the line of code, translates the next line, and so on. This type of translator is slower than a compiler, but easier for the development of new applications, because it helps with error elimination. Table 1–1 shows some of the languages available on microcomputers.

Code
The use of symbols or numbers to represent letters, numbers, or special meanings.

Syntax
The manner in which a code must be put together for the computer to understand, including spelling.

Table 1–1
Selected Microcomputer Languages

Language	Application
Assembly[a]	Used to create machine language programs.
BASIC	Beginner's All-purpose Symbolic Instruction Code; available for most microcomputers.
C	Structured programming language; can perform many tasks that would normally require the use of assembly machine programs.
COBOL	COmmon Business Oriented Language; for business programs such as accounting.
FORTH	FOuRTH-generation language; for business, scientific, process control, and robotics use; contains a resident assembly language.
FORTRAN	FORmula TRANslator; for engineering and science applications.
LOGO	Education; an easy-to-program language that has outstanding graphics capabilities.
Pascal	Simple and structured for general applications.

[a] Assembly language is almost always available on microcomputers. It is generally the language used to create high-level language compilers and interpreters.

Legal and Ethical Issues

As the computer is integrated into our lives and economic activities, the number of legal and ethical questions increases. Currently, the issues of most concern to the microcomputer user include ownership of programs, ownership of data, data security, misuse of data, and viruses.

Ownership of Programs

It is easy to copy programs for backup and other purposes. However, when a program is sold, you purchase the right to use it on a single computer or in a single location. You do not purchase the right to resell it or give it to your friends. Always take the time to look at the current software licensing agreements that accompany all software packages and stick to the terms for their use.

It is estimated that as much as 80 percent of the software being used in corporations and by individuals was not purchased legally. The software has been copied in violation of the licensing agreement. There are no accepted solutions to this problem, and now that you are entering the world of computers, it has become your problem.

Whatever the legal resolution of unlicensed software copying is, you should do everything in your power to act within the law. After all, you would not like to lose your job and destroy your career by stealing a piece of software. In addition, obeying the law is also the ethical thing to do.

Ownership of Data

Software belongs to the developer and designer. Data belongs to the individual or institution that collects it. To enter a database without the consent of the owner or to view, copy, or damage the information in any manner is neither moral nor legal in most instances. State and federal laws addressing the unauthorized entry of individuals to databases are under development.

Data Security

Data security systems and procedures are difficult to create and maintain. It is said that whenever a better security system is created, someone will come up with a method of breaking it. Many individuals earn their livings creating and maintaining data security systems.

Misuse of Data

Data are a valuable asset of a business or individual. Data can represent power to earn money and control the activities of individuals. When used wrongly, by error or by intent, data can also harm individuals. Government databases have long been a concern of individuals who worry about possible invasion of privacy.

The increasing capabilities of microcomputers mean that individuals and businesses are able to maintain their own databases. Many problems will be created by the proliferation of electronic databases.

As a manager or user of a database, you have a responsibility to use the data in a professional manner. The laws on how these databases can be used and the responsibility of the owners are just now being written. You will be judged by their standards once they are implemented. Now you have the opportunity and obligation to participate in the development of these standards.

Viruses

A computer virus is a program introduced into a computer, usually without the knowledge of the user, for the purpose of damaging or destroying the

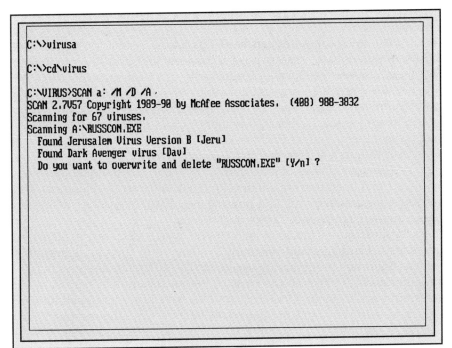

Figure 1–20
Computer Virus in a University
Computer Laboratory

operating system, application programs, and data. Viruses can save random numbers on hard disks until the disks are full, reformat the hard drive on or after a given date, or attach themselves to programs and destroy their capability to operate. Figure 1–20 illustrates McAfee Associates' virus scanning program Scan 2.7V57 which identifies and removes two viruses: the Jerusalem Virus Version B, and the Dark Avenger virus (names given to common viruses tend to be colorful). These viruses were found on a student's disk. The viruses did considerable damage to both student and instructor disks in a university computer laboratory.

Viruses may be introduced on purpose or by accident. The introduction of a virus can cost users time and money. The developer can go to jail and/or pay a large fine.

Summary

The microcomputer and its programs combined to form tools that may be used to increase personal and business productivity. The computer program instructs the computer to perform a variety of applications. Among the important application programs available for microcomputers are word processing, spreadsheets, data-driven graphics, file management, database management, image-driven graphics, desktop publishing, communication, and integrated programs. In addition, there are many programs available to help in management decision making. The user is aided in learning how to operate the computer through the use of printed documentation.

The microcomputer can be defined from several points of view. Microcomputers have various physical aspects that contribute to making the microcomputer productive. For instance, a typical microcomputer system hardware purchase price is affordable (the hardware is that part of the microcomputer you can see and feel). The essential parts are the system box (microprocessor, PC-boards, memory), input devices, output devices, and on-line memory devices. Microcomputer size variation makes it easy for a user to find a system that fits a particular need.

The main phases of microcomputer history are premicroprocessor, hardware and operating system development, software development, professional use, connectivity, and power tools. These phases are delineated by an ongoing emergence of new technology.

Hardware is the foundation upon which operating systems are developed. Hardware and operating systems form the foundation upon which application programs are designed. The disk operating system is the program used to make all the parts of the microcomputer hardware and software work together. Operating systems have been developed for computers to help users and program developers control the computer's operation. Computer programming languages have been developed to fit different user needs.

The social, moral, and legal issues associated with the use of microcomputers are important considerations. Some legal and ethical questions of microcomputer use include the ownership of programs, data, data security, misuse of data, and the need to protect a system against computer viruses.

Key Terms

Code
Communication
  Software
Data-driven graphics
  program
Database
Database management
  program
Desktop
  microcomputer
Desktop publishing
  software
Documentation

File management
  program
Hardware
Hierarchy
Image-driven graphics
  program
Integrated program
I/O
Laptop
  microcomputer
Operating system
Peripheral

Pocket computer
Program
Programming
  language
Scan
Software
Spreadsheet program
Syntax
Transportable
  microcomputer
Word processing
  program

Review Questions

1. What is a program?
2. What is software?
3. What does an operating system do?
4. Why is computer program documentation important?
5. What does a word processing program do?
6. What does a spreadsheet program do?
7. What does a data-driven graphics program do?
8. What is a file management program? What is a database management program? What are the differences between the two? What is a database?
9. What is an image-driven graphics program?
10. What can you use a communication program for?
11. Why would you want to buy and use a desktop publishing program?
12. What is I/O? Why is I/O important?
13. Give several examples of computer peripherals.
14. What is a desktop computer? What is a transportable? What is a laptop? What is a pocket computer? When would you select one type versus the others?
15. Why is syntax important?
16. Identify some legal and ethical issues in microcomputer use.
17. What is the estimated amount of illegal software being used?
18. Who own software? Who owns data?
19. What is the responsibility of the manager/user of a database?
20. What is a computer virus? What does one do?

CHAPTER **2**

Hardware

Goals

Upon completion of this chapter, you will be able to do the following:

- Identify the important features of hardware.

- Identify and name the parts of a microcomputer.

- Explain how each part of the microcomputer fits into the overall system.

- List some of the systems currently available.

- Review the significance of compatibility.

Outline

Selecting a System for Manufacturing

Tipi Makers, Inc., is a small manufacturing company located in the Southeast. Its product is the American Indian tepee in a variety of sizes, tribal representations (styles), and prices. The company has a total of 17 employees, including the owners. Output has grown over the 14 years of Tipi Makers' existence to the point where it can no longer handle its record keeping using manual methods, and the company began investigating the use of computers.

First on the list of requirements is the need for customer records listing the customer's name, address, date of purchase, style, serial number, fabric weight, fabric treatment, vat lot number (waterproof, flame retardant, and dye), cutting, sewing, and inspection (quality control) approval, and method of sale (direct, distributor, or retail).

Next on the list of priorities are the needs for two kinds of inventory control: raw materials for manufacturing, and completed goods. Accounting, word processing, desktop publishing (newsletters), and bar coding for delivery inventory round out the requirements.

The hardware requirements indicate the need for a network of four computer workstations: one file server and three desktop units. The file server is to be used to download files to the bookkeeping, shipping, and manufacturing departments.

Microcomputers come in different sizes and shapes. They have many parts that are joined together to form a system. **Hardware** is that part of the microcomputer you can see and feel. It is difficult to determine the function of microcomputer hardware from its outside appearance. Gaining knowledge of the importance, parts, and availability of microcomputer hardware; typical **configurations**; and **compatibility** with other brands of microcomputers is a step in the process of learning how to evaluate and select the appropriate hardware for a specific need. Configuration is the act of matching hardware, software, and operating system settings so that all the parts work and communicate with all the other parts of a system. Compatibility is the capability of microcomputers to work together as a system and to exchange physical parts. Micros in Action "Selecting a System for Manufacturing" indicates how one manufacturer determined its hardware needs.

A microcomputer (Figure 2–1) is a collection of parts that form a system. This chapter will discuss how the parts of the system work together.

Hardware
The part of a microcomputer you can see and feel.

Configuration
The matching of hardware, software, and operating system settings so that all the parts work and communicate with all the other parts of a system.

Compatibility
The capability of microcomputers to work together as a system and to exchange physical parts.

Figure 2–1
Microcomputers in Use

Why Microcomputer Hardware?

The microcomputer is an answer to problems. The user must learn about hardware in order to select the best combination of capabilities and cost to match problem-solving needs. A microcomputer system consists of application software built upon a hardware foundation. The remaining chapters of this book are devoted to software; this chapter studies the hardware foundation.

In order to purchase a system intelligently, the user must know his or her needs, the capabilities of a typical system, and its cost. The user must also know what can be added and how the system can be expanded to satisfy current and future needs.

One decision users must make is the selection and justification of microcomputer hardware and software. This book is designed to help users learn about microcomputer hardware, operating systems, and available programs. It will be your responsibility as a user to study your needs. The microcomputer salesperson can help you match hardware and software with your problems.

It is best to ask questions before you spend your money. For example, late one evening a business associate called. He announced that he was about to purchase a second word processor for his office. His partner had an Apple Macintosh, and he wanted to use similar programs and to exchange files and data with his partner. He had been told to purchase an IBM Personal System/2 and wanted to know how difficult it would be to exchange files and data between the two machines. We answered that there could be problems. Many software companies produce both Macintosh and IBM Personal System/2 versions of their software, but not all do. Data files can be moved between the Macintosh and the IBM Personal System/2 using either a special disk drive (available on the Macintosh) or communication programs and cables. We recommended a Macintosh if our associate wanted to share data files. Thus, a simple question before buying saved him frustration and dollars.

Hardware: The Parts of a Computer

The parts of a microcomputer in the system case include the following:

> A microprocessor (on the motherboard).
> RAM and ROM.
> Printed circuit (PC) boards or cards (expansion capability).
> Controllers.
> Dual in-line package (DIP) switches.
> Input devices, including keyboards, pointing devices, scanners, bar code readers, voice recognition devices, and modems.
> Output devices, including monitors (CRTs, screens) and printers.
> On-line storage devices and media.

Each manufacturer uses a design philosophy, called **design architecture,** or architecture, to create its microcomputers. Many designs use the concept of a **motherboard.** A motherboard is a **printed circuit (PC) board** containing the microprocessor; some computer memory; selected controller circuits to direct the signals that are received from external connectors; and often the ability to be expanded. Figure 2–2 examines the inside of a microcomputer.

The concept of design architecture may be illustrated by comparing the Apple IIe and the IBM PC. Both of these microcomputers have a number of slots into which are inserted cards with special capabilities. The Apple IIe looks at slot 1 for the printer controller card; the IBM PC seeks a printer card in whatever slot it may be. Thus, the Apple IIe looks for slots; the IBM PC looks for function.

Design architecture
The design philosophy used to create a specific microcomputer.

Motherboard
A printed circuit board containing the microprocessor, computer memory, and selected controller circuits to direct the signals that are received from external connectors.

Printed circuit (PC) board
A flat piece of material with circuits (electronic connections) printed on it plus electronic components to add special capabilities to a microcomputer.

Figure 2–2

Inside a Microcomputer

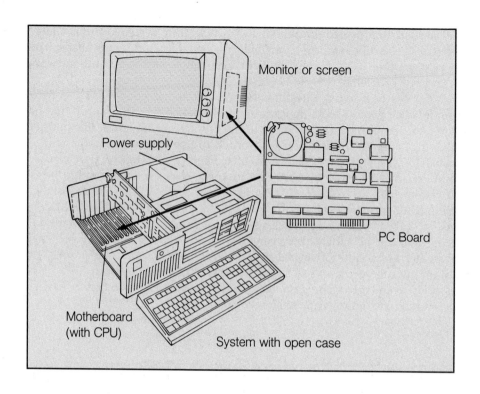

Monitor or screen

Power supply

PC Board

Motherboard
(with CPU)

System with open case

Micro Channel Architecture (MCA)
A design architecture built around
an internal communication system
that speeds operation and reduces
the problems associated with
communication with host
computers.

Industry Standard Architecture (ISA)
The original open architecture
design of the IBM PC.

**Extended Industry Standard
Architecture (EISA)**
A design architecture built around
an internal communication system
that speeds operation and reduces
the problems associated with
communication with host
computers. EISA motherboards
accept expansion boards used in
ISA motherboards.

Bit
The smallest component in binary
code. A bit is a single binary digit
(0 or 1). The microcomputer uses a
binary number system consisting of
0 and 1.

Six years after IBM developed "open architecture" for a personal computer, it released a PS/2 motherboard, Personal System/2, with **Micro Channel Architecture (MCA).** An open architecture design may be used by anyone with concern about copyright or patent limitations. MCA is a design architecture built around an internal communication system that speeds operation and reduces the problems associated with communication with host computers. MCA is not compatible with hardware used in systems with the original architecture, **Industry Standard Architecture (ISA).** The two motherboards do not accept the same add-on boards and are generally not compatible. The PS/2 motherboard accommodates coprocessor boards, device controllers, and other specially designed functional boards not available for the PC/XT/AT or compatible computers.

The **Extended Industry Standard Architecture (EISA)** motherboard was developed by a group of nine manufacturers led by COMPAQ Computer Corporation as an alternative to the IBM's PS/2 MCA mother board. EISA is an extension of the basic architecture of the original IBM PC/XT/AT and compatibles.

The EISA standard allows producers to develop their own "extended" specifications for product differentiation. The EISA standard requires that input/output (I/O), such as the 32 **bit bus** boards, remain compatible. A bit is a single binary digit (0 or 1), the smallest component in binary code. Multiple processor and memory support can be proprietary among developers.

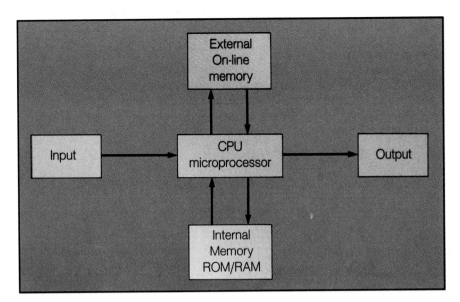

Figure 2–3
Diagram of a Computer System

Another part of microcomputer design architecture determines how the microcomputer is packaged. The microcomputer may be in one container or come in a number of parts. Figure 2–3 shows an overall diagram of a microcomputer system.

Bus
A pathway or channel for data and instructions between hardware devices.

The System Case

The system case usually contains a microprocessor mounted on a printed circuit board, a math co-processor, memory, other printed circuit boards, and configuration switches. Input, output, and on-line storage devices may or may not be in the system box, depending on the design architecture.

Microprocessor

The **microprocessor** is commonly found on the motherboard inside the system case. A microprocessor is the **central processing unit (CPU),** a single chip that contains an arithmetic and logic unit, a control unit, and registers. With the addition of a power supply, memory, and other circuitry, the microprocessor becomes a complete microcomputer. Figure 2–4 illustrates a microprocessor, the Intel i486™.

Eight binary digits, called bits, are combined to create characters, or **bytes. Word size** refers to the number of bits a microprocessor handles at one time. Common word sizes are 8, 16, 24, or 32 bits. Table 2–1 shows some

Microprocessor
An integrated circuit on a silicon chip that is the central processing unit (CPU).

Central processing unit (CPU)
A silicon chip that includes the arithmetic, logic, control, and memory units.

Figure 2-4
A Microprocessor—The Intel
i486™

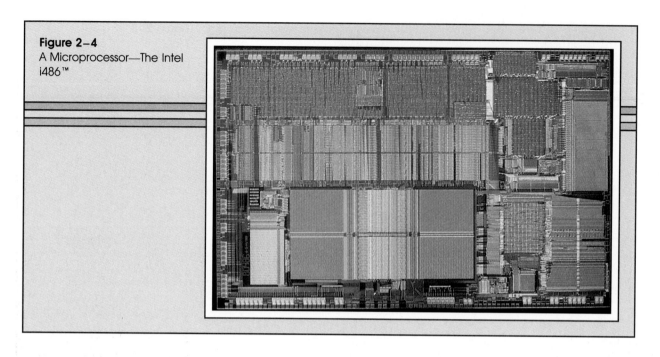

Byte
A sequence of eight binary digits
(bits) taken as a unit.

Word size
The number of bits a
microprocessor can handle at one
time.

of the more popular microprocessors, the number of bits they use per word size, and the operating systems that are available for them. Microcomputers commonly process 8, 16, or 32 bits at one time. A 16-bit microcomputer may process two 8-bit bytes (characters) at one time. A 32-bit microcomputer may process four 8-bit bytes at one time. The overall speed of a microcomputer is a function of the number of bits per word, or word size.

To be useful in many applications, a microprocessor needs a minimum word size of 8 bits. The word size determines the potential speed of a computer, the maximum memory that may be used directly, and to a large degree, the sophistication of programs that can be handled.

The development of the Intel 8086 microprocessor in 1979 led to the microcomputer revolution. Early microprocessors, such as the Zilog Z80 and MOS Technology 6502, could use only a limited amount of memory. When IBM introduced the Personal Computer in 1981, Apple Computer Corporation ran ads saying that the microcomputer industry had been legitimized. During the next seven years, 40 million microcomputers were produced. The open architecture of the IBM PC spurred the development of hardware and software for this new environment.

The Intel 8088 microprocessor was selected by IBM for its original PC because it used both 8- and 16-bit word sizes. There were only a limited number of 16-bit devices available at the time. The 8088 has a speed of 4.77 megahertz (Mhz). The Intel 8086, with a speed of 6Mhz, was selected by COMPAQ Computer Corporation. After five years, the 8086 became the industry standard.

The next microprocessor was the Intel 80186. It was used in a few computers, but primarily on co-processor boards (a second microprocessor added to the system to speed selected operations such as mathematical

Table 2–1
Microprocessors

Microprocessors	Address Bus Width[a]	Internal RAM	Word Size (arithmetic-logic unit and external data-bus width)[b]	Operating System
Intel 4004			4	None
Intel 8008			8	None
Intel 8080	16	64K[c]	8	CP/M
Zilog Z80	16	64K	8	CP/M, TRS-DOS
Motorola 6800	16	64K	8	Commodore DOS
MOS Technology 6502	16	64K	8	Apple, Commodore DOS
Intel 8088	20	640K	16/8	MS-DOS, PC DOS
Intel 8086	20	640K	16	MS-DOS, PC DOS
Intel 80286	24	16MB[d]	16	MS-DOS, PC DOS, OS/2
Motorola 68000	24	16MB	16	Macintosh DOS
Motorola 68020	32	4 GB[e]	32	Macintosh DOS
Intel 80386	32	4 GB	32	MS-DOS, PC DOS, OS/2
Motorola 68030	32	4 GB	32	Macintosh DOS
Intel 80486	32	16 GB	32	MS-DOS, PC DOS, OS/2

[a] The address bus width is the number of bits for internal addressing memory. This value determines the maximum amount of memory a computer may directly address. MS-DOS limits some systems to 640K.

[b] The arithmetic-logic unit width is the maximum number of bits manipulated during one instruction. The external data-bus width is the number of bits transferred in one clock cycle.

[c] K = kilobytes, or 1,024 bytes.

[d] MB = megabyte, or 1 million bytes.

[e] GB = gigabytes, or 1 billion bytes.

computations or graphics displays). Next was the 80286 microprocessor, upon which IBM based its AT series. The amount of usable memory was extended to 16MB (1 megabyte equals 1 million bytes), and the operating speed was increased to 6Mhz. Some manufacturers increased the speed of their systems to 8, 10, 12, 16, and 20Mhz.

In 1987 the Intel 80386 microprocessor made its debut; it runs at a speed of 16Mhz, and offers its users up to 4GB (1 gigabyte equals 1 billion bytes) of directly addressable memory. Operating speeds of 16, 20, 25, and 33Mhz are available. A lower-cost 80386SX is also available in smaller-footprint versions; it offers fewer capabilities than its big brother, the 80386. Footprint refers to the space used on a desk.

The Intel 80486 (i486) microprocessor chips are available in operating speeds of over 25 megahertz. This microprocessor is used in advanced personal computers, high-speed graphics/scientific terminals, and multiuser networks. The Intel 80586 (i586) microprocessor is being tested and will offer operating speeds from 50 to 100 megahertz. The i686 is expected to offer operating speeds from 100 to 200 megahertz, whereas the proposed i786 microprocessor will operate at 250 megahertz, occupy only 1 square inch of space, and be binary compatible all the way down to the software designed to run on the 8086 machines.

The microprocessor, combined with an operating system, determines the maximum file size and the programs available to solve problems. You will learn more about operating systems and how they perform their tasks in Chapter 3.

Math Co-processor

Math co-processor
A chip that reduces the amount of time required to perform mathematical operations.

A **math co-processor** is a chip that reduces the amount of time required to perform mathematical operations. A math co-processor may be added to most microcomputers to speed up mathematical calculations and graphics operations. A socket for the math co-processor has been available since the earliest IBM PC. However, only recently has the use of math co-processors become more popular. With the addition of a math co-processor, calculations or redrawing of graphic illustrations can be accomplished in up to 80 percent less time than without the co-processor.

It is best to match the speed of the math co-processor to the speed of the CPU (Table 2–2). The 80287 co-processor chip is available in 6- to 8-, 8- to 10-, and 12-megahertz ratings, but the 80286 microprocessor chip also comes in 16- and 20-megahertz versions. If you have a nonmatching co-processor, it is recommended that you use the speed closest to that of your microprocessor.

RAM and ROM

Random access memory (RAM)
Memory used for data and program storage by the user. The user can write and read data in RAM.

Read-only memory (ROM)
Memory with instructions (programs) needed when operating the microcomputer. The user cannot write data into ROM.

Microcomputers contain both **random access memory (RAM)** and **read-only memory (ROM)**. RAM is available for the user to store programs and data. ROM contains instructions for the microcomputer. The user cannot write data into ROM but can write and read data in RAM.

The amount of ROM needed depends on the manner in which the microcomputer is to be used. In transportables and desktop microcomputers, ROM may be used for getting the system started and for containing special-purpose programs (Table 2–3). ROM contains a "bootstrap" program that is used to load the operating system into the RAM of the micro computer from external devices where it is stored. Loading the operating system from an on-line storage device is often called booting.

Microcomputers use ROM, programmable read-only memory (PROM), and erasable programmable read-only memory (EPROM) to store

Table 2–2
Math Co-processor Speeds

Co-processor Chip	Speed of Compatible Microprocessor (megahertz)
8087	4.77 or less
8087-1	10 or less
8087-2	8 or less
80287	6 or less
80287-8	8 or less
80287-10	10 or less
80C287-12	12 or less
80387-16	16 or less
80387-20	20 or less
80387-25	25 or less
80387-33	33 or less
80387SX	16 or less

Table 2–3
Use of ROM

Type of Microcomputer	Start System	System	Word Processing Programs	Spreadsheet Programs	Communications Programs	Custom Programs[a]
Pocket	X	X		X	X	X
Laptop	X	X	X	X	X	X
Transportable	X					
Desktop	X					

[a]Custom programs are special applications supplied on PROMs or EPROMs.

selected application programs. Pocket (Figure 2–5) and laptop microcomputers often use PROMs or EPROMs to store word processing, database, and communications programs. A popular method of supplying insurance sales professionals with programs for pocket and other portable microcomputers is through the use of EPROMs.

Figure 2–5
Atari Pocket Computer

The problems that may be solved by microcomputers depend on the application programs available. The programs available are a function of the amount of RAM and the programming skill of the program's creator. The amount of RAM needed by specific programs will be examined in later chapters.

Measuring RAM and ROM

Microcomputer memory, RAM and ROM, is measured in kilobytes (K), units of 1,024 bytes (Table 2–4). Most 8-bit microcomputers contain 64K, or 65,536 bytes (2^{16}, or 64 × 1,024). The 8 bits are called a byte. Some 8-bit microcomputers can use over 64K, but only with the use of special programming procedures. Sixteen-bit computers can use over half a million bytes of memory.

Generally, only pocket microcomputers and starter systems have less than 2K of RAM. Programs using such limited memory may do many tasks in small increments. They use small amounts of data at a time. Despite these limitations, these machines have many applications. For example, real estate sales professionals use them for calculating mortgage information, and insurance sales professionals use them in lieu of rate books.

Pocket microcomputers often contain RAM that maintains its memory when the machine is turned off. They contain a complimentary metallic oxide semiconductor (CMOS) that requires little power, as well as bubble memory, a thin magnetic recording film, which requires no power. This means the microcomputer maintains its programs and data when

Table 2–4
Measuring Memory

Power of	Bytes	Kilobytes (K)
2^6	1	0
2^{10}	1,024	1
2^{16}	65,536	64

turned off. When the sales professional walks in to give a sales presentation or perform an analysis, the microcomputer is ready. An on-line storage device is not required for the storage of programs and data using bubble memory.

Microcomputers with 48 to 64K were the business standard for several years. These machines could do word processing, electronic spreadsheets, database maintenance, graphics, and communication. Each application was generally created as a stand-alone (not an integrated) program. Most business applications, such as general ledger programs, were available for these machines.

With the introduction of the IBM PC, available RAM expanded from 64 to 640K. At first, the only programs available were expanded versions of the ones used in 64K microcomputers. Soon, however, integrated programs started to appear. Integrated programs now combine word processing, spreadsheet, database, graphics, and communications programs. Programs that allow multitasking (operating more than one program at a time) and multiusers (two or more people sharing the same microprocessor) have been developed.

The amount of memory a user requires is a function of the programs available and the tasks to be performed. Prior to 1981, most users needed only 64K. Between 1981 and 1990, most users needed 640K or less. Most users still use many programs that operate in 640K, but some programs require up to 5MB of memory. Users who want to use the more powerful programs must have the additional memory.

When selecting a microcomputer, you must determine the maximum amount of RAM needed by the specific programs you plan to use. Some programs will often not be able to take advantage of extra memory in your computer. Generally, electronic spreadsheet, database, and engineering/scientific graphics programs require the most RAM.

PC Boards or Cards

The capabilities of the microcomputer can be expanded with internal cards or boards called printed circuit (PC) boards. Some boards or computers can be expanded with chips as well. Many microcomputers have slots for additional circuits on microcomputer boards (cards) to give expanded capabilities, including the following: adding memory, connecting to telephones, communicating (out of specified ports), using voice recognition units, using bar code readers, operating laboratory equipment, and filling other special needs. Some cards are referred to as multifunction cards, because they add a number of functions rather than just one. Many manufacturers produce microcomputers that accept the same physical cards as the IBM PC.

Controllers

Controller board
A PC board that controls specific devices.

In addition to the motherboard, other individual **controller boards** control various peripheral devices. Some individual controllers, such as those for monitors and on-line storage devices, may be built into motherboards, but most controllers are found on separate boards. For example, color graphics monitors require color graphics controllers, monochrome graphics monitors require monochrome graphics controllers, and so on.

DIP Switches

Dual in-line package (DIP)
A housing to hold a chip or other items on a printed circuit board.

DIP switch
A series of toggle switches mounted on a DIP that is in turn mounted on a PC board. The switches are used for system configuration.

A **dual in-line package (DIP)** is a housing commonly used to hold a chip on a PC board. A **DIP switch** is usually a series of toggle switches mounted on a DIP approximately the same size as a chip. DIP switches are found on ISA personal computers, printers, and peripherals.

DIP switches must be set to tell the microcomputer the amount of memory installed, the peripheral devices connected, and the communication procedures used between devices in most microcomputers. Setting the DIP switches (configuring the parts of the microcomputer system) is usually done by the seller of microcomputers.

DIP switches are not used in the IBM Personal System/2. Instead, the configuration is set using software and the battery-powered memory that is used to remember the settings when the computer is powered down.

Input Devices

Input device
A device connected to the microcomputer through which data and instructions are entered.

An **input device** is a device for entering data and instructions into a computer. Input devices include keyboards, pointing devices, scanners, bar code readers, voice recognition devices, and modems. Most keyboards look like typewriters with the addition of a numeric keypad and function keys. Different manufacturers produce different keyboards. Some keyboards are better used for word processing, whereas others are better for programming.

The most common keyboard layout, QWERTY, is named for the order in which the letters are arranged in the uppermost row containing letters. The arrangement of keys on QWERTY keyboards was designed to slow down the users of early (slow) typewriters. The Dvorak keyboard layout is designed to assign the most-used letters to the stronger fingers. Both QWERTY and Dvorak keyboards are available for microcomputers.

Pointing devices, including the mouse, joy stick, track ball, pad, and touch-sensitive screen, are popular input devices for making menu selections (selections from a display of options on the screen) and locating the cursor on the screen. Pointing devices are almost a requirement when working with image-driven graphics and are integrated into some operating systems.

> **Pointing device**
> A device that moves the menu pointer and cursor on the screen.

A **scanner** is a device that senses printed material or images and enters the material into a computer. Scanners include hand, roller, platform, and video cameras. The hand scanner costs the least. Roller and platform scanners can scan an entire page at a time. Video scanners may be still or motion picture cameras. Most scanners require a PC board to connect them to the computer. A few operate using available **I/O ports.** An I/O port is a connection found on most computers that connects the computer to printers, plotters, and communication devices. Generally, standard I/O ports are found on printers, plotters, and communication devices.

> **Scanner**
> A device for sensing printed material (text and graphics) or images and entering them into a computer system.

> **I/O port**
> A connection found on most computers that connects the computer to printers, plotters, and communication devices.

Bar code readers are devices for reading the meaning of specially produced lines called bars. Each bar has a special meaning, and the bar code reader is able to determine the width of the bar and its meaning. Bar code readers are commonly found in supermarkets and warehouses. Figure 2–6 illustrates four types of input devices.

> **Bar code reader**
> A device that reads the codes associated with bars.

Voice recognition devices (Figure 2–7) allows the computer to input human speech. For example, these devices are used to identify individuals for security purposes, for the selection of options in a menu, or for the input of text into a word processor. Rapid technological advances are being made in this field, especially for special users who have a hearing or sight impairment.

> **Voice recognition device**
> A device that can understand human speech.

Microcomputers can receive input from (and can send output to) other computers over telephone lines using **modems** (both input and output devices). Modems convert the signals that come over the telephone lines so the computer can understand them.

> **Modem**
> A device to connect a microcomputer to a telephone. Modems change binary code to a signal that can be sent over telephone lines.

Output Devices

An **output device** is a device connected to the microcomputer through which data, information, and other communications are sent to users or to other devices. The most common microcomputer output device is the monitor, and the second most common is the printer.

> **Output device**
> A device connected to the microcomputer through which data and instructions are communicated to users or to other devices.

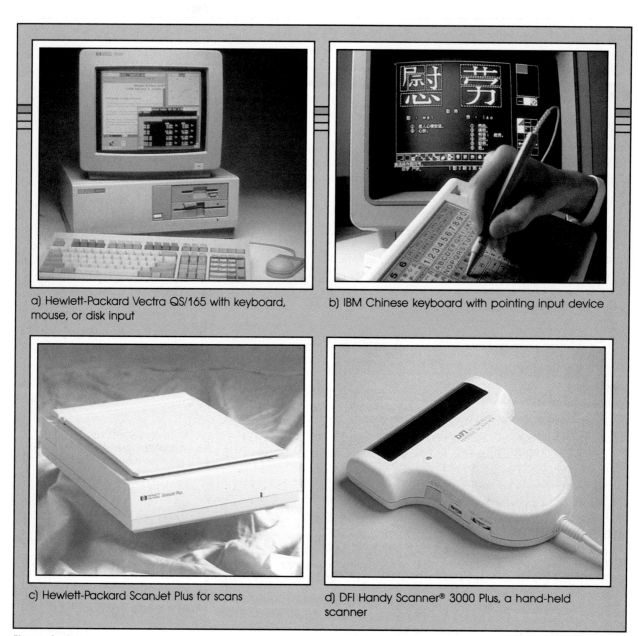

a) Hewlett-Packard Vectra QS/165 with keyboard, mouse, or disk input

b) IBM Chinese keyboard with pointing input device

c) Hewlett-Packard ScanJet Plus for scans

d) DFI Handy Scanner® 3000 Plus, a hand-held scanner

Figure 2–6
Types of Input Devices

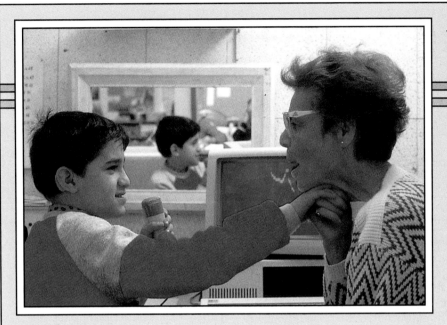

Figure 2–7
Voice Recognition Used in Speech Training

Monitors

Monitors are television-like devices for displaying the output of computers. Many computers use television sets to display output. Computer monitors are often called **cathode ray tubes (CRTs)** and **video display tubes (VDTs)**.

Computer users may select from monochrome or color/graphics monitors by installing a card to work with one of these output devices. Generally, the quality of the screen display depends on the number of **pixels** (picture elements) displayed on the screen. Pixels are dots used to create letters and graphic displays.

The original screens on pocket and laptop computers were liquid crystal displays (LCDs). They were followed by electroluminescent gas plasma, video graphics array (VGA), color, and transflective screens. These screens are compact, flat, and easy to transport and store. In addition, their clarity and sharpness of resolution continue to improve.

Monochrome monitors display varying shades of color using amber, green, paper white, white, and yellow on a black background. They use up to 64 shades of gray scale measurements, or the equivalent shades in amber, green, or yellow. PC boards offer monochrome with or without graphics capabilities, and some manufacturers offer monochrome and color on the same board.

Color monitors require adapter boards different from those used on monochrome monitors, except for the combination board just mentioned. Table 2–5 lists the types of color monitors and their accompanying

Monitor
A television-like device for displaying the output of computers.

Cathode ray tube (CRT)
A computer monitor.

Video display tube (VDT)
A computer monitor.

Pixel
A picture element; screen dots used to create letters and graphics.

Table 2–5
Color Monitors

Type	Name	Resolution	Pixels[a]
CGA	Color graphics adapter	Low	320 × 200
EGA	Enhanced graphics adapter	Medium	640 × 350
VGA	Video graphics array	High	640 × 480
Super VGA[b]		Superhigh	800 × 600 (up to 1,024 × 768)[c]
Ultra			2,048 × 2,048

[a] The pixel counts vary between manufacturers.

[b] Super VGA is not yet standard.

[c] IBM's 3415/A monitors display up to 1,024 × 768 pixels.

adapter boards. Color graphics adapter (CGA) monitors can display four colors from a palette of eight colors. Some VGA controller cards allow a display of up to 256 colors from a palette of 2,640,000 colors.

Printers

Printer
A device for producing text and graphics on paper.

A computer **printer** is a device for producing text and graphics on paper. The most common method of getting hard copy from a microcomputer is through a printer. The common types of printers are the dot-matrix, formed-character, laser, ink-jet, and thermal printer, along with the plotter. The selection of a printer depends on the printer type and user needs, as shown in Tables 2–6 and 2–7.

Dot-matrix printer
A printer that uses small pins to make marks on paper to form text and graphics.

The **dot-matrix printer** uses small pins that produce dots on paper to form letters and other characters (Figure 2–8). The quality of the letters is a function of the number of dots used per letter. The newer and more expensive models produce the highest-quality output. Some dot-matrix printers produce characters at the rate of 500 to 600 characters per second.

The dots are created using a print head. Figure 2–9 illustrates a dot matrix printer nine pin print head. The quality of output is incremented as the number of pins in the print head are incremented. Figure 2–10 illustrates how the pins are used to create the letter W: the pins are fired (activated) after a half or full position move.

Dot-matrix printers can produce small letters in compressed or condensed mode to increase the number of characters outputted per line on standard paper. Businesses using databases and spreadsheets often need this feature. Special sideways-printing programs also output a greater number of characters per line.

Table 2–6
Types of Printers

Type of Printer	Method of Letter Creation	Quality			Graphics Variable Letter Size	Approximate Characters per Second	Price Range
		Draft	NLQ[a]	Letter Quality			
Dot-matrix	Dots	X	X		X	80 to 600	$100 to $2,000
Formed-characters	Typewriter style			X		12 to 90	$300 to $3,000
Laser	Dots	X	X	X	X	8 pages/ minute	$1,000 plus
Ink jet	Ink dots	X	X	X	X	80 plus	$300 to $1,500
Thermal	Heat-sensitive paper/ribbons	X	X	X	X	High speed	$50 and up
Plotter	Pen				X	Slow	$350 to $11,000

[a] NLQ = near-letter quality.

Note: The performance and pricing of printers are changing constantly. Computer magazines are a good source for the latest performance specifications and pricing.

Table 2–7
Uses of Printers

Application	Printer Needs
Word processing	Letter or near-letter quality (formed characters)
Spreadsheets	Many characters per line
Databases	Many characters per line
Graphics	Dot-addressable control or plotter

Many dot-matrix printers can produce special characters, including Greek and other foreign languages, scientific symbols, and graphic characters. Some printers allow users to define their own characters.

Formed-character printers produce letter-quality results using thimbles, balls, and daisy wheels. The letter formed looks exactly like that produced by a typewriter. These printers are generally slower than dot-matrix printers. Speeds vary from 12 to 90 characters per second.

Formed-character printer
A printer that uses a thimble, ball, or daisy wheel to produce characters.

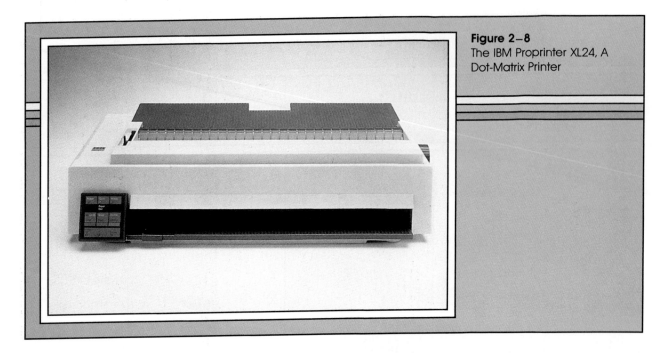

Figure 2–8
The IBM Proprinter XL24, A
Dot-Matrix Printer

Figure 2–9
Dot Matrix Print Head

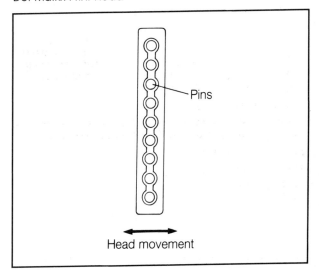

Figure 2–10
Creating a W

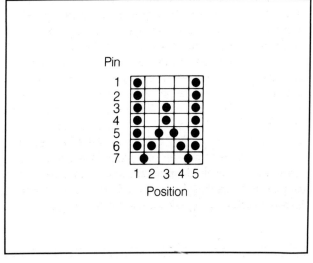

Laser printer
A printer that uses light and an electro-statically controlled toner (ink) to produce characters and graphics on paper.

Ink-jet printer
A printer that uses dots of ink to produce text and graphics.

The **laser printer** uses light technology similar to some copying machines (Figure 2–11). The slower, low-cost models have maximum output of eight pages per minute. The quality of output is competitive with traditional letter-quality printers. Unlimited kinds of images can be produced by a laser printer.

The **ink-jet printer** produces letters by spraying a jet of ink through small pinholes (Figure 2–12). Its use is not limited to letters, and it can produce many special effects. The speed is in the same range as dot-matrix printers.

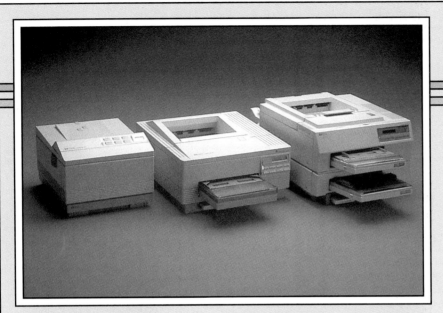

Figure 2–11
Laser Printers—Hewlett-Packard
LaserJet I, II, and III
(left to right)

Thermal printers use a heating element to make a letter or character on either heat-sensitive paper or on regular paper with a heat-sensitive ribbon. The units vary from low-priced units designed for home and traveling microcomputers to high-quality, high-speed, and high-priced units. A common use of thermal printers are as part of facsimile (FAX) communication machines used for the long-distance transfer of documents.

Plotters use pens to produce their images (Figure 2–13). Some hold the paper and move the pens, whereas others hold the printing head in a fixed position and move the paper. Some use drums, whereas others print on a flat surface. Generally, a plotter is much slower than other output devices. It is primarily used for graphics, computer-aided design (CAD), computer-aided design and drafting (CADD), and special effects.

Printer paper-feeding methods include single-sheet friction feed, automatic sheet feed, pin feed, and tractor feed. Any and all types of paper may be fed in using friction feed. Pin or tractor feed require that the paper have a tractor along the outside edge to guide it in.

> Thermal printer
> A printer that uses a heating element and either heat-sensitive paper or heat-sensitive ribbons to produce text and graphics on paper.

> Plotter
> A device that uses pens to produce text and graphics on paper.

On-Line Storage Devices

Program and data storage devices may be either **on-line** or **off-line,** depending on how they are connected to the CPU. On-line devices operate under the control of the CPU. Off-line devices operate independently of the CPU. **On-line storage devices** are devices containing memory that is available to the microcomputer through communication cables. The memory is not part of the internal RAM or ROM. On-line storage devices are

> On line
> Operated at the same time as other equipment under the control of the microprocessor.

> Off line
> Independent of the microprocessor in the computer.

Figure 2–12
Hewlett-Packard Think Jet

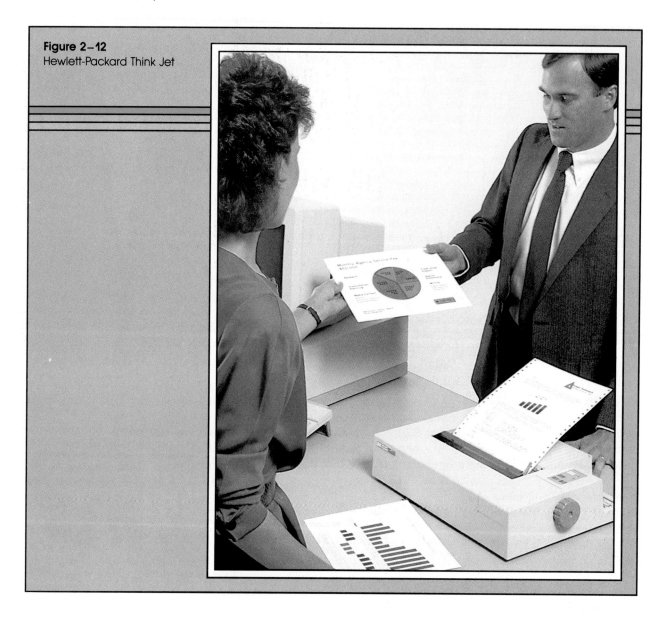

On-line storage device
A device containing memory
available to the microcomputer
through communication cables.

considered to be external to the microcomputer, even though they are commonly built into the same case. The Apple IIc, Apple look-alikes, IBM PC, IBM look-alikes, and most other microcomputers use cards, called disk controller cards, for controlling on-line storage devices. Usually, each type of data storage device requires its own card.

Among the storage devices used on computers are cassette tape recorders, 5¼-inch floppy disk drives, 3½-inch floppy disk drives, 8-inch floppy disk drives, hard (fixed and removable) disk drives; quarter-inch (streaming) tapes, 2½-inch disk drives (slowly winning acceptance), RAM cards, and CD-ROM.

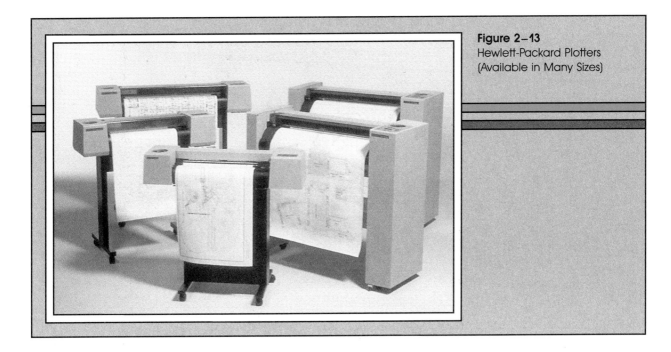

Figure 2–13
Hewlett-Packard Plotters
(Available in Many Sizes)

Cassette Tape Recorders

Some home and pocket computers use the cassette tape recorder as a low-cost on-line storage device. A few laptop computers include a cassette recorder as an internal part of their system.

Five and One-Quarter (5¼) Inch Disk Drives

The most common data and program storage device is the **five and one-quarter (5¼) inch floppy disk drive.** This electromechanical device rotates a 5¼-inch disk and feeds signals into and accepts signals from the disk as directed by the controller circuits. The controller circuits are managed by the microcomputer through its operating system.

Five and one-quarter (5¼) inch floppy disk drive
A disk drive that reads and writes computer data on a 5¼-inch disk covered with a paperlike cover.

Three and One-Half (3½) Inch Disk Drives

The Apple Macintosh introduced the **three and one-half (3½) inch disk drive** to the U.S. market. Since its introduction, the 3½-inch disk drive has found favor with laptop (Figure 2–14), portable, and desktop manufacturers due to its economy, lightweight (all-plastic) construction, storage capacity of more than 700K, compact-sized disk drive, compact-sized disk, and disk's hard shell (for the protection of stored data).

Three and one-half (3½) inch disk drive
A disk drive that reads and writes computer data on a 3½-inch disk covered with a hard plastic shell.

Many MS-DOS/PC DOS microcomputers now use the 3½-inch disk drive. When IBM used this smaller drive on its Personal System/2 series, it became a second standard.

Figure 2–14
Laptop Computers with
3½-inch Disk Drives
(Compaq LTEs)

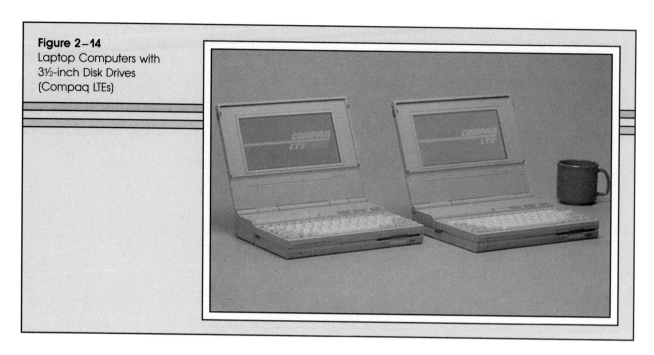

The 3½-inch disk drive is available in 720K, 800K, 1.44MB, and 2.88MB capacities. The use of these disk drives is dependent upon the version of MS-DOS/PC DOS, some controller chips, and the software being used. Among the many computers using the 3½-inch drives is the COMPAQ LTE, which may be equipped with a 20MB hard drive and a 1.44MB 3½-inch drive. In addition, a 2½-inch disk drive is being offered for some lightweight IBM-compatible laptop computers.

A 3½-inch disk cannot fit into a 5¼-inch disk drive, and vice versa. Many leading software manufacturers are producing software in both sizes.

Eight (8) Inch Disk Drives

The Radio Shack Models II, 12, and 6000 microcomputers, among others, use 8-inch floppy disk drives. The trend in on-line storage devices is toward smaller ones. The dominance of the 5¼-inch floppy disk drive over the 8-inch drive seems to be primarily due to its smaller size and its compatible technology.

Hard Disk Drives

Hard disk
A high-capacity data storage device that may be fixed or removable.

The **hard disk** (Figure 2–15) provides mass storage of data in an efficient manner and, thus, greater operating speed, convenience, and economy. A 10MB hard disk can store the equivalent of 39 floppy disks and save the user hundreds of hours of time in not having to switch disks in search of

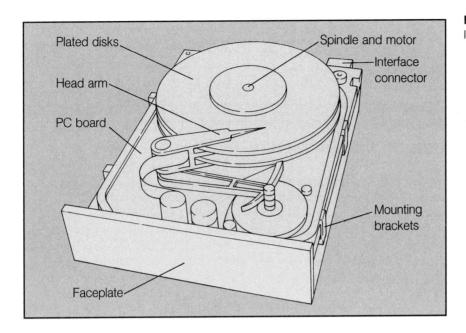

Figure 2–15
Inside a Hard Disk Drive

one special disk, or in not forgetting on which disk a particular file was stored. Many programs require the availability of a hard disk.

Hard disk drives may be found in 3½-, 5¼-, and 8-inch sizes, with the 5¼-inch drive being most popular. The 5-to-10MB standard size has given way to the 20, 30, and 40MB capacities. Manufacturers put more than 900MB into a hard disk drive. **Half-height** disk drives fit into half the space as the original IBM PC disk drives. Internal hard disk drives with 680MB and external drive units with up to 16 GB are available.

Not only have the capacities changed, but access speed has also quickened with the increase in megabytes. Early technology used the stepper motor, or incremental method of searching for data. Access time varies from 85 to 65 milliseconds.

Present technology uses a voice coil method of access that has reduced search time to 65 to 25 nanoseconds for a 40MB hard disk drive versus 65 milliseconds for the stepper motor. Access time depends on the technology and disk capacity.

Hard disk drives in 10 to 80MB plus capacities may also be found mounted on PC boards that fit into a slot on the motherboard. These drives come in varying thicknesses. Some require a single slot, some two slots. Many require one and a half slots.

Half-height
The space available for a disk drive that is equal to half the height of the original IBM PC disk drive.

CD-ROM

Compact disk-read only memory (CD-ROM) is a compact disk similar to the compact disk used for audio and video recording. A CD-ROM player uses laser (light) technology to store files. It is a write once-read many times storage media-device which is used for selected applications such as storing and distributing census data and encyclopedias. One company markets a database of over 8 million names, addresses, and telephone numbers on a single CD-ROM disk.

On-Line Storage Media

On-line storage media
Material used to store microcomputer files.

Floppy disk
A plastic circle with a coating of magnetic material that rotates within an outer sleeve.

Track
A magnetic circle on a disk for storing data.

Sector
A division of a track on a disk.

On-line storage media are used to store microcomputer files. Many different types of media are used. The **floppy disk** is a plastic circle with a coating of magnetic material that rotates within an outer sleeve. Users must be careful not to touch the magnetic surface, as the oil from the fingers will damage the surface. Figure 2–16 identifies the parts of two types of disks. Figure 2–17 shows the **track** and **sector** divisions of a disk. A track is a magnetic circle on the disk that stores data, and a sector is a division of a track.

On the upper right side is a square cutout, the write-protect notch. On 8-inch disks it must be covered for writing, and on 5¼-inch disks it must be uncovered for writing. On 8-inch disks it is uncovered for read only, and on 5¼-inch disks it is covered. The index hole on disks is used by some microcomputers to locate the data on the media. The rotation hole is in the middle of the disk and is used by the disk drive to rotate the media.

The 3½-inch disk is similar internally to the larger disks and has a hard plastic shell that opens automatically when inserted into the disk drive. It does not require a paper case or sleeve but must be treated with care.

Figure 2–16
Two Types of Disks

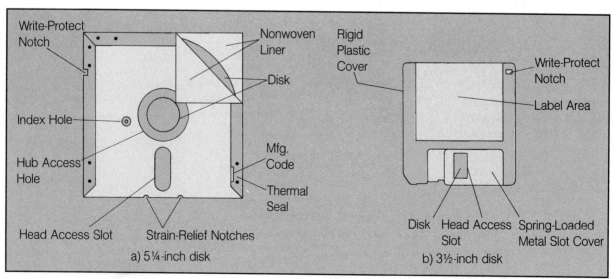

a) 5¼-inch disk

b) 3½-inch disk

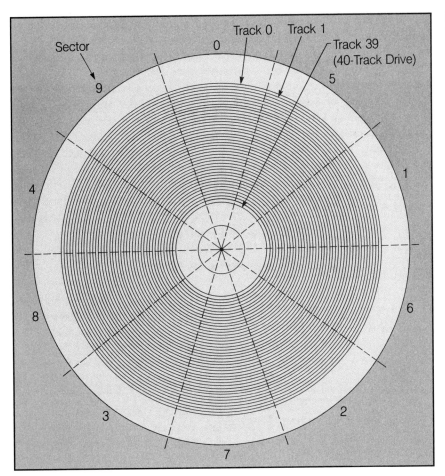

Figure 2–17
The Tracks and Sectors of a Disk

Handling rules for disks include the following:

Do not allow the disk to come near magnetic fields such as those generated by television sets and electric motors.

Do not remove the disk from the microcomputer when it is operating. (A red light indicates when a disk drive is moving.)

Do not force the disk into the drive.

Do not write on the disk with a hard device. It is best to write on the label before placing it on the disk.

Do not touch the magnetic part of the disk.

Do not expose the disk to the direct heat of the sun (for example, by storing it on the dashboard of a car).

Do not expose the disk to extreme cold.

Do keep the disk in its protective envelope except when in use.

Do handle the disk by its edges.

When placing a disk in a disk drive, hold the disk by the edge with the write-protect notch to the left and the label facing up. Gently place it in the disk drive, and close the door.

When a microcomputer is started, it will look for the operating system in a particular disk drive, called the default drive. When the disk drives lie side by side, the default drive on U.S.-manufactured microcomputers is located on the left. When drives sit on top of one another, you must learn the disk drive designations, since they vary among manufacturers.

The size of a disk is not the only factor that determines the amount of data that can be stored. Disks may be single sided/single density (SSSD), single sided/double density (SSDD), double sided/double density (DSDD), quad density (QD), and high density. Single sided means that only one side of the disk is used to store information. The density rating indicates the closeness in which data are stored and determines the capacity of the storage media. For disks with storage densities greater than double density, the number of tracks is used as a measure of the potential storage capacity. Disks store from 50,000 to over a billion characters (Table 2–8).

The type of disks you purchase should match your system specifications. For example, if you are using a microcomputer such as the IBM AT with high-density 1.2MB disks, you must use that type of disk.

Even carefully handled disks will fail at times. Thus, make a copy of all program and data disks, and store these in a separate location for insurance.

Review of Selected Systems

A wide selection of microcomputers with varying capabilities is available in each size class: pockets, laptops, transportables, and desktops. The systems available change constantly as technology changes. For example, the IBM Personal System/2 series of microcomputers, released in April 1987, compares with the original IBM PC, released in 1981, as follows. It has approximately 1,000 times more internal (RAM) memory, 1,000 times more

Table 2–8
Capacity of Commonly Used On-Line Storage Media

Type of Disk	3½ Inch	5¼ Inch	8 Inch
Single sided/single density		50 to 90K	92K
Single sided/double density	720K	160 to 200K	
Double sided/double density		300 to 400K	500K
Quad density		750K to 3MB	
High density	1.44 to 5MB		

external (on-line) memory, 4 times more data-carrying capacity, 6 times the number of communication protocols, 5 times more speed, 5 times more disk retrieval speed, 4,000 times the number of colors, 4.8 times more screen resolution; a 50 percent reduction in price; and a 50 percent reduction in size. Micros in Action "Selecting a System" illustrates how one company wrote the specifications for its microcomputer system.

Micros in Action

Selecting a System

Tipi Makers, Inc., selected an IBM-compatible 80386 computer with 33Mhz as its file server due to the need to work with three workstations. It also selected Novell Netware for the system operations and MS-DOS as the operating system. For the file server, the on-line storage include a 320MB hard disk drive, a 1.2MB (5¼-inch) floppy disk drive, and a 1.44MB (3½-inch) floppy disk drive. The monitor selected was a 14-inch VGA superresolution (1,024 × 768 pixels) with a TVGA adapter card.

For the workstations, Tipi Makers selected three 80286 systems with 40MB hard drives and one 1.44MB (3½-inch) disk drive. The monitors were identical to the file server. Software selected included network, manufacturing, accounting, word processing, spreadsheet, data-driven graphics, image-driven graphics, database, and desktop publishing.

Microcomputer Compatibility

When a business requires more than a single microcomputer, it is important that the microcomputers selected be able to function as a system. **Operational compatibility**—the capability of microcomputers to work together as a system—is one important aspect that must be considered where more than a single microcomputer is used. **Physical compatibility** involves the capability to exchange physical parts, such as the PC boards used to add capabilities.

The office with only one microcomputer does not need to be concerned with compatibility except when expansion is anticipated or data are being transferred from an outside source. When the business professional must work with others who are using microcomputers, the need for compatibility begins. When a second or third microcomputer is added, the problem of compatibility becomes critical. The number of offices with multiple microcomputers is increasing rapidly.

The problem of compatibility exists between different brands, and even within the same brand of microcomputers produced at different times. The capabilities of microcomputers have grown. A five-year-old

Operational compatibility
The capability of microcomputers to work together as a system.

Physical compatibility
The capability to exchange physical parts between computer systems.

4. What is a motherboard?
5. What is a printed circuit board? What is a PC board used for?
6. Identify MCA, ISA, and EISA.
7. What is a bit? What is a byte? How are they related?
8. What does a microprocessor do?
9. What is a math co-processor? Why would a user want one?
10. What is random access memory? What is read-only memory? How are they related? How do they differ?
11. What is a controller board? Why would a user want one?
12. What are DIP switches used for?
13. Identify some microcomputer input devices.
14. Give some examples of pointing devices and how they are used.
15. What does a scanner do?
16. What is an I/O port? What is one used for?
17. What is a modem? What is one used for?
18. Identify some output devices.
19. What is a pixel? Why should a user know about pixels?
20. What is the difference between the operation of a dot-matrix and a laser printer?

Discussion and Application Questions

1. In your local newspaper, find some advertisements for microcomputers. Identify the microcomputers being sold, and prepare a short discussion of the nature of these microcomputers.
2. Obtain a copy of a microcomputer magazine from your library, local computer store, or bookstore. Select any article relating to microcomputer hardware, and prepare to discuss the information contained in the article.
3. Examine several copies of the *Wall Street Journal* or national news magazines. Identify some articles about microcomputer hardware, and prepare a short discussion.
4. Identify the radio and television advertisements for microcomputer hardware currently being run. What type of hardware or store is being advertised in each case?
5. Identify the type of hardware sold through the following:
   a. Local retail stores.
   b. Discount and department stores.
   c. Mail-order outlets.
   d. Office supply outlets.
6. Look up the hardware outlets listed in the yellow pages of your telephone book. What equipment might you expect to be able to purchase locally?

CHAPTER 3

Operating Systems

Goals

Upon completion of this chapter, you will be able to do the following:

- Define the tasks of an operating system.

- Identify and examine operating system features.

- Understand the importance of the operating system to the user.

Outline

Operations Research

An operations research analyst for the Corps of Engineers, Economic Analysis Section, identified his microcomputer needs as follows: statistical analysis, database maintenance, word processing, spreadsheet analysis, graphical presentation, and project management. For his particular job, the statistical analysis, combined with database maintenance, was the most critical. He obtained copies of statistical programs to maintain and analyze data for lock use, water supply and quality, economic impact of housing and employment, military base adjustments and closings, and relocation of naval and other military bases. The programs made analysis easier, reduced the time required to do the job, and resulted in better decision making.

Because of software site licenses and the many computers at the Corps of Engineers, the capability to use the available software and compatibility with other computers were critical. The decision was limited to MS-DOS computers.

An **operating system** is a program that controls printers, monitors, disk drives, and hard disk drives connected to a central processing unit so they all work together. The user works through the operating system to control microcomputer parts to obtain useful results. As noted in the Micros in Action "Operations Research," software is designed to operate on computers with a given operating system.

A **routine** is part of a program that performs a specific task. Internal to the operating system are a number of **functions**. Functions are routines that are part of the operating system (internal) and are always available. When the operating system is started, all functions are **loaded** (transferred from disk to memory) into RAM.

Utilities are external programs that usually come with the operating system but can also be purchased separately. The terms used to define the concepts of functions and utilities have changed constantly over the history of microcomputers. Some texts or magazines call functions *internal utilities* or *resident utilities*, whereas they call utilities *external utilities* or *transient utilities*. Functions and utilities are the terms most commonly used.

Many functions and utilities involve **saving, retrieving,** moving, changing, copying, and keeping track of **files.** A file is a collection of related data or program code. Saving or **storing** is the recording of a data or program file on a disk or other recording media. Retrieving is the loading or recalling of a file from disk or other storage media into computer memory. Routines are either functions or utilities depending on the operating system. Examples of routines include preparing a disk to receive data or programs, copying a disk; saving a data or program file, retrieving a data or program file into RAM, and removing data or program files from the directory.

Operating system
The program that controls the printers, monitors, disk drives, and hard disk drives connected to a central processing unit so that they work together.

Routine
A part of a program that performs a specific task.

Function
(operating system): A routine that is part of the operating system. These routines provide the user with the capability to perform often-needed tasks. Functions are loaded into RAM with the operating system and remain there.

Load
To transfer a program from disk to RAM.

Utility
An external program available on the disk with the operating system. Utilities often include programs that support the operation of the operating system by adding capabilities.

Saving
To record a data or program file on disk or other recording media.

Retrieving
The loading or recalling of a file from disk or other storage media into computer memory.

File
A collection of related data or program code.

Storing
To save a file.

Currently, popular operating systems include the Apple Macintosh operating system, the Apple Disk Operating System used on the Apple Macintosh; the Microsoft Disk Operating System/Personal Computer Disk Operating System (MS-DOS/PC DOS) used on the IBM PC, XT, AT, and compatibles; Operating System 2 (OS/2) for multitasking and multiuser operation on the high-end IBM Personal System/2 microcomputers and compatibles; and UNIX, the multiuser operating system developed by Bell Laboratories. Versions of UNIX include Venix and Xenix.

Why Operating Systems?

The operating system controls the microcomputer. Some of the output the user of a microcomputer might produce are letters, financial reports, evaluations, market surveys, invoices, and checks. Many users are not interested in how the program and data files are saved, but they must know what to do and what not to do to ensure that errors are not made that may damage these files. In addition, knowledge about the operating system makes the performance of selected tasks easier, helps solve operating problems if they occur, and often saves time. Usually, application programs interface with the operating system, but sometimes users must do so directly.

Backup
A copy of a disk or file.

The user of any operating system must know how to make **backup** copies of programs and data files. Having backup copies eliminates the potentially devastating effects of storage media failures, loss, or destruction.

The creation and maintenance of a data set entails costs for hardware, software, time, and effort. These dollars may be wasted if data are lost due to the lack of backup copies and poor operating practices. Once a user becomes experienced in using a data set, it is difficult to do without it even for a short period of time.

Problems occur even with the best-designed systems and programs. When these problems occur, the user's knowledge of the operating system can turn a disaster into a simple inconvenience. For example, operating systems often are upgraded. When an earlier operating system is used to read a high-capacity disk, a lot of junk appears on the screen, but no damage is done to the disk. When an older system is used to change or write something on a new disk, however, program and data files can be damaged. Knowing that an error has occurred and what not to do can prevent the loss of valuable programs and data.

The original version of MS-DOS/PC DOS was capable of controlling single-sided disk drives (160K). Version 1.1 added the capability of controlling double-sided drives (320K). With the MS-DOS/PC DOS version 2.0 came the capability to increase the amount of storage on a disk from 320 to 360K. Version 2.1 enabled the PC Jr. to read and write to a cassette drive. With the MS-DOS/PC DOS version 3.0 came the ability to store 1.2MB on disk and to read and write the 360K disk on the 1.2MB disk drive. Version 3.2 brought with it the capability to read and write 3½-inch disks, thus adding the possibilities of new tasks.

A user can perform a task in a number of ways. Knowledge of the operating system makes it easier to select the best method. In MS-DOS/PC DOS, for example, a text file can be examined by using a word processor or by typing the word **TYPE** followed by the file name specification and **<CR>**. The characters <CR> and the symbol ↵ are used to represent the return or enter key on the keyboard.

TYPE
MS-DOS/PC DOS instruction to display a file on the screen.

<CR>
Press the return or enter key.

↵
Press the return or enter key.

Tasks of Operating Systems

Operating system tasks are performed using internal functions and external utilities. The operating system functions, utilities, and hardware define the limits of a microcomputer system's capabilities. For example, you cannot obtain printed output unless you have an operating system with the capability and the hardware to do the job.

As already described, internal functions are loaded into RAM when the system is loaded and are always available. Utilities are programs recorded separately in files on a disk. The user must tell the computer to load utilities into RAM when they are needed. That disk must be available when these utilities are used.

A set of **operating system conventions** (operating rules) makes it easier to use functions and utilities. There are conventions for communication between all the parts of the microcomputer system.

Operating system convention
A standard and accepted abbreviation or symbol, with its meaning, for users of microcomputer operating systems.

Internal Functions

Internal functions include booting the system, storage and retrieval of files, examining the directory, and controlling communications.

Booting the System

The first thing that must happen when a computer is started is to start the operating system. There are two methods, a **cold boot** and a **warm boot.** A cold boot is the starting of the operating system by turning the microcomputer on. A warm boot is the restarting of the operating system when the microcomputer is running.

A small **bootstrap program** recorded in the ROM of the microcomputer loads the operating system code from disk or hard disk into RAM. The Apple and MS-DOS/PC DOS microcomputers start with a cold boot, while in older operating systems (CP/M and TRS-DOS), the microcomputer is first turned on, and then the disk is inserted before starting the booting process.

Most microcomputer operating systems look for a program or data file on the disk drive that is the currently **logged drive.** When a system is started, the **default drive** that becomes the logged drive is the lower-numbered or lower-lettered drive. The default drive is the disk drive from which data and programs are read unless the microcomputer is instructed

Cold boot
The starting of a microcomputer operating system by turning the microcomputer on.

Warm boot (Ctrl / Alt / Del)
The restarting of the microcomputer operating system while the computer is running.

Bootstrap program
A program (set of instructions) used to load the operating system from disk to RAM when the system is started.

Logged drive
The disk drive from which data and programs are read.

Default drive
The disk drive from which data and programs are read unless the microcomputer is instructed otherwise. The default drive is the logged drive if no additional instructions are given.

otherwise. The default drive is the logged drive, if no additional instructions are given. Table 3–1 lists the default drive by operating system.

To perform a cold boot, place a disk with an operating system in the default drive, and turn the microcomputer on. When the machine starts, the disk is read, and the operating system is loaded. The warm boot, which most microcomputers can use, starts with the microcomputer running, a disk with an operating system in the default drive, and a reset instruction. Table 3–2 lists the reset instructions for selected systems. After giving the reset command, the bootstrap program will take over in the same manner as a cold boot.

The operating system may be loaded directly from some hard disks. Usually, the microcomputer first looks for a disk in the default drive, and if one is not found, it then changes the default drive to the hard drive and continues with the process of loading the system into RAM. Some hard disk drive systems do not boot from the hard disk drive, but require that the user load the operating system from the default drive or a preboot program (which transfers control to the hard disk drive.)

Some MS-DOS/PC DOS versions ask that the user enter the date and time at the beginning of an operating session. In some cases the user can to press and not actually enter the date. If a version requires that the user enter certain information, it will not let the user continue until this has been done.

CONFIG.SYS
An MS-DOS/PC DOS file that contains data used by the operating system to setup the system environment.

In MS-DOS/PC DOS, after the operating system is loaded, the operating system then looks for a **CONFIG.SYS** file on the logged disk. The CONFIG.SYS file contains data on how to set up the system. For example, some programs use a large number of data files. A statement such as FILES = 20 in the CONFIG.SYS file tells the operating system to reserve space to open up to twenty data files at one time.

AUTOEXEC.BAT
A computer program file that is executed when the system is started.

After the CONFIG.SYS file is read, the MS-DOS/PC DOS operating system loads and executes the **AUTOEXEC.BAT** file. The AUTOEXEC.BAT file contains a set of instructions that tell the operating system what to do next. AUTOEXEC.BAT files are commonly used to clear the screen and present a menu.

Table 3–1 Default/Logged Drives	
Operating System	Default Drive
Apple Macintosh	Internal drive
MS-DOS/PC DOS	A drive on floppy disk systems C drive on hard disk systems
OS/2	Same as MS-DOS/PC DOS computers
UNIX	C drive on most systems

Table 3–2
Reset Methods

Operating System	Reset Method
Apple Macintosh	Press the reset key on the side.
MS-DOS/PC DOS	Press the \<Ctrl\>, \<Alt\>, and \<Delete\> keys together. (Many newer models have reset buttons on the front panel of the computer.)
OS/2	Follow the procedure for MS-DOS/PC DOS computers.
UNIX	Follow the procedure for MS-DOS/PC DOS computers.

Table 3–3
Steps Required to Save a File

Step	How/Who
1. Prepare recording media.	Media is placed in disk drive, and a preparation program is executed.
2. Prepare file to save.	This is a user task.
3. Place recording media in disk drive.	This is a user task.
4. Locate starting location for file.	Task is performed automatically by the operating system.
5. Store file.	Task is performed automatically by the operating system after user starts the process.
6. Keep record of where saved.	Task is performed automatically by the operating system in a disk directory.

Storing and Retrieving Files on Disk

After the system is booted, the task of organizing, indexing, and locating data and program files on data storage devices is one of the most important operating system functions. Most of the work is performed automatically by the operating system. The steps in saving a file are shown in Table 3–3.

When the microcomputer records the material, it starts by placing a beginning-of-file code marker; it then records the information, followed by an end-of-file marker (often called EOF). The operating system records where on the disk to save the file in order to prevent the overwriting of valuable information.

FORMAT.COM
A program that tells the microcomputer to prepare a disk for use. Magnetic marks are made on the media to identify tracks and sectors where data are to be stored.

Extension
In MS-DOS/PC DOS a three character addition to a file name to indicate the file type.

.COM
Extension for a command program file. This file may be executed by typing its name and pressing ↵.

.EXE
Extension for an execute program file. This file may be executed by typing its name and pressing ↵.

.BAT
Extension of a batch program file. The file contains disk operating system instructions. This file may be executed by typing its name and pressing ↵.

Hierarchical file structure
A file structure consisiting of a top-down organization. Files are organized in what is often referred to as a tree structure. Some operating systems allow sophisticated security to be established for hierarchical files.

The disk **FORMAT.COM** program tells the microcomputer to prepare a disk for use. It includes instructions to prepare a directory (a list of programs, data, and other files) for the disk. The disk operating system records the name and location of each file on the disk in the directory.

In MS-DOS/PC DOS, a three-character **extension** is included on file names to indicate file type. The extension **.COM** on the FORMAT.COM file means that the file is a command file. A command file is a small program that may be executed by typing the name of the file such as, FORMAT and then pressing ↵. Other common extensions are **.EXE** (execute file-larger program), **.BAT** (batch file-direct disk operating system instruction file), and **.BAK** (backup file).

Once the material is stored on disk, you may shut off your microcomputer. The program or data may be reloaded into the RAM of your microcomputer. The microcomputer disk operating system checks the disk's directory to find the file, which is then loaded. The operating system uses the directory to go directly to where the file is stored.

There are a number of different methods for organizing files on a disk or hard disk. The most popular method for disks has been a series of individual files. For hard disks, a **hierarchical file structure** is popular (Figure 3–1). A hierarchical file structure has a top-down organization, often referred to as a tree directory structure (to be discussed later). Some operating systems allow sophisticated security to be established for hierarchical files.

Examining the Directory

Disk operating systems contain directories, files which keep lists of the programs, data, and other files stored on media. Examining a directory is

Figure 3–1
Hierarchical Files

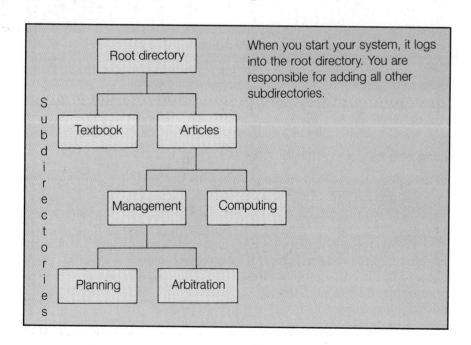

When you start your system, it logs into the root directory. You are responsible for adding all other subdirectories.

simple (Figure 3–2). In MS-DOS/PC DOS, you simply type **DIR** ↵ to get the directory of the disk in the logged drive.

When the instruction DIR ↵ was given to create Figure 3–2, the file list scrolled off the screen telling us that the numer of files in the directory is greater than can be displayed on a single screen. The user may use DIR/W ↵ for a wide display or DIR/P ↵ for paging (examining one screen at a time) to examine all the items in the directory. Figure 3–3 illustrates the DIR/W ↵ results. In MS-DOS/PC DOS, you may type the instruction DIR in uppercase or lowercase letters. The microcomputer tells you what files are on the disk, the size of each file, the date and time the file was started, and the number of bytes still free to use on the disk. DIR/W ↵ results in the names of the files, the number of files, and the free bytes available.

To get the directory of any other drive, the instruction is usually DIR n: ↵ in MS-DOS/PC DOS, where n stands for the letter of the drive (A, B, C, and so on) or the name of the subdirectory. For example, if you are logged into drive A and the prompt A> is displayed on the screen, typing DIR :C ↵ displays the list of files on the disk in drive C.

Most operating systems allow you to give instructions to your operating system using either uppercase or lowercase letters. There are some exceptions. For example, UNIX uses lowercase letters for system instructions.

For hard disks with large volumes of files, a tree directory structure has been developed. UNIX was the first microcomputer operating system to use this type of directory, which is now used by MS-DOS/PC DOS 2.0 and newer versions, among others. The number of branches (subdirectories) is limited in some operating systems. The set of subdirectories from the main directory to the one of interest is called a path. In MS-DOS/PC DOS, utilities are available to help examine the tree structure of a disk.

DIR
The MS-DOS/PC DOS instruction that tells the operating system to display a listing of the files on a disk.

```
PAINTPLU BAT      117    1-18-90    2:35p
PBRUSH   BAT      121   10-16-89    8:02a
PROCOM   BAT      179   10-21-89   11:07a
QFONT    BAT      169    9-29-89    9:00a
QMS      BAT       19    9-22-89    3:58p
QUIKMEM2 SYS     3956   10-28-88    7:57a
RUNKM    EXE     7030   11-21-86
SCAN     BAT       62   12-06-89    9:00p
SERIAL   BAT       84    6-15-87    6:12a
SK       COM    38021   12-06-85    1:15p
SKETCH   BAT       69   12-06-89    9:00p
SMALL               3    2-07-89    8:38p
SMARTDRV SYS    10224    9-07-89    4:29a
TREEINFO NCD      587   12-31-88    2:33a
USA      BAT      113    9-27-89    6:14a
VDISK    SYS     3550    2-06-87   12:00p
VIDEO    BAT       60    8-31-89    1:45p
WIN386   BAT      134   10-04-89   11:20a
WIN86    BAT      133   10-04-89   12:04p
WORD5    BAT      126   12-29-89    9:01a
WORDM    BAT      129    9-07-89   10:42a
WORDP    BAT      149    9-07-89   10:14a
        78 File(s)     49152 bytes free

C:\>
```

Figure 3–2
Disk Directory Using MS-DOS/PC DOS

Figure 3–3

The Results of Typing `DIR/W`

```
C:\>dir /w

 Volume in drive C is DISK1_VOL1
 Directory of  C:\

A&Z              COMPAQ           CONFIG           DOS              HIJAAK
INSET            JUNK             LAPLINK          LIGHT            MOUSE
PAINT            PAINTPLU         PBRUSH           PROCOM           QMS
READR            SK               SKETCH           TEMP             TEST
USA              UTILITIE         VIDEO            WIN386           WP44
WP51             WS4              ANSI     SYS     AUTOEXEC BAT     AZ       BAT
CHSYS    BAT     CLOCK    SYS     COMMAND  COM     CONFIG   SYS     COREDSK  COM
DM       EXE     DMDRVR   BIN     DRIVER   SYS     EGA      SYS     EMM      SYS
GRAFTABL COM     HIJAAK   BAT     HPSCANER SYS     INSET    BAT     LAPLINK  BAT
LIGHT    BAT     MENU             MENU     BAT     MODE     COM     MODE     DAT
MOUSE    BAT     MOUSE    SYS     ONLINE   HLP     PACOLOR  BAT     PAGRAY   BAT
PAINT    BAT     PAINTPLU BAT     PBRUSH   BAT     PROCOM   BAT     QFONT    BAT
QMS      BAT     QUIKMEM2 SYS     RUNKM    EXE     SCAN     BAT     SERIAL   BAT
SK       COM     SKETCH   BAT     SMALL            SMARTDRV SYS     TREEINFO NCD
USA      BAT     VDISK    SYS     VIDEO    BAT     WIN386   BAT     WIN86    BAT
WORD5    BAT     WORDM    BAT     WORDP    BAT
          78 File(s)      34816 bytes free

C:\>
```

Figure 3–4 illustrates the use of VTREE.COM, examining the same hard disk root directory that was illustrated in Figures 3–2 and 3–3.

If you are using a MS-DOS/PC DOS system with a hard disk divided into subdirectories, you must either log into a subdirectory or use a path instruction to obtain the directory listing in a subdirectory. To log into a subdirectory, type `CD\subname` ↵. CD is the change directory instruction. To return to the root directory, type `CD\` ↵. Once the system is logged into a subdirectory, the directory can be examined as noted above.

The path instruction is used to examine the directory of one subdirectory when the system is logged into another subdirectory. The path instruction is similar to the change directory instruction. For example, if you are logged into a subdirectory DOS on disk drive C, you can type `DIR C:\PAINT` ↵ to examine the directory of the subdirectory PAINT without changing the logged subdirectory.

Controlling Communication Functions

The microcomputer communicates with printers, monitors, plotters, and communication devices through ports. Some of the more common ports found on microcomputers are the parallel printer port, RS-232C serial communication port (see Micros in Action, "Tracking the Use of a Waterway"), and printer port, disk drive port, keyboard port, monochrome monitor (one-color) port, RGB (red-green-blue; color) monitor port, RS-422 serial port, and IEEE-488 parallel port for laboratory equipment. Outlet ports are discussed in detail in Chapter 10.

Figure 3—4
VTREE.COM

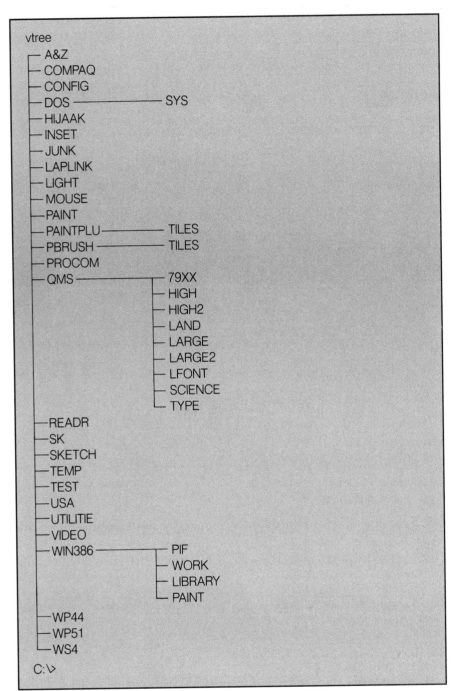

One job of the operating system is to control the communication between the CPU and the ports. Before this control can be executed, the hardware and software must be configured to operate with the operating system being used. As a user, you need not concern yourself with the communi-

Tracking the Use of a Waterway

The data for the Tennessee Tombigbee Waterway were maintained on the Corp of Engineer's mainframe computer. A modem was used to connect the telephone to the serial communication port of the microcomputer system and then to the mainframe computer through lines. The waterway data were downloaded from the mainframe and then analyzed using statistical software available.

The waterway data required the use of a hard disk drive, because the file size was over 2 million bytes. The microcomputer was able to analyze the data despite its volume.

cation process. For example, when you type on the keyboard, the operating system is controlling the communication from the keyboard to the other parts of the system. Your concern is simply to type the characters correctly on the keyboard.

A default communication procedure in MS-DOS/PC DOS requires the user to enter the time and date at the beginning of a session. The time and date entered are used by all programs that require such information. Some microcomputer systems have PC boards with clocks and batteries that provide this information automatically.

Housekeeping Functions

Housekeeping functions include the required system organizational adjustments as needs change over time. No matter how careful you are in setting up a microcomputer system, it will require adjustments eventually. For example, a new application will require a different or an improved collection of programs. MS-DOS/PC DOS housekeeping functions such as **COPY** and utilities such as **DISKCOPY.COM,** make it easier to move files to reorganize for the new needs. COPY is a MS-DOS/PC DOS function for copying the files on one disk to another or for copying a file to a second file using a new name. DISKCOPY.COM is MS-DOS/PC DOS utility used to make a copy of a disk.

It is often convenient to erase files that are no longer wanted and to rename files to fit a new pattern. ERASE zzz ↵ is the internal MS-DOS/PC DOS function that removes the file zzz. RENAME zzzl zzz2 ↵ is the internal MS-DOS/PC DOS function that changes the name of zzzl to zzz2. During moving, erasing, and renaming, the operating system will keep track of what files are available and where on the disk they are stored.

COPY
A MS-DOS/PC DOS function for copying the files on one disk to another or for copying a file to a second file using a new name.

DISKCOPY.COM
A MS-DOS/PC DOS utility used to make a copy of a disk.

Additional Operating System Functions

Operating system windows are an additional feature of operating systems (Figure 3–5). The use of windows allows you to use the operating system to split the screen into two or more parts. You may view different combinations of files, parts of files, and different activities. One application of windows is in word processing. The capability to look at two word processing documents and to transfer text between them may speed the creation of new documents.

Another operating system feature is **multitasking,** the capability of a microcomputer to do more than one task at a time. For example, a user can maintain communications with another computer while creating a document. Information from the second computer may be transferred into the document periodically.

Multiusing is the capability of two or more users to use the same computer at one time. Multiusing gives the microcomputer **time-sharing** capabilities so that more than one **terminal** can share the same microprocessor. Terminals are computer input/output devices. A microcomputer can be used as a terminal for a multiusing computer. Individuals using these terminals share the microcomputer's microprocessor, data, program files, and peripherals.

Microcomputers may be connected in a local area network (LAN, or **computer network**) to share files and peripherals. Networks are important to the business office where a number of individuals must use the same files or where the number of peripherals, such as printers, is limited.

Operating system windows
An operating system capability to divide the screen into parts.

Multitasking
The capability to instruct the microcomputer to perform more than one task at a time.

Multiusing
The capability of using a microcomputer system for more than a single user at one time.

Time-sharing
The capability of having more than one terminal connected to, and operated at one time by the same computer.

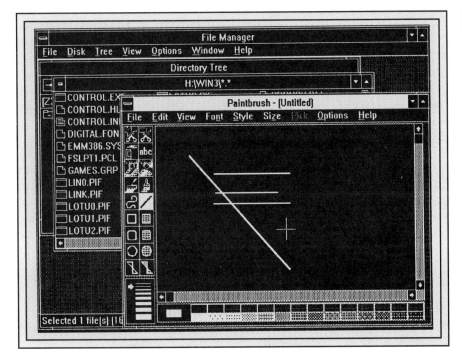

Figure 3–5
Microsoft Windows

External Utilities

Utilities are external programs that add to the capabilities of an operating system; they are stored on a disk, not in RAM. Utilities include housekeeping utilities and other utilities.

Housekeeping Utilities—FORMAT

One utility that must be used each time a new data disk is created is FORMAT. This utility has a variety of names in different operating systems. Formatting is the process by which magnetic markers are placed on a disk to identify where data are to be stored. These locations are divided into tracks and sectors. One track, the directory track, maintains the list and location of all files. The amount of data that can be stored on a disk is a function of the manner in which it is formatted (organized).

A common application problem stems from the use of unformatted disks or the user's forgetting to place a disk in a disk drive. When this occurs, an error message like the following is displayed:

```
Not ready error reading drive A

Abort, Retry, Fail?
```

This message should not bother you. You might want to keep a small supply of formatted disks ready to use, just in case you make an error of this type. When the error occurs, place a formatted disk in the drive required, and keep working. The key is to read the screen instructions carefully and then to take corrective action to reduce the consequence of your error.

Most operating systems offer file copy, disk copy, and hard disk backup routines. The file copy routine copies individual files to a formatted disk. The DISKCOPY.COM routine copies an entire disk to a second disk. The hard disk **BACKUP.COM** program copies the files from a hard disk to one or more floppy disks. In MS-DOS/PC DOS, the individual file copy routine is an internal function, whereas the DISKCOPY.COM and the hard disk BACKUP.COM routines are utilities.

When you purchase or create a program, your first task should be to make a copy in case the original is damaged. Some programs are sold **copy protected**, with limits on the number of copies that may be made to prevent illegal copying (usually zero to five copies). The producers of these programs often provide a backup service to owners who register their purchases with the sellers. After you copy a program or data disk, store one copy at a different location in case of fire or theft.

Making a Backup

Disks and hard disks fail, so backup copies of disks are needed to prevent loss of data and program files. Ironically, most failures seem to occur when you do not have a backup copy. The process of making backup copies varies from system to system. When you first purchase a microcomputer, the manual instructs you to make a backup copy of the operating system disk, store the master, and use the backup as the working disk. However, the documentation for this task is often poor, misleading, or missing, and you may have no microcomputer knowledge. Sometimes experience and knowledge gained on one system works to your disadvantage because of the manner in which the task is performed.

The backup routine can be started after the system has been loaded and the date and time questions answered, as required. Always place the master disk in a specific drive and the new disk in the other. You might want to copy from A to B on MS-DOS/PC DOS microcomputers.

If you live in an area where power is unstable during storms, be careful to save your files more often or do not use the computer during these periods. When a storm approaches and you cannot stop working, make extra backups, and keep an extra disk copy separate from the microcomputer.

Specific routines may be part of the operating system, or they may be independent programs. The location varies between systems and versions of systems. Most backup routines are separate utilities. It is usually necessary to have the system disk in the microcomputer when the utility is executed.

In MS-DOS/PC DOS, the DISKCOPY A: B: ↵ instruction results the instruction shown in Figure 3–6. Following these instructions carefully results in a copy of the disk in drive A being produced on the disk in drive B. In MS-DOS/PC DOS it is not necessary to format the disk in drive B before executing DISKCOPY.COM. If any files were stored on the disk in drive B, they are destroyed during the diskcopy process.

Additional Utilities

Almost any program can be added as a utility in a given operating system. One utility added to MS-DOS/PC DOS is **SORT.EXE** (or SORT.COM in some systems) which sorts lists rapidly. It may be used to alphabetize the directory of files on a disk.

SORT.EXE
MS-DOS/PC DOS utility to sort lists.

The MS-DOS/PC DOS **MODE.COM** utility may be used to instruct the computer to use the serial port rather than the parallel port for printing. It can also be used to configure the serial communication, change the screen mode, and change the printer time-out error message duration, among other things. Because computers are faster than printers, if the computer gets too far ahead of the printer a time-out error will occur. MODE.COM may be used to control the time before the message is generated. A full discussion of serial communication appears in Chapter 10.

MODE.COM
MS-DOS/PC DOS utility to change printer ports, serial communication parameters, screen displays, and printer time-out duration.

```
Insert source diskette in drive A:
Insert target diskette in drive B:
Strike any key when ready
```

Figure 3–6
MS-DOS/PC DOS Backup Procedures

Communication Conventions

Communication requires conventions for two partners to understand each other. Conventions are used to communicate in four instances: from microcomputer to user, from user to microcomputer, between microcomputers, and from microcomputer to peripherals. As a user, you must learn what is expected by the microcomputer when certain messages appear on the screen.

From Microcomputer to User

The communication conventions from the microcomputer to the user include the following. ↵ means press the carriage return or enter key. Usually, ^n means to press the <Ctrl> (control) key while simultaneously pressing the other key (n). ^C is the break instruction in some operating systems. <Esc> means to press the escape key or to send the code number 27 to a device.

The filename is the name of a data or program file. A filespec contains the disk drive where the file is located, a colon, the path (if any), the filename, a decimal point, and an extension. A path is needed on hard disks that are divided into subdirectories (Figure 3–7). When .BAK is the extension on a filename, the file is a backup file. As the extension on a filename, .COM means the file is a command file. It is usually run by typing its name and pressing ↵. A BASIC program file has .BAS as the extension on the filename.

From User to Microcomputer

Communication conventions exist from the user to the microcomputer. The filename must fit the limitations of the operating system. Some systems accept blanks, but most do not. Some do not limit characters such as commas, whereas others do.

Most systems start on the default or logged disk drive. Drives are identified as A, B, C, and so on; each operating system has a convention.

Most programs do not allow the use of commas in numbers entered into the microcomputer. For example, the number 1,000 must be entered as 1000 ↵.

When using a word processor, a carriage return is needed at the end of each paragraph. If you enter ↵ on each line, the program usually will not work as expected. There is a special code at the end of each file,

Figure 3–7
Sample Filespec

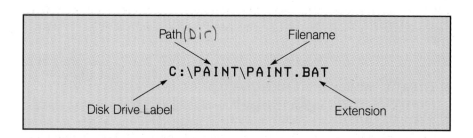

called an end-of-file (EOF) marker. In a word processing file it is usually necessary to press the enter key to make the program expand beyond the end of file. The down arrow will not work to expand a word processing file.

Between Microcomputers

Microcomputers use a number of communication conventions to communicate with each other. The **American Standard Code for Information Interchange (ASCII)** is often part of the convention. In ASCII, numbers are used to represent a set of fixed characters. For example, Z is represented by the number 90, while z is represented by 122. The microcomputer records the numbers 90 and 122 as a **binary file** (a file using on-off **binary numbers**); it does not record the uppercase and lowercase letters.

Microcomputers save program and data files in special binary code (machine language) and in ASCII. Most binary files are specific to a microprocessor and an operating system. ASCII files may be transferred between microcomputers.

From Microcomputer to Peripherals

The communication of data from microcomputer to printers, plotters, and most other peripherals uses the same ASCII code that is used for communication between microcomputers. This is why one printer can be operated by many different microcomputers.

American Standard Code for Information Interchange (ASCII) A seven-bit binary code. Numbers from 00 to 127 can be produced with a seven-bit number. The decimal number 90 is 1011010. Each number in ASCII stands for a character or control.

Binary file Programs stored in machine language form using Os and Is. A binary file may be directly executed by the microcomputer.

Binary number A number consisting of 0 and 1. Each 0 or 1 is a bit. The decimal numbers 0 to 127 require 7 bits. To add the decimal numbers 128 to 255 requires the eighth bit.

Microcomputer Families

The combination of microprocessor and operating system forms the basis for microcomputer families such as Apple DOS and PRO-DOS; Apple Macintosh operating system; MS-DOS/PC DOS; OS/2; UNIX; and two older systems, CP/M and TRS-DOS. Operating systems are created for a specific microprocessor. They are a series of programs usually written in the basic **instruction set** of the microprocessor. An instruction set are instructions built into the computer. The instruction set is contained in the microprocessor.

Each family is built on a different microprocessor (Table 3–4), hardware system, and operating system. In general, families are compatible. Families can use the same machine language programs, high-level language programs, and data files. The MS-DOS/PC DOS family can read, write, and format the same disks. In general, the only method of transfer between families is by use of ASCII files. The data files that can be saved in ASCII and estimates of the percentage that can be saved in this manner are shown in Table 3–5.

The methods of transferring files between families include communication over cables and telephone lines, the use of special programs to read different disk formats, and the purchase of special PC boards that give

Instruction set Instructions built into the computer. The instruction set is contained in the microprocessor.

Table 3–4
Microprocessors and Operating Systems

Microprocessor	Apple DOS	Macintosh DOS	MS-DOS/PC DOS	OS/2	UNIX
Motorola					
6502	X				
68000 Series		X			X
Intel					
8086			X		X
8088			X		X
80286			X	X	X
80386			X	X	X
80486			X	X	X

Table 3–5
Use of All ASCII Files

Type of File	Percentage of Programs Using ASCII Files
Word processing	90
Spreadsheets	90
Database	70
Data-driven graphics	60
Image-driven graphics	10
Communication	100
Special applications	80

a microcomputer in one family the capabilities of those in another family. Special PC boards can use machine language programs from one family in a computer from another family. High-level programs, such as BASIC programs, can sometimes be transferred by converting them to ASCII and then correcting them to work in the second family.

There are many versions of each operating system. An operating system is like a language; it is alive and constantly growing and improving. As the capabilities of hardware improve, operating system programs are

spend the additional money for memory upgrades, thereby holding back the growth of the GUI. In addition, visually handicapped users with keyboarding skills may not find GUIs easier to use because vision is required to use a GUI.

Summary

The operating system is the program that controls the printer, monitors, disk drives, and hard disk drives connected to a central processing unit so that they all work together. The operating system includes both internal functions and external utilities. Among the internal functions are DIR to display the contents of a disk and COPY to copy data and program files from one location to another. Once the operating system is started, its jobs include loading and unloading programs into and out of RAM and keeping track of where programs are stored on disk.

Most operating systems come with a good selection of external utilities. However, additional utilities may be purchased when needed as the computer system changes and grows. Among the utilities usually included are FORMAT.COM, DISKCOPY.COM, SORT.EXE, and MODE-.COM. These utilities are used to prepare disks for use, to copy one disk onto another, to sort lists, and to change the operating environment of the system. To use a utility, the name is typed, followed by pressing ↵, the return or enter key. The operating system will not perform any action until it is told to do so.

The computer system may be started by turning on its power (cold boot) or by pressing a combination of keys on the key board (warm boot). When a system is started, the computer first loads the operating system located on the default drive, checks the CONFIG.SYS file (if available) and then executes the AUTOEXEC.BAT file (if available).

Communication conventions are needed for communication from the microcomputer to user, from user to microcomputer, between microcomputers, and from microcomputers to peripherals. The operating system controls this communication.

Key Terms

American Standard Code for Information Interchange (ASCII)	.BAT	Computer network
	Binary file	CONFIG.SYS
	Binary number	COPY
	Bootstrap program	Copy protected (program)
AUTOEXEC.BAT	.EXE	
Backup	Cold boot	<CR>
BACKUP.COM	.COM	Default drive

DIR
DISKCOPY.COM
Extension
File
FORMAT.COM
Function
Graphical user
   interface (GUI)
Hierarchical file
   structure
Icon
Instruction set

Load
Logged drive
Menu
MODE.COM
Multitasking
Multiusing
Operating system
Operating system
   convention
Operating system
   windows

Retrieving
Routine
Saving
SORT.EXE
Storing
Terminal
Time-sharing
TYPE
Utility
Warm boot
↵

Review Questions

1. What does an operating system do?
2. What is a function? What is a utility? Identify some alternate names used for functions and utilities.
3. When a program is loaded, what happens?
4. Why would you want to make a backup copy of a disk or file? Identify some alternate commands for making backups.
5. Identify what each of the following MS-DOS/PC DOS functions or utilities does: TYPE, FORMAT.COM, DIR, COPY, DISKCOPY.COM, BACKUP.COM, SORT.EXE, and MODE.COM.
6. What does ↵ cause the computer to do?
7. What is the difference between a cold boot and a warm boot? What happens when you perform either one?
8. What does the bootstrap program do?
9. What is the importance of knowing which is the logged drive?
10. What is a default drive?
11. What is a hierarchical file structure?
12. What does operating system windows do?
13. What is time-sharing?
14. What is a computer terminal? What does it do? How is it used?
15. What is a computer network?
16. Review some of the features of the American Standard Code for Information Interchange (ASCII), and explain how the code is used.
17. What is a binary file?
18. What is a computer menu?
19. What is a graphical user interface (GUI)? Identify some operating systems that use GUI.
20. What is an icon? How are icons used?

Discussion and Application Questions

1. Find a microcomputer magazine with an article on disk operating systems in the library or local bookstore. Prepare a short discussion of the material in the article.
2. Survey organizations (business, academic, and government), and identify the type of microcomputer and the operating system in use. Why do you think each type of hardware and operating system was selected?
3. Interview a faculty member or other microcomputer user who is an advocate of a particular operating system, and summarize his or her views.
4. From a recent issue of a microcomputer magazine, identify current developments in operating systems and their meanings for the user.
5. From material in the chapter and your library, review the operating systems currently in use and their features. Prepare a forecast of future developments in operating systems.

Laboratory Assignments

1. To get you started, do the following:
   a. Make a backup (DISKCOPY.COM) of the operating system disk.
   b. Examine the directory of the disk, and if possible, type a copy of the directory.
   c. Identify the routines performed by three of the utilities or programs listed in the directory.

2. Use the FORMAT.COM command to prepare a disk for use.

3. Use your operating system to copy a disk file from one disk to another.

4. Use the TYPE instruction in MS-DOS/PC DOS to examine the contents of individual files. Which files are ASCII? Which are not?

5. The following is a list of MS-DOS/PC DOS utilities. Use them or their substitutes in the available operating system:
   a. SORT.EXE.
   b. DISKCOPY.COM.
   c. MODE.COM.
   d. TREE.COM.

   Explain the tasks performed by each of these routines.

PART II

Microcomputer Applications

CHAPTER 4

Word Processing

Goals

Upon completion of this chapter, you will be able to do the following:

- Understand why word processors are valuable to both individuals and organizations.

- Identify what a word processor can do.

- List some commercial word processing programs.

- Review and explain the need for specific hardware for word processing.

- Learn about the many capabilities of word processors.

Outline

The Need for Word Processing

Commercial Investors Services, Inc. is a two-person real estate office consisting of one broker and one associate. The agency's business is primarily concerned with the sale of commercial investment property— hotels, motels, apartments, and large tracts of land for development.

When evaluating the feasibility of starting a new business, the broker and associate identified their microcomputer word processing needs as follows:

- Contacting potential sellers.
- Organizing the property list.
- Developing "packages" describing the financial picture (market and income analysis), physical location, and values of similar properties.
- Aiding in handling the closing details.

In addition, they identified needs for spreadsheet and database programs. They expected that most of the associate's time would be spent communicating with buyers and sellers. This communication places a heavy demand on word processing and requires a letter-quality printer.

The prime use at the outset was to prepare a form letter that was to be mailed to known commercial real estate investors. The letter was to announce a new office location, its affiliation, and the services being offered from this location.

Because one of the partners had experience with WordStar, that word processing program was chosen. It offered them the capability to prepare lists of names and addresses and salutations, as well as to personalize the letters at certain locations within the text. They could then print the letters one after another, with the envelopes' being addressed as well, while they attended to other matters.

This capability allowed them to produce nearly 200 two-page letters efficiently and economically, in a matter of hours. This would normally require two days of a typist's time.

Word processing is the creation of documents for professional or other purposes. Micros in Action "The Need for Word Processing" illustrates how one company, Commercial Investors Services, Inc., identified its word processing needs. Electronic word processing is the creation of documents on a microcomputer using a **word processing program.** Word processing programs are used to create/edit/format, save/retrieve, display (on the screen) and print (on the printer) **text files.** A text file is a computer file that usually contains words and characters (**text**). Some **word processing program files** include both text and graphics or references to graphics files to be used. You will learn about graphics and graphics files in Chapters 6 and 8. The user can start a document, save it, and then return to complete it at some future time.

Word processing program
A program used to create, edit, and format text; save and retrieve files to and from a disk; display results on the screen; and print results on a printer or plotter.

Text file
A computer file that contains words and characters. Such files are commonly created during word processing.

Text
Characters found on paper or the screen, or stored in a microcomputer text file. Text may be a letter or a manuscript-length book.

Word processing program file
A file that contains text, text and graphics, or a reference to graphics files.

This chapter will first review why word processing is important to the microcomputer user. It will then examine word processing program features that aid users in the creating, editing, and formatting of text files. It will also review the saving/retrieving and displaying/printing features of word processors. There are more features than any single user will likely need. You will be asked to learn about the features so that you may select the ones that best help you perform your word processing tasks.

Many word processing and word processing support programs exist. Specific word processing tasks are performed differently in each program. WordPerfect, Microsoft Word, WordStar, PC Outline, OmniPage, ReadRight, InSet, and SideKick are used to illustrate how selected word processing and word processing support programs perform specific tasks. These programs are among the more popular ones available.

Why Word Processing?

Many surveys indicate that the availability of word processing programs is the primary reason for the initial purchase of a microcomputer system. Word processors are valuable tools for both users who do their own typing and those who have secretaries or other assistants. The time needed to produce an individual letter becomes important as the number of letters created becomes large. Some users spend over half their time producing letters. Microcomputer word processing reduces the time between the creation and production of a printed document. The use of word processing changes the skills needed by the typist from speed and accuracy on the keyboard to knowledge in the use of the microcomputer and its programs.

A completed document with an error, an excessive amount of correction fluid, or any other mark of poor quality makes a negative impression on a reader. Word processing helps produce quality documents by allowing screen editing for easy correction of errors and by creating hard copies quickly without introducing new errors that might need correction fluid or overtyping with correction tape.

Many users have some typing training but are not expert typists. Users with marginal typing skills, when aided by word processors, may take over the entire typing and letter creation process and produce quality documents exactly the way they are wanted.

A document produced on a word processor needs to be proofread once, and then only the changes need be proofed as they are made. Errors may be introduced during editing, but no new errors are introduced with the printing of the revised document. The time to prepare the first copy of a document may not be significantly reduced with word processing, but if a second or third draft is needed, the word processor can turn them out with ease.

Creating, Editing, and Formatting

Creating, editing, and **formatting** include the initial input of text using the keyboard and **file transfer.** Creating is the initial entry of characters into a text file using a word processing program. Editing is changing, correcting, deleting, and adding to the characters in a text file using a word processing program. Formatting is the controlling of the screen display and future printer output using the capabilities of a word processing program. File transfer is the movement of computer files to a word processor from another application.

Word processing includes the methods used to control program operations using **function keys, menus,** and **pointing devices.** The function keys are the keys on the left or top of a computer keyboard labeled F1, F2, and so on. Computer menus are screen displays of selected alternate actions. The arrow keys, a mouse, a track ball, or similar devices are used as screen pointing devices to move the screen **cursor.** The screen cursor is a line or small box on the screen that indicates where text will be typed.

A **text editor** is software used to perform the creating, editing, and formatting tasks. It enables the user to insert or delete characters, words, or complete paragraphs anywhere in the text file. Using a text editor, the user can make changes with ease and see the changes on the monitor as they are made.

The microcomputer monitor is an ideal place to accomplish the editing task. Most word processors allow for **full-screen editing.** This means you may move the cursor to any location on the monitor and make whatever changes, additions, or corrections are needed. You may **scroll** (display different parts of a word processing program file on the screen) through a document (text file), looking at it over and over again.

One advantage of electronic editing is that once you have entered the text, you do not need to type the material a second or third time. You enter the text once and save it as a text file on computer storage media. Creating, editing, and formatting includes the methods used to do the following:

Input text (using keyboard, pointing devices, and function keys).
Overwrite, insert, and delete characters.
Format, control text margins, and select fonts.
Search and replace letters, words, or blocks of characters.
Enter and control hyphens and spaces.
Define, format, copy, move, and erase blocks of text.
Control page numbers and page breaks.
Display and use rulers and tabs.
Use headers, footers, and endnotes.
Create tables of contents, indexes, and outlines.
Check spelling, use a thesaurus, and use style checkers.
Create and use macros.
Create lines and boxes.
Create and locate graphics.

Creating
The initial entry of characters into a text or word processing program file using a word processing program.

Editing
Changing the characters in a text or word processing program file using the capabilities of a word processing program.

Formatting
Controlling the screen display and printer output using the capabilities of a word processing program.

File transfer
The movement of a computer file from one application to another. If the text is changed in the original program after a transfer, it has no effect on the second program.

Function key
A computer keyboard key labeled F1, F2, and so on.

Menu
A screen display of alternate actions from which the computer user makes a selection.

Pointing device
An input device that moves the screen cursor in a manner similar to the arrow keys. It usually includes keys that duplicate the function of the arrow, <ESC>, and ↵ keys.

Cursor
A symbol on the monitor that indicates where an action will be started (such as drawing a line) or text will be typed. The cursor is often a dot (.), line (_), base line (_), or a box. It may be steady or blinking.

Text editor
Software that makes creating, editing, formatting, saving, and retrieving of text in a file possible.

Full-screen editing
The capability to move the cursor anyplace on the computer screen and make changes.

Scroll
To display different parts of a word processing program file on the screen. Generally, text is moved up or down to display text that cannot be shown on the monitor at one time.

Control the printer and use the page preview.
Use windows.
Use scanning devices for text input.

Pointing Devices and Function Keys

The keyboard's arrow keys and pointing devices such as a mouse or track ball are used to locate the cursor on the screen. Many MS-DOS/PC DOS word processing programs use both the function keys and a pointing device to send special instructions from the user to the microcomputer. Most Macintosh word processors use pointing devices to send instructions to the microcomputer. On the original IBM PC keyboard, the function keys were on the left side (left portion of Figure 4–1). On many newer keyboards, the function keys are along the top (right portion of Figure 4–1). Originally, most keyboards had ten function keys. Some new keyboards have 12, but many programs use only the first ten.

WordPerfect uses every function key alone and in combination with the <Shift>, <Alt>, and <Ctrl> keys. F3 is the help key in WordPerfect. Figure 4–2 illustrates the initial WordPerfect help screen called by pressing function key F3.

Microsoft Word (a word processing program) uses both function keys and menus with a mouse. Figure 4–3 illustrates a Microsoft Word screen with the mouse controlling the arrow. The square is the character pointer. Menu selections in Microsoft Word and other word processing programs using pointing devices may be made in these ways:

1. Moving the mouse arrow to the bottom of the screen
2. Pointing to a selection
3. Pressing (clicking) the left mouse key (button)

or

1. Pressing the <Esc> key
2. Moving the menu pointer to the desired selection by pressing the space bar
3. Pressing ↵

There are some limitations on how text is entered into a word processing file. For example, the ↵ key (carriage return key) should not be used at the end of each line. If ↵ is pressed, the word processor cannot control **word wrap.** Word wrap occurs automatically in most word processing programs when the text reaches the end of a line. The last word is moved to the next line when there is no more room on that line, according to the margins the user specifies. The user may override the automatic word wrap by entering a ↵ at the end of a line.

Word wrap
The moving of the last word in a line to the next line below when there is no room between margins.

Overwrite, Insert, and Delete

A word processing program may be in the **overwrite** (typeover) or **insert** mode. Overwrite means the character you are entering from the keyboard

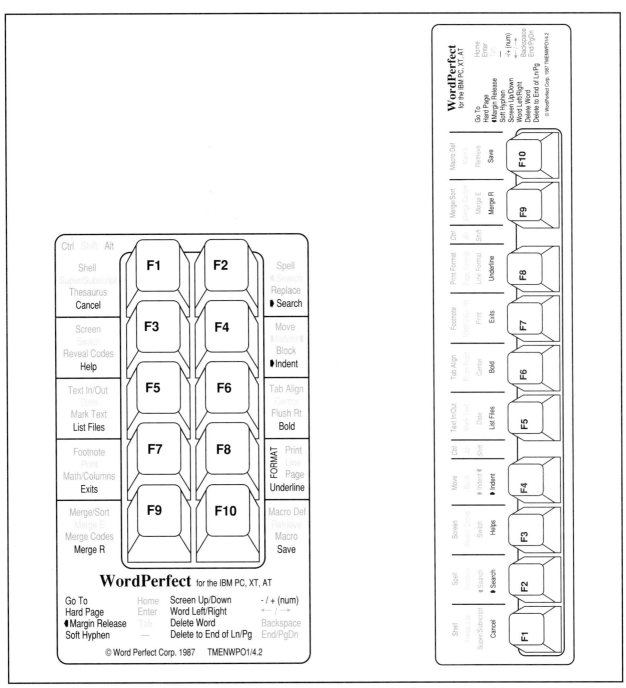

Figure 4–1
WordPerfect Function Keys

Figure 4–2
WordPerfect's Initial Help Screen

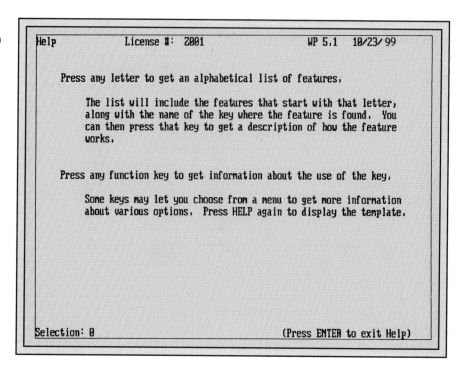

```
Help                 License #:  2001              WP 5.1   10/23/99


    Press any letter to get an alphabetical list of features.

        The list will include the features that start with that letter,
        along with the name of the key where the feature is found.  You
        can then press that key to get a description of how the feature
        works.


    Press any function key to get information about the use of the key.

        Some keys may let you choose from a menu to get more information
        about various options.  Press HELP again to display the template.












Selection: 0                              (Press ENTER to exit Help)
```

Figure 4–3
Microsoft Word Using a Mouse

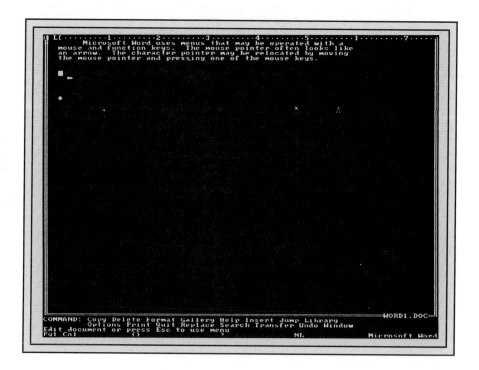

replaces the character that was formerly at the location of the cursor. Insert means that when a character is typed into existing text, the text following it is moved to the right to make room. Some word processors control the shape or size of the cursor to let you know which mode they are in, while others display the words `INSERT ON` or `TYPE OVER`. Pressing the `<Insert>` key toggles between the overwrite and insert modes in most word processing programs.

Located near the `<Insert>` key is the `<Delete>` key. In most word processors, a **delete** instruction erases the character from the screen at the cursor location. When characters are removed in most word processing programs, the text closes up. In WordStar, the **reformatting** command is under the control of the user. Reformatting is the redisplay of the screen text around the characters that were changed or deleted.

Figure 4–4 illustrates a computer screen with some text that needs to be edited. It includes a misspelled word (*diskette*) to illustrate how corrections are made. Figure 4–4 shows a word processing screen in insert mode. The cursor is located at the character *t* in the word *text*. Starting at that location, the words `OVERWRITE ON` were typed (in the insert mode). Figure 4–5 illustrates how the text moved to make room for the new characters.

Many word processing programs switch from the insert mode to the overwrite mode when the `<Insert>` key is pressed. Figure 4–6 illustrates the WordPerfect screen after the `<Insert>` key has been pressed. Notice that the line where the words `OVERWRITE ON` were added is automatically reformatted and the word `Typeover` appears in the lower left of the figure.

Figure 4–7 illustrates the results that occur when the following steps are followed to correct the misspelling:

1. Locate the cursor under the letter *e* in the collection of characters `ONext` (Figure 4–6)
2. Type `***WE ARE OVERWRITING***`
3. To correct the spelling, move the cursor under one of the *t*'s and then press the `<Delete>` key

WordPerfect makes it easy to delete characters and make corrections in the overwrite mode.

Format, Margins, and Fonts

Many word processors use **formatting codes** that are saved in the document to control line spacing, type of **justification,** margins (left, right, top, and bottom), changes in **font** (size and shape of a character set) and **pitch** (characters per inch), and **proportional spacing** (providing each character with the space it needs rather than a fixed amount of space). Figure 4–8 illustrates a Microsoft Word screen with two different line spacings and three types of justification. The first paragraph at the top of the screen is formatted ragged right using the **default** line spacing. Default values are the original setting. For line spacing, the default is single spacing. Before

Overwrite
The mode in which a character typed replaces the character formerly at the location of the cursor. Some word processors use the term *typeover* rather than *overwrite.*

Insert
The mode in which a character typed into existing text causes the text that follows it to move to the right to make room.

Delete
An instruction to remove a character, a collection of characters, or a file. When characters are removed, the text closes up.

Reformatting
The redisplay of the screen text around the characters that were changed or deleted.

Formatting code
Code placed in a word processing file to instruct the printer to change fonts, spacing, and so on.

Justification
Text formatting control of right margin. May be ragged (not lined up), even (right justified), or centered (word located evenly between margins).

Font
Size and shape of a character set.

Pitch 10 ᴏᴜ 12
Number of characters per inch.

Proportional spacing
Characters spaced according to the form and size of each individual letter.

Default
The original settings for line spacing, formatting, and so on.

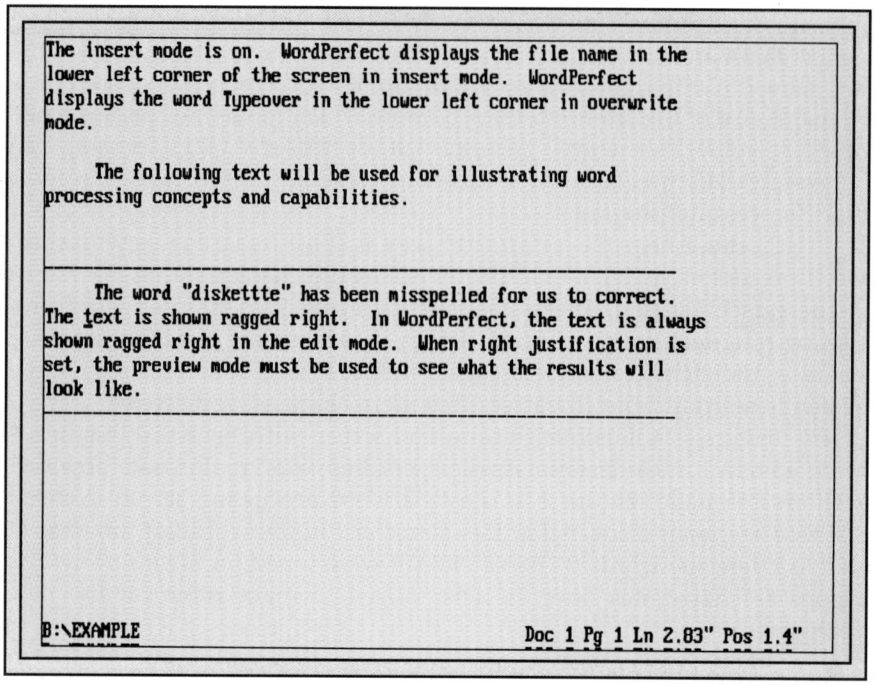

Figure 4–4
Diskette Misspelled

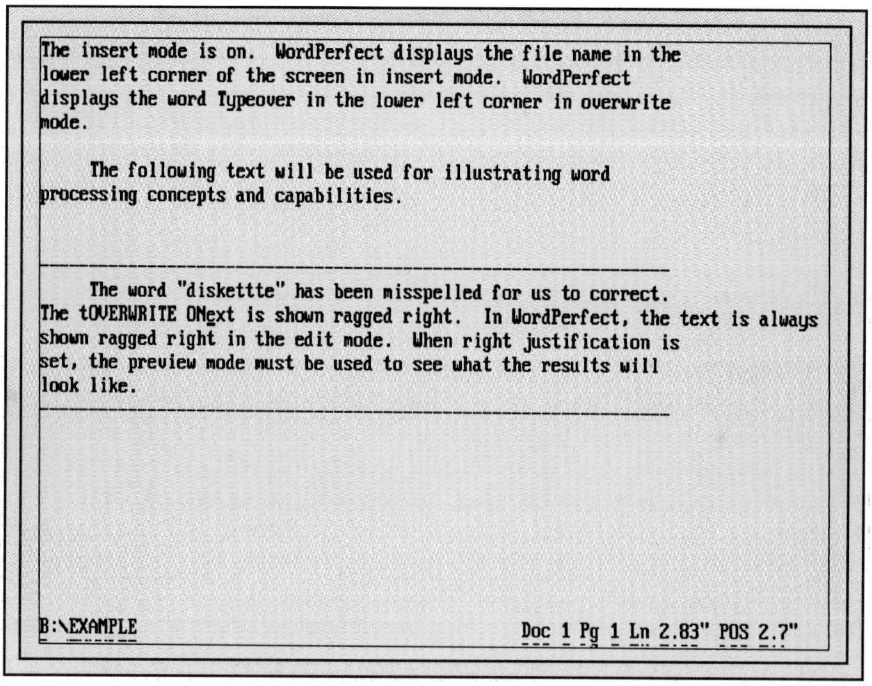

```
The insert mode is on.  WordPerfect displays the file name in the
lower left corner of the screen in insert mode.  WordPerfect
displays the word Typeover in the lower left corner in overwrite
mode.

     The following text will be used for illustrating word
processing concepts and capabilities.

_____

     The word "diskettte" has been misspelled for us to correct.
The text is shown ragged right.  In WordPerfect, the text is always
shown ragged right in the edit mode.  When right justification is
set, the preview mode must be used to see what the results will
look like.
_____




B:\EXAMPLE                                    Doc 1 Pg 1 Ln 2.83" Pos 1.4"
```

Figure 4–5
Insert Mode

```
The insert mode is on.  WordPerfect displays the file name in the
lower left corner of the screen in insert mode.  WordPerfect
displays the word Typeover in the lower left corner in overwrite
mode.

     The following text will be used for illustrating word
processing concepts and capabilities.

_____

     The word "diskettte" has been misspelled for us to correct.
The tOVERWRITE ONext is shown ragged right.  In WordPerfect, the text is always
shown ragged right in the edit mode.  When right justification is
set, the preview mode must be used to see what the results will
look like.
_____




B:\EXAMPLE                                    Doc 1 Pg 1 Ln 2.83" POS 2.7"
```

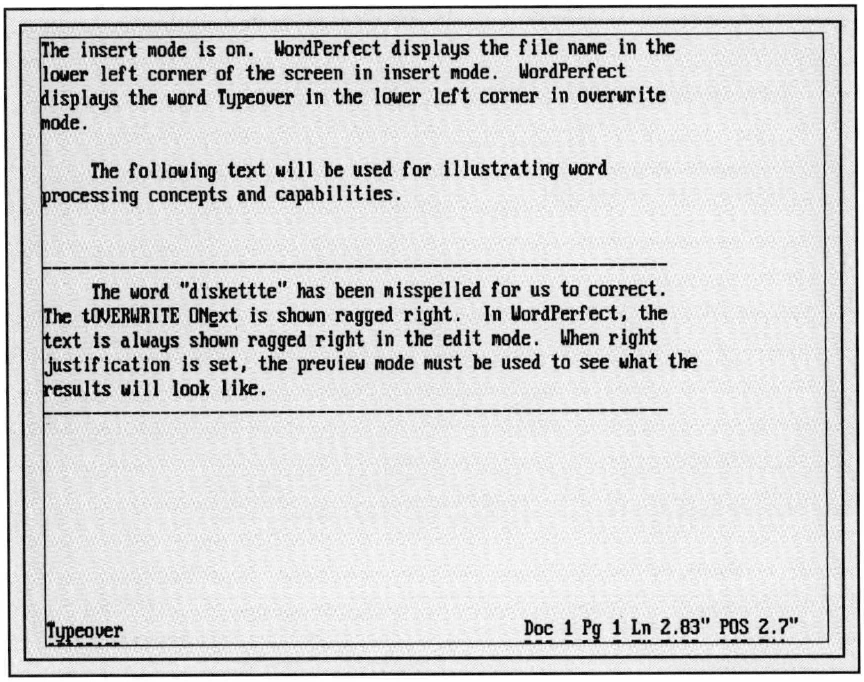

```
The insert mode is on.  WordPerfect displays the file name in the
lower left corner of the screen in insert mode.  WordPerfect
displays the word Typeover in the lower left corner in overwrite
mode.

     The following text will be used for illustrating word
processing concepts and capabilities.

     _____

     The word "diskettte" has been misspelled for us to correct.
The tOVERWRITE ONext is shown ragged right.  In WordPerfect, the
text is always shown ragged right in the edit mode.  When right
justification is set, the preview mode must be used to see what the
results will look like.
     _____

Typeover                                Doc 1 Pg 1 Ln 2.83" POS 2.7"
```

Figure 4–6
Overwriting Is Called
`Typeover` in WordPerfect

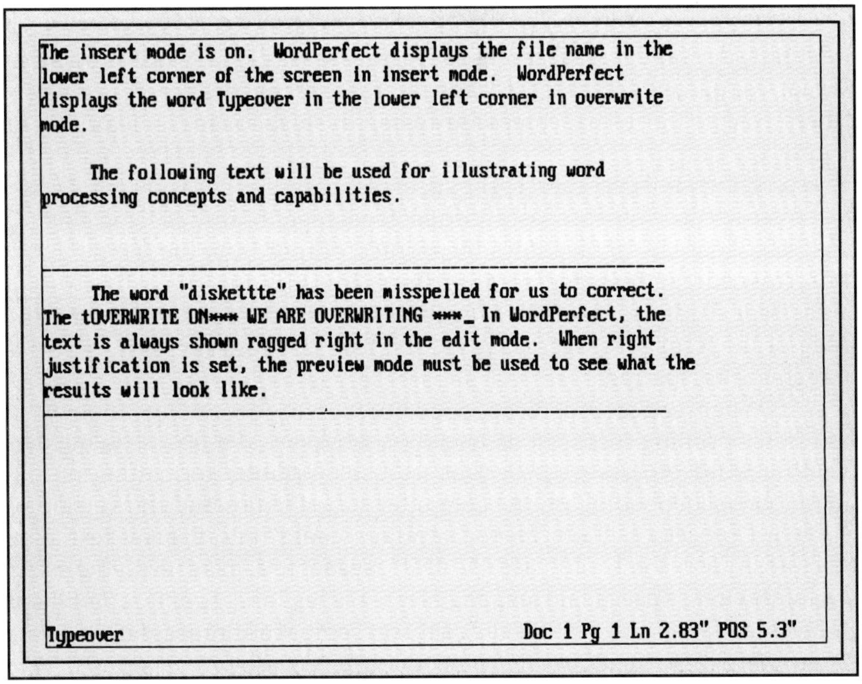

```
The insert mode is on.  WordPerfect displays the file name in the
lower left corner of the screen in insert mode.  WordPerfect
displays the word Typeover in the lower left corner in overwrite
mode.

     The following text will be used for illustrating word
processing concepts and capabilities.

     _____

     The word "diskettte" has been misspelled for us to correct.
The tOVERWRITE ON*** WE ARE OVERWRITING ***_ In WordPerfect, the
text is always shown ragged right in the edit mode.  When right
justification is set, the preview mode must be used to see what the
results will look like.
     _____

Typeover                                Doc 1 Pg 1 Ln 2.83" POS 5.3"
```

Figure 4–7
Results of `WE ARE OVERWRITING` and the
Correct Spelling

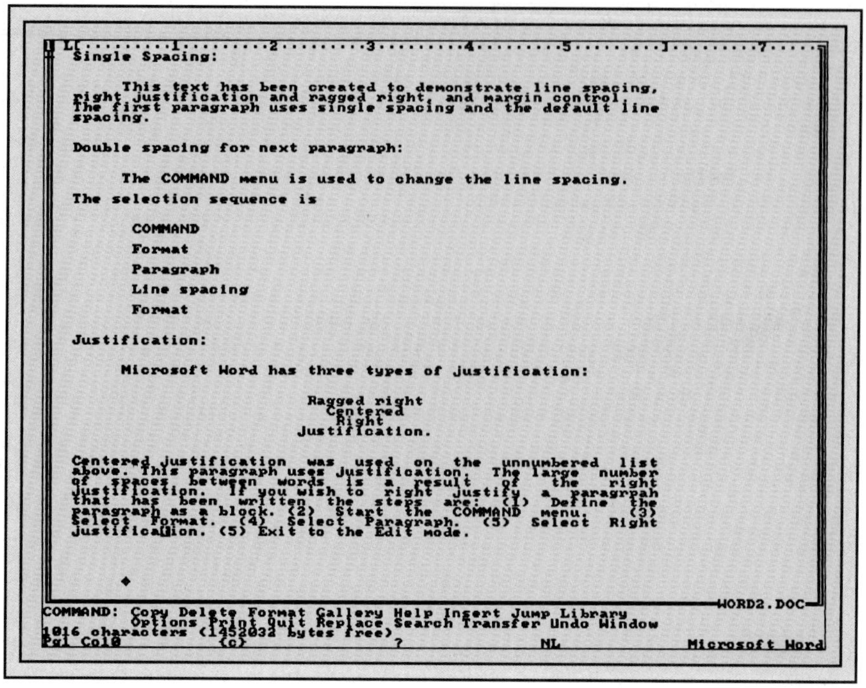

Figure 4–8
Formatting Codes

the second paragraph was typed the line spacing was changed to double spacing. Before the word Justification the spacing was reset to single spacing and an extra line space added underneath it. Each word in the list at the bottom of the page is centered between margins and the last paragraph is right justified.

Printer instructions in the form of formatting codes may be visible at all times or only in special modes (Figure 4–9). Some word processors format completely, or at least partially, the text on the screen, whereas others execute the format commands when the text is sent to the printer or to preview output.

The code <27>[300;0;1s<27>[950;0;1s shown in Figure 4–9 instructs a QMS Kiss laser printer to change to font 300 and then to font 950. Figure 4–10 illustrates the printed output from the file in Figure 4–9. Notice how the letters in A Number One Head overlap. In addition to the font change instruction, it is necessary to send a code to control the pitch of the fonts. WordPerfect gives the user control over both the word and character spacing.

When text is sent from the computer to the printer, formatting and other printing instructions usually accompany the text. The method used by word processing programs to display printer formatting on the screen varies depending on the computer's capabilities and the version of the word processor. Early microcomputers could only display text. The Macintosh and some MS-DOS/PC DOS systems display text, the exact size of the font, special line and character spacing, and graphics. **Bold** and **underlined** letters are displayed exactly on some word processing systems while others use shading or colors. Bold letters are letters printed in a

Bold
Letters printed in a darker font and often displayed on the screen in a special shade or color.

Underlined
Letters printed with a line under them and often displayed on the screen in a special shade or color.

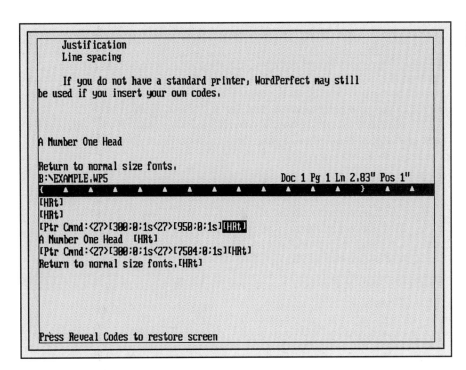

Figure 4-9
Reveal Codes in WordPerfect

```
This text has been created to demonstrate the method used by WordPerfect to
inset printer codes to control:

        Fonts
        Justification
        Line spacing


        If you do not have a standard printer, WordPerfect may still be used if
you insert your own codes.

A Number One Head

Return to normal size font.
```

Figure 4-10
Printer Output

darker font. Underlined letters are letters printed with a line under them. Some word processors that do not display font sizes and graphics while editing use a preview mode to display the printer results on the screen.

Some printers are capable of adjusting the spacing of letters so that the space provided is proportional to the size and shape of the letter. Few word processors are currently capable of displaying this proportional spacing on the screen.

Search and Replace

Search is the capability of a word processor to find the next occurrence of a **string** of characters. A string of characters is a collection of characters treated as a unit. **Search and replace** is the capability to find characters, words, or groups of characters and replace them with another.

Figure 4–11 illustrates a search in a Microsoft Word screen. The word *and* occurs a number of times in the document. The steps to find the next occurrence of *and* follow:

1. Start the COMMAND menu by pressing `<Esc>`
2. Select search by moving the menu pointer to the word `Search` and press `↵`
3. Type the collection of characters and
4. Select the direction options using the arrow keys
5. Execute by pressing `↵`

The menu area at the bottom of the Figure 4–11 illustrates part of the search process.

Soft Hyphens and Hard Spaces

Word processors help users with hyphenation. They use two types of hyphens: **hard hyphens** and **soft hyphens.** A hard hyphen is a dash that is always included where placed. A soft hyphen is only entered by the word processor when it is needed by a word break at the end of a line.

Figure 4–11
Search in Microsoft Word

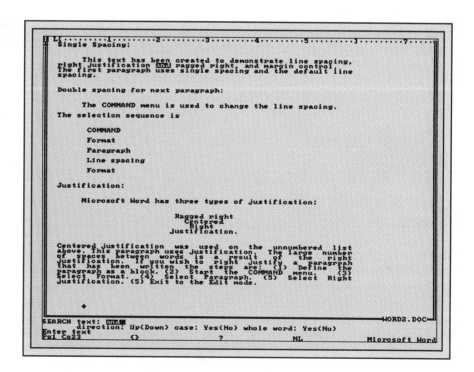

Some word processors will aid you in the placement of hyphens during the editing process by identifying words that need them. Others allow you to place a soft hyphen in a word or words to be used if that word or words appear at the end of the line.

You may wish to control the location of two or more words so they are on the same line. In some word processors, the placement of a **hard space** between two words forces the programs to handle the string as a single word during formatting. The two words then will always appear on the same line. A soft space between words allows the word processor to separate the words on two lines if required by the formatting process.

Soft hyphen
A dash that is used only by the word processor when needed at the end of a line for a word break.

Hard space
A space that does not allow two words to be separated at the end of a line.

Blocks

A **block** is a section of text identified with beginning and ending markers that the user enters. The marker at the beginning of the block may be identical to the marker at the end. Once identified, the block may be **copied** (duplicated at another location), be **moved** (duplicated at another location and erased from the current location), be **erased (deleted),** be formatted, be sorted, be checked for spelling and style, be saved to a disk file, have some mathematical operation executed, and so on. Figure 4–12 illustrates a WordPerfect screen with a block being defined in both the normal mode and the word [Block] in the reveal code mode (see portions reversed in black). After the instruction is given that definition is complete, the character [b] appears at the end of the block in the reveal code mode.

Block
A collection of text defined by a marker at the beginning and end.

Copy
To duplicate an image of a block at a new location.

Move
To relocate a block.

Erase (delete)
To remove a marked block or character.

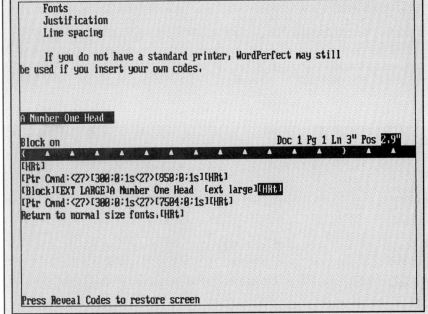

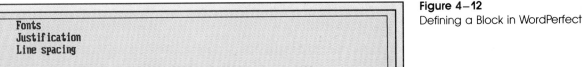

Figure 4–12
Defining a Block in WordPerfect

Page Numbering and Page Breaks

Word processors give the user the option of adding page numbers to printed output. Many word processors print page numbers in the default mode, while others will not do so unless instructed. Some locate the page number on the top of the page while others put it on the bottom. The user who plans to create letters and other such documents can instruct the word processor not to print page numbers.

Generally, only word processors that format on the screen will be able to display **page breaks** during the editing process. A page break shows when the instruction (code) will be sent to the printer to feed in a new sheet of paper. If page breaks and other on-screen formatting are important, an on-screen formatting word processor should be selected.

Rulers and Tabs

A **ruler** is a marked line that counts the number of characters displayed on the screen. Figure 4–12 displays the ruler in WordPerfect. Figure 4–13 shows the ruler in WordStar (a word processing program). The **tab** settings are indicated by the exclamation point (!) character on the ruler. A tab is a mark on the ruler to indicate cursor movement when the <Tab> key is pressed. In Figure 4–13, the tabs were used to locate the position of the indented heading in the table of contents listing shown. Tab locations may easily be changed. Some users find tab setting controls useful when designing custom forms. WordStar allows you to determine how the ruler is displayed.

Page break
A code entered into a word processing file to tell the printer to feed a sheet of paper. Often a line will be drawn across the screen to indicate the page break location to the user.

Ruler
A line on the screen with marks to indicate locations.

Tab
A mark on the ruler line to indicate cursor movements when the <Tab> key is pressed.

Figure 4–13
Ruler in WordStar

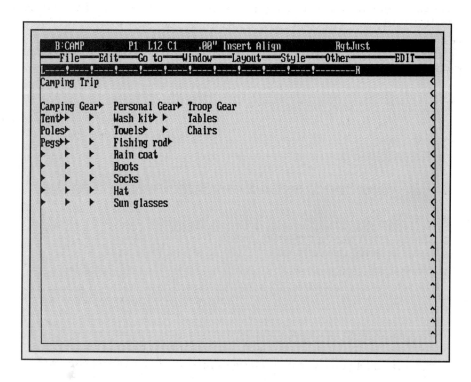

Headers, Footers, and Endnotes

The addition of page **headers,** page **footers,** and chapter **endnotes** can be important when you are assigned the task of producing a document in a specific format. Headers are blocks of text placed at the top of selected printed pages. Footers are blocks of text placed at the bottom of selected printed pages. Endnotes are similar to headers and footers, except they are placed at the end of a document. Page titles, footnotes, and references are examples of headers, footers, and endnotes, respectively.

In the past, most publishers and universities had specific methods for handling headers and footers. The trend is for them to be more flexible. However, you may still find yourself faced with the problem of a specific location and format requirement for footnotes and page titles.

Header
Text placed on the top of a printed page in a document.

Footer
Text placed at the bottom of a printed page in a document.

Endnote
Text placed at the end of a document.

Tables of Contents, Index Generators, and Outliners

Completing a manuscript involves many details. The creation of a table of contents; the searching for, and identification of, terms for an index; and the creation of an outline are a few of these details.

Table of contents routines are routines available in word processors that will automatically add (and adjust) page numbers to a table of contents as changes are made in a manuscript. The routine requires that the text be stored in a single file.

There are three approaches to an **index generator,** a routine that creates an index with page numbers. All words can be indexed, all words not on an exclusion list can be indexed, or words on an index list or words that are specially marked in the text can be indexed. The index is produced using the page numbers of the document. If the text created is changed or combined with other text before publishing, the index must be adjusted.

An **outline program** combines outlining and planning. These programs allow you to enter information in any order and then help you organize the concepts. Once organized, you can examine different levels of the structure. Some outline programs include their own text editors (Figure 4–14) while others are integrated into the operation of a word processor.

Table of contents routine
A routine that automatically adds page numbers to a table of contents.

Index generator
A routine that creates an index with page numbers.

Outline program
A program that allows the user to enter information in any order and then helps in the organization of the concepts and text.

Spelling Checkers, Thesauri, and Style Checkers

Spelling checkers have become part of most word processors. A spelling checker examines a text file and identifies words as being misspelled that are not in its dictionary. Figure 4–15 illustrates the use of WordPerfect's spelling checker. In the text, the word *return* had an extra *u.* WordPerfect identifies the misspelled word and lists possible correct spellings.

A word may not be in a spelling program's dictionary because it is a proper name, is not included in the dictionary or is misspelled. Some spelling programs will help you find the correct spelling for a word by displaying similar words on the screen. Other programs point out the problem and let you solve it. Spelling programs can find misspelled words,

Spelling checker
A routine that helps the user correct the spelling of text in a file.

Figure 4–14
An Outline Program
(PC Outline)

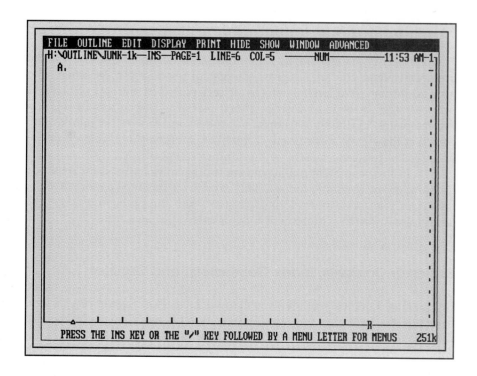

Figure 4–15
Using WordPerfect's Spelling
Checker

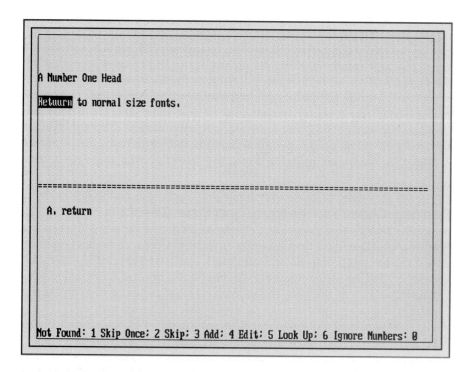

not misused words. For example, if you spell the word *computer* as *commuter*, this error will not be identified, since *commuter* is a word.

Have you ever noticed that errors seem to leap off the page? Errors are often the prime thing readers remember about a document, not what the document was about. If you are unsure about the spelling in your document or letter, take the few extra minutes required to run it through the spelling checker. Micros in Action "Spelling Checker" illustrates how Commercial Investors Services, Inc. used a spelling checker.

Micros in Action

Spelling Checker

The employees of Commercial Investors Services, Inc. found that a spelling checker reduced the amount of time required for proofreading the letters and contracts they produced. The spelling program helped improve the quality of documents and was well worth its purchase price.

They made use of two spelling programs: one external to, and one part of, their word processor. The combination of the two spelling programs helped them create documents that were more professional looking.

In addition to spelling checkers, many word processors include the capability to find alternate words with a **thesaurus program.** The operation of a thesaurus is similar to a spelling checker.

Style checker (grammar) programs will check a document for common typographical errors, writing style, and sentence level. Common errors, such as writing the word *cannot* as two words rather than one, will be found by grammar programs but not by spelling programs. Words such as *very* will be identified by grammar programs as being unnecessary. Wordy phrases such as *in the case of* will be found by a grammar program. Double words such as *the the* also will be found. This error is common in word processing.

These style programs make great teaching aids. They point out questions and problems without becoming annoying, as may happen with a human proofreader. Many of the current versions cannot correct errors; they just alert the writer to possible stylistic errors.

> **Thesaurus program**
> A program that helps the user find alternate words.

> **Style checker**
> A program that helps correct grammar and style problems.

Macros

Macros are special files that contain a record of keystrokes (text and commands) for later use. A macro may contain your name and address, for example. This macro may be used by pressing a small number of keys (`<Alt> + <F10>` followed by the macro's name in WordPerfect). The instruction `<Key> + <key>` is a computer instruction that means hold down

> **Macro**
> A file containing a record of keystrokes for future use.

<Key> + <key>
A computer instruction telling the user to hold down the first key usually the <Alt>, <Ctrl> or <Shift> keys and then press the second key. The instruction <Key> – <key> is an alternate method of giving the instruction.

the first key (<Alt>, <Ctrl>, or <Shift>) while pressing the second key. When the macro is used, your name and address will appear on the screen at the cursor location.

If a font requires a margin and pitch change, a macro may be created to perform the set of commands. Most current word processors have special procedures for creating macros.

Line and Box Draw

Line draw
The capability to display and print lines.

Box draw
The capability to display and print boxes.

Line draw and **box draw** routines give the user the ability to draw lines and boxes. Printers can print lines and boxes around selected areas on a page. Screens may display lines and boxes. WordPerfect makes the creation of text with lines and boxes easy. Figure 4–16 illustrates a simple form being created in WordPerfect. Pressing <Ctrl> + <F3> and selecting option 2 starts the line draw mode. WordPerfect allows you to select from a variety of lines (single, double, and so on). The arrow keys are used to place the lines where desired.

Graphics

Graphics integrating routine
A routine that integrates the output of graphics with text.

Word processing programs include **graphics integrating routines** to integrate graphics with text output. Dot-matrix, laser, and ink-jet printers can output both letters and graphics of high quality. Using **terminate and stay resident (TSR)** programs such as InSet (**a graphics screen capture routine and integrating program**) or built-in capabilities, a word processor can

Figure 4–16
WordPerfect Line Draw

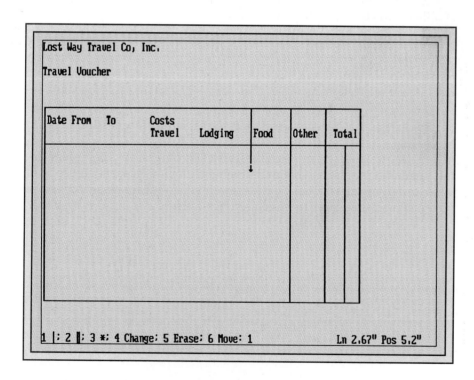

output text and graphics to a printer. A TSR program is a program that is loaded into memory and remains in memory while other programs are loaded and used. Once loaded, a TSR program may be recalled using a series of **hot keys,** while some other program is running. The steps in using a TSR graphics capture routine are: load the program in memory, select a graphics program to create and display selected graphics, call the TSR program to capture the screen, and save a file containing the image on disk.

Usually data- or image-driven graphics programs are used to create graphics images. An image is captured or the image file is transferred to a file that can be used by the word processor before being integrated with text output. Figure 4–17 illustrates a text-graphics screen using InSet.

Printer Controls and Page Preview

Word processing programs may be used to send instructions (codes) to printers to tell them to change fonts (character sizes and shapes), to insert graphics, to page (instruct the printer to feed a sheet of paper), and so on. In some word processors, the codes appear on the screen, while in others, the codes are not visible to the user. Most newer versions allow the user to control the display of the printer codes.

Printers are not screens. There are many different printers and many different screens and screen control boards. What you see is what you get **(WYSIWYG)** formatting occurs when a word processor produces exactly the same thing on the screen as on the printer. In order to duplicate the screen exactly, the word processor must know the exact capabilities of the printer.

Terminate and stay resident (TSR)
Programs that are loaded into memory and remain in memory while other programs are loaded and used. Once loaded, a TSR program may be recalled using a series of keys, while some other program is running.

Graphics screen capture routine
A routine that may be used to capture a computer graphic screen display and then save it as a file. Most screen capture routines are part of TSR programs.

Hot keys
The key combination that calls a TSR program.

WYSIWYG
Screen formatting in which what you see (on the screen) is what you get (out of your printer).

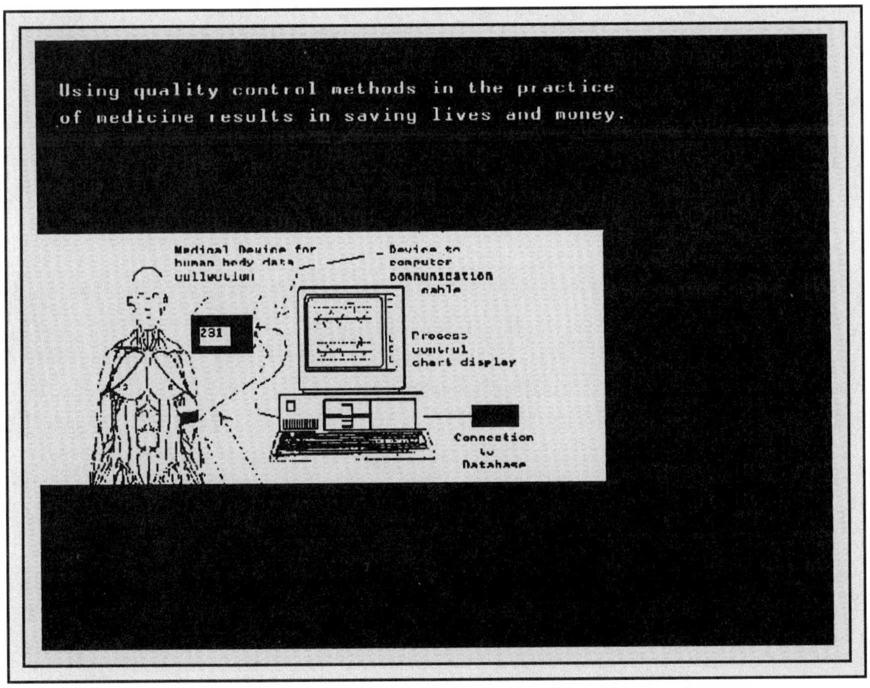

Figure 4–17
Integration of Text and Graphics Using InSet

One of the reasons for the growth of interest in the Apple Macintosh was that the screen and printer output were matched. In MS-DOS/PC DOS microcomputers, there are many different printers and screens. The large variety slowed down the process of matching the output of the two devices.

Page preview
A display on the screen of exactly what is sent to the printer, including unusual fonts and graphics.

Some word processors create a screen environment that matches the printers. Others use a **page preview** routine for viewing on the screen exactly what is being sent to the printer. Figure 4–18 illustrates WordPerfect's page preview. Figure 4–19 illustrates a close-up of the page preview.

Word processors often require the use of a combination of keys. The <Ctrl> key is used in combination with other keys; for example, Ctrl + S is often written ^S. The <Esc> key is used to back out of a menu and initiate special printer instructions.

One reason why combinations of keys are needed is that there is only a limited number of keys on the keyboard. Each key sends to the microcomputer a number that instructs it to perform a specific function. There are simply not enough keys to control all of the functions of a printer. Some special functions require numbers that can be produced only with a combination of the <Ctrl> key and some other key being pressed at the same time. For example, the number 26 is produced by pressing ^Z. It is used to signify the end of file in some systems. Most programs insulate the user from such details by entering the end-of-file markers automatically.

The <Esc> key creates the number 27. Often, combinations of numbers, such as 27 + 21 (<Esc> + 021), are sent to printers to give them special instructions. The 27 + 21 combination, when sent to the printer, tells it to line feed as needed by an IBM PC type of microcomputer. The 27 + 21 combination must be sent to the printer each time it is turned on. These numbers, called codes, may be sent by a special program and by many word processing programs. Often, the word processor user does not see the printer control codes. When a word processor is installed (initialized) for a given printer, the word processor is instructed on the use of printer control codes. If a new printer is added or features are added to the current printer, it may become necessary to use the <Esc> code. Usually, the codes are listed in the back of each printer manual.

Windows

Window
The division of the screen into parts where different documents or different parts of the same document are displayed.

Active window
The window where editing can be performed and where the cursor is located.

The **windows** feature gives the user the ability to split the screen into parts, or windows. Figure 4–20 illustrates a WordPerfect screen with two windows and two documents showing (one at the top of the screen and one at the bottom). Pressing <Shift> + <F3> in WordPerfect moves the cursor between the two windows. The **active window** is the one where the cursor is located and where editing can be performed. Each word processor with windows uses them a little differently. In general, each window may display a part of the same document or entirely different documents. Text may be transferred between windows. Windows are most useful when creating a custom document from a series of other documents.

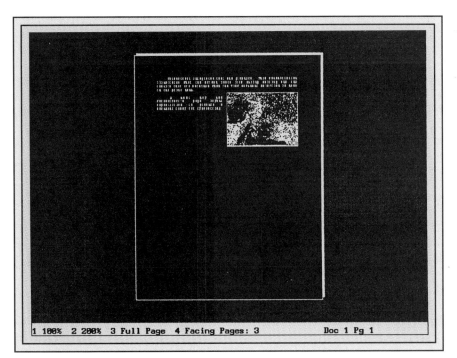

Figure 4–18
WordPerfect's Page Preview

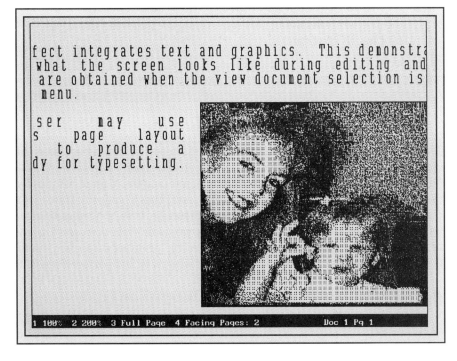

Figure 4–19
WordPerfect's Close-Up Page Preview

Figure 4-20
Word Processing Windows in
WordPerfect

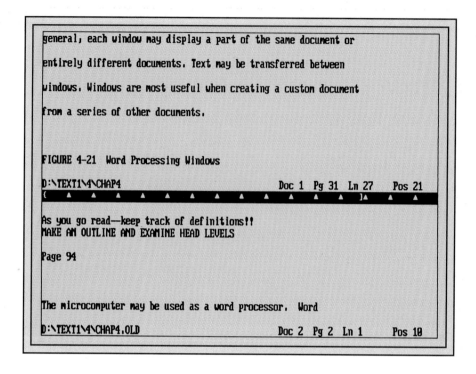

general, each window may display a part of the same document or

entirely different documents. Text may be transferred between

windows. Windows are most useful when creating a custom document

from a series of other documents.

FIGURE 4-21 Word Processing Windows

D:\TEXT1\4\CHAP4   Doc 1 Pg 31 Ln 27   Pos 21

As you go read—keep track of definitions!!
MAKE AN OUTLINE AND EXAMINE HEAD LEVELS

Page 94

The microcomputer may be used as a word processor. Word

D:\TEXT1\4\CHAP4.OLD   Doc 2 Pg 2 Ln 1   Pos 10

Scanning

Scanner
A device used to copy material
(text or images) into a computer
file.

**Optical character recognition
(OCR)**
A term used to describe programs
that read the characters
represented by graphic images.

Scanners are used to copy material (text or images) as graphic images.
Optical character recognition (OCR) programs are used to examine the
graphic images and find their character codes (ASCII code numbers). Figure 4–21 illustrates the menu of an OCR program that reads images directly into text without going through a graphic display. OmniPage is an
example of an OCR program.

Saving and Retrieving

Text may be saved in files and then retrieved for future editing and use. All
word processing programs save text files, some include graphics with text.
File formats are usually either ASCII or some custom format. Generally,
custom files may only be used by a single word processing program. Files
containing ASCII code can be used for transferring between programs. As
long as you use a single word processing program the file format is not
important. When you change word processing programs, the file format
becomes important.

File Transfer

Most of the word processors that do not use the ASCII format are capable
of the file transfer (importing and exporting) of ASCII files. Often, when

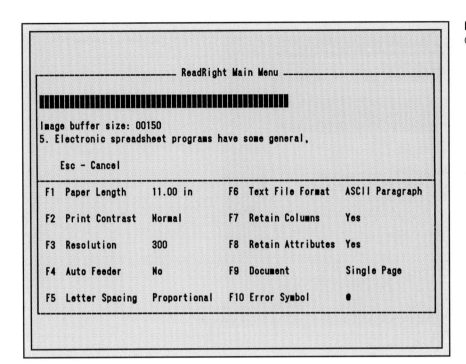

Figure 4–21
OCR Program Menu

files are imported or exported, the text is transferred but the format and special printing instructions are lost. An important use of ASCII files is the transfer of text between two different word processors.

Most spreadsheet programs (Chapter 5) and database programs (Chapter 7) are capable of creating ASCII files that may be imported into word processing programs. There are programs that will read a text file created by one word processing program and then create a new text file to be read by a second word processing program (Figure 4–22).

One popular method of transferring text material from one program to another is the use of **screen capture** programs such as BOR-LAND's SideKick (a text screen capture and editing program). Screen data capture is the capability to capture a screen display and transfer it into a second program or save it as a computer file. Figure 4–23 illustrates Side-Kick (bottom of screen) being used to capture a block of text from a word processing program, WordStar (on the top of screen). SideKick saved its file in an ASCII format that can be imported into most word processing programs.

Screen capture
The capability to capture data from a screen display and transfer it into a second program or save it as a file.

Backup Files

A backup is a copy of a disk or file. Backup copies are needed to protect against damaged disks. Some word processors produce backup files automatically using the extension .BAK (or BA!) and save the current working text file under its original name. Users should use the disk utilities to make copies of their disks periodically. A copy on two physically separate disks is better than two copies on the same disk.

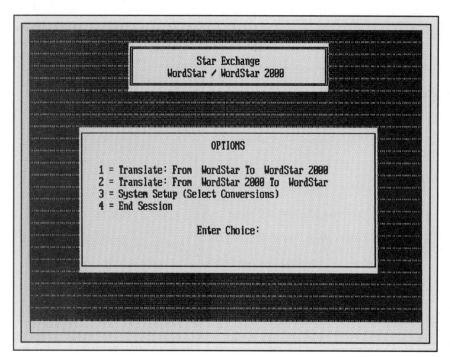

Figure 4—22
WordStar File Conversion

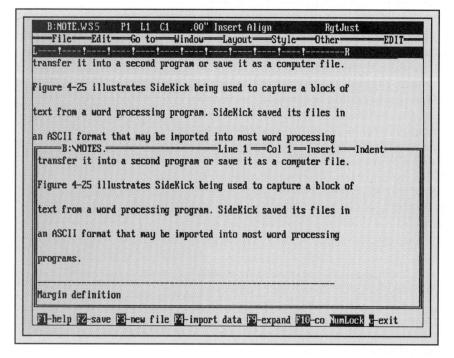

Figure 4—23
SideKick Screen Capture of
WordStar

Printing

The final step in a word processing program is the production of a **hard copy,** a printed copy of the word processing file that matches the screen display. Printer controllers, which are programs or routines that are part of the word processor, send code to printers according to the instructions from the creating and editing activities.

Hard copy
Printed copy on paper of a file.

Special Printing Effects

A number of popular printer control languages can be used to transfer instructions from the computer to a printer. The code language created by Epson is one of the most popular for dot-matrix printers. Postscript and HPGL are the most popular for laser printers.

The <Esc> codes discussed earlier are used to control the Epson and Hewlett-Packard printers. Postscript uses a similar coding system. Dot-matrix printers usually transmit a line at a time, while laser printers (Postscript and HPGL) transmit a page at a time.

When editing, some users find a printed draft unnecessary. However, no matter how much editing is done on the monitor, most users always find changes they want to make after the text is printed. Examination of the screen helps find some errors, while examination of a printed document helps find others.

Text may be assembled during the printing process. A master text file is created that includes instructions to link specified text files. When the parent file is printed, the most current version of the linked file is printed. Some word processing programs allow you to link part of a spreadsheet or database, as well as text files.

Merge Print for Mass Mailing

Merge print is the integration of two or more files during the printing process. An example of a merge print program for mass mailing is Mail-Merge, an add-on to the word processing program WordStar. It allows the preparation of mailing list data files that may be used to produce multiple letters addressed to different individuals. MailMerge aids in the preparation of envelopes, document assembly, and the continuous printing of multiple files. Merge print programs allow the use of names and addresses for business applications. Some mailing programs personalize mass mailings by addressing mail to individuals.

File linkage is similar to merge printing. File linkage is the joining of two files during the printing process (document assembly). A master text file is created that includes instructions to link specified text files. When the master file is printed, the most current version of the linked file is printed. Some word processing programs allow you to link part of a spreadsheet or database, as well as text files.

File linkage
The joining of two files. Whenever the second file is used, the latest version of the sending file is transferred.

Word Processing Hardware

Word processing requires a microcomputer, a word processing program, and a printer. The minimum hardware requirements include enough RAM to support the word processing program; an input device such as a keyboard; a monitor upon which to edit; a printer that can produce output of the desired quality; and a storage device, such as disk drives or memory, that retains text when the microcomputer is turned off. In addition, all word processors operating on the Macintosh take advantage of a mouse. Many new versions of word processors operating in MS-DOS/PC DOS are adding mouse capabilities.

RAM Needs

The amount of RAM required for a particular word processing program depends on how the program is written, the number of features it contains, and the operating system being used. In addition, more RAM may be needed if an operating system shell, such as Microsoft Windows, is used. TSR may also be used. These programs also require more RAM.

Input Devices: Keyboards and Pointing Devices

All microcomputers have some type of input device. The one most often used for word processing is the keyboard. Keyboards can have different layouts. The QWERTY keyboard was originally designed to slow down typing and the Dvorak keyboard was designed to increase typing speed. Other devices, such as optical character readers and voice recognition devices, are also available. Many word processors allow the user to use a mouse or some other pointing device in addition to the keyboard.

Monitors

Monitors are either (1) monochrome monitors, which are green, amber, yellow, or black and white, or (2) color monitors, which are composite or RGB (red, green, and blue). All types of monitors can be used for word processing. Some monitors produce higher-quality characters than others. Some monitors designed for graphics will not produce letters as sharp as those produced by monitors designed for text. Some color monitors produce poorer-quality letters than monitors with black and white, amber, or green screens. Generally, a monitor's price reflects its quality. High-resolution color monitors are available at additional cost.

For word processing, the standard monitor produces 80 characters across, and either 24 or 25 lines down. A full page (8½ by 11 inches) is 66 lines in length. Microcomputer monitors combined with printed circuit boards are available to handle up to 66 lines (down) and 132 or more characters (across), allowing the user a bigger view of the page.

Most word processors work with all combinations of color or monochrome monitors, but in different manners. Many word processors display underlining and boldface type correctly on one or the other configuration, but some display the output correctly on both. If you want to take advantage of all the features of a word processor, you must make sure you have the correct configuration.

Printers

A word processing microcomputer must be able to control a printer. This is done through ports. Printers are available for both parallel and serial ports.

All types of printers may be used for word processing. The most commonly used printers include daisy wheel and similar printers (sometimes called letter-quality printers), laser printers, dot-matrix printers, and ink-jet printers. Daisy wheel and similar printers produce documents in the same manner as a typewriter using a daisy wheel, ball, or thimble. Laser printers are similar to copy machines, except the images are formed by the computer rather than by a copying mechanism.

Dot-matrix, laser, and ink-jet printers produce dots that are organized to create characters and symbols. The form and style of the character produced is called a font. Figure 4–24 shows how the dots are placed to form the character, as compared with the solid image created by the letter-quality daisy wheel, ball, or thimble. Printers that produce characters from dots come with fonts that make it possible to produce a variety of type styles (Figure 4–25).

Dot Matrix   Letter Quality

Figure 4–24
Comparison of Dot-Matrix and Impact-Created Fonts

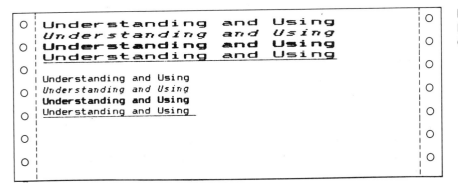

Figure 4–25
Font Variations in Dot-Matrix Output

Storage Devices

Word processing requires a method of saving text when the microcomputer is turned off. Any of the devices discussed in Chapter 2 may be used. Two common configurations are (1) a two-drive system and (2) one disk drive and one hard drive. Users of two-drive systems must select a word processor that will work with two drives. Many newer word processors require a hard drive.

Summary

Word processing is one of the more important programs to computer users. Word processing capabilities make it easy to produce letters and documents of high quality. There are many creating/editing/formatting, saving/retrieving, and printing features in word processing programs. Generally, an individual user will use only a fraction of the features available.

The creating/editing/formatting capabilities of word processing programs include the use of pointing devices and function keys; overwrite, insert, and delete capabilities; format, margin, and font control capabilities; search and replace capabilities; control over hyphenation and hard spaces; the use of blocks; page numbering and page break control; ruler and tab use; header, footer, and endnote capabilities; table of contents, index generator, and outline aids; spelling, thesaurus, and style checker routines; macros to reduce finger motion; line and box draw capabilities; graphics integration and location procedures; printer control codes and page preview capabilities; the capability to divide the screen into windows; and the use of scanning devices.

The saving/retrieving features include file transfer; file linkage for ease of document assembly; and the generation of backup files to reduce the consequences of user errors. Printing features include special printing effects and merge print for mass mailing. The hardware needs for word processing programs are input devices, storage devices, internal RAM, monitors, and printers.

Key Terms

Active window	Delete	Formatting
Block	Editing	Formatting codes
Bold	Endnote	Full-screen editing
Box draw	Erase	Function key
Copy	File linkage	Graphics integrating
Creating	File transfer	routine
Cursor	Font	Graphics screen
Default	Footer	capture routine

Hard copy
Hard hyphen
Hard space
Header
Hot keys
Index generator
Insert
Justification
<Key> + <key>
Line draw
Macro
Menu
Move
Optical character
  recognition (OCR)
Outline program
Overwrite

Page break
Page preview
Pitch
Pointing device
Proportional spacing
Reformatting
Ruler
Scanner
Screen capture
Scroll
Search
Search and replace
Soft hyphen
Spelling checker
String
Style checker
Tab

Table of contents
  routine
Terminate and stay
  resident (TSR)
Text
Text editor
Text file
Thesaurus program
Underlined
Window
Word processing
  program
Word processing
  program file
Word wrap
WYSIWYG

Review Questions

1. What is a word processing program? What does it do?
2. What is a text file? What is a word processing program file? How can a text file differ from a word processing program file?
3. What usually happens to a text or word processing program file when it is transferred?
4. Give an example of a computer screen menu. How are selections made from the menu?
5. What is a cursor used for?
6. What is word wrap?
7. What is a font?
8. What is proportional spacing?
9. What is a string?
10. What is the difference between a hard and soft hyphen? What is a hard space?
11. What is the function of a page break?
12. What is a header, footer, and endnote?
13. What are the three ways an index generator program works?
14. What is an outlining program? What does one do?
15. How does a spelling checker work?
16. What is a style checker program?
17. Why are line and box draw capabilities useful?
18. Why would a word processor user want WYSIWYG?
19. What is a word processing window? Why would a user want one?
20. Why would a user want a screen capture program such as SideKick?

Discussion and Application Questions

1. Find a magazine advertisement for a word processor. How much does one cost? What kind of features are being advertised?
2. Survey an office that uses electronic word processing. What kind of word processor is being used? Why was this one selected for this office? Was it a good choice?
3. Use the yellow pages of your telephone book to identify where word processing programs and equipment may be purchased.
4. Identify alternate equipment and techniques to word processing. Where are they available locally?
5. After being introduced to the use of word processing in your laboratory, use magazines and other sources to study electronic typewriters. How do the two compare?
6. If your school's mainframe computer has a word processing program, find out about it. How does it compare with the one available on your microcomputer?
7. Examine the school's bulletin board for advertisements for typing and word processing services. What do they cost? What is being offered?
8. Examine your local newspaper and the yellow pages for word processing services. What is available?

Laboratory Assignments

All assignments start with the same letter. The DOS copy utility should be used to make copies of the original letter for the additional assignments.

1. Enter the following letter, and save it on your disk:

```
                    John Quartize
                     President
            American Indian Foundation
                 123 Far West Lane
               Way Out, Arizona 55555
                  212 555-1234


                 January 3, 1999

Mr. William Snodgrass
Office of Senator Avert
Capitol Building
Washington, DC 55551
```

```
Dear Sir:

The research on the farming conditions on the XZP
Indian Reservation has been completed and forwarded
to your office under separate cover. We feel the
results justify additional investigation and a
grant to develop new crops for the particular soil
conditions found on the reservation.

We would like an appointment to meet with you in
May during our trip to Washington.

Sincerely,

John Quartize, President
```

2. Starting with the letter in assignment 1, create a memo telling members of the tribal council that a letter has been written to the office of Senator Avert. Save the memo on your disk.

   The organization of this memo should be as follows:

   ```
   Date:_____
   Subject:_____
   From:_____
   To:_____

   Subject: . . . . . . .
   ```

3. Starting with the letter in assignment 1, restyle the letter with paragraphs that are indented and with the *sincerely* and name placed in the middle of the page rather than the left side. Save the memo on your disk.

4. Create the following letter:

```
                    John Quartize
                      President
             American Indian Foundation
                  123 Far West Lane
                 Way Out, Arizona 55555
                    212 555+1234


                  January 3, 1999
```

```
Mr. William Snodgrass
Office of Senator Avert
Capitol Building
Washington, DC 55551
```

```
Dear Sir:

We are inviting all candidates for the office of
senator to join us on our radio station for a
debate on local issues. We have made arrangements
with all local newspapers to cover the event and
help us in getting out support.

Your participation will be appreciated. We will
schedule the event to meet your requirements.

Sincerely,

John Quartize, President
```

5. Prepare a newspaper release based on assignment 4. Assume a date has been set by the senator.

6. Prepare a memo to the tribe on the XZP Indian Reservation on the debate from assignment 4.

7. Redo assignments 4 through 6 using margins of left 10, right 50. Assume the material will be included in a newsletter.

8. Change all words *the* to *help* in assignment 4.

9. Use the block move capability of your word processor, and make ten copies of paragraph 2 in assignment 4.

10. Add three user-controlled page breaks to assignment 9.

11. If your word processor does not automatically put in page numbers, add them to the letter in assignment 4. If your word processor does put in numbers, delete them.

12. Make a copy of assignment 1. Import into the middle of this assignment a copy of the letter from assignment 4.

13. Type a short description of how to import a file in your word processor. Create a README file from this description.

14. Mark the second paragraph of the letter prepared in assignment 4 as a block. Save the block as a separate file.

15. Make hard copies of the editing assignment. Create a new document to experiment with the capabilities of your printer.

16. Prepare a memo detailing the capability of your word processor's printer to bold face, underline, use compressed print, use expanded print, use special characters, and use superscripts and subscripts.

17. Prepare a meeting announcement for a local club. Use the power of your printer.

18. Prepare a program for class presentation. Use the power of your printer to create different size fonts.

19. Prepare a set of handouts to be made into overhead slides for a classroom presentation. Use the power of your printer.

20. Prepare a report showing a formula. Use superscripts and subscripts.

CHAPTER 5

Spreadsheet Programs

Goals

Upon completion of this chapter, you will be able to do the following:

- Learn how spreadsheets are used.

- Identify what a spreadsheet program can do.

- List some commercial spreadsheet programs.

- Review and explain the need for specific hardware for use with spreadsheet programs.

Outline

Using Spreadsheets

Scott Paper Company, including its international operations, is the world's leading manufacturer and marketer of sanitary tissue paper products. In the United States, through the Packaged Products Division, Scott sells a broad range of products for the home and away from home. Scott's international operations are located in 20 countries and primarily manufacture and market sanitary paper products similar to those produced in the United States.

Scott's S.D. Warren Division produces coated and uncoated printing, publishing, and specialty papers, principally for U.S. markets. The National Resources Division is responsible for Scott's 3.3 million acres of woodlands in the United States, Canada, and Brazil, and it directs the company's land management, pulp and forest products marketing, and mineral activities. Scott also manufactures nonwoven materials in its Nonwoven Division. The Scott family includes approximately 20,600 employees in consolidated operations and more than 19,700 in affiliated companies.

Scott's initial application of electronic spreadsheets started in the accounting department. An advertisement for an electronic spreadsheet indicated that a microcomputer program that solved problems using the same structure as the manual method was available. An electronic spreadsheet program and a microcomputer were purchased to try it out.

The use of electronic spreadsheets grew throughout the company. Spreadsheets and spreadsheet graphics are now used for applications in financial analysis, monthly accounting statements, budget control, production planning, engineering analysis, quality control, inventory tracking and labor and organizational performance tracking. Electronic spreadsheets have proved to be an economical method of doing accounting jobs. Many different brands of electronic spreadsheets are now used at Scott Paper, including VisiCalc, SuperCalc, Multiplan, and Lotus 1-2-3.

A **spreadsheet** is a method for organizing, calculating, and presenting numerical data for decision making. A **spreadsheet program** divides the screen into **columns** and **rows.** It helps users create, edit, and format; calculate, handle data, and create graphs; use labels and values; save and retrieve files; and print the results of numerical operations on printer or plotters. A column is a vertical division of the screen, and a row is a horizontal division of the screen. A column-row position on a spreadsheet screen is a **cell.** Most spreadsheet programs use capital letters (A, B, C, etc.) to identify columns that appear across the top of the screen. A row extends across the screen and is usually identified by numbers down the left side of the screen. Cells are identified by their column-row position; for example, G4 means column G, row 4.

Spreadsheet
A method for organizing, calculating, and presenting numerical data for decision making.

Spreadsheet program
A program that divides the screen into columns and rows and helps users create/edit/format; calculate/handle data/create graphs; use labels and values; save/retrieve files; and print results on printers or plotters.

Column
A vertical division of the screen and spreadsheet.

Row
A horizontal division of the screen and spreadsheet.

Cell
The column and row intersection on a spreadsheet screen.

Label
A word identifying columns, rows, or overall titles in a spreadsheet.

Value
The number appearing in a cell as the result of entering a formula or a number.

Number
A mathematical value.

Formula
A rule defining the relationship (outcome) between numbers. Spreadsheet program formulas use cell references as their source for numbers.

Spreadsheet (electronic)
The model consisting of labels and values, sometimes called a worksheet.

Template
A complete spreadsheet or other model saved on disk to be recalled into a spreadsheet or other program as a pattern for future applications. Templates can be created by a user, purchased on disk, or copied out of books for many applications.

Micros in Action "Using Spreadsheets" illustrates how spreadsheet programs are used at Scott Paper Company. A spreadsheet program solves problems using **labels** (words that describe what is on the spreadsheet) and **values (numbers** and **formulas).** A number is a mathematical value and a formula is a rule defining the relationship (outcome) between numbers. Spreadsheet program formulas use cell references as their source for numbers. The **spreadsheet (electronic),** sometimes called a worksheet, is used to aid individuals in creating spreadsheets that consist of labels and values. A completed spreadsheet ready to add new values is often called a **template.** Lotus Development Corporation refers to the template as a worksheet.

Many spreadsheet and spreadsheet support programs exist. Specific spreadsheet program tasks are performed differently in each program. Allways, Lotus 1-2-3 (Versions 2.2 and 3.0), Microsoft Excel, Quattro, Quattro Pro, SeeMore, SuperCalc5, VP-Planner, and V-P Planner 3D are used to illustrate how selected spreadsheet and spreadsheet support programs perform specific tasks. These programs are among the more popular ones available.

Why Spreadsheet Programs?

Spreadsheet programs are among the most valuable programs available. They are best-sellers, because they allow the user to solve business, finance, and other numeric problems without the help of programmers. The programs perform calculations at high speed without errors, and they format the results for screen and printer output.

Spreadsheet programs have been modeled after manual accounting ledger sheets. Both use labels and values. Table 5–1 summarizes the applications of spreadsheet programs.

Dividing the Screen

A spreadsheet program divides the screen into columns. A column-row position is called a cell. The cell (commonly nine characters wide) and rows (commonly one line high) is highlighted by reverse video (white on black, for example) or a box. This highlighted cell, the **active cell,** is where characters may be entered from the keyboard. The arrow keys may be used to relocate the highlighted indication **(cell pointer).**

Common methods for relocating the cell pointer follow:

Active cell
The cell into which characters may be entered.

Cell pointer
The display that indicates which cell is the active cell.

1. Use the arrow keys to move the cell pointer from cell to cell.
2. Press function key F5 to call a goto option. Enter the cell to which you wish to move the cell pointer, and press the ↵ key.

Table 5–1
Spreadsheet Program Applications

Professional Area	Application
Accounting	General ledgers, trial balances, checkbook balancing, data collection reports, amortization schedules, depreciation schedules
Banking	Ratio analysis, cash budgets, capital budgeting–net present value, internal rate of return, profitability index, optimization analysis, loan analysis
Finance and economics	Ratio analysis, cash budgets, capital budgeting–net present value, internal rate of return, profitability index, optimization analysis, amortization schedules, depreciation schedules
Marketing (transportation and logistics)	Analysis of marketing surveys, marketing projections, inventory control analysis, location evaluation, marketing mix analysis, distribution analysis
Personnel administration	Personnel needs analysis, personnel use analysis, insurance needs, job analysis and evaluation
Quantitative management	Optimization applications, inventory analysis and control, production control, Program Evaluation and Review Technique (PERT)
Retail merchandising	Pricing, inventory control, marketing mix, turnover analysis
Statistics	Analysis of variance, regression analysis, calculations of averages and standard deviations
Training	Training records, tests records, performance analysis

3. Use the `<PgUp>`, `<PgDn>`, `<Home>`, `<End>`, arrow, `<TAB>`, `<Shift-Tab>`, and `<Scroll lock>` keys. In Lotus 1-2-3 and many other programs, these keys result in the following:
   a. `<PgUp>` moves the cell pointer one screen up.
   b. `<PgDn>` moves the cell pointer one screen down.
   c. `<Home>` moves the cell pointer to cell A1.
   d. `<End>` and arrow keys move the cell pointer to the end of a list or to the beginning of the next list.
   e. `<TAB>` moves the cell pointer one screen right.
   f. `<Shift-Tab>` moves the cell pointer one screen left.
   g. `<Scroll lock>` changes the screen relocation method between the normal mode and moving the screen around the cell pointer.

Figure 5–1 illustrates the layout of a spreadsheet. Cell C2 is identified by asterisks and the character C2.

Figure 5–1
Spreadsheet Layout

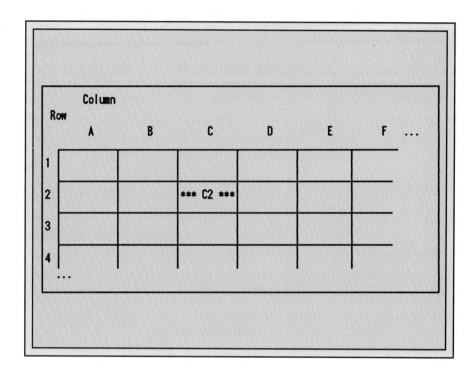

Creating, Editing, and Formatting

A spreadsheet is created by entering labels and values. After the initial labels and values are entered, the spreadsheet can be formatted by organizing the cells or controlling the display of the material in a cell.

Labels

To enter a label, first, use arrows to locate the cell pointer at the desired cell. Next, type the instruction that a label is being entered. Finally, type the label and press ↵.

Figure 5–2 is a spreadsheet with the title "Commission Report" and the cell pointer in cell A1. The spreadsheet example in Figure 5–2 will be expanded to illustrate additional concepts.

A name and date may be entered so a spreadsheet is usable for different months by changing the input data. The next steps in development of the spreadsheet example follow:

1. Move the cell pointer to cell D1
2. Type January 1999 ↵
3. Move the cell pointer to cell A4
4. Type the salesperson's name, Pia Martin ↵
5. Move the cell pointer to cell A6
6. Type the label, Type Sales ↵

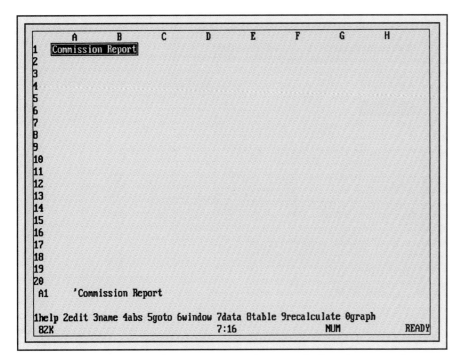

Figure 5–2
Entering a Label

The spreadsheet used assumes labels overflow to the next cell when they are too large to fit into a column. Some spreadsheet programs truncate (shorten) the display to the number of characters available in a cell. The characters not shown are still in the computer's memory.

The results are shown in Figure 5–3.

Column labels Rate, Sales, and Commissions are entered in row 6 (cells C6, D6, and E6). The row labels Computers, Software, and Furniture are entered in column A (cells A7, A8, and A9). The spreadsheet shown in Figure 5–4 is ready for number and formula entry.

Values: Numbers and Formulas

The steps needed to enter some numbers in the spreadsheet example follow:

1. Move the cell pointer to C7
2. Enter the number 8 (for 8 percent commission)
3. Move the cell pointer to C8
4. Enter the number 10 (for 10 percent commission)
5. Move the cell pointer to C9
6. Enter the number 12 (for 12 percent commission)
7. Move the cell pointer to D7
8. Enter the number 23000 (amount of sales)
9. Move the cell pointer to D8
10. Enter the number 1200 (amount of sales)
11. Move the cell pointer to D9
12. Enter the number 5466 (amount of sales)

Figure 5–3
Entering Dates and Names

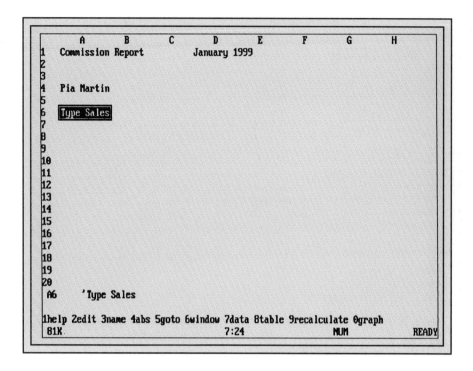

Figure 5–4
Spreadsheet Ready for the
Numbers and Formulas

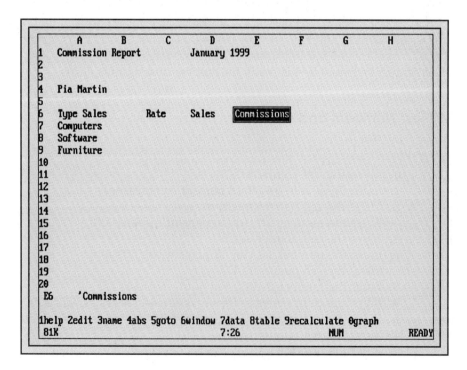

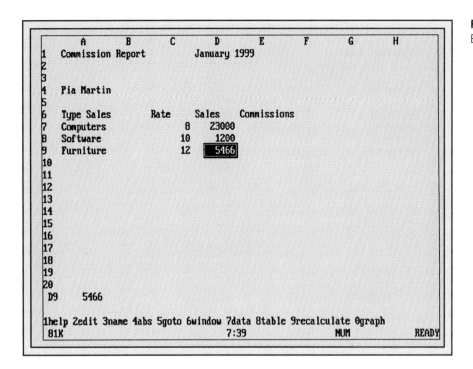

Figure 5–5
Entering the Numbers

Figure 5–5 shows the spreadsheet with all numbers entered.

Note that the numbers are located on the right side of the cell, while the labels are located on the left. Numbers usually default to being right **justified,** and labels default to being left justified. Examine the first character in cell C6. In most spreadsheet programs, it will be a single quote (**'**). Spreadsheet programs often use **'** to mean left label justification, **"** to mean right label justification, and ^ to mean center label. Use the edit mode or retype the single quote (**'**) to change it to a double quote (**"**) in cells C6, D6, and E6. This will help line up the text and numbers in columns C, D, and E.

> **Justified**
> Lined up. Left justified means lined up evenly on left side, and right justified means lined up on the right side.

The commission dollar amount can be calculated in cells E7, E8, and E9. The spreadsheet formula for calculating commission is

> Commission = sales * percent commission * 0.01

The asterisks are used for multiplication. Multiplication by 0.01 changes the percent commission to a decimal. For sales of computers, the commission formula in spreadsheet terms is +C7*D7*0.01 in cell E7. Cell C7 contains the percent commission, and cell D7 contains the amount of sales. The percent commission was entered as a whole number in location C7. The steps to enter the formula follow:

1. Move the cell pointer to E7
2. Type the formula +C7*D7*0.01 ↵

Among the ways to enter the formulas in cells E8 and E9 are to (1) type the formulas in individually or (2) copy the formulas from cell E7 to cells E8 and E9. Enter the formulas in cells E8 and E9 using the method of your choice. Figure 5–6 is the spreadsheet including all commission for-

Figure 5–6
Formula Results

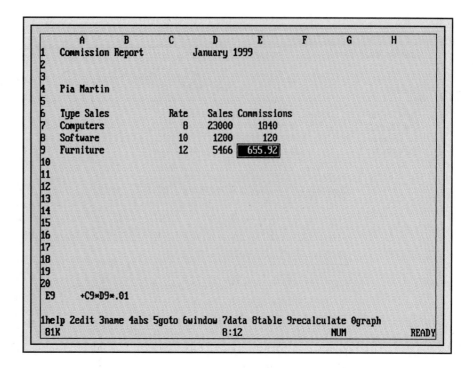

mulas. Cell E7 shows the number 1840, not the formula. The formulas are invisible; only the results of the calculations are displayed. The results of the formula for Software, +C8*D8*.01 (cell E8), and the results of the formula for Furniture, +C9*D9*.01 (cell E9), are also in Figure 5–6.

Range

Range (of cells)
Cells in a spreadsheet identified by the specification of the cell in the upper left position and the cell in the lower right position. For example, the range A5..C7 identifies the cells A5, A6, A7, B5, B6, B7, C5, C6, and C7.

Protected cell
A cell that has been protected from change by the spreadsheet designer. It is good practice to protect the cells with labels when a standard form is created.

Range name
Name assigned to a range of cells.

Format
To control the display and printer output.

A **range (of cells)** is a group of cells defined by the cell in the upper left position and the cell in the lower right position. Ranges are used for format control, creating **protected cells,** and printing, among other purposes. A protected cell is a cell that the user has instructed the program not to allow future users to enter new material from the keyboard. Figure 5–7 is a spreadsheet with a range of cells (C7 through E11) defined. Table 5–2 illustrates the range commands of Lotus 1-2-3. Many spreadsheet program users assign **range names** so they can refer to a range by name, rather than defining them each time they are used.

Format

Formatting is controlling the display and printer output. Cell formats are controlled using features of the spreadsheet program. An example of a format change are the values in the range defined in Figure 5–8. The format of the range was changed to fixed with two values to the right of the decimal point.

Figure 5–8 illustrates numbers (values) presented using the following cells formats Fixed, Scientific, Currency, (comma), General,

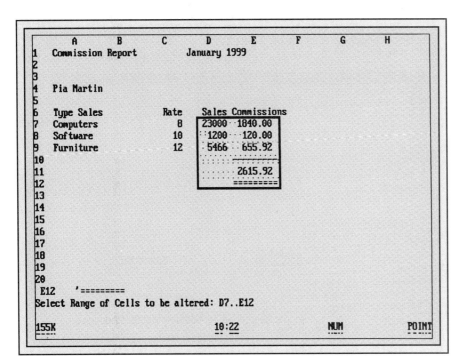

Figure 5–7
Range Defined (C7 through E11)

Table 5–2
Range Commands of Lotus 1-2-3

Command	Application
Format	Number/formula display
Label-prefix	Align labels
Erase	Erase cell entries
Name	Maintain set of names for ranges
Justify	Adjust width of label "paragraph"
Protect	Disallow changes to cells (if protection enabled)
Unprotect	Allow changes to cells
Input	Restrict pointer to unprotected cells

+/-, Percent, Date, Text, and Hidden. In spreadsheets where the +/- format is not available, the * character can be used for bar charts on the spreadsheet. The width of the columns was changed to 11 characters in order for the value to fit using the formats specified. The format steps in Lotus 1-2-3 are listed in Table 5–3.

Figure 5–8
Cell Format Options

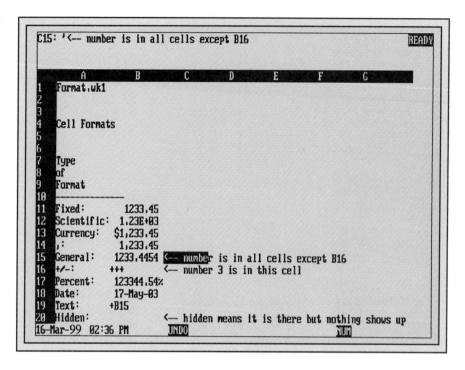

```
C15: '<-- number is in all cells except B16                         READY

         A          B         C        D        E        F        G
 1  Format.wk1
 2
 3
 4  Cell Formats
 5
 6
 7  Type
 8  of
 9  Format
10  ------------
11  Fixed:        1233.45
12  Scientific:   1.23E+03
13  Currency:     $1,233.45
14  ,:            1,233.45
15  General:      1233.4454  <-- number is in all cells except B16
16  +/-:          +++        <-- number 3 is in this cell
17  Percent:      123344.54%
18  Date:         17-May-03
19  Text:         +B15
20  Hidden:                  <-- hidden means it is there but nothing shows up
16-Mar-99  02:36 PM         UNDO                              NUM
```

Table 5–3
Steps to Format a Range in Lotus 1-2-3

Steps
1. / To start menu
2. R To select range
3. F To select format
4. n Where n is the character associated with the format selected
5.   The next steps vary depending on the format selected

Menus

Menu
A screen display of alternate actions from which the computer user makes a selection.

Formats can be controlled using spreadsheet program **menus,** screen displays of alternate actions from which the user makes selections. Menus are started by pressing / in most spreadsheet programs. The format of the output in the commission report is not consistent. Figure 5–9 illustrates the screen menu before step 5. The steps for formatting column E are listed in Table 5–4.

In Figure 5–10, a line consisting of nine minus signs as a label in cell E10 and a second line consisting of nine equals signs as a label in E12 are used to indicate that the column is summed. Most spreadsheet pro-

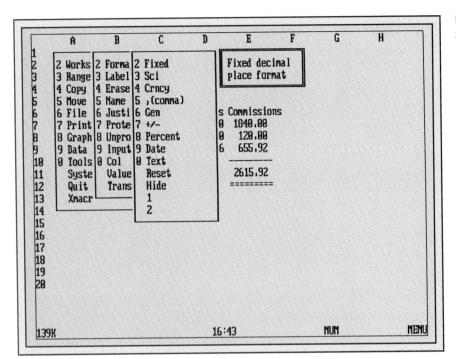

Figure 5–9
Screen Menu Display

Table 5–4
Using a Menu

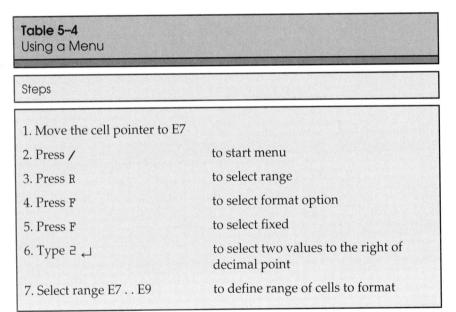

Steps	
1. Move the cell pointer to E7	
2. Press /	to start menu
3. Press R	to select range
4. Press F	to select format option
5. Press F	to select fixed
6. Type 2 ↵	to select two values to the right of decimal point
7. Select range E7 .. E9	to define range of cells to format

Many spreadsheet programs allow you to move the cell pointer to E7 (press the decimal point to anchor (start the range); move the cell pointer to E9 and press ↵ to end the range definition).

grams require a quotation mark when using a mathematical operator (^), *, /, +, −, or =) as a label. (Mathematical operators will be discussed in a later section.)

One more formula in cell E11 (Figure 5–10) completes the spreadsheet. Two alternate forms are possible: +E7+E8+E9 or @SUM(E7..E9). The second form varies between spreadsheet programs. The @SUM(start

Figure 5–10
One More Formula Is Added

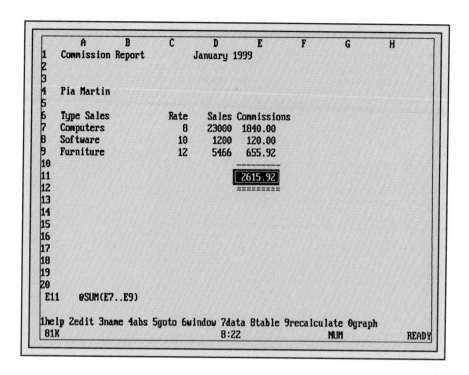

`cell..end cell`) form means to add the values in the range defined from the starting cell to the ending cell, inclusive. For adding large columns of numbers, the `@SUM` method is more convenient.

Function Keys and Modes

Function key
A computer keyboard key labeled F1, F2, and so on.

Function keys are found on the left side of the keyboard or along the top. In some spreadsheet programs, the use of the function keys is displayed on the screen. Usually, pressing function key `F1` recalls a help screen that aids in the performance of the task being performed by the spreadsheet. In Lotus 1-2-3, pressing `F1` for "help" produces different results, depending on the spreadsheet **mode** (Table 5–5). The mode determines the options available to the spreadsheet program user.

Mode
Manner of operations. The mode determines the optional action available to the spreadsheet program user.

Table 5–6 lists the use of function keys in Lotus 1-2-3. The same or similar function keys are used in many other spreadsheet programs.

Editing Cells

The spreadsheet edit mode allows the user to change, add, or delete the individual characters that make up the labels and formulas in a cell. These steps are commonly used:

1. Place the cursor in the cell to be edited
2. Press function key `F2`

Once you are in the edit mode, use the cursor keys such as `<Home>`, arrows, `<Delete>`, and `<Insert>` to change the text or numbers in the cell.

Table 5–5
Lotus 1-2-3 Modes (Release 2.2)

Mode	Explanation
Edit	Pressing F2 allows you to edit the contents of a cell
Error	Indicates an error has occured; pressing F1 displays a help screen
Files	Displays menu of file names; press F3 for full screen display
Find	Repeats the last / Data Query Find
FRMT	Selects / Data Parse Format–Line Edit to edit format line
Help	Help screen appears after pressing F1
Label	Entering a label
Menu	Menu appears after pressing / or <
Names	Menu of range, graphs, or attached add-in names
Point	Prompt to specify a range
Ready	Program ready for an instruction
Stat	Status screen for / Worksheet Status or / Worksheet Global Status
Value	Entering a value
Wait	Program completing a command or process

Inserting and Deleting Columns and Rows

If you make an error and do not leave enough room on a manual spread-sheet, you will have to copy it over. In a spreadsheet program, however, you can insert a column or row when needed with a few simple menu-driven instructions. Most spreadsheet programs adjust all formulas when columns or rows insert. However, errors may be introduced and the spreadsheet should be checked.

You can delete a column or row. If you delete a cell that contains a number or formula used by other cells, you may get an error. The commands used to delete columns or rows are similar in all spreadsheet programs.

Cell Copying

Cell copying (replication) is the copying of the contents of cells from one range on a spreadsheet to another. When copying a cell that contains a formula, pay attention to how the formula uses other cells. A cell formula may refer to other cells using either an absolute or relative reference. With

Cell copying
Replicating (copying) the contents of cells form one range to another.

Table 5–6
Function Keys in Lotus 1-2-3 (Release 2.2)

Function Key	Application
F1:Help	Display content-sensitive Help screens; press <Esc> to return to prior mode.
F2:Edit	Switch to/from Edit Mode for current entry.
F3:Name	Display menu of range names (Point Mode only).
F4:Abs	Toggle between relative and absolute addressing (Point and Edit Modes).
F5:Goto	Move cell pointer to a particular cell.
F6:Window	Move sell pointer to other window (Split screen only).
F7:Query	Repeat most recent Data Query operation.
F8:Table	Repeat most recent Data Table operation.
F9:Calc	Ready Mode: Recalculate worksheet. Value and Edit Modes: Convert formula to its current value.
F10:Graph	Draw active graph according to most recent graphing specification.
<Alt>+F1:Compose	Display characters in addition to those produced by the keyboard.
<Alt>+F2:Step	Toggle macro step mode; execute macros one step at a time.
<Alt>+F3:Run	Display list or range names for you to select to run (Ready Mode).
<Alt>+F4:Undo	Cancel any changes made since last ready mode (Ready Mode).
<Alt>+F5:Learn	Toggle on recording of keystrokes.
<Alt>+F6:	
<Alt>+F7:App1	Activate add-in program.
<Alt>+F8:App2	Activate add-in program.
<Alt>+F9:App3	Activate add-in program.
<Alt>+F10:App4	Activate add-in program.

Absolute referencing (absolute addressing)
In a spreadsheet, a cell or range reference that always refers to the same cell when copied or moved. A dollar sign ($) placed before the column letter and row number, such as A2, is often used to indicate absolute reference. The term addressing is often used in place of reference.

absolute referencing, or absolute addressing, no matter where a formula is copied or moved on a spreadsheet, the formula will always use the values in a specific cell or cells. The top example in Figure 5–11 uses the value in cell A2. No matter where the formula is copied or moved, cell A2 is the cell of reference.

Relative referencing refers to a cell that is a fixed number of columns and rows away from the cell containing the formula. In the bottom example in Figure 5–11, the formula in cell C18 is +A13*B2. Cell A13 is five rows up and two columns to the left of C18. Cell B2 is 16 rows up and one column to the left of C18. When the formula is moved to cell F17, it

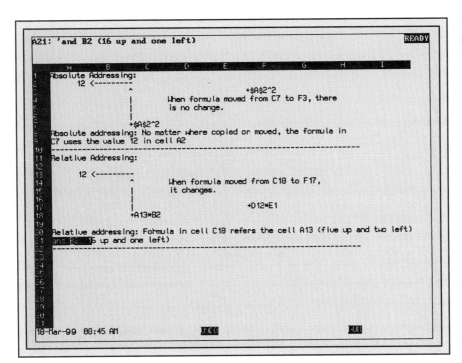

Figure 5–11
Absolute and Relative
Referencing

Table 5–7
Common References for the Formula in Cell Z3

Type of Reference	Cell Reference
Relative	B4
Absolute	B4
Relative column, absolute row	B$4
Absolute column, relative row	$B4

changes to $+D12*E1$. Cell D12 is five rows up and two columns to the left of F17. Cell E1 is 16 rows up and one column to the left of F17. The formula uses cells that are always 5 up and 2 left and 15 up and 3 left.

Cell formulas may contain both absolute and relative references (Table 5–7). A formula may refer to a series of cells in a given row; that is, the column reference is relative, and the row is absolute.

Undo

Undo, the capability to back up to a prior version of a spreadsheet when an error is made, is found in most new versions of spreadsheet programs. If

Relative referencing
In a spreadsheet, a cell or range reference that refers to a cell a set number of columns and rows away in a specified direction. When the formulas in a cell are moved or copied, the relative references are changed to maintain their relative position.

Undo
The capability to back up a step and eliminate a change, returning to the old version of the spreadsheet work.

the undo function is selected while performing an edit, the old version of the spreadsheet is restored. In Lotus 1-2-3 version 2.2 and 3.0, pressing <Alt>+F4 performs the undo function. In SuperCalc5, the undo function is a menu selection.

Macros

Macros are sets of instructions for performing a task or tasks. Usually, macros consist of a record of the keystrokes used to perform the task. Macros are often started by pressing <Alt>+n, where n is a specified key. In Lotus 1-2-3, n may be any letter from A to Z, or 0 (zero). If n is 0, the macro automatically executes when the spreadsheet template is loaded. Lotus macros are part of the spreadsheet template.

Figure 5–12 includes four macros. The macros operate in Lotus 1-2-3 (Release 2.01 and 2.2), Lotus 1-2-3 (Release 3.0), Quattro (using the 123 menu mode), and VP-Planner Plus, among other spreadsheet programs. The first macro, @today~/rfd1/wcs10~ is located in a cell with the range name \D. When you press <Alt>+D, the current date is entered in the cell where the cell pointer is located. The commands performed by the macro are listed in Table 5–8.

The second macro, /FS~R, is located in a cell with the range name \S. The macro assumes the file has been saved at least once and has a name. When <Alt>+S is pressed, the steps listed in Table 5–9 are performed.

The third and fourth macros print the spreadsheet. The fourth macro uses the setup code \015 to tell the printer to switch to compressed

Figure 5–12
Four Spreadsheet Macros

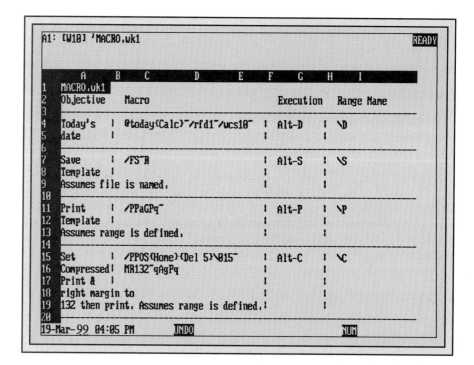

Table 5–8
Date Macro

Instruction	
@today	Enter the day's number based on the date entered when DOS was started, or obtain it from the computer's time clock
~	Enter
/	Start the menu
r	Range
f	Format
d	Date
1	First format (DD-MMM-YY)
~	Enter
/	Start the menu
W	Worksheet
C	Column
S	Set-Width
10	Ten characters wide
~	Enter

Table 5–9
Saving the Spreadsheet Macro

Instruction	
/	Start the menu; when entering this macro, you must first type an apostrophe (') to tell the spreadsheet program that text is being entered
F	File
S	Save
~	Enter
R	Replace

mode. This code does not work on all printers. If you try this macro, change the code to match your printer.

Windows and Multiple Spreadsheets

A window is the divison of the screen into parts to display (1) parts of the same spreadsheet, (2) a spreadsheet and a graph, (3) pages of a given spreadsheet, (4) multiple (linked or unlinked) spreadsheets, or (5) one or more spreadsheets and other applications. Spreadsheets are linked when formulas in one spreadsheet refer to cells in a second spreadsheet. Figure 5-13 illustrates spreadsheet windows dividing the screen into two parts. Figure 5-14 illustrates a spreadsheet with windows containing an individual spreadsheet. In additon, spreadsheet programs can divide the screen into windows containing a spreadsheet and a graph and Windows 3.0 may be used to display a spreadsheet and some additional applications.

Calculating, Handling Data, and Creating Graphs

Spreadsheets perform calculations using mathematical operators, use special functions, and use logical functions. They provide warning messages, use menu-driven data analysis, handle data, and create graphs. Spreadsheets also can perform "What if?" investigations and sensitivity analysis.

Mathematical Operations

Mathematical operator
A symbol that indicates a mathematical process such as power (∧), multiplication (·), division (/), addition (+), and subtraction (−).

Mathematical operators are symbols that provide instruction on what mathematical operations to perform. Mathematical operators include raising to a power (∧), multiplication (*), division (/), addition (+), and subtraction (−). All mathematical operations can be performed by spreadsheet programs. In addition, most programs provide special mathematical capabilities, such as adding all values in a column or row, most trigonometric functions, and others.

A number is a value you place in a cell to be used in your calculations, such as the cost of an item, the volume sold, and so on. A mathematical formula is a defined relationship that you place in a cell to calculate the desired results. The formula will appear in a section of the screen on the top or bottom, but not in the body of the spreadsheet. In the body of the spreadsheet you will see a value, the results of the formula. A number is a mathematical formula equal to a constant, the number.

Mathematical precedence
The order in which mathematical operations are executed. The standard order is operators in parentheses, power, calculations, multiplication and division, and addition and subtraction.

Spreadsheet programs may or may not use all the **mathematical precedence** rules. Precedence is the order in which mathematical operations are executed. It requires all operators (∧, *, /, +, and −) inside parentheses to be performed first, followed by power calculations, then multiplication and division, and finally addition and subtraction. Operations at a common level of precedence are performed from left to right. For

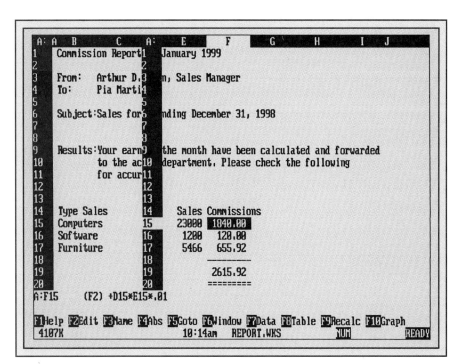

Figure 5–13
VP-Planner 3D: Two Parts, Same Spreadsheet

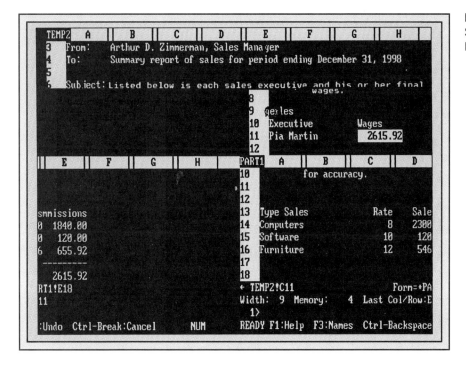

Figure 5–14
SuperCalc5: Display of Two Linked Spreadsheets

example, the formula A = 5 + 2 * 4, yields the result 28 when executed from left to right. It yields the result 13 when the order of precedence is considered. The 2 * 4 operation should be executed first, and then the value 5 added to that result. Table 5–10 shows the operators used on most spreadsheet programs in order of precedence.

Table 5–10
Spreadsheet Operators in Order of Precedence

Operation	Operator
Parentheses	( )
Power	^
Multiplication	*
Division	/
Addition	+
Subtraction	−

Table 5–11
Calculating −1^2

Spreadsheet	Result
Excel	+1
ExpressCalc	−1
Lotus	−1 (all releases)
Multiplan	+1
Quattro	+1
SuperCalc	+1
VisiCalc	+1
VP Planner	+1

Take care when using precedence. For example, the square of a negative number may or may not be a positive number (Table 5–11). When calculating −1^2, some spreadsheet programs square the 1 and then consider the negative sign. Other spreadsheet programs square −1. All spreadsheet programs obtain +1 when calculating (−1)^2. It is best, therefore, to use parentheses to control the order of calculations.

Functions

A variety of special functions are built into spreadsheet programs. Some spreadsheet financial functions are shown in Table 5–12.

Table 5–12
Spreadsheet Financial Functions

Financial Function	Application
IRR(guess, range)	Internal rate of return
NPV(x, range)	Net present value
FV(pmt, int, term)	Future value
PV(pmt, int, term)	Present value
PMT(prn, int, term)	Payment

Note: Lotus 1-2-3 requires an @ preceding all functions.

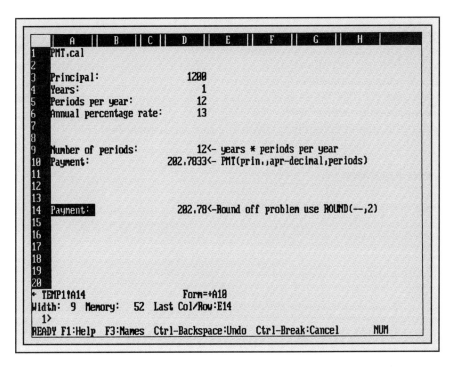

Figure 5–15
Financial Functions

The PMT (*prn,int,term*) function (Figure 5–15) finds the equal payment required to pay off a loan for the value *prn,* at a periodic interest rate of *int* (in decimal format), in *term* payments. The variables may be either numbers or numbers found in cells. To use a function found in a specific spreadsheet program, you must know how the data are entered into the function. When calculating loan payments, it is necessary to round off the results to the nearest penny. A @ROUND(value,number) function rounds off values (placed in the first position) to a number of figures to the right of the decimal point (placed in the second position). Figure 5–15 illustrates the use of both the PMT and ROUND functions.

Logical Functions

Logical function
A conditional statement that evaluates a condition in the form of an equation.

A **logical function** is a conditional statement that evaluates a condition in the form of an equation. Spreadsheets may contain logical functions such as conditional "if" statements, among others. Table 5–13 lists the logical and special functions found in Lotus 1-2-3.

The logical function allows you to direct the actions of the spreadsheet program with the values entered. For example, the @IF(cond, x,y) function calculates the formula entered into the conditional position and if the number is nonzero, executes the instruction in the x position. If the number is 0, the instruction in the y position is executed.

Some spreadsheets include logical operations in their precedence rules. The arithmetic and logical operators of a spreadsheet program and their precedence are shown in Table 5–14.

Warning Messages

Warning message
A warning displayed on the screen to tell users about a potential problem.

Spreadsheet programs provide **warning messages** to tell users when potential problems may be occurring. A warning message will be displayed when circular calculations are used. A circular reference is when the value in a cell depends on the original value in that cell (Figure 5–16). In general, don't use circular references, always check your results to be sure the spreadsheet formulas are performing the way you want them to, and watch the screen carefully for warning messages such as CIRC.

Data Analysis

Data analysis
Techniques for the evaluation of ranges of data.

Data analysis includes a number of techniques for evaluating ranges of data. Among the data analysis techniques is **regression analysis.** Regres-

---

Table 5–13
Lotus 1-2-3 Logical and Special @ Functions

Logical Function	Application
@False	0 (FALSE)
@ True	1 (TRUE)
@IF(cond, x, y)	x if cond is TRUE (nonzero) y if cond is FALSE (0)
@ISNA(x)	1 (TRUE) if x=NA
@ISERR(x)	1 (TRUE) if x=ERR

Note: When determining the true value of a formula, Lotus 1-2-3 considers any nonzero value to be TRUE. Only 0 itself is FALSE.

Table 5-14
Arithmetic and Logical Operators of a Spreadsheet Program

Operator	Application	Precedence Number
^	Exponentiation	7
+	Positive	6
−	Negative	6
*	Multiplication	5
/	Division	4
+	Addition	4
−	Subtraction	4
=	Equals	3
<	Less than	3
<=	Less than or equal to	3
>	Greater than	3
>=	Greater than or equal to	3
<>	Not equal to	3
#NOT#	Logical not	2
#AND#	Logical and	1
#OR#	Logical or	1

Note: Operators with larger precedence numbers are performed first, unless overridden by parentheses. Operators with equal precedence are performed left to right.

sion analysis is a procedure for fitting a line or a curve to a data set and calculating statistical information about the relationship between the line and the data set. Some spreadsheet programs have built-in capabilities to perform regression analysis. Figure 5–17 illustrates spreadsheet regression analysis.

Another data analysis procedure is a frequency count of a range of data relative to a set of defined cells. **Cell counting** is the capability to define a group of cells and then to count (in a range) the number of data points that fall into each cell. Cell counting is needed in many data analysis situations. Figure 5–18 illustrates the `/Tools-Frequency` selection in Quattro Pro. The data in the range A1..A20 is counted using the cells in the range C2..C11 with the results displayed in the range D2..D12. For example, the number 3 in cell D4 counts the value between 10 and 20, and the value 16 (D3), 17 (D4), and 19 (D16).

Regression analysis
A procedure for fitting a line or curve to a data set and calculating statistical information about the relationship between the line and the data set.

Cell counting
The capability to define a group of cells and count (in a range) the number of data points that fall into each cell.

Figure 5–16
Circular References in
Quattro Pro

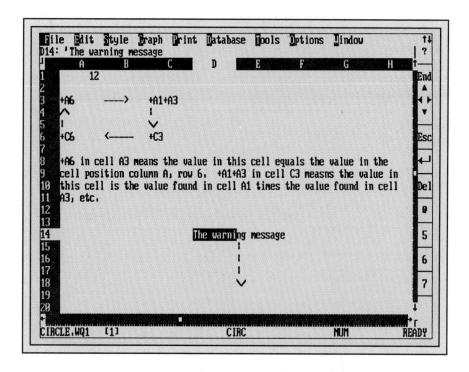

Figure 5–17
SuperCalc5 Regression Analysis

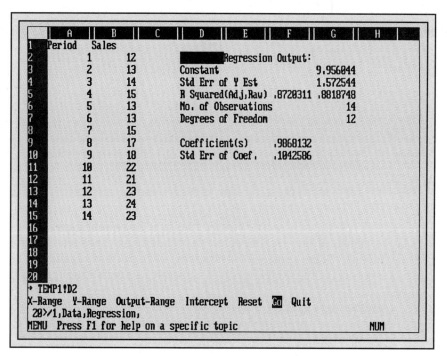

Data Handling

Data handling
The use of the database functions
included in many spreadsheet
programs.

Many spreadsheet programs include basic **data-handling** (database) maintenance capabilities such as sorting and querying. Spreadsheet programs
allow you to sort a range of rows with the Data-Range menu selection

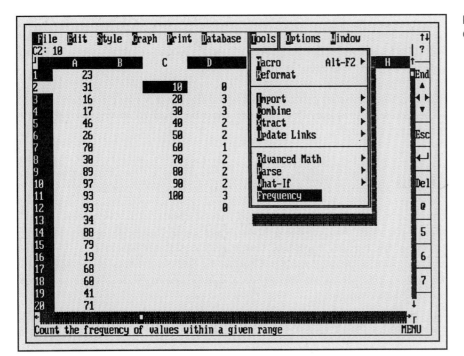

Figure 5–18
Cell Counting in Quattro Pro

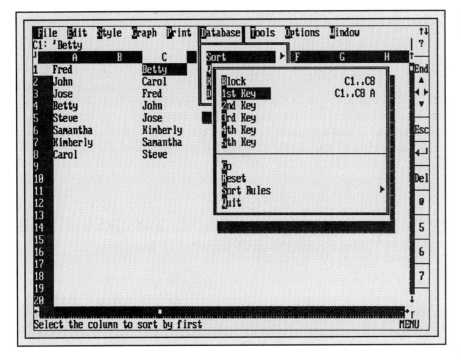

Figure 5–19
Sorting a List

using a primary and secondary key in ascending or descending order (Lotus 1-2-3). Some spreadsheet programs include three keys (Excel and SuperCalc5), four keys (VP-Planner), and even five keys (Quattro). Figure 5–19 illustrates sorting. The names in column A were copied into column C and then sorted from low to high. The menu selections used are shown.

Most spreadsheet programs include a `/DataQuery` or similar command sequence for locating and editing selected records. When making queries, spreadsheet programs allow for global searches using selected criteria, deletes, extracts, finds, and so on.

In addition to query capabilities, some spreadsheet programs (VP-Planner, for example) can read and write files in a format that can be read by a database program. VP-Planner may be used to maintain a multidimensional database.

Graphs

The type and variety of graphs that can be created vary between spreadsheet programs. Among the graphs available are line, bar, xy, stacked bar, pie, area, dual scales, high-low, radar, and text. Examples and explanations of each graph type are found in Chapter 6. The charts may be displayed on the screen, printer, or plotter. When a value is changed on the spreadsheet, the graph is changed.

The following steps are required in a spreadsheet program to create a graph:

1. Enter the labels and values.
2. Start the graph routine.
3. Select the graph type.
4. Identify the range of cells for the x scale (if the graph type uses an x scale).
5. Identify the range of cells for each variable graphed.
6. Instruct the program to display the graph.

In addition, the labels and special options (such as three dimensions), if available, must be specified. Functions may be graphed by calculating their values into a range of cells. Being able to see what a function looks like helps in the understanding of mathematical concepts. Figure 5–20 is a graph of the normal distribution (used in statistical analysis) and its rate of change. The quality and accuracy of spreadsheet graphs are beyond the manual ability of most individuals.

"What If?" Investigations and Sensitivity Analysis

"What if?" investigation
The study of the changes in the values of an output variable or variables as the values of a selected input or inputs are changed.

Sensitivity analysis
The determination of how fast an output variable changes for a given change in an input variable.

A **"what if?" investigation** is the study of changes in the values of an output variable or variables as the values of a selected input or inputs are changed. A **sensitivity analysis** is the determining of how fast an output variable changes for a given change in an input variable. Micros in Action "What If?" illustrates how a "what if?" analysis is used in industry. In many business, economic, and engineering situations, the exact values of selected input variables are often not known. Sometimes the extreme (lowest and highest) values of an input variable can be estimated. Spreadsheet templates can be created to allow the user to enter different values for a given variable and then examine the values of output variables. Important "what if?" and sensitivity questions include the following: What if the

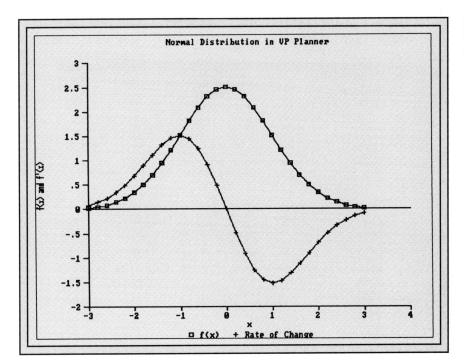

Figure 5–20
Normal Distribution and
Rate-of-Change Equation

value of the (input) variable approaches one extreme or the other? How fast do the values of the output variables change as the value of an input variable is changed by 1 percent, 5 percent, 10 percent, and so on? What is the best setting for a decision variable in order to maximize some measure of value or minimize some cost measure?

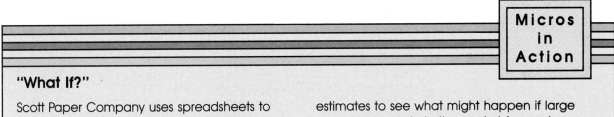

Micros in Action

"What If?"

Scott Paper Company uses spreadsheets to make "what if?" evaluations. For example, sales forecasts are often uncertain when Scott performs an evaluation on the profitability of investing in a new piece of production equipment. Evaluations are often performed using 50, 100, and 150 percent of the best-sales estimates to see what might happen if large errors were made in the market forecast.

The risk and profitability of each level of sales is evaluated. Only with the use of spreadsheets can "what if?" investigations be performed in minutes rather than hours, days, or even weeks.

Figure 5–21 displays an analysis of the profits earned by a hotel. Figure 5–22 is a graph of the daily profits for each of the five months shown. The key unknown variables are the average daily rate and the average daily occupancy rate. Management knows that as it increases the average daily rate, the average daily occupancy rate will decrease. The cost

Figure 5–21
Hotel Profit Analysis

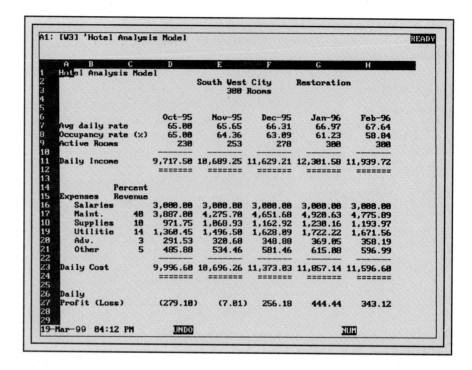

Figure 5–22
Graph of Hotel Profit or Loss

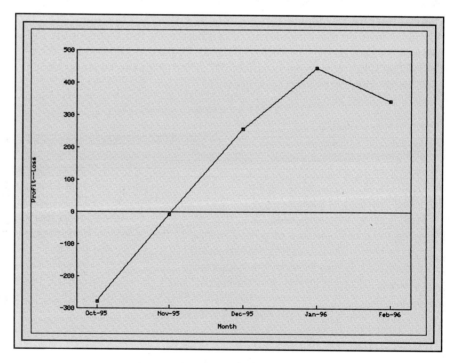

of wages and salaries is fixed. The costs of maintenance, supplies, utilities, advertisements, and others are known from experience to be a percentage of income. Using this spreadsheet, management may answer such questions as, What if we increased the average daily rate to $70? What if we decreased the average daily rate to $60?

A sensitivity analysis determines how fast an output variable reacts to changes in an input variable. For example, in the spreadsheet illustrated in Figure 5–21, if the starting average daily rate were increased by 10 percent to 71.50 (65 + 0.10 * 65), then the daily profit for Feb–96 would change from $343.12 to $677.43, an increase of more than 97 percent. The spreadsheet user must decide if this is a good prediction or if the spread sheet template needs correction. If the spreadsheet model reflects actual occurrences, management has a good guide to action.

Saving and Retrieving

Spreadsheet programs allow users to save and retrieve all or parts of a spreadsheet and to import and export spreadsheet files to other spread-sheet programs and applications.

Saving and Retrieving Spreadsheets

Spreadsheet programs allow users to save spreadsheets as files on a disk. When a spreadsheet is being used as a template, the labels and formulas only are saved. All data must be saved in a completed form. Once saved, the spreadsheet file can be recalled for use at any time. By editing or overtyping, new data are entered, and the analysis is updated for the next period. Saving a spreadsheet file is simple and often menu driven. Table 5–15 lists the commands in the file menu of Lotus 1-2-3.

Table 5–15
File Menu of Lotus 1-2-3

Instruction	Function
Save	Store entire worksheet in worksheet file
Retrieve	Restore data from worksheet file
Combine	Incorporate (part of) worksheet file into Current worksheet (Methods: Copy, Add, Subtract); use Entire-file or Named-Range only
Xtract	Store range of entries in worksheet file; save Formulas or current values only
Erase	Erase one or more Lotus 1-2-3 data files
List	List names of Lotus 1-2-3 data files; report disk space
Import	Incorporate print file into worksheet; treat lines as Text or as Numbers and quoted text
Directory	Change current directory assignment

Spreadsheet programs create files with special extensions. Many spreadsheet programs use a three-character extension on the filename to identify the type of file stored on the disk. Table 5–16 identifies the extension used in spreadsheet programs, and Table 5–17 illustrates the use of **.WK*** files. The asterisk in the extension is a wild card; you may expect to see a number of different characters in this location.

.WK*

An extension for Lotus 1-2-3 spreadsheet files. The * is a wild card meaning that a number of different characters will appear in this position.

Transferring Data and Output

Spreadsheet results and data can be transferred to or from (exported to and imported from) other spreadsheet programs, word processing programs, database programs, graphics programs, and special-purpose programs.

When you first develop applications with a spreadsheet program, the need to transfer data between programs may not seem important. After a number of years, however, you will find yourself with a collection of spreadsheets and data in many different formats. You may also find the

Table 5–16
Spreadsheet File Extenders

Extender	Application
.CAL	SuperCalc spreadsheet file
.COM	Program file
.DAT	Program data file
.DOC	Text file with documentation [a]
.EXE	Program file
.HLP	Help file
.MSG	Message file
.OVL	Program overlay file
.PIC	Graph (picture) file
.PRN	Print (text) file
.PRO	Program file
.WKS	Lotus V.1 spreadsheet file
.WK1	Lotus (Release 2.0, 2.01, 2.2) file
.WK3	Lotus (Release 3.0) file
.XQT	SuperCalc macro-execute file

[a] Programs that have documentation on the disk.

Table 5–17
Spreadsheet Template Formats

Developed For	Extender
Lotus 1-2-3 (Release 1A)	.WKS
Lotus 1-2-3 (Release 2.0, 2.01, 2.2)	.WK1[a]
Lotus 1-2-3 (Release 3.0)	.WK3

[a].WK1 files saved by Lotus 1-2-3 (Release 2.01 and earlier) are not exactly the same as the files saved by Lotus 1-2-3 (Release 2.2).

need to transfer spreadsheet formulas and data into word processing or database programs. For example, say you have a report to prepare based on the output of calculations performed in an electronic spreadsheet. The output of the spreadsheet may be saved as an ASCII (DOS or text) file and then transferred into a word processor text file to save your typing.

Most spreadsheet programs can print files to a disk. This capability usually produces an ASCII file that may be transferred to a word processing program for report preparation. If a spreadsheet program can read ASCII files (and most can), it is generally easy to transfer data in.

In addition to ASCII files, a number of other "standard" formats are used in spreadsheet work. DIF (data interchange format file), first developed for VisiCalc, is used by a number of programs to aid in interfacing. DIF files are ASCII files in a specific format. Many spreadsheet programs allow you to save your spreadsheet in DIF format.

Printing

The commission calculation spreadsheet presented earlier in the chapter has been edited with the addition of memo information and prepared for printing. The printing instruction is given in Table 5–18.

Figure 5–23 illustrates the screen in Lotus 1-2-3 (Release 2.2) with the printing range defined. After the printing range is defined, options can be selected to specify such things as setup codes and margins. Many spreadsheet outputs require the use of compressed mode and changes in margins due to the spreadsheets' size.

The next step is to press A (for "align") to tell Lotus that the paper is ready in the printer and then to press G (for "go"). Figure 5–24 shows the Lotus 1-2-3 printout for the spreadsheet in Figure 5–23. When using some printers, pressing P (for "page feed") may be necessary. Users of Lotus 1-2-3 (Release 2.00, 2.01, and 2.2) may use Allways (an **add-in program**) to enhance their printer output. An add-in program is a program

Add-in program
A program created for use with a program (such as Lotus 1-2-3) to add features and extend its capabilities.

Table 5–18
Printing Instructions

Steps	
/	Start menu
P	Select Print
P	Select Printer
R	Define the range

that may be attached to a spreadsheet program to add features. The All-ways screen displays fonts of different sizes on the screen before printing. The overlay of the title ("Commission Report") and the date previews the printer results.

Lotus 1-2-3 is not the only spreadsheet program with special formatting and printer output capabilities. Figure 5-25 illustrates a VP-Planner 3D screen using box draw to enhance the memo illustrated in Figure 5-23 and 5-24 (Lotus 1-2-3). Figure 5-26 illustrates the printed results obtained from VP-Planner 3D.

Often, the number of columns or rows to be printed is greater than the standard page format of the printer. Some programs allow you to print spreadsheets sideways to obtain better fit.

The printer instructions are menu driven in most spreadsheets and are specific to a particular spreadsheet program (Table 5–19). Many spreadsheet programs allow printing (saving) to a file as well as to a printer. The file printed (saved) is an ASCII file, which may be transferred to a word processor or used with a sideways printing program.

Printer setup codes can be used to control spacing, pitch, fonts, and other variables. The printer setup codes (strings of characters) are sent in a variety of ways. For example, compressed mode on an Epson printer requires the code 015. The Lotus stepup string is \015. In older versions of SuperCalc, the setup string is ^O (the 15th letter of the alphabet sends a 15 to the printer). Newer versions of SuperCalc use either ^O or \015.

Spreadsheet Hardware

Spreadsheet programs are created to run on a specific microprocessor with a specific operating system using standard computer hardware. The microcomputer hardware needs for spreadsheet programs include a micro processor and operating system, RAM, input devices, a monitor, a printer, and on-line storage.

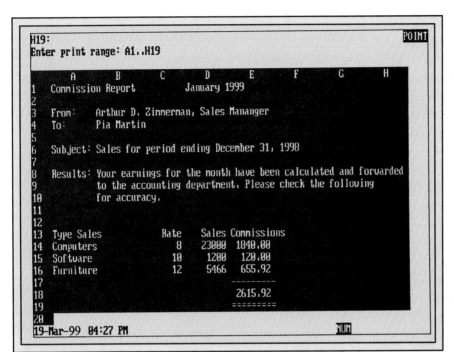

Figure 5–23
Lotus 1-2-3 (Release 2.2) Report,
Print Range Defined

```
Commission Report          January 1999

From:    Arthur D. Zimmerman, Sales Manager
To:      Pia Martin

Subject: Sales for period ending December 31, 1998

Results: Your earnings for the month have been calculated and forwarded
         to the accounting department. Please check the following
         for accuracy.


Type Sales         Rate    Sales Commissions
Computers            8     23000  1840.00
Software            10      1200   120.00
Furniture           12      5466   655.92
                                 ---------
                                   2615.92
                                 =========
```

Figure 5–24
Lotus 1-2-3 Report Printout

Figure 5–25
VP-Planner 3D Box Draw

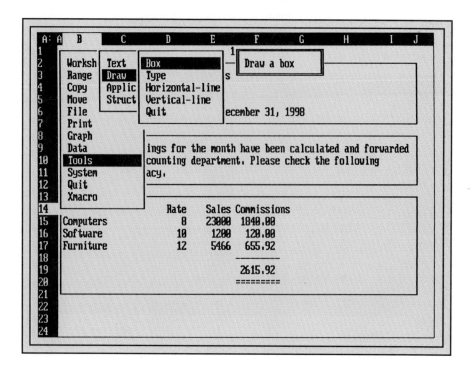

Figure 5–26
VP-Planner Printout

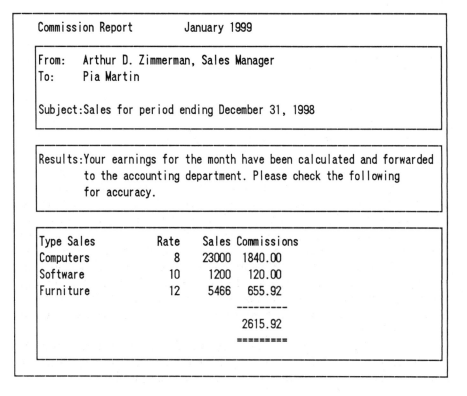

Table 5–19
Printer Menu for Lotus 1-2-3

Function	Application
Printer vs. File	Direct output to printer or print file
Range	Range to be printed
Line	Advance printer one line
Page	Advance to top of next page

Options
  Headers, Footers
  Margins
  Borders
	Page formatting
	Set page header/footer line
	Left, right, top, bottom
	Graft extra columns or rows to print range

Setup	Set printer control characters
Page-Length	Set number of lines
Other	As displayed versus cell formulas Printing of formula texts Unformatted versus formatted Suppress headers, footers, page breaks
Clear	Cancel print settings
Align	Reset line number counter to 1
Go	Print the selected range

Microprocessors and Operating Systems

Early spreadsheet programs, such as VisiCalc and SuperCalc, had versions for the Apple (6502 microprocessor using Apple-DOS), the Osborne (Z80 microprocessor using CP/M), and the IBM PC and workalikes (8088 microprocessor using MS-DOS/PC DOS). SuperCalc5, Quattro Pro, and Lotus 1-2-3 (Release 2.2) operate on the IBM PC, XT, AT, and their workalikes using the 8088, 8086, 80286, 80386, and 80486 microprocessors. Lotus 1-2-3 (Release 3.0) requires an 80286 or better microprocessor. All versions of Lotus 1-2-3 require MS-DOS/PC DOS or OS/2 operating systems. Microsoft's Excel has versions available for MS-DOS/PC DOS using the 8088 or better microprocessors, as well as most versions of the Apple Macintosh.

Spreadsheet programs were originally developed on microcomputers. Spreadsheet versions are now available for systems of many different sizes, including minicomputers and mainframe computers.

RAM Needs

Electronic spreadsheet programs are limited to the number of columns and rows (cells), number of cells with characters, amount of data entered into the spreadsheet, and number of features (such as graphics). There are no simple rules for determining the number of columns and rows (cells) and number of cells with characters for a specific program on a specific computer with a given amount of RAM. Each spreadsheet program requires a minimum amount of RAM to begin operation; Lotus 1-2-3 (Release 2.2) requires 320K, and Lotus 1-2-3 (Release 3.0) requires 1MB. Most student assignments are small and do not need extra RAM.

MS-DOS and PC DOS spreadsheet programs use up to 640K of RAM. Some spreadsheet programs are able to use add-on expanded memory storage (EMS) on special PC boards of 1MB or more. Some Apple Macintoshes, Amigas, and others have over 1 million bytes of RAM that may be used by spreadsheet programs.

Monitors

Spreadsheet programs use many types of monitors, including CGA, Hercules Monochrome, EGA, MCGA, and VGA monitors. The number of columns displayed is a function of the spreadsheet program's configuration, the type of monitor, and the width of each column. The number of rows displayed is a function of the spreadsheet program's configuration and the type of monitor.

Add-in programs such as Personic's SeeMore for Lotus 1-2-3 can be used with many monitors to control the number of columns and rows displayed on the screen. Figure 5–27 illustrates a CGA screen using See-More with Lotus 1-2-3.

Monitors with 80 columns and 25 lines are sufficient for many spreadsheet needs. As the size of the spreadsheet increases, the availability of the bigger displays become desirable. SeeMore's capability for changing the screen display using a simple menu helps users making presentations to large groups using overhead projectors.

Printers

Spreadsheet applications often require a large number of columns and rows. Dot-matrix, laser, ink-jet, and other printers can change the size of the fonts and produce from 80 to 132 characters on paper of normal size. Most laser printers print sideways on command. Many dot-matrix printers can print sideways with the addition of special software.

Table 5–20 identifies the number of nine-character spreadsheet columns that selected printers can produce using **compressed print** (approximately 17 characters per inch rather than 10 or 12). If add-in programs such as Allways (sold with Lotus 1-2-3 [Release 2.2]) are used, the number, shape, and size of characters printed can be controlled.

Compressed print
Printing with approximately 17 characters per inch rather than the standard 10 or 12.

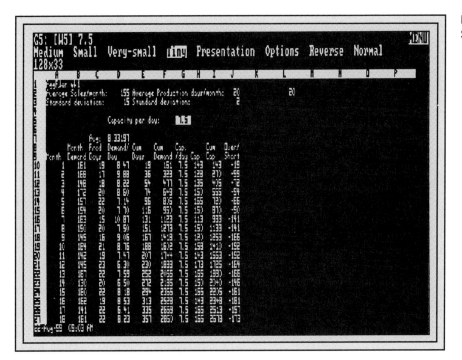

Figure 5–27
SeeMore with Lotus 1-2-3

Table 5–20
Printer Size versus Spreadsheet Columns

Printer Size	Number of Characters	Number of Nine-Character Spreadsheet Columns
Normal carriage		
Regular-size print	80	8
Compressed print	132	14
Wide carriage		
Regular-size print	132	14
Compressed print	220	24[a]

[a] Some printers can print as many as 255 characters, resulting in 28 columns of nine characters each.

Note: Wide-carriage printers are usually more expensive than smaller-carriage printers of the same type.

On-Line Storage

The minimum amount of storage for spreadsheet programs and data ranges from a single 360K disk to a hard disk. Table 5–21 lists the hard disk space required to store complete versions of popular spreadsheet programs, including some popular add-ins. Most spreadsheet programs can

Table 5–21
Hard Disk Storage Needs

Program	Hard Disk Space Used (bytes)
Lotus 1-2-3 (Release 2.01), including SeeMore	1,363,077
Lotus 1-2-3 (Release 2.2), including Allways	1,562,591
Lotus 1-2-3 (Release 3.00)	3,246,604
Quattro	1,210,174
Quattro Pro	2,864,348
SuperCalc5	2,421,479
VP-Planner Plus	401,787
VP-Planner 3D	657,828

be configured to operate on a floppy disk system by eliminating some features, dividing the program among several disks, or both.

The disk storage needs of some large spreadsheet applications may exceed the capacity of a single floppy disk. A few spreadsheet programs allow you to save a spreadsheet application on more than a single disk.

Summary

A spreadsheet is a method of organizing, calculating, and presenting numerical data for decision making. A spreadsheet program is a program that divides the screen into columns and rows. It helps users create/edit/format labels and values (formulas and numbers); calculate/handle data/graph; use labels and values; save/retrieve files to and from the disk; and print results on printers or plotters. A column is a vertical division of screen and spreadsheet. A row is a horizontal division of screen and spreadsheet. A cell is the column and row intersection on a spreadsheet screen.

Spreadsheet programs use labels, values, numbers, and formulas. A label is a word that identifies columns, rows, or overall titles in a spreadsheet. A value is the number appearing in a cell as the result of entering a formula or a number. A number is a mathematical value. A formula is a rule defining the relationship (outcome) between numbers. Spreadsheet program formulas use cell references as their source of numbers. An electronic spreadsheet is the model consisting of labels and formulas, sometimes called a worksheet. A template is a complete spreadsheet or other model saved on disk to be recalled into a spreadsheet program or other program as a pattern for future applications. Templates can be created by a user, purchased on disk, or copied out of books for many applications.

The active cell is the cell into which characters may be entered. The cell pointer is the display that indicates which cell is the active cell. Spreadsheet operations often refer to a range of cells. A range of cells are cells in a spreadsheet identified by the specification of the cell in the upper left position and the cell in the lower right position. For example, the range A5..C7 identifies the cells A5, A6, A7, B5, B6, B7, C5, C6, and C7. Often a range name is given to a range of cells. Cell copying is usually performed from one range to another.

Spreadsheet formulas use absolute and relative addressing. Absolute addressing (reference) is a cell or range reference that always refers to the same cell when copied or moved. A dollar sign ($) placed before the column letter and row number, such as A2, is often used to indicate absolute reference. Relative reference is a cell or range reference that refers to a cell a set number of columns and rows away in a specified direction. When the formula in a cell is moved or copied, the relative references change to maintain their relative position.

Macros may be created for spreadsheet programs. A macro is a set of commands and keystrokes to perform a spreadsheet task. Macros can be created by the user and stored for future use. Spreadsheet formulas may include mathematical and logical operators. Macros can be used to create and move spreadsheet formulas. Spreadsheet programs include a number of data analysis techniques such as frequency and regression analysis, sorting, and searching for selected words.

Key Terms

Absolute reference	Justified	Relative reference
Active cell	Label	Row
Add-in program	Logical function	Sensitivity analysis
Cell	Macro	Spreadsheet
Cell copying	Mathematical operator	Spreadsheet program
Cell counting	Mathematical	Spreadsheet
Cell pointer	precedence	(electronic)
Column	Menu	Template
Compressed print	Mode	Undo
Data analysis	Number	Value
Data handling	Protected cell	Warning message
Format	Range of cells	"What if?"
Formula	Range name	investigation
Function key	Regression analysis	.WK*

Review Questions

1. What is a spreadsheet? What is the difference between a manual and an electronic spreadsheet?
2. What does a spreadsheet program do?
3. Define a column, row, and cell.
4. What is a label?
5. What are the two types of values?
6. What is a spreadsheet template? How is one used?
7. What is the difference between the active cell and all other cells?
8. What is a spreadsheet range? Why is the concept of a spreadsheet range important? Give some examples of how a range is used.
9. What is a protected cell? Why would you want to protect a cell?
10. Identify some of the choices available in spreadsheet program menus.
11. Why is the mode of a spreadsheet important? Identify some different modes.
12. What is the difference between absolute reference and relative references? Why are these concepts important when cells are being copied?
13. What happens when you select the undo function?
14. What is a spreadsheet macro?
15. Identify the mathematical operators used in spreadsheets.
16. What is mathematical precedence? Why is this concept important?
17. Give an example of some logical spreadsheet functions.
18. Give examples of some data-handling spreadsheet capabilities.
19. Why are "what if?" investigations and sensitivity analysis performed using spreadsheet programs?
20. What is an add-in program? Give some examples of add-in programs.

Discussion and Application Questions

1. Identify what courses, if any, you have taken and several you plan to take in which spreadsheet programs could help you complete the assignments.
2. Select a problem from a math, statistics, finance, or similar course that can take advantage of spreadsheet graphics. Identify how spreadsheet graphics help in the solution of the problem.
3. Examine advertisements in a microcomputer magazine for electronic spreadsheet programs. What features are now being pushed?
4. From the advertisements reviewed in question 3, determine the amount of RAM that can be used by electronic spreadsheet programs.

5. Use the yellow pages of your telephone book to identify several businesses that have uses for electronic spreadsheet programs. How do you think the programs might be used?
6. Use the yellow pages to find where electronic spreadsheet programs can be purchased in your area.

Laboratory Assignments

1. Load a spreadsheet program (or clear one that has already been loaded) into a microcomputer. Enter a label, enter two values, enter an equation based on the values entered, and then check the results.

2. Start with a clear spreadsheet. Enter the number 1 in cell A1. Enter the formula +A1+1 in cell B1. Use the copy or replicate routine to replicate the equation for 12 cells.

3. Start with a clear spreadsheet. Place the label Help in cell A1. Replicate the label into cells A2 through A12.

4. Start with a clear spreadsheet. Enter the number 3 in cell A1 and the number 10 in B1. Enter the formula +A1+B2 in cell B3. The cell A1 is assumed to be absolute, whereas cell B1 is relative. Copy the formula to cells B4 through B12.

5. Place a label in cell A1. Copy it both down and across the page.

6. Start with a clear spreadsheet. In cells B2, B3, . . . B10, enter the following values: 12 23 43 12 23 12 15 14 24.
   a. In cell B11, enter the label "". In cell B12, enter the formula @SUM(B2..B10) in the format required by the spreadsheet being used. In cell B13, enter the label "=====.
   b. In cell A15, enter the label Average:. In cell B15, enter the formula @AVG(B2..B10) in the format required by the spreadsheet being used.
   c. In cell A16, enter the label Standard:. In cell B16, enter the formula @STD(B2..B10) in the format required by the spreadsheet being used.
   d. Check all calculations by calculator to determine if you have made any errors.
   e. (Statistics background recommended) Determine whether the equation used for standard deviation used n or $n-1$.
   f. Use the formulas @MAX(B2...B10) and @MIN(B2,,B10) in the format required by the spreadsheet being used to determine the maximum and minimum values in the data.

7. Develop a spreadsheet to calculate gasoline mileage. The output should be similar to the following:

```
           A        B        C         D          E        F        G        H
 1   GAS.wk1
 2
 3   Tank     Miles    Gallons   Miles/Gallon
 4      1       300      11.8 25.42373
 5      2       334      12.4 26.93548
 6      3       333      12.3 27.07317
 7      4       288      11.9 24.20168
 8      5       345      10.3 33.49515
 9      6       355      12.1 29.33884
10      7       301      12.1 24.87603
11
12
13
14
15
16
17
18
19
20
 A1      'Gas.wk1


1help 2edit 3name 4abs 5goto 6window 7data 8table 9recalculate 0graph
  96K                                    10:11                   NUM        READY
```

Column A is the counter for the tank number. Column B is the number of miles driven on the tank. Column C is the amount of gasoline purchased to fill the tank. Column D is the calculation of miles divided by the number of gallons used.

8. Develop a spreadsheet to calculate the batting average of the members of a baseball team. The output should be similar to this:

```
        A       B       C       D       E       F       G       H       I       J
1   BAT.wk1
2
3
4
5   Player          Number  Number of                       Total  Batting
6   Last    First   at bats Singles Doubles Triples Homers  Hits   Average
7   Jones   Jim       22      2       0       2       3       7      318
8   Smith   Stan      55      5       2       4       5       16     291
9   Kim     Carol     45      6       1       2       1       10     222
10  Rodrege Andy      29      4       2       4       1       11     379
11  Smith   Samual    65      8       6       7       4       25     385
12  Able    Andres    65      9       0       9       5       23     354
13
14
15
16
17
18
19
20
    A1      'BAT.wk1


    1help 2edit 3name 4abs 5goto 6window 7data 8table 9recalculate 0graph
        95K                             10:22               NUM             READY
```

Column A is the last name of the team member. Column B is the first name of the team member. Column C is the number of at bats. Columns D through G are the numbers of each kind of hit. Column H is the sum of the number of hits. Column I is the batting average.

9. In the spreadsheet developed for problem 8:
   a. Sort the spreadsheet in alphabetic order (last name–first name), and print the results.
   b. Sort the spreadsheet in order of batting average, and print the results.
   c. Sort the spreadsheet in order of the number of hits, and print the results.

10. Enter your own data for the gasoline spreadsheet in problem 7. Print the results.

11. The election for the president of the senior class is conducted by sections. There are five sections and three candidates. Develop a spreadsheet as follows:

```
          A        B          C          D        E        F        G        H
 1   Elect.wk1
 2
 3
 4   Section Names
 5            John     July       Manuel
 6            Jones    Fransisco  Rodrigus
 7        1      102        132        122
 8        2      122        255        345
 9        3      200        234        322
10        4      123        122        344
11        5      333        234        546 Total
12            -------    ------    ------- Votes
13              880        977       1679      3536
14            =====    =====    =====
15   Percent:   24.89      27.63      47.48  ←Format to two decimal places
16
17
18
19
20
 A1      'Elect.wk1


1help 2edit 3name 4abs 5goto 6window 7data 8table 9recalculate 0graph
  96K                                        10:33                NUM           READY
```

Cells B13, C13, and D13 contain formulas to sum the number of votes. Cell E13 is the sum of the sums of votes. Cells B15, C15, and D15 contain formulas to calculate the percentage of votes obtained by each candidate.

12. A class consists of 12 people. The following are their names and student numbers:

Number	Student	Student Number
1	Mary Lenissa	12234
2	Ivan Petrushian	22445
3	Stanley Michel	12554
4	Neal Roberts	43223
5	Bruce Davis	11447
6	Kim Aguilar	43556
7	Kim McCreary	45669
8	Sven Torgeson	19854
9	Wayne Bonnana	18888
10	Anna Spatulski	16431
11	Jean Angstreich	25647
12	Chang Ho Quon	54678

Set up a class roll and grade sheet that can be used by the instructor. Identify headings for each column, including spaces for roll checking, grades for quizzes, final exams, and course grades.

There are five grading criteria in the class. The first two are reports, with a weight of 5 percent each. The third and fourth are quizzes, with a weight of 10 percent each. The fifth is the final exam, with a weight of 70 percent. The class meets twice a week for five weeks.

Identify the formulas used to calculate the student's average for the term, the class average, and the class standard deviation. Lay out the grade sheet on a piece of paper in preparation for making a spreadsheet. Identify the location of these formulas.

13. Develop a budget in the form of a spreadsheet for a dual-career couple with the wife working as an accountant for $22,000 per year and the husband attending graduate school full-time at a nearby university. The following are monthly costs for various budget items:

Number	Item	Monthly Budget
1	Rent	$344
2	Food	280
3	Babysitting	100
4	Utilities	200
5	Books	30
6	Tuition	200
7	Clothing	200
8	Travel/Auto	200
9	Savings or Entertainment	
10	Miscellaneous	
11	Gifts/donations	

Using spreadsheet format, lay out this budget for the year on a month-by-month basis. Assume that church donations will total $50 a month except during December, when a donation of $300 is planned. Also include a special birthday present for the couple's daughter, costing $200 in June. In the spreadsheet, locate all labels and formulas. Identify the formulas needed. The objective is to determine the cash available per month.

14. (General) The couple in problem 13 has a ten-year-old girl who is a member of a youth group. The group is planning a three-day 300-mile trip to the state capital. The costs include the following:

Number	Item	Cost
1	Rent on bus	$600
2	Meals per day per person	18
3	Camping fees for group	50
4	Museum entrance fees per person	8
5	Insurance	75
6	Camping supplies	50

Lay out a spreadsheet to determine the total cost for the group and to identify the cost per individual if there are 22 children and 4 adults making the trip. Identify all labels, numbers, and formulas.

15. (General business) A checkbook check register contains the following information:

Date	Check Number	Description of Transaction	Credit/ Deposit	T	Fee (if any)	Payment/ Debt	Balance
—	—	Original balance		x			2000.00
8/13	202	Rent				150.00	
8/15	203	Utilities				125.36	
8/16	204	Phone				39.87	
8/17	—	Salary check	1500.26				
8/18	—	Gift	12.15				
8/18	205	Cash				175.00	
8/18	206	Food store				97.83	

The bank records show the following:

Balance Last	We Have Added		We Have Subtracted			Balance
Statement	Number	Deposits	Number	Checks	Serv Chg	
2000.00	1	1500.26	8	587.01	1.22	
2912.03						

Checking Account Transactions

Date	Amount	Description
8/19	1500.26	DEPOSIT

CHECKS

DATE	AMOUNT
8/15	100.22
8/19	39.87
8/19	5.21
8/19	12.55
8/20	6.33
8/24	175.00
8/25	97.83
8/25	150.00

At the beginning of the period, your balance and the bank's balance were the same. There were no outstanding transactions of any type.

Set up a spreadsheet to start with your balance, add the not-cleared checks, subtract the unrecorded checks, subtract the not-cleared deposits, add the unrecorded deposits, make adjustments for errors in recording and service charges, and produce a final balance to be compared with the bank's.

16. (Accounting) Set up and organize a spreadsheet for the ledger of Western with the following chart of accounts:

Balance Sheet	Debit	Credit
Cash account	5,000	
Accounts payable		7,000
Accounts receivable	1,200	
Building	100,000	
Equipment	59,800	
Reserve for depreciation		30,000
Land	75,000	
Notes payable		55,000
Capital		150,000
Retained earnings		9,000
Supplies	10,000	

Place the accounts in order of current assets, fixed assets, current liabilities, and long-term liabilities followed by stockholders' equity. Locate where all labels and formulas will be, and identify these formulas in terms of spreadsheet location.

17. (Marketing) You have a job working for the local computer store to determine the number of spreadsheet users on your campus. A questionnaire has been designed. Most questions are designed to be answered with "yes," "no," or "I do not know." Some questions require the respondent to identify the type of computer or program being used. The questions to be answered by the survey include these:

> Do you know what a spreadsheet is?
> Are you currently using an electronic spreadsheet?
> Do you have a microcomputer available?
> What kind of microcomputer do you use?
> Do you have an electronic spreadsheet program available?
> What electronic spreadsheet program do you have?
> How long have you had the program?
> How much did you pay for the program?
> If you do not have a spreadsheet program, are you planning to purchase one?
> How often do you use your program?
> Do you plan to purchase a microcomputer? When?

Organize the questions onto a spreadsheet. Identify all questions, the numbers you generate, the formulas needed, and their location. The objective is to give the store management some idea of how large a market exists for electronic spreadsheet and microcomputers on campus.

18. (Statistics) The formulas for the average and standard deviation of a sample follow:

$$\text{Average} = (\Sigma\, X(i))/N$$

$$\text{Standard deviation} = \text{square root}$$
$$((\Sigma(\text{average} - x(i))\char`\^2)/(N - 1))$$

Set up a spreadsheet for a sample size of 10 to do the following:

a. Find $\Sigma\, X(i)$.
b. Identify where N is.
c. Find $\Sigma\, (\text{average} - X(i))$.
d. Find the average.
e. Find the standard deviation.

Analyze the following sample data set:

Number	Data
1	12.32
2	12.99
3	13.55
4	16.55
5	11.23
6	12.24
7	13.66
8	12.45
9	12.54
10	12.00

Identify the labels, the numbers, the formulas, and the location of each item.

19. (Accounting/finance) Lay out a spreadsheet for the preparation of an amortization schedule for the first 12 months of an equal-monthly-payment mortgage. The mortgage is for $40,000 with a 30-year payout at a 12.5 percent annual percentage rate. Identify the location of all labels, all numbers entered, and all formulas. Specify the formulas needed.

20. (Other courses) From any course being taken this term or last term, propose a spreadsheet application for the instructor's approval. After approval, lay out a spreadsheet for the selected application.

21. (General) Create a macro that places your name, street address, city–state–zip code, and telephone number in five rows, starting with the location of the cell pointer.

22. (General) Create a macro that sums the values in a column of numbers, places a single line under the last number in the column, places the sum under that line, and then places a double line under the sum when the cell pointer is placed in the cell under the lowest number in the column.

23. (Accounting) Create an invoice using the following model:

```
        A          B          C          D          E          F          G            H
 1 Invoice.wk1
 2
 3                         INVOICE
 4 ----------------------------------------------------------------------------------
 5 From:                                      To:
 6 Professional Sales and Services, Inc.      A1Z Management Services, In
 7 3545 West Brook Lane                       233 Bay Road
 8 Santa Clara, CA 55555                      Atlanta, AL 55555
 9 555-555-55555                              Atten: A.D. Zimmerman
10 ----------------------------------------------------------------------------------
11 QUANTITY DESCRIPTION                       PRICE     AMOUNT
12 ----------------------------------------------------------------------------------
13
14
15
16
17
18 ----------------------------------------------------------------------------------
19                                                      TOTAL
20                                                                = = = =
```

24. (Accounting) Create a spreadsheet for accounting working papers. Use
    this model:

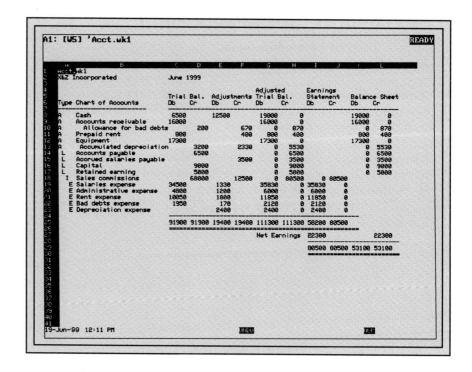

Column A identifies the type (asset, liability, income, or expense), column B is the chart of accounts, and columns E and F are the trial balance. The numbers in the trial balance columns E and F and the numbers in the adjustments columns (G and F) are input data.

Column G is the sum of columns C and E. Column H is the sum of columns D and F. Column I transfers the data in the range G18..G23, and column J transfers the information in the range H18..H23.

The balance sheet includes columns K and L. Column K transfers the information in the range G8..G17, and column L transfers the range H8..H17. Adjustments must be made in the ending balance sheet for the net earnings for the period.

CHAPTER 6

Data-driven Graphics

Goals

Upon completion of this chapter, you will be able to do the following:

- Review the importance of data-driven graphics.

- List the types of charts produced by spreadsheet programs.

- List the types of charts produced by data-driven graphics programs.

- Define each type of chart.

**Micros
in
Action**

A Sales Aid

Jean King and Associates, a public relations and advertising agency, is approximately 11 years old and employs five individuals. It has maintained a rapid growth in sales and client base.

Among other activities, the staff prepares presentations for meetings and publications in which graphics play an important part. The staff identified its microcomputer needs as follows:

- Graphics for client presentations.
- Word processing for letters, presentations, and contracts.
- Database for client characteristics and advertising outlets.

The types of graphics needed include bar charts, pie charts, and some special presentation capabilities that combine microcomputer outputs with pictures.

Data-driven graphics programs are tools for illustrating the relationships between numbers. Usually, a data-driven program is used to create, edit, and format data that is represented graphically. The microcomputer is a tool for creating graphic displays on the screen, paper, film, and other media. As indicated in Micros in Action "A Sales Aid," data-driven graphics programs are useful for sales presentations. Data-driven graphics are often referred to as standard charts and graphs, or business graphics. Data-driven graphics can be used to illustrate both discrete (1, 2, 3, . . .) and continuous (1.23, 1.44, . . .) numbers.

Remember, graphic displays and software capabilities should be matched. When a program requiring a color graphics adapter (CGA) is run on a system with a video graphics array (VGA), the program may or may not work. Usually, if the software creator has not put some special checks in the program, a VGA system will automatically display EGA and CGA. Some VGA boards will even display Hercules monochrome (half-page, full-page, or both) graphics programs.

Three types of programs produce graphs from numeric data: spreadsheet programs, data-driven graphics programs, and analytical programs. All of the spreadsheet programs studied in Chapter 5 have graphing capabilities. The following types of charts can be produced by spreadsheet programs: area, horizontal bar, vertical bar, high-low, grouped bar, high-low volume, line/xy, organization, pie, exploded pie, three-dimensional pie, radar, scatter, stack-bar, text, bar-line, pie-bar, dual scales, and three-dimensional. Micros in Action "Graphics Stories" indicates how pie charts are used in professional presentations.

> **Data-driven graphics program**
> A program to create/edit/format data for area, bar, high-low, line, and similar types of graphs; to save/retrieve data; and to print results on a printer or plotter.

Many data-driven and data-driven support programs exist. Specific data-driven program tasks are performed differently in each program. The spreadsheet programs that are used for data-driven graphics in this chapter are Lotus 1-2-3 (Release 2.2 and 3.0), Microsoft Excel, Quattro, Quattro Pro, SuperCalc5, and VP-Planner. The data-driven programs that are used are Atlas*Graphics, DPac, Graph-in-the-Box, Graph-in-the-box Analytic, Map-Master, Lotus Freelance, Harvard graphics, Microsoft Chart, and VP Graphics. Programs used to transfer data are pfs:Graph, Multiplan, pfs:Professional Write, InSet, and HiJaak. These programs are among the more popular ones available.

Micros in Action

Graphics Stories

The employees at Jean King and Associates often use the exploded pie chart, because it allows them to highlight a selected factor when making a presentation for fund-raising campaigns and government analysis. They also use bar charts and line charts for many business clients.

In addition, Jean King and Associates require specialized custom presentations for specific business objectives. They prepare slides using screen copy equipment for meetings and hard copy for stockholder reports and similar publications. They use slides, film, and VCR tapes for audiovisual presentations.

Why Data-driven Graphics?

Academic and professional reports can be enhanced through the use of data-driven graphics. Reports enhanced with data-driven graphics earn better grades, sell more products, help obtain jobs, and usually result in benefits that far outweigh the effort used to produce the graphics.

Spreadsheet Graphics

Line/xy chart
A chart that shows the behavior between two variables. A line chart requires even divisions of the x scale, while the xy chart performs scaling.

Spreadsheet programs produce a large variety of data-driven graphics. Table 6–1 lists the data-driven graphics produced by six spreadsheet programs. A **line/xy chart** is a chart that shows the relationship between two variables. A line chart requires even divisions of the x scale, while the xy chart performs scaling. An **area chart** is a line graph in which the area under the horizontal line represents a quantity. A **bar chart** compares parts

Table 6–1
Spreadsheet Data-driven Graphics

Chart	Excel	Lotus 1-2-3 (Release 2.2)	Lotus 1-2-3 (Release 3.0)	Quattro Pro	SuperCalc5	VP-Planner
Area	x		x	x	x	
Bar						
Vertical	x	x	x	x	x	x
Horizontal	x	x	x	x	x	x
Grouped					x	
Stacked	x	x	x	x	x	x
High-low	x			x	x	
High-low volume			x			
Line/xy	x	x/x	x/x	x/x	x/x	x/x
Pie	x	x	x	x	x	x
Exploded	x	x	x	x	x	x
Three-dimensional				x	x	
Radar					x	
Scatter diagram	x	x	x	x	x	x
Text				x	x	
Three-dimensional				x (single variable)	x	
Bar-line	x		x			
Pie-column					x	
Dual scales			x			
Customized	x			x		

of the whole using bars. Bar charts may be horizontal, vertical, stacked, grouped, or three-dimensional. A **high-low chart** is a line graph showing the high, low, open, and closing values of a stock over time. A **high-low volume chart** is a high-low chart and a bar chart using the same time scale. A **pie chart** compares parts to the whole using a circle. It may be exploded and three-dimensional. A **radar chart** is a 360-degree-axis chart that displays data in polar coordinates (angle versus radius). A **scatter diagram** is a line chart with points plotted only; it may be two- or three-dimensional. A **text chart** displays using words rather than images. A **bar-line (combination) chart** is a bar and line chart using a common x scale. A **pie-column (combination) chart** is a pie and column chart showing parts of a whole and parts of a part in a single bar. A **dual scales chart** is a line or bar chart with two y scales. Figure 6–1 shows many of the above types of charts.

Area chart
A line graph in which the area under the horizontal line represents a quantity.

Bar chart
A chart that compares parts of the whole using bars. Bar charts may be horizontal, vertical, stacked, grouped, or three-dimensional.

High-low chart
A line graph showing the high, low, open, and closing values of a stock over time.

Figure 6–1
Spreadsheet Data-driven
Graphics—Types of Charts

Line xy chart (Lotus 1-2-3 [Release 2.2])

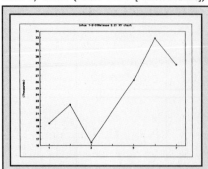

Area chart (Excel)

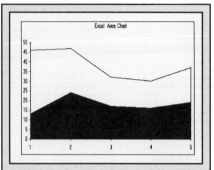

Bar chart (Quattro)

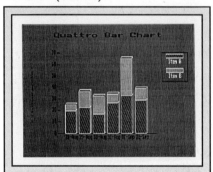

High-low volume chart
(Lotus 1-2-3 [Release 3.0])

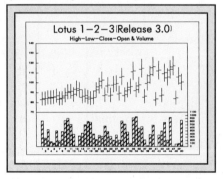

Exploded pie chart (VP-Planner Plus)

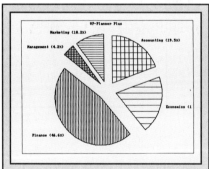

Radar chart (SuperCalc5)

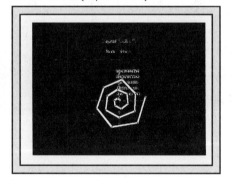

High-low volume chart
A high-low chart and a bar chart
using the same time scale.

Pie chart
A chart that compares parts to the
whole using a circle; may be
exploded or three-dimensional.

The steps for creating spreadsheet graphics follow:

Specify the range of the x variable.
Specify the range of each y variable.
Add headings and other identifying text.
Specify the options (colors, three-dimensions, and so on) wanted.
View the graph.
Save.
Print the results.

Many spreadsheet graphics programs can define all the graph ranges as a group:

1. Select the range to define x, A, B, and so on by moving the menu pointer to the range letter
2. Press ↵
3. Move the cell pointer to the beginning of the range
4. Press the decimal point
5. Move the cell pointer to the end of the range
6. Press ↵

In Excel, Lotus 1-2-3 (Release 2.2), Lotus 1-2-3 (Release 3.0), and Quattro Pro, the entire range of graphing variables may be defined at one time. The number of ranges may be important. For example, in quality control graphing, an average and standard deviation chart requires eight graphing variables. Most spreadsheet programs may graph up to six variables. SuperCalc5 is the only program in our sample set that can handle the quality control application.

Spreadsheet programs use menu-driven selection methods to add graph titles and scale text information. Some spreadsheet programs, such as Excel, Lotus 1-2-3 (Release 2.2) with Allways, Lotus 1-2-3 (Release 3.0), Quattro Pro, and SuperCalc5, have the capability to control the size and type of the fonts used.

The graph can be viewed a number of times to examine the results and determine if changes are wanted. If you are working on a system that cannot display graphics, it may be possible to set up the specification for a graph and print it on your printer without viewing the results on the screen.

Data-driven Graphics Programs

Data-driven graphics programs create charts from labels and numbers. The most common methods of data entry include the keyboard and file transfer from spreadsheet and database programs. Data-driven graphics programs often have capabilities not included in spreadsheet programs. For example, the **step chart** illustrated in Figure 6–2. A step chart is a line chart that changes in increments.

Table 6–2 lists some popular data-driven graphics programs and their capabilities. Table 6–3 lists the types of graphics produced by graphics programs. Few programs are pure data-driven graphics programs. Some have some image-editing capabilities and a **symbol** (icon) library. A symbol is a saved image which may be used to represent a menu selection on the screen. The addition of symbols to a data-driven chart helps direct the viewers' attention to desired details. Symbols will also be discussed in Chapter 8. Image editing allows the user to customize charts created from numeric data, as well as to create images. A discussion of image drawing (creating) and editing capabilities will appear in Chapter 8.

Radar chart
A 360-degree-axis chart that displays data in polar coordinates (angle versus radius).

Scatter diagram
A line chart with points plotted only; may be two- or three-dimensional.

Text chart
A display using words rather than images.

Bar-line (combination) chart
A bar and line chart using a common x scale.

Pie-column (combination) chart
A pie and column chart showing parts of a whole and parts of a part in a single bar.

Dual scales chart
A line or bar chart with two y scales.

Step chart
A chart that shows the behavior between two variables as a series of incremental changes.

Symbol
A saved image; may be used to represent a menu selection on the screen.

Figure 6–2
A Step Chart

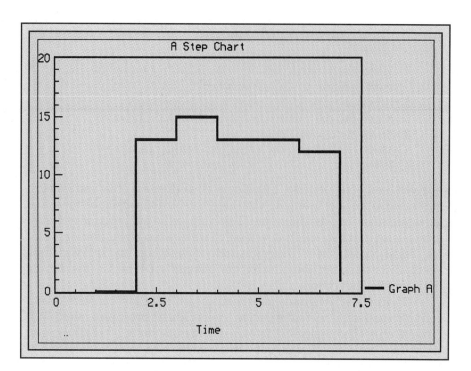

Table 6–2
Data-driven Graphics Program Features

Capability	Graph-in-the-Box	Graph-in-the-Box Analytic	Lotus Freelance Plus 3.0	Harvard Graphics	Microsoft Chart	VP Graphics
Charts	x	x	x	x	x	x
Drawing and editing			x	x		x
Symbol library			x	x		
Linkage			x		x	
Scanning images			x			
Slide show	x	x	x	x	x	
Spelling checker				x		
Templates			x	x		
Math capabilities		x		x	x	
Sort		x			x	

Table 6–3
Data-driven Graphics Program Charts

Chart	Graph-in-the-Box	Graph-in-the-Box Analytic	Lotus Freelance Plus 3.0	Harvard Graphics	Microsoft Chart	VP Graphics
Area	x	x	x	x	x	
Bar						
Vertical	x	x	x	x	x	x
Horizontal	x	x	x	x	x	
Stacked	x	x	x	x		x
High-low		x	x	x	x	
High-low volume			x			
Line/xy	x	x	x/x	x	x	x/x
Logarithmic		x	x			
Exponential		x	x			
Organization*				x		
Pie	x			x	x	x
Exploded	x		x	x	x	x
Three-dimensional			x	x	x	
Scatter diagram	x		x	x		
Step						
Open	x	x				
Filled		x				
Text		x	x	x		x
Combination			a	a	b	c
Three-dimensional				x		
Bar-line	x	x	x	x	x	
Bar-area		x		x	x	
Bar-pie				x	x	
Pie-pie				x	x	
Bar left/right				x	x	
Symbol			x	x		
Dual scale		x	x		x	

* An organizational chart is usually not data driven. An organization chart is a display in boxes of positions in an organization with text to explain the relationship between the positions.

a Lotus Freelance Plus and Harvard Graphics include a large set of charts and symbols. In addition, in Harvard Graphics, chart books can be purchased that contain many more chart types, and a number of charts can be merged.

b Microsoft Chart allows you to merge any number of charts.

c The graphics editing capability of VP Graphics allows you to integrate the output of several different charts.

The capabilities of data-driven graphics programs to create charts are similar to those of spreadsheet programs. However, the variety and options are usually greater. Figure 6–3 illustrates some of the results obtainable using data-driven graphics programs.

Harvard Graphics includes a **spelling checker.** You might think this an unnecessary feature on a data-driven graphics program. However, the first time you use a slide with a spelling error, the advantage of the spelling checker becomes apparent.

Three programs, Graph-in-the-Box Analytic, Microsoft Chart, and Harvard Graphics, have mathematical capabilities. The first two also have sorting capabilities. These packages are included in data-driven graphics programs because the primary function is the creation of graphics from numbers and values, not because calculations need to be performed. Among their mathematical capabilities are finding averages, determining confidence levels, descriptive statistics, determining goodness of fit, and matrix transformations. Linear regression analysis can be performed using a spreadsheet program such as Excel, Lotus 1-2-3, Quattro (Figure 6–4), Quattro Pro, or SuperCalc5, or data-driven graphics programs such as Graph-in-the-Box Analytic or Harvard Graphics.

Spelling checker
Routine that helps the user correct the spelling of text in a file.

Creating, Editing, and Formatting

The data (labels and numbers) can be entered directly into the data-driven graphics program, transferred from other programs using data files (nu-

Figure 6–3
Data-driven Graphics Program Screens

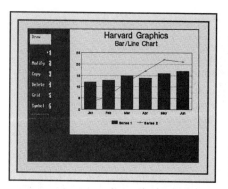
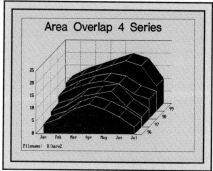

Figure 6–4
Quattro Linear Regression Analysis

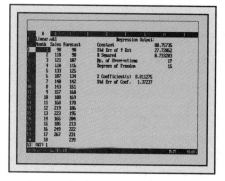
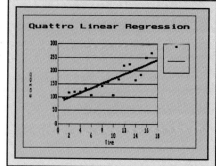

meric and graphic), and/or captured from the screen using **screen data capture** routines. Figure 6–5 illustrates data entry and the resulting chart in selected data-driven graphics packages. The three-dimensional option in Harvard Graphics was obtained by pressing function key F8 ("Options") and making some simple menu selections. VP-Planner uses pull-down menus for task selection. Data input in Microsoft Chart is menu driven. The menu system looks and operates similarly to Microsoft's Multiplan spreadsheet.

Graph-in-the-Box is a **terminate and stay resident (TSR)** program. After Graph-in-the-Box is started, it remains in memory and can be called to the screen by pressing the <Alt> and G keys at the same time (<Alt> G).

Screen data capture
The capability to capture data from screen display and transfer them into a second program or save them as a file.

Terminate and stay resident (TSR)
Programs that are loaded into memory and remain in memory while other programs are loaded and used. Once loaded, a TSR program can be recalled using a series of keys while some other program is running.

Harvard Graphics

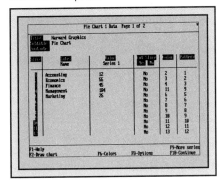

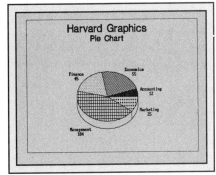

Figure 6–5
Data Entry into Data-driven Graphics Programs

Microsoft Chart

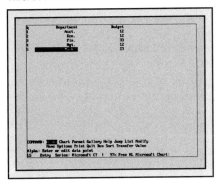

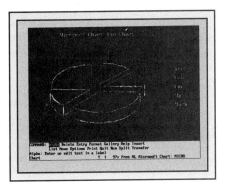

Lotus Freelance Plus

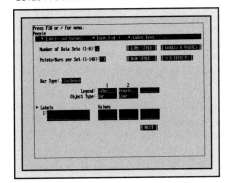

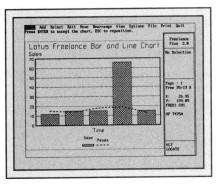

Figure 6–5
Data Entry into Data-driven
Graphics Programs, continued

VP-Planner

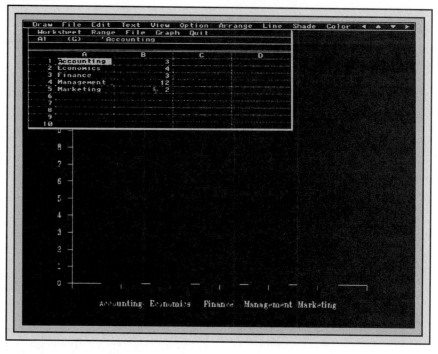

Hot keys
The key combination that calls a
TSR program.

The key combinations that start a TSR are called **hot keys.** An important feature of Graph-in-the-Box is its screen data capture capability; it can capture labels and numbers off the screen. Figure 6–6 illustrates data capture by Graph-in-the-Box from VP-Planner Plus, the data display, the chart selection display, and a graph in Graph-in-the-Box.

In addition to data capture and direct data input, data-driven graphics programs often are able to import data saved by spreadsheet programs. Table 6–4 lists a number of popular files used to save data or pictures that can be read by the data-driven graphics programs being discussed in this chapter.

Saving and Retrieving

.WK*
An extension for Lotus 1-2-3
spreadsheet files. The * is a wild
card meaning that a number of
different characters will appear in
this position.

Data-driven graphics programs can save and retrieve a variety of file types. An objective of this type of program is to support other programs. Among the files retrieved are the Lotus 1-2-3 **.WK*** files. The * in the extension means a wild card, i.e. you may expect to see a number of different characters in this location. The importing of Lotus 1-2-3 .WK1 files created in Lotus 1-2-3 (Release 2.2) may be a problem in some data-driven graphics programs. Lotus made adjustments in Lotus 1-2-3 (Release 2.2) .WK1 files. If you expect to import .WK1 files created in Lotus 1-2-3 (Release 2.2) regularly, check to see that the graphing program you select is not subject to the problem.

Some programs accept **American Standard Code for Information Interchange (ASCII)** files that consist of numbers separated by spaces.

a) Starting Graph-in-the-Box

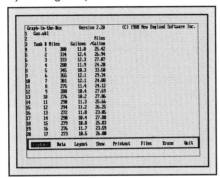

b) Range of data to capture

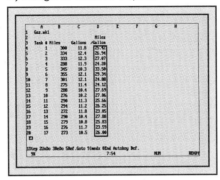

Figure 6-6

Graph-in-the-Box Data Capture

c) Data captured

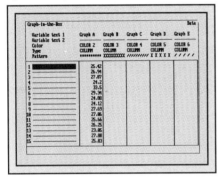

d) Graph of data

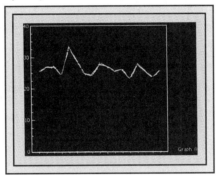

Others use ASCII files where the numbers are delimited (separated) by commas or other characters. Harvard Graphics uses both ASCII and delimited ASCII files. Some programs only use the standard ASCII characters based on the code numbers 00 to 127. These are often called 7-bit files, because a 7-bit binary number can be used to create the decimal numbers 00 to 127. Some programs accept characters based on the code numbers 00 to 255. An eighth bit is needed to create the added decimal numbers. These files are often called 8-bit ASCII files.

Data Interchange Format (DIF) files are ASCII files saved in a specific manner where the type of data is identified. The DIF was a popular method used to transfer numbers, formulas, and labels between spreadsheet programs. The popularity of DIF files has been declining. Microsoft's **Symbolic Link (SYLK)** format was popular at one time for the transfer of numbers, formulas, and labels between spreadsheet programs.

A graph may be saved in a **Hewlett-Packard Graphic Language (HPGL) file** ready to be used by an HP plotter. HPGL files are used to transfer charts to desktop publishing programs such as Aldus's Page-Maker. Metrafiles, **Computer Graphics Metrafiles (CGM)** and **Graphic Metrafiles (GMF)** files, are used in Lotus Manuscript and other word processors to integrate graphics into their output.

Lotus developed a number of file formats that use the extension .WK*: .WKS, .WKR, .WK1, and .WK3. The file used by data-driven graphics depends on the version of the program. When Lotus develops a new format, most manufacturers of data-driven graphics add that format to

American Standard Code for Information Interchange (ASCII)
A seven-bit binary code. Numbers from 00 to 127 can be produced with a seven-bit number. The decimal number 90 is 1011010. Each number in ASCII stands for a character or control Binary Number: A number consisting of 0 and 1. Each 0 or 1 is a bit. The decimal numbers 0 to 127 require 7 bits. To add the decimal numbers 128 to 255 require the eighth bit.

Data Interchange Format (DIF)
A standard ASCII file format for transferring data between spreadsheet programs.

Symbolic Link (SYLK)
A standard file format for transferring data between spreadsheet programs.

Hewlett-Packard Graphic Language (HPGL)
A graphics language file used for printing to plotters, CAD drawing, and desktop publishing.

Table 6–4
Data-driven Graphics Program I/O

Type of File	Graph-in-the-Box	Graph-in-the-Box Analytic	Lotus Freelance Plus 3.0	Harvard Graphics	Microsoft Chart	VP Graphics
Input						
ASCII (ASC)				x	x	
DIF	x	x			x	
pfs:Graph				x		
Links			x			
Lotus			x	x	x	
Multiplan					x	
PIC files			x	x		x
Screen Data Capture	x	x				
SYLK					x	
TIFF (TIF)			x	x		
VPG (special VP Graphics)						x
Output						
ASCII (ASC)						x
DIF	x	x				x
Harvard (TPL) (special Harvard Graphics)				x		
HPGL	x	x		x		
Metrafiles (CGM)			x	x		
pfs:Professional Write				x		
Postscript: (EPS)	x	x	x	x		
TIFF (TIF)			x			

Computer Graphics Metrafiles (CGM)
A graphics file used for the transfer of graphics to some word processing programs.

their input/output routines. In addition, when a graph is created in a Lotus 1-2-3 spreadsheet program, it can be saved as a **.PIC file,** a graphics file that can be edited using a graphics editor.

Encapsulated Postscript (EPS) files and **Tagged Image File Format (TIFF) files** are used in many desktop publishing programs. The PostScript file uses the desktop publishing page description language format and carries a volume of text and graphics information. TIFF files include both black-and-white and gray scale images. Some programs only support black-and-white images. TIFF files are a widely used format.

Multiplan, pfs:Graph, and pfs:Professional Write are programs that have specific file formats supported by some data-driven graphics programs. The more file formats a program may read or write, the greater the number of packages it can be used with. If it is necessary to transfer files between programs that do not support each other, it is sometimes possible to use a transfer program such as InSet System's HiJaak or InSet. HiJaak transfers one file to another, and InSet captures graphic screen displays. These programs are reviewed in detail in Chapter 8.

File linkage (joining) can be established between a data-driven graphics program and a spreadsheet or database. The graphics produced are automatically updated when next used after the base spreadsheet or database is updated.

Printing

Printing is mostly menu driven in data-driven graphics programs. Most programs can be configured to print on a variety of printers, (including dot-matrix and laser) and plotters. Figure 6–7 illustrates how to select the print option in a data-driven graphics program.

Graphic Metrafiles (GMF)
A graphics file used for the transfer of graphics to some word processing programs.

.PIC
A graphics file created in Lotus 1-2-3 and some other spreadsheet programs. The .PIC extension is used by some image-driven graphics programs and is not usually compatible with Lotus files.

Encapsulated PostScript (EPS) file
A graphics files using the PostScript language format.

Tagged Image File Format (TIFF) file
A graphics file carrying gray scale information.

File linkage
The dynamic joining (linkage) of two files. Whenever the second file is used, the latest version of the sending file is transferred.

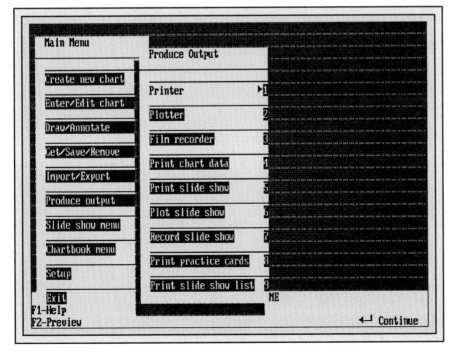

Figure 6–7
The Print Option in Harvard Graphics

Data-driven Mapping Programs

Thematic mapping programs are driven by statistical data collected about geographical regions. Figure 6–8 illustrates a map of the United States from STSC's Atlas*Graphics library. Both Atlas*Graphics and Aston Tate's Map-Master have population data files that can be retrieved and then displayed on the map (Figure 6–9). Map-Master allows you to select the states for graphing. Figure 6–10 illustrates how the chart titles are created and how the menu for selecting the graph is displayed.

An additional feature of a mapping program is the capability to **zoom** in on part of the display. In many programs you can zoom out for an overall view or zoom in for an enlarged view of a local area.

Zoom
To move out for an overall view of move in to a small portion of an image for an enlarged view of a small area.

Additional Data-driven Graphics Applications

Many organizational problems and applications can be presented graphically: breakeven analysis, linear programming, economic order size analysis, financial analysis, Gantt scheduling and control charts, inventory levels, aggregate scheduling, operations research, Program Evaluation and Review Technique (PERT), quality control, safety stock analysis, and statistical analysis. Figure 6–11 illustrates some of these applications.

Figure 6–8
Atlas*Graphics Map

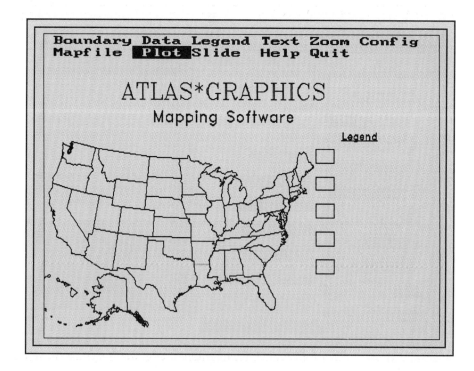

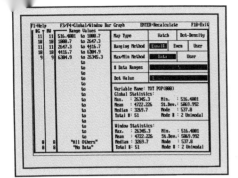
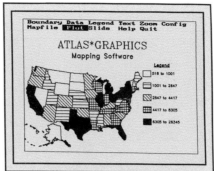

Figure 6–9
Data and Map with Population Data Using Atlas*Graphics

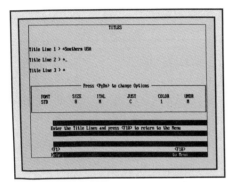
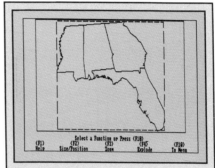

Figure 6–10
Selection of States Using Map Master

Data-driven Graphics Hardware

Data-driven graphics hardware needs are similar to spreadsheet program needs. The specific program used determines the need for internal memory (RAM), input devices, output devices, and on-line storage devices.

RAM Needs

Table 6–5 illustrates the amount of RAM storage needed for various levels of screen graphics display resolution. The PC boards that control 640 × 200 pixel screens often use the RAM memory of the computer to store the video data. The PC boards that control monitors requiring large amounts of RAM often come with their own dedicated RAM. One reason for the increase in cost of the PC boards for higher-resolution monitors is the additional memory.

Input Devices

The keyboard and mouse are the most common data input devices for data-driven graphics programs. Often, when the graph required is not

Figure 6–11
Additional Data-driven Graphics
Applications

Breakeven analysis

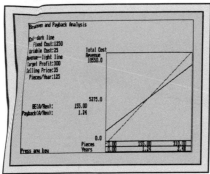

Linear programming
graphical analysis

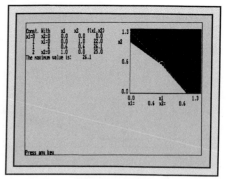

Transportation method of
linear programming

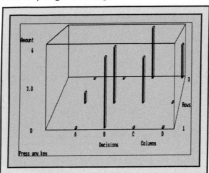

Inventory levels

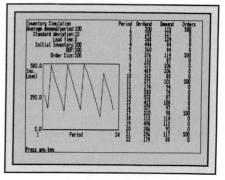

Aggregate scheduling

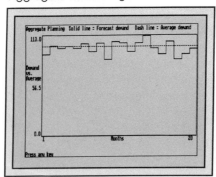

Gantt scheduling and control charts

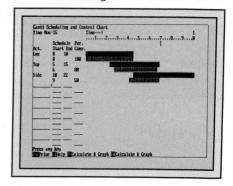

available in a given spreadsheet program, the data are transferred directly to the required graphics program without the need to reenter them. The bar code reader is becoming a popular device for entering numeric data.

Output Devices

Graphics output devices include monitors, printers, plotters, cameras (photographic slides), facsimile (fax) machines, and videocassette recorders (VCRs). The prime output device of the microcomputer is the monitor. For

Table 6–5 Resolution versus RAM			
Screen Pixels	Number of Colors	Bits (Pixels)	Bytes (8 bits per byte)
320 X 200	16	1,024,000	128,000
640 X 200	2	256,000	32,000
720 X 350	2	504,000	63,000
640 X 350	2	448,000	56,000
640 X 350	16	3,584,000	448,000
640 X 350	256	57,344,000	7,168,000
640 X 480	2	614,400	76,800
640 X 480	16	4,915,200	614,400
640 X 480	256	78,643,200	9,830,400
800 X 600	2	960,000	120,000
1,024 X 1,024	2	2,097,152	262,144
1,024 X 1,024	16	16,777,216	2,097,152
1,024 X 1,024	256	268,435,456	33,554,432

graphics output, the higher the resolution, the better. As the resolution and output complexity increase, the amount of time required to display an image increases. Some graphics packages require higher-speed computers and the use of a math co-processor. Graphics displays require many calculations, and the displays are sped up with the use of a math co-processor.

Dot-matrix, laser, ink-jet, and other printers that create characters by printing dots can be used to output graphics characters. The resolution depends on the number of dots per inch. Generally, dot-matrix printers produce the fewest dots per inch, followed by ink-jet and then laser printers. However, some dot-matrix printers produce 360 dots per inch.

The first group of laser printers produced 300 dots per inch. The number of dots per inch for laser printers can be increased by the use of special printer controller cards. In general, the more expensive the printer, the better the resolution.

Plotters use line-drawing devices to produce graphic images. Computers equipped with PC boards with **FAX machine** capabilities can output both text and graphics to FAX machines at remote locations as if they were long-distance printers. The quality of the FAX output is a function of the FAX board and the FAX machine at the receiving end. A FAX machine transmits a copy of a document from one location to another, usually over a telephone line.

FAX machine
A machine that transmits a copy of a document from one location to another usually over telephone lines. There are PC boards available that allow a computer to act as a FAX machine.

On-Line Storage

Generally, storing a graphic image requires a lot of memory. If only the data used to create the image are stored, data storage needs are reduced. Graphics data are stored in approximately the same way as spreadsheet data are stored.

Summary

A data-driven graphics program is a program that can be used to create/edit/format data for area, bar, high-low, line, and similar types of charts and graphs; save/retrieve data; and to print results on a printer or plotter. Generally, the user controls the data which is then sent to the program for graphing. Among the charts that may be created are line/xy charts, area charts, bar charts, high-low charts, high-low volume charts, pie charts, radar charts, scatter diagrams, text charts, step charts, and combination charts. Data-driven graphics programs may be used to combine data-driven graphics with symbols from a symbol library. Some programs allow the user to enhance the output using graphic editing commands.

Some data-driven graphic programs include spelling checkers and screen data capture routines. Usually, the screen data capture routines are TSR. Often data-driven graphic programs may be used to import data from other programs using DIF, SYLK, HPGL, CGM, GMF, .WK*, EPS, TIFF, and other file storage formats.

In addition to typical charts and graphs, there are a number of data-driven graphic programs that produce maps and other special presentations such as breakeven and quality control analysis. Data-driven graphics programs require monitors, internal data storage, and on-line storage capacities adequate for the graphics images generated.

Key Terms

American Standard Code for Information Interchange (ASCII)

Area chart

Bar chart

Bar-line (combination) chart

Computer Graphics Metrafiles (CGM)

Data-driven graphics program

Data Interchange Format (DIF)

Dual scales chart

Encapsulated PostScript (EPS)

FAX machine

File linkage

Graphic Metrafiles (GMF)

Hewlett-Packard Graphic Language (HPGL)

High-low chart

High-low volume chart

Hot keys

Line/xy chart
.PIC
Pie chart
Pie-column
  (combination) chart
Radar chart
Scatter diagram

Screen data capture
Spelling checker
Step chart
Symbol
Symbolic Link (SYLK)
Tagged Image File
  Format (TIFF)

Terminate and stay
  resident (TSR)
Text chart
.WK*
Zoom

Review Questions

1. What is a data-driven graphics program? Where does it get its name?
2. Sketch a line/xy chart. Identify the difference between a line chart and an xy chart. Research some places where this type of chart would be useful.
3. Sketch an area chart. Research some places where this type of chart would be useful.
4. Sketch a bar chart. Research some places where this type of chart would be useful.
5. Sketch a high-low and a high-low volume chart. Research some places where these types of chart would be useful.
6. Sketch a pie chart. Research some places where this type of chart would be useful.
7. Sketch a radar chart. Research some places where this type of chart would be useful.
8. What is the difference between a scatter diagram and a line chart?
9. What is a text chart? How is one used?
10. What are the available chart combinations? Give examples, and show how they are used.
11. What is a symbol? How is a symbol useful when creating a data-driven chart?
12. What is a spelling checker? Why would you want one when creating a data-driven chart?
13. How does screen data capture help in the creation of a data-driven chart?
14. What is a terminate and stay resident (TSR) program? How is one used for data-driven graphics?
15. Identify the file formats ASCII, DIF, and SYLK. What functions do these files perform in data-driven graphics?
16. Identify the file formats HPGL, CGM, GMF, EPS, and TIFF. What functions do these files perform in data-driven graphics?
17. Identify the file formats WK* and PIC. What functions do these files perform in data-driven graphics?
18. How is file linkage used for data-driven graphics?
19. What is the zoom capability?
20. In what type of application would you use zoom?

Discussion and Application Questions

1. Find a magazine advertisement for data-driven graphics programs. What are their costs? What features are highlighted?
2. Survey an office that uses data-driven graphics programs. What program or programs is it using? What was the reason for its choice? Is the office satisfied it made a good purchase?
3. Find out where data-driven graphics programs can be purchased using the yellow pages of the telephone directory.
4. What data-driven graphics programs are available for use in your laboratory? In your department? In your school?

Laboratory Assignments

1. (General) Enter the following data into your spreadsheet program, data-driven graphics program, or both, and produce a line and pie chart:

Month	Sales
April	1000
May	1100
June	900
July	700

2. (General) Use the month number (for example, 4 for April) and your spreadsheet program, data-driven graphics program, or both to produce an xy chart of the data in assignment 1.

3. (General) Enter the following data into your spreadsheet program, data-driven graphics program, or both, and create a stack-bar chart:

Month	Sales Product A	Product B
April	1000	1200
May	1100	900
June	900	1200
July	700	1300

4. (General) Examine the capabilities of your data-driven graphics program. Either perform each of the following exercises or demonstrate that your program cannot do them. Use the data from assignments 1 through 3.
   a. Create a pie chart and add a symbol.
   b. Create a combination pie and bar chart.
   c. Create a bar chart that looks three-dimensional.

5. (General) Use the following data to create one each of the types of charts available in your spreadsheet program, data-driven graphics program, or both:

Data Set A		Data Set B		Data Set C	
Andy	12	July	22	12	122
Judy	22	August	24	13	133
Carol	21	September	33	14	123
Andress	17	October	34	15	155

   Produce a chart with headings on both screen and printer.

6. (General) The class budget for a party follows:

Drinks	$34.00
Hot food	23.00
Cold food	12.00
Treats	10.00

   Make a pie-bar chart of the budget using your spreadsheet program, data-driven graphics program, or both.

7. (Accounting) Using the data from the following income statement and balance sheet, create a pie-bar chart to compare these four items using your spreadsheet program, data-driven graphics program, or both:
   a. Sources of income.
   b. Alternate expenses.
   c. Assets.
   d. Liabilities.

```
          Income Statement for the Three-Month Period Ending

December 31, 19xx

REVENUE
   Rent Unit 1                            $   35710 Rent Unit 2
                 $26590
                                          --------
      Total Revenue                       $  62300

EXPENSES
   Wages Expense                 $ 750
   Rent Expense                   2500
   Advertising Expense            2430
   Travel Expense                  920
   Supplies Expense               1700
   Insurance Expense               700
   Depreciation Expense           2400
                                --------
      Total Expenses                            11400
                                              --------
NET INCOME                                     $50900
                                              ========


Balance Sheet As of December 31, 19xx

ASSETS
   Cash                                   $56300
   Supplies                                2900
   Prepaid Wages                           2100
   Equipment                    $93500
   ...Depreciation               34900    58600
   Accounts Receivable                     1800
                                         --------
                                          121700
                                         =====

LIABILITIES
  Accounts Payable                        $ 3900
  Loans                                     550
  Wages Payable                             750

STOCK HOLDERS EQUITY
  Retained Earnings                        86500
  Capital                                  30000
                                         ---------
                                         $121700
                                         ======
```

8. (Algebra) Use a spreadsheet program, data-driven graphics program, or both to chart the following functions:
   a. $f(x) = SIN(x) /x$ for $-22 \le x \le 22$ in steps of 22
   b. $f(x) = x^2 + 3 * x + 2$ for $-10 \le x \le 10$

9. (Economics) The quantity demanded and the amount supplied are functions of price:

   $$Demand = -price * 22 + 300$$
   $$1.00 \le price \le 25.00$$

   $$Supply = price * 12 + 22$$
   $$1.00 \le price \le 25.00$$

   Graph the supply and demand curves as a function of price using your spreadsheet program, data-driven graphics program, or both.
   Using algebra to find the price as a function of quantity, the results follow:

   $$Price (demand) = -(quantity - 300)/22$$

   $$Price (supply) = (quantity + 22)/12$$

   Graph the supply and demand curves for quantities from 0 to 280 in steps of 10 units.

10. (Management) The economic order quantity formula is

    $$f(Q) = 122 * 1200 / Q + (Q/2) * 12.33$$

    for values of Q greater than 0. Graph the formula from $Q = 20$ to $Q = 500$ in steps of 20.

11. (General) Look through your local newspaper. Find some data that fit the form of the data in laboratory assignment 2. Make a pie-bar chart with headings from the data.

CHAPTER 7

Database Programs

Goals

Upon completion of this chapter, you will be able to do the following:

- Understand why database programs are important to the user.

- Define the tasks of a database program.

- Understand the steps needed to set up and operate a database system.

Outline

Insurance Customer Database

An agent for the Schneider-Fleming Insurance Agency identified his microcomputer needs as customer database files, word processing (letters, proposals, and contracts), custom programs or spreadsheet client analysis, and communication capability with the central office.

The database file need was the most critical, because research had shown that appointments per telephone call and sales per appointment could be increased if the calls could be coordinated with events in the clients' lives. Among the more important events were the birth of a child, the graduation of a family member from high school or college, obtaining a new job, the purchase or sale of a house, a family member's death, a serious illness of a family member, a marriage or divorce of a family member, and a child's first car.

A database also made sales easier by providing the knowledge necessary to maintain contact with a client. If contact is not made for one year, the probability of client loss to another agency is increased.

One agent for Schneider-Fleming Insurance set up her own database. She entered her clients' names and the life information needed to provide insurance services into the database. The extra work slowed down the number of sales calls at first but resulted in a good long-term relationship and repeat business from the client base, once it was established.

Some of the data needed were identified as name, how called (how the individual wants to be addressed), address, telephone number, date of last contact, number in family, names and dates of birth of each family member, approximate date of next life event, home ownership, automobile ownership, and unusual or serious illness of a family member.

A **fact** is something having a real, demonstrable existence. Facts are everywhere. Your name, weight, and address are facts. **Data** are facts stored in a database. Facts become data when they are selected and stored. A **database** is a collection of data used for one or more purposes. Usually the data are stored in a number of unique **files.** A file is a collection of related data or program code. A **data file** is a collection of data that have some relationship stored together. Micros in Action "Insurance Company Database" illustrates how the Schneider-Fleming Insurance Agency needed to know about its customers. A database provided the data it needed.

A **database management program** can be used to create/edit (update) screen input format, the data storage structure, data, and the report-output format; to process/save/retrieve data saved in one or more files; and to print reports. These programs include flexible commands to control all aspects of database operation, including the screen display for data input, processing (data searches, sorting, calculating, and so on), creating/editing the internal data structure and the output (report) format, and printing the results.

Fact
Something having real, demonstrable existence.

Data
Facts stored in a database.

Database
A collection of data used for one or more purposes. A database usually consists of a number of data files.

File
A collection of related data or program code.

Data file
A collection of related data.

Database management program
A program to create/edit (update) input format, data structure, data, and output format; to process and save/retrieve data saved in one or more files; and to print reports.

Knowledge
The assignment of meaning to information by a human being.

Information
Data that have been processed and recalled from a database in an organized manner.

Report generator
The program that creates a formatted report to output information from a database.

Record
A collection of data about an entity.

Entity
Something that has a separate and distinct existence.

Field
A unit of data about an attribute of an entity.

Attribute
An inherent characteristic.

Alphanumeric
Including both characters and numbers.

Knowledge and Information

Knowledge is the assignment of meaning to information by a human being. **Information** is the organized, processed output of a database. The **report generator** part of the database management system is used to create and print the formatted report. When the information is read and used by a human being, knowledge is gained.

Files, Records, and Fields

A database file is a collection of similar **records.** A record is a collection of facts about an **entity.** An entity is something that has a separate and distinct existence. An example of a file is a file cabinet containing all the data pertaining to a group of housing units owned by a real estate investor. A database file is stored on your disk in the same manner as text or program files. The rent record form in a file folder in a housing unit file cabinet may contain historical rental facts about a particular housing unit. This form is a record. A collection of records constitutes a file. A **field** stores data about an **attribute** (an inherent characteristic) of the entity. For example, if there is a location to enter the telephone number of the current occupant of a housing unit on the rent record form, this location could be considered a field. The telephone number is an attribute. Figure 7–1 illustrates a file, record, and field.

Say a database of personnel records consists of a series of files. In the file are different job skills. The record or entity would be an individual. The fields in the record would contain the individual's name, sex, pay rate, number of dependents, address, telephone number, and so on. The more information in the database, the more potential applications of the database. The more information, however, the greater the cost of setup and maintenance.

In many databases, fields and records contain a fixed number of **alphanumeric** characters (both characters and numbers). If the data in a field do not take up the entire field, the remaining space is wasted. Every wasted character cuts the amount of data that can be stored in a given file on a given type of computer storage media. When you assign characters to fields, you must be careful to balance the loss of information in small fields with the waste of space caused by too large a field. An example of wasted space is a last name field of ten characters with the name JONES in it. JONES uses only five characters. The extra space for the five additional characters is wasted. A name such as WILLIAMSON requires ten characters. If a field size of less than ten is selected, part of the WILLIAMSON name is lost.

Many database and support programs exist. Specific database program tasks are performed differently in each program. The database pro-

Figure 7–1
a) File b) Record, and c) Field

grams used in this chapter are dBASE III PLUS, dBASE IV, and PC File III. These programs are among the more popular ones available.

Why Database Programs?

Information is a resource. Database programs help individuals manipulate information. Businesses require many different databases—for example, accounts payable, accounts receivable, customer or client lists, vendor lists, employee records, inventory, product information, sales records, suppliers, and year-to-date accounting performance data. The availability of accurate, up-to-date information can help management earn or save dollars. Management decisions must often be made immediately, and the availability of information from the database can mean additional profit (as long as the database is kept up to date). Errors in judgment can occur when working without key facts. The cost of creating and maintaining a database must be balanced against the value of the data to the organization.

Some questions cannot be answered by a database. For example, the question "What would be the potential size of the college microcomputer market if the current price of equipment were reduced by 50 percent?" cannot be answered by a database because it asks for a prediction. The question "What are the current and past sales of microcomputer equipment in different types of colleges in different locations around the country?" can be answered by a database because it requires a simple collection of facts. Having the answers to the second question can aid a manager in making a better decision about how to service the college microcomputer market.

Artificial intelligence applications such as expert systems with a knowledge base and database are needed to answer a prediction question. A knowledge base is a database that contains decision rules. An expert system includes an inference (decision making) program which draws conclusions based on the rules in the knowledge base, data in a database(s), and the data entered by the user. Additional material on expert systems and knowledge base concepts may be found in Appendix B.

The principal limitations to the creation of databases are the needs and imagination of the user. Database design begins with an in-depth understanding of user needs.

Creating and Editing

Database users can use a database program to design and create the screen format used for data entry, design and create the reports to be generated, select the facts to be stored, input facts, update data, generate reports as needed, sort the data, and query the database for specific data. The plan and organization determine the database reports, other outputs, and their frequency. The desired output of a database determines how it must be designed and operated. Output includes reports and screen displays.

The steps in designing a database are as follows:

1. Identify the user.
2. Identify output needs (reports and other output).
3. Identify the data required, sources, and the input format.
4. Design the structure and size for data storage (identify file, records, and fields).
5. Identify what must be done with the input data to generate the reports and output required.
6. Identify data security needs.
7. Select and use a database program to do the following:
   a. Create the data structure.
   b. Design the data input formats.
   c. Enter preliminary data.
   d. Design procedures for processing the data.
   e. Design outputs.

   f. Perform a trial run.
   g. Evaluate the performance.
   h. Redesign and repeat steps a through g until satisfied.
8. Operate and manage the database.
9. Select a database manager.

There are constraints on all steps. Some of the facts needed may not be available. In the health care business, for example, information on personal health is restricted. Some financial facts are also often difficult to obtain.

Starting a Database Management Program

Microcomputer users create and maintain databases for their own personal and professional needs by acquiring one of the many database programs currently available. Some databases such as dBASE IV operate using menu-driven programs (Figure 7–2).

Identifying User and Output Needs (Reports)

Databases are tools for the user to accomplish specific objectives. The reports and other outputs are the physical manifestations of the objectives and government regulations. Government regulations result in mandatory sales tax reports, income tax reports, reports on the race, sex, and age of employees, fire inspection reports, and other record keeping. User needs

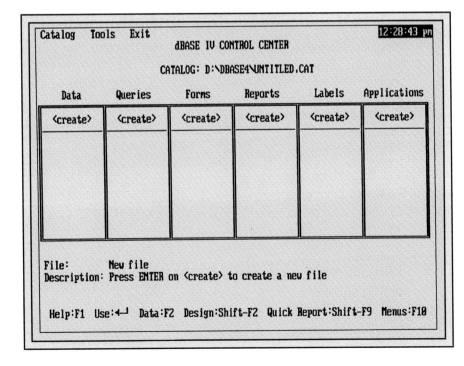

Figure 7–2
dBASE IV Opening Screen

will dictate the direction of a database. Examples of reports and outputs include lists of customers, employees, church members, or property for sale; mailing lists; mailing labels; and automatic addressing of letters.

Figure 7–3 illustrates a report design with records referring to an individual and the following fields: last name, first name, how called (how the individual wants to be addressed), telephone number, company, address, city, zip code, state, numeric code, and alphabetic code. The form in Figure 7–3 is controlled by the database program. Figure 7–4 illustrates how fields are defined in dBASE III PLUS, and Figure 7–5 illustrates how fields are defined in PC File III.

Last	First	Call	Phone	Company	Address	City	Zip	1T	Num	Alp
Prieto	Juan	Smitty	205-555-1212	Able Computer Company	11 First Street	Mobile	12345	AL	1255	99AA
Snodgrass	Mary	Leni	123-555-1111	AZ Management Service	4151 Bay Avenue	Atlanta	44445	NJ	5555	A1BB
Timbalov	Stephanie	Dr. T	123-555-1111	AZ Management Services In	4151 Bay Avenue	Atlanta	44445	NJ	5555	82BB
Rockable	Betty	Rocky	333-555-1111	Lost Lane School	55 Byte Drive	Miami	11112	NY	2222	A3CC
Duval	Robert	Bob	333-555-2222	Western Wear Clothes Inc.	12 Label Lane	Miami	11112	NY	2223	A3CC
Kahn	Joe	Joe	205-555-1233	Able Computer Company	11 First Avenue	Mobile	12345	AL	5555	A1AA
Cheng	Thuc	Thuc	333-666-1111	Boston Computer Company	11 First Avenue	Western	11115	AL	5555	A2BB
Anderson	Steve	Mr. Anders	222-444-5555	Eastern Microcomputer Co.	1 Computer Lane	Boston	99995	CA	5555	B6XX

Figure 7–3
Required Report in dBASE III PLUS

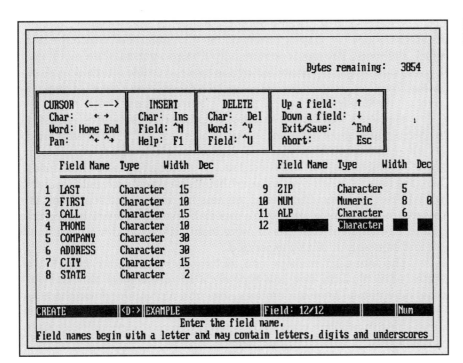

Figure 7−4
Defining Fields in dBASE III PLUS

```
                                                    Bytes remaining:   3854

 ┌──────────────┬──────────────┬──────────────┬─────────────────────┐
 │ CURSOR <──── ──>│   INSERT   │   DELETE   │ Up a field:    ↑    │
 │ Char:    ← →    │ Char:  Ins │ Char:  Del │ Down a field:  ↓    │  ↓
 │ Word: Home End  │ Field: ^N  │ Word:  ^Y  │ Exit/Save:   ^End   │
 │ Pan:    ^← ^→   │ Help:  F1  │ Field: ^U  │ Abort:        Esc   │
 └──────────────┴──────────────┴──────────────┴─────────────────────┘

     Field Name  Type      Width Dec        Field Name  Type      Width Dec
  1  LAST        Character   15         9  ZIP         Character    5
  2  FIRST       Character   10        10  NUM         Numeric      8    0
  3  CALL        Character   15        11  ALP         Character    6
  4  PHONE       Character   10        12  ▆▆▆▆▆▆▆▆   Character   ▆▆  ▆▆
  5  COMPANY     Character   30
  6  ADDRESS     Character   30
  7  CITY        Character   15
  8  STATE       Character    2

 CREATE        |<D:>|EXAMPLE              |Field: 12/12    |      |Num
                         Enter the field name.
 Field names begin with a letter and may contain letters, digits and underscores
```

Figure 7−5
Defining Fields in PC File III

```
 (Alt)H for help.  Define the database.
  FIELD NAME          LENGTH                FIELD NAME        LENGTH
 [Last       ]      [15  ]               [          ]      [     ]
 [First      ]      [10  ]               [          ]      [     ]
 [Call       ]      [15  ]               [          ]      [     ]
 [Phone      ]      [10  ]               [          ]      [     ]
 [Company    ]      [30  ]               [          ]      [     ]
 [Address    ]      [30  ]               [          ]      [     ]
 [City       ]      [15  ]               [          ]      [     ]
 [State      ]      [2   ]               [          ]      [     ]
 [Zip        ]      [5   ]               [          ]      [     ]
 [Num        ]      [5   ]               [          ]      [     ]
 [Alp        ]      [6   ]               [          ]      [     ]
 ▶           ◀      [    ]               [          ]      [     ]
 [           ]      [    ]               [          ]      [     ]
 [           ]      [    ]               [          ]      [     ]
 [           ]      [    ]               [          ]      [     ]
 [           ]      [    ]               [          ]      [     ]
 [           ]      [    ]               [          ]      [     ]
 [           ]      [    ]               [          ]      [     ]
 [           ]      [    ]               [          ]      [     ]
 [           ]      [    ]               [          ]      [     ]

 Enter data. Press (F10) when complete.
```

Microcomputer database programs include **nonprocedural languages** and other high-level microcomputer languages. A nonprocedural language is a programming language that does not require programming techniques to be used. It allows the user to send instructions to the computer in English-like statements. These languages are capable of producing customized documents

Nonprocedural language
A programming language that does not require programming techniques to be used. It allows the user to send instructions to the computer in English-like statements.

such as general ledgers, income and expense statements, inventory reports, lists of telephone calls, graphic presentations, communication with other computers, and more. The most common output from a database is a report on a piece of paper. Reports are limited by the space available on the screen and printer. Some programs allow you to print sideways on a sheet of paper to overcome the limitations of paper size in a printer (Figure 7–6).

Figure 7–7 shows a 65-column report layout. Sixty-five columns is the default limitation on many word processors, so reports with more columns create problems. Figure 7–8 illustrates the report described in Figure 7–7. Note that the titles and data are too long for some of the fields. There are no spaces left over to insert blanks between each field, and the data will run together. Database programs are not limited to storing the same information that is printed in a report. If an output device is used that handles more than 65 columns or more than a single line for output, both data and title output can be expanded.

The four-digit numeric and alphanumeric codes are included in Figure 7–8 to illustrate how this type of data is used. Most database programs differentiate between numeric data and alphanumeric or character data. The alphanumeric codes may represent an income level; a credit rating; a health problem type; or a preference in cars, computers, copiers, television sets, cameras, or other items.

Figure 7–6
Sideways-printed Report

Last Name	First Name	How Called	Phone	Company	Address	City	St	Zip Code	Numeric Code	Alpha Code
5	5	4	9	8	7	6	2	3	3	3

Figure 7–7
Definition of Field Size for 65-Column Report

Last Name	First Name	How Calle	Phone	Company	Address	City	St	Zip Code	Num Code	Alph Cod
Prieto	Juan	Smitt	2055551212	Able Com	11 First	Mobile	AL	12345	1255	99AA
Snodgra	Mary	Leni	1235551111	AZ Manag	4151 Bay	Atlanta	NJ	44445	5555	A1B8
Timbalo	Steph	Dr. T	1235551111	AZ Manag	4151 Bay	Atlanta	NJ	44445	5555	82BB
Rockable	Betty	Rocky	3335551111	Lost Lan	55 Byte	Miami	NY	11112	2222	A3CC
Duval	Rober	Bob	3335552222	Western	12 Label	Miami	NY	11112	2223	A3CC
Kahn	Joe	Joe	2055551233	Able Com	11 First	Mobile	AL	12345	5555	A1AA
Cheng	Thuc	Thuc	3336661111	Boston C	11 First	Western	AL	11115	5555	A2BB
Anderso	Steve	Mr. An	2224445555	Eastern	1 Comput	Boston	CA	99995	5555	B6XX

Figure 7–8
The 65-Column Report
Some report generators truncate while others wrap-around the data into multiple lines.

The limitation of 65 columns reflects the users' decision to design a report that will fit on normal-width paper. Most database programs allow the user to enter a greater number of characters in a given field than are printed.

Examine each field in Figure 7–8 to see if the output would be useful for your application. Because the space is limited, the data printed will not be usable for many applications. As a user, you must determine your output needs and the limitations of the equipment used and then make a careful trade-off between them if a conflict occurs, as in this case. Some fields are fixed, such as the telephone number and zip code. The code fields must also be shown in their entirety. Some database systems allow you to add spaces and the extra characters in telephone numbers and zip codes that make them more readable. The layout of a report requires a lot of careful counting and consideration for each output.

Data Structure and Screen Input

Data structure includes the number of fields in a record, the size of each field, and the number of records in a file. The database output defines the needed input. The report of our example includes the last name, first name, how called (for personal letters), telephone number, company name, address, city, state, zip code, and two codes for customer information. These

Data structure
The number of fields in a record, the size of each field, and the number of records in a file. The number of records per file may or may not have a limit.

facts must be found someplace. Sources include salesperson reports, other databases, and copies of orders. Once located, the data must be entered into the database. Figure 7–9 illustrates a typical input screen for these facts.

The facts, once obtained, must be entered into the database. Most entries will be through the keyboard onto a form designed and displayed on the screen. Some data can be entered directly from other databases by **downloading** the data electronically into your computer. Data can also be **uploaded** to a database from your computer to another computer.

The database user usually must define the data entry screen format. The same care used in laying out the output format pays dividends when defining the input format. The data entry task is made easier by a careful layout. Following the layout of the source documents, if there is a consistent one, is often useful.

Data Input

On-screen editors allow you to enter and update data in a database. No database remains fixed; constant update is needed. Most programs allow you to make changes with ease and to see the changes on the computer's monitor. One advantage of many electronically maintained databases is that once you have entered the data, you need only update the changes and then press a key to produce a new report.

PC File III uses the function keys on the IBM PC, found on the left side or top of the keyboard, in combination with screen selection menus. A menu is a list of different actions that may be taken. For example, the menu for the use of function keys in PC File III is illustrated in Figure 7–10.

Downloading
Transferring data from another computer into yours.

Uploading
Transferring data from your computer to another computer.

Figure 7–9
Input Screen

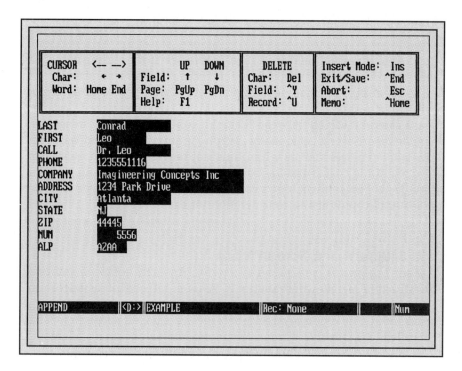

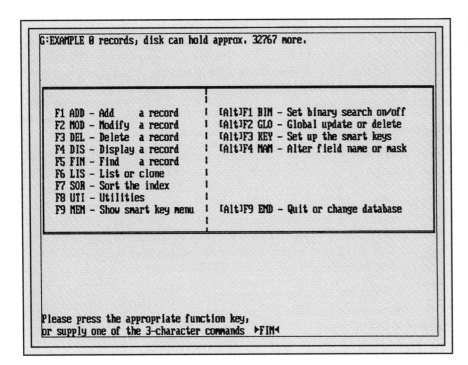

Figure 7-10
PC File III Menu

The PC File III menu allows you to enter add, modify, delete, display, find a record, and so on. This program places all the text in the random access memory (RAM), and it can be cleared with ease.

Processing

Among the many processing capabilities of a database management program are sorting, querying, calculating report design, report generation, addition of new records, and structure changing (addition of new fields). Most database programs provide all these capabilities with the exception of addition of new fields. You must examine your requirements, determine what you plan to do with the data, and then eliminate from consideration all database programs that do not have the capabilities required.

Classification/Types

Database programs may be simple file managers, complete languages in which many applications can be created, or something in between. The classification (general type) of database management programs determines the type of problem the program can solve: file management–report generator databases, relational databases, hierarchical databases, network databases, free-format databases, multiuser databases, and computer languages.

Although most of the database programs currently available for microcomputers are either file management–report generators or relational types, all types are available. The number and quality of network and multiuser databases have increased as the hardware to support these types of databases has improved and the costs have decreased.

File Management–Report Generator Databases

File management–report generator program
A program to create/edit (update), save/retrieve, process data saved in a single file, and to print reports.

The needs of many users are satisfied by the **file management–report generator program.** A file management–report generator program is a program to create/edit (update), save/retrieve, process data saved in a single file, and to print reports. This type of program is not a true database. It is often used to create and manage a single file for some single purpose with limited on-line storage capacity. A file management-report generator program controls a file that is organized into records and fields, and it produces reports from the data. Figure 7–11 illustrates a file management file layout.

Relational Databases

Relational database
A database that organizes data into files as arrays of rows (records) and columns (fields) and includes at least one field that is keyed into at least one other file.

Ad hoc
Formed or created as needed, with little or no preplanning.

A **relational database** organizes data into files as arrays of rows (records) and columns (fields) and includes at least one field that is keyed into at least one other file. Relational databases do not have to be as carefully organized as file management systems, but the poorer the organization, the slower the system will operate. Figure 7–12 shows a relational data file layout. The objective of a relational database is to make **ad hoc** requests for information easy to accommodate.

The organization of relational and file management databases looks the same. The difference is that relational database programs have a "join" command that allows searching for all individuals with a given characteristic in a specified field in two or more data files, and combining in a variety of ways the data pertaining to that characteristic. For example, with a relational database program, you may produce a list of all individuals in a file who live in the same zip code area.

Figure 7–11
File Management File Layout

```
File — scoutmasters in a district
     Record — a scoutmaster
     Fields — troop/name/street/city/
                  zipcode/telephone
```

Figure 7–12
Relational Database File Layout

```
File — scoutmasters in a district
     Record — a scoutmaster
     Fields — troop/name/street/ . . .
You may join all records that pertain to a
given city.
```

Hierarchical Databases

A **hierarchical database** is organized from the top down. These databases do not have to be divided into fields. The hierarchical structure allows you to search the database without being limited to searching each field. The record contents are not limited by the nature of the search procedures. The file organization, not the contents of the file, determines the location of a record in the hierarchy. The organization is similar to the hierarchical organization of MS-DOS files. In the hierarchical system (Figure 7–13), each record is related to the next higher level by its location.

Hierarchical database
A database organized from the top down.

Network Databases

A **network database** (Figure 7–14) is similar to a hierarchical system, with the exception that it allows for multiple relationships among levels. Microcomputer programs for this type of database are limited.

Network database
A hierarchical database with the additional capability of allowing multiple relationships at different levels.

Free-Format Databases

Free-format databases (Figure 7–15) combine different forms of data entry, including text, lists, tables, charts, and graphs. Key words located in the stored database are used to retrieve the material. Programs for microcomputers that handle this type of database are not readily available.

Free-format database
A database that combines different types of data structures, such as text, lists, tables, charts, and graphs.

Multiuser Databases

A **multiuser database** allows more than a single user access to the database at the same time. This means that two or more microcomputers are connected and use the same on-line storage device. The problems of two users'

Multiuser database
A database that allows more than a single user access to the database at the same time.

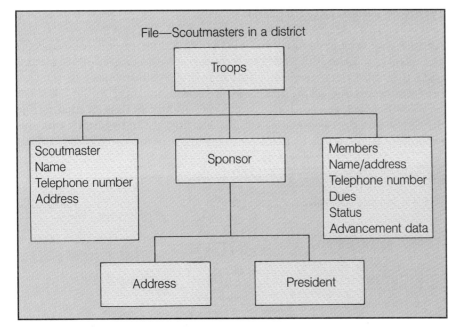

Figure 7–13
Hierarchical Database File Layout

Figure 7–14
Network Database File Layout

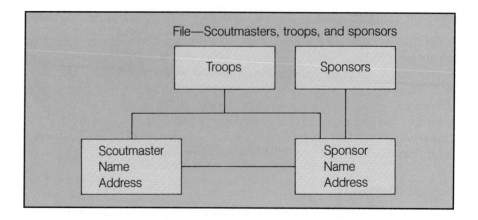

changing a record at the same time and of file security become more complex when more than one person uses a database.

Computer Languages

There are few limits to the problems that can be solved by some database programs. Complete accounting systems can be created entirely in a database program. Computer language database programs fit the definition of a high-level computer language: a set of near-English codes is used to give instructions to a computer. These database programs (all versions of dBASE) often include specialized statements that make the creation and use of databases easier than if a general-purpose language were used in their creation.

Types of Index Organization

Indexing scheme
A method of creating a directory of where records and files can be found.

An **indexing scheme** is a method of creating a directory of where records and files can be found. Indexing schemes reduce the amount of time needed to find data in a database. Indexing is the manner in which a program orders the records in a file. It is often invisible to the user. The important aspect of record indexing is the amount of time needed to find the data wanted. A sequential search—starting at the beginning of a file, examining each record in turn, and seeking a particular record—quickly

Figure 7–15
Free-Format Database

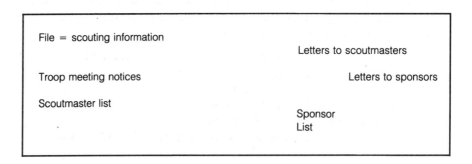

results in long delays for even small databases and is not an acceptable method for most databases. The schemes commonly used for indexing are detailed in Appendix C.

Security

Management has a professional, social, moral, and legal obligation to control the quality and use of the data in its database. A database must be protected from both internal and external contamination and misuse. Equipment must be protected from damage and theft. The loss of equipment is the least crucial loss, however, although it can be expensive. A database with contaminated data can lead to decisions that hurt both the individuals whose data are in the database and the company. The misuse of data by either employees or outsiders can damage all involved.

Data can be contaminated by the entry of bad data. This can happen in the normal course of business, and management must develop methods to prevent the addition of bad data, if possible, and then to detect and purge bad data if any get around the controls. Data contamination can also occur when an employee who is unhappy deliberately enters bad data to damage the company. If a system uses telephone communication input, an unauthorized outsider can break into the system and enter bad data. Bad data could result in millions of dollars of funds being transferred to an account out of the country, or a company could injure someone because of the bad data and find itself on the receiving end of a lawsuit.

Data can be destroyed by individuals who are part of an organization or external to it, or by an electronic power or hardware failure. Good backup procedures help protect against these problems. With good backup procedures, it is not difficult to replace data that have been destroyed. It is often less costly to have all data destroyed than to have data polluted or misused.

For individual users of microcomputers, data security may mean locking up the floppy disks when they are removed from the microcomputer, locking up the microcomputer that uses a hard (fixed) disk system, adapting a software protection scheme, using passwords that are changed periodically and account numbers, or a combination of these measures. The security problem becomes more complex when there are a number of users of the same microcomputer with a fixed (nonremovable) hard disk. If you have an automatic telephone-answering device on your microcomputer or use the microcomputer as part of a network, you will have the same security problems as a large computer time-sharing system. Suggested security procedures include the following:

Long passwords to make exhaustive searches difficult.
Passwords containing random characters.
Limited number of trials (three or less).
Invisible passwords during operation.
Careful administration of passwords.
Multilevel system: one password for read only and a second
    password for read and write.

Monthly changing of passwords.

Special operating procedures for use when the security system is attacked.

Holding area for new data (data check before adding database).

Remote access limited to read only or input limited to holding area.

Dial-back devices.

Logs of data use and access.

It is difficult to protect yourself completely from other computer users who wish to break into your system when it is on line with an auto-answer telephone-answering device and in an unattended mode. Time-sharing managers spend many hours developing schemes to protect their computers from outsiders. If you are concerned with data security, do not use an automatic answering device.

A company is responsible for what is in its database and for the use of that data. Social attitudes toward information about individuals recorded in databases are changing, along with the laws governing the use of such information. Users must make sure they operate within current legal and moral constraints. It is important to enter accurate data into a database and to control the data's distribution carefully.

Operating and Managing the Database

To be useful to the user, a database must produce results that are relevant, accurate, reliable, timely, available, secure, flexible, and economical. The relevancy of the output of a database often depends as much on how the database is managed and operated as on the selection of the database program. Only the user can determine if the facts contained in a database are of value in a given situation. The expression "garbage in, garbage out" (GIGO) has been picked up for popular use in the computer field. GIGO refers to the necessity of carefully controlling and selecting the facts that go into a database to make sure the information wanted is available when requested. The facts entered into a database must be both accurate and measured in a consistent manner for the facts to be reliable for decision making.

If a database requires constant update, management must make sure the updates are made. Old data often have no value, or even a negative value, in a given decision-making situation. One reason for the growth of microcomputer databases is that they provide the user with a method of getting the information needed to perform. The facts stored in the databases are readily available. "User-friendly" database programs are designed to make it easy for the computer beginner to get started. However, user-friendly programs also tend to be "abuser-friendly" programs; that is, unauthorized individuals can break in and get information out of such systems.

A database program must be flexible. Organizations exist in an ever-changing environment. Objectives change as the environment changes. Databases must change and adapt to the changing objectives. This means a continual management commitment to operating and directing the database is necessary.

Information has value. It costs money to create and manage a database. If at any time the value of the information generated by a database is less than the cost of operating the system, the continued existence of the database must be questioned.

Organizations sometimes find that some standardization in database design helps reduce training time and helps eliminate errors. Field names, record designs, and input and output formats help users get the maximum benefits from databases when they are transferred within an organization.

Saving and Retrieving

Database management programs save input formats, data structure, data, processing instructions, and output formats. Database programs use a variety of file types to save the required information. File types may be identified by their extensions. Table 7–1 lists some of the extensions used by dBASE files.

Saving Structure

In dBASE, file structure information can be saved as part of the data file. At the top of a dBASE's .dbf file are stored header, data record, flag, and end-of-file marker information. The header includes information about the file structure. dBASE saves this information when the structure is created, before data are entered. Figure 7–4 illustrates the task of creating/editing the size of each field and the number of fields. Also displayed on the screen is the ^END instruction, which indicates how to save the results.

Compatibility

Compatibility is the capability of two different items to work together. The capability of transfer files to and from databases is a form of compatibility. A database program is more useful if you are able to transfer files between it and other applications. Table 7–2 illustrates the variety of files handled by dBASE and their extensions.

Your ability to take advantage of new database programs will be limited if your file cannot be transferred. Retyping a database is expensive and subject to the introduction of costly errors. Database programs are often combined with other programs such as word processing, spreadsheet, communication, graphics, or other programs. These integrated programs, which include one or more functions, are often selected because they take care of file transfer. All parts of the program use the same data file and operate using similar menus or functions.

Compatibility
The capability of two different items to work together.

Table 7–1
Selected dBASE File Extensions

Working and Configuration Files

Extension	File Use
.$$$	Temporary file; action was not complete
.BAK	Command, procedure, or database backup file
.BIN	Binary file
.CAT	Catalog file
.COD	Template source file
.CPT	Encrypted memo file; used with password information (.crp) file
.CRP	Password information file; created with PROTECT only
.CVT	Convert file; for multiuser change detection file
.DB	Configuration file; for defaults on dBASE IV start-up
.DBF	Database file
.DBO	Command and procedure object file
.DBT	Database memo file
.DB2	Renamed old dBASE II file; used for import and export
.DEF	Selector definition file
.FIL	Files list design object file
.FMO	Compiled format (.fmt) file
.FMT	Generated format file; from screen (.scr) file
.FRG	Generated report form file; from report form (.frm) file
.FRM	Report form file
.FRO	Compiled generated report form (.frg) file
.FR3	Renamed old dBASE III report form (.frm) file
.GEN	Template file
.KEY	Keystroke macro library file
.LBG	Generated label form file; from label form (.lbl) file
.LBL	Label form file
.LBO	Compiled label form (.lbl) file
.LB3	Renamed old dBASE III label form (.lbl) file
.LOG	Transaction log file

Printing

Some database programs have special report forms and output procedures for the printer. Others, such as dBASE, allow you to format a report on the screen and then transfer it to the printer with a simple command. Printer format controls may be included in the database printing instructions.

Table 7–1
Selected dBASE File Extensions, continued

.MDX	Multiple index file
.MEM	Memory file
.NDX	Single index file
.NPI	Reports, forms, label files; template interpreter only
.PRF	Print form file
.PRG	dBASE command or procedure file
.PRS	dBASE/SQL command or procedure file
.PRT	Printer output file
.PR2	Printer driver file
.QBE	Query file
.QBO	Compiled query (.qbe) file
.QRY	Query file
.SCR	Screen file
.SC3	Renamed old dBASE III screen (.scr) file
.TBK	Database memo backup file
.T44/.W44	Intermediate work files; used by SORT and INDEX
.UPD	Update query file
.UPO	Compiled update query (.upd) file
.VUE	View file
.WIN	Logical window save file

Applications Generator Files

Extension	File Use
.APP	Application design object file
.BAR	Horizontal bar design object file
.BCH	Batch process design object file
.DOC	Documentation file
.POP	Pop-up menu design object file
.STR	Structure list design object file
.VAL	Values list design object file

Database Hardware

The development and application of microcomputer databases depend upon the capabilities and capacities of the available hardware. The hardware needed for a microcomputer database includes RAM, input devices, monitors, printers, and on-line storage devices.

Table 7–2
Selected dBASE Support File Extensions

Extension	File Use
.CHT	CHART-MASTER file; used with dBASE/CHART-MASTER Bridge
.DIF	Data Interchange Format, or VisiCalc file;
.FW2	Framework spreadsheet/database file; used for import/export
.RPD	RapidFile file; used for import/export
.TXT	ASCII text output file
.WKS	Lotus 1-2-3 file; used with `APPEND FROM/COPY TO`

RAM Needs

Many database programs, both file maintenance and very high level language programs, have no special RAM requirements. A number of programs that were transferred and rewritten from larger computers do have large RAM needs. In addition, as programmers add features to newer versions of database programs, the amount of RAM required increases. For example, dBASE II could be stored on a single low-capacity disk (approximately 180K), dBASE III required two larger-capacity disks (approximately 526K), and dBASE IV can only run on a hard disk (approximately 2.8MB).

Input Devices

The most often used method of data entry and database update is the keyboard. However, database programs can be designed to take advantage of many other methods. Point-of-sale data entry (cash registers), light pens, and optical character readers are often used for inventory control.

Microcomputer databases are often used in conjunction with central computer databases. Communication and transfer of files between the central computer and the microcomputer are common; they will be covered in more detail in Chapter 10.

Monitors

The monitor is a primary output device for database programs. Almost any monochrome or color screen will satisfy the database user's needs. If the data are to be used for color or high-resolution graphics, a monitor with the required capability is needed.

Printers

Databases are often used to produce reports, lists, and tables. Users of databases and spreadsheets often have the same need for wide-carriage printers. The discussion of printers in Chapter 5 applies to databases as well as to spreadsheets. In addition, if graphs of the contents of the database are needed, or if graphic images are stored in the database, a graphics printer may be needed.

On-Line Storage

Databases need on-line storage devices that can handle large amounts of information. As the amount of on-line storage availability has increased and its costs decreased, the numbers of programs and applications of databases on microcomputers have increased as well. Early databases on microcomputers were simple due to the limited hardware capacity and software capability. Only when low-cost (under $1,000) hard disk devices (over 5 million bytes) and increased RAM (beyond 64K) became available did the number of programs and applications expand.

If you have a small database, it may fit on floppy disks. The capacity of floppy disks started at 50,000 bytes and has grown to over 1.44 million bytes. Even with the increased capacity, many database systems require the use of a hard disk.

In database programs using ASCII files, the number of bytes equals the total number of characters in the database, including control codes and spaces. Most database programs use ASCII files. Database programs using compressed code are able to store more data in the same space as an ASCII file. The storage requirements of files created by a database program can be determined only from studying its specifications.

Many database applications are initially set up using floppy disks and then moved to hard disks as the system grows. Hard disks or hard disk cartridges can store from 5MB to over 16,000MB of data. The greater the capacity, the greater the absolute cost but the lower the cost per byte.

Summary

A fact is something having real, demonstrable existence while data are facts stored in a database. A database is a collection of data used for one or more purposes. Usually the data are stored in a number of unique files which are collections of related data or program code. A database usually consists of a number of data files which are collections of related data. A database management program is a program to create/edit (update) input format, data structure, data, and output format; to process and save/ retrieve data saved in one or more files; and to print reports.

Knowledge is the assignment of meaning to information by a human being. Information is data that have been processed and recalled from a database in an organized manner. A report generator is the program that creates a formatted report to output information from a database.

A record is a collection of data about an entity which is something that has a separate and distinct existence. A field is a unit of data about an attribute of an entity. An attribute is an inherent characteristic.

The types of databases include file management-report generator, relational, hierarchical, network, free-format, and multiuser databases, and computer languages. A file management-report generator database can be used to create/edit (update), save/retrieve, process data saved in a single file, and print reports. A relational database is a database that organizes data into files as arrays of rows (records) and columns (fields) and includes at least one field that is keyed into at least one other file. A hierarchical database is a database organized from the top down. A network database is a hierarchical database with the additional capability of allowing multiple relationships at different levels. A free-format database is a database that combines different types of data structures, such as text, lists, tables, charts, and graphs. A multiuser database is a database that allows access to the database to more than one user at the same time.

Key Terms

Ad hoc	Entity	Knowledge
Alphanumeric	Fact	Multiuser database
Attribute	Field	Network database
Compatibility	File	Nonprocedural
Data	File management-	language
Data file	report generator	Record
Data structure	program	Relational database
Database	Free-format database	Report generator
Database management	Hierarchical database	Uploading
program	Indexing scheme	
Downloading	Information	

Review Questions

1. What is a fact?
2. When do facts become data?
3. What is a database? How many data files are usually in a database?
4. What is a file? What is a data file? What is the difference between a file and a data file?
5. What does a database management program do?
6. What is knowledge?
7. What is information? What is the difference between knowledge and information?
8. What does a report generator do?
9. What is a record?
10. What is an entity?

11. What is a field? Give some examples of fields.
12. What is an attribute?
13. What is included in an alphanumeric character set?
14. What is a nonprocedural language?
15. Why is the data structure of a database important? Give some examples of data structure.
16. What is the difference between downloading and uploading?
17. Identify a file management–report generator program.
18. Identify each type of database: relational, hierarchical, network, free-format, and multiuser databases.
19. What is indexing? Why is it used?
20. Identify some database security problems.

Discussion and Application Questions

1. Identify some databases where you would expect to find information about yourself listed.
2. Identify some databases maintained by your university.
3. Identify some databases maintained by religious or social organizations.
4. Identify some databases maintained by your local government.
5. Visit a local business and identify some databases it maintains.

Laboratory Assignments

1. Load your database program into a microcomputer. Enter the following structure:

Field	Size	Type	Decimal Places
Last Name	22	Characters	
First Name	22	Characters	
How Called	15	Characters	
Identification Number	9	Characters	
Telephone Number	10	Characters	
Street Address	22	Characters	
City	15	Characters	
State	2	Characters	
Zip code	5	Characters	
Amount	9	Number	
Date Due	6	Special	

Use the procedure in your database for handling dates under "Date Due." If there is no procedure, enter the date as a single number YYMMDD. Save, display, and print a copy of the structure.

2. Enter and save the following data into the structure developed in assignment 1:

Last Name	First Name	How Called	ID No.	No.	Street Address	City	St	Zip	Amt.	Date Due
Booth	Frank	FB	15526	2055555	123 West Lane	Atlanta	Al	35555	$450.77	12/12/99
Armenable	Leanoria	Leo	11122	1112223	64 Lost Lane	Mobile	NJ	11111	$122.00	01/11/99
Poser	Judy	Judy	22211	9992221	112 Bay Road	New Orleans	GA	22222	$12.03	02/12/99
Renser	Raymond	Ray	99922	8882221	65 Red Lane	New York	WI	44444	$947.22	02/02/99
Candely	Fred	Candy	22233	5556667	66 West Wood	Miami	FL	24442	$342.77	03/06/99

Print the data entered to demonstrate that it was entered and saved.

3. Identify the help routine in your database, and make a screen copy of one of the help screens.

4. Develop a database to store the amount of miles traveled and the amount of gasoline used per tank. The objective is to calculate the gasoline mileage of each tank. Use the field size and type indicated.

Field	Size	Type	Decimal Places
Miles	7	Numeric	1
Gallons	7	Numeric	1

The gasoline mileage report follows:

Tank $	Miles	Gallons	Miles per Gallon
1	220.3	11.9	
2	234.5	11.0	
3	263.3	11.1	
4	248.2	12.2	
5	245.1	11.3	
6	256.3	11.4	
7	266.4	11.5	

The last column must be calculated by your database.

5. Develop a database to calculate the batting average of the members of a baseball team. The output should be as follows:

Player	Number at Bat	Singles	Doubles	Triples	Homers	Batting Average
Jim Jones	34	4	1	2	3	
Stan Smith	45	5	3	3	1	Calculate in
Carol Kim	33	4	2	2	2	database
Andy Rodrege	20	2	3	0	0	
Samual Smith	12	1	1	0	1	
Andres Able	44	4	1	1	0	

Add to the database the players' telephone numbers and addresses. Produce a report sorted by batting average from high to low.

6. Print an ASCII text file for one of the assignments you have completed. Transfer the file to your word processor, and use it to create a report including a number of different fonts available in your printer.

7. Set up a database for a company with the following fields:

Field	Size	Type	Decimal places
Date	6	Number or special	
Stock Name	22	Character	
Price	15	Numeric	3 beyond decimal point
Shares	5	Numeric	0 beyond decimal point

After creating the database, enter the closing value of the stock's selling price for 15 days. Produce a report that calculates the average closing value of the stock.

8. Print an ASCII file from assignment 2 above. Prepare the data for transfer to some other program.

9. Develop a method to produce a mailing label from a database containing names and addresses.

10. In assignment 1, a database was created that included the following: last name, first name, how called, identification number, telephone number, street address, city, state, zip code, amount, and date due. Sort the records in the database according to last name. Create an index for city, state, zip code, amount, and date due. Print reports in order of the database records and each index item.

11. Use the baseball team database in assignment 5 as a foundation for a database of your favorite team. Maintain the records in last-name

order. Add indexes for the number of times at bat, batting average, and position. Print the database according to last name, number of times at bat, batting average, and position.

12. Create (program) a grade sheet for a class. Include freshmen, sophomores, juniors, and seniors. Calculate the average of each grading criterion, each student's average, and the class average. Produce a report of the grades of all freshmen separated from all other members of the class. Produce a grade sheet for the class.

13. Create (program) a database to maintain the finances of a student club or other activity. Develop a report on the finances. Use any manual finance report as a model.

14. (General business) Set up a database for inventory control with the following fields: stock number, description, wholesale unit cost, quantity on hand, quantity on order, reorder point, sales this month, and sales year to date. Enter the following data:

Stock Number	Description	Wholesale Unit Cost	Quantity on Hand	Quantity on Order	Reorder Point	Sales Month	Sales Year to Date
15525	RS-232 cable	9.55	8	12	12	5	36
15684	Parallel cable	8.22	15	0	12	9	44
14871	Null modems	20.11	2	0	1	0	8
12322	Cable ends	1.00	22	30	24	12	78
23202	Cable roll	5.22	5	6	5	3	22

Produce reports of the entire inventory and stock numbers with orders outstanding.

15. (Clubs) Use your database to set up a club membership record-keeping procedure. Each member must be listed, with telephone number, academic division, dues status, and attendance record.

16. (Education) Create a database for a class roll:

No.	Name	Student$	Exam$1	Exam$2	Exam$3	Final	Report
1.	Mary Priero	11122					
2.	Leo Anderson	12345					
3.	Fred Prieto	54123					
4.	Bill Cheng	15487					
5.	Jean Beirel	78451					
6.	Carol Baker	02635					
7.	Fred Osborne	11220					

Add equations to find the sum, average, and standard deviation of each grading criterion, each student, and the total class effort.

17. (General Business) A checkbook register contains the following information:

Date	Check#	Checks/Deposits	Deposit	Check	Balance
—	—	Original balance			1,225.22
9/1	210	Rent 1		50.00	
9/2	211	Utilities		101.00	
9/3	212	Telephone		31.22	
9/6	—	Salary check	1,500.26		
9/7	213	Cash		160.00	
9/11	214	Food		102.33	

The bank record shows the following:

Balance	We have added		We have subtracted			Current Balance
Statement	Number	Deposits	Number	Checks	Service Charges	
$1,225.22	2	$2,000.26	6	$644.55	1.22	$2579.71

Checking Account Transactions		
Date	Amount	Description
9/6	$1,500.26	Deposit
9/8	500.00	Deposit

Checks	
Date	Amount
9/2	$150.00
9/5	101.00
9/8	31.22
9/8	100.00
9/12	160.00
9/15	102.33

At the beginning of the period, your balance and the bank's balance were the same. There were no outstanding transactions of any type.

Set up a database program to start with your balance, add the not-cleared checks, subtract the unrecorded checks, subtract the not-cleared deposits, add the unrecorded deposits, make adjustments for errors in recording the service charges, and produce a final balance to be compared with the bank's.

18. (Accounting) Set up and organize a database to enter the chart of accounts (below) a debit field, and a credit field. Add the capability to sum both the debits and credits.

Chart of Accounts	Type	Liquidity	Debit	Credit
Cash account	A	L	9,200	
Accounts receivable	A	L	1,200	
Accounts payable	L	C		1,400
Retained earnings	E	T		2,000
Capital stock	E	T		4,000
Supplies	A	L	500	
Building	A	F	12,000	
Build-reserve for Depreciation	A	F		4,000
Trucks	A	F	8,000	
Truck-reserve for Depreciation	A	F		3,000
Equipment	A	F	21,000	
Equip-reserve for Depreciation	A	F		6,000
Notes payable	L	C		8,000
Loans payable	L	T		24,500

Under "Type," A is an asset, L is a liability, and E is stockholders' equity.
Under "Liquidity," L is for liquid, C is for current, T is for long term, and F is for fixed.

19. Database number 1 contains the following:

Field	Size
Company Name	22
Street Address	22
City	15
State	2
Zip	5
Contact	22
Code Number	9

Database number 2 contains the following:

```
Field                 Size

Code Number            9
Date of Transaction    6
Quantity              12  with 2 values beyond decimal point
Description           22
Price                 12  with 2 values beyond decimal point
```

One objective is to create an invoice using the following model:

```
         INVOICE

From:                              To:
Professional Sales and Services, Inc.   A&Z Management
Services, In
3545 West Brook Lane               233 Bay Road
Santa Clara, CA 55555              Atlanta, AL 55555
555-555-55555                      Atten: A.D. Zimmerman


QUANTITY DESCRIPTION               PRICE    AMOUNT



                                   TOTAL
                                   = = = = =
```

The amount should be calculated by multiplying the quantity times the price. The total is the sum of all the individual amounts.

20. The club budget report contains the following fields:

> Date received from or paid to.
> Dues income.
> Registration income.
> Magazine income.
> Other income.
> Registration cost.
> Magazine cost.
> Insignia cost.

Supplies cost.
Special fund cost.
Materials cost.
Activities cost.

In addition to the detailed field data, the report is required to have a sum of the incomes, a sum of costs, and a balance. Prepare a structure. Use your best estimates for size and type of fields. Enter the following data, and prepare a report.

Date	Activity	Income	Exp.	Balance	Income Dues	Reg	Other	Expenses Reg	Logo	Supplies
	Special Mat Act									
	Original			855.44						
	Balance									
12/1	Annual dues	122.34			122.34					
12/8	Headquarters		98.00					98.00		
12/15	Material		5.45							5.45

21. Create a database to model a checkbook. A checkbook register contains the following information:

Date	Check#	Check/Deposit	Deposited	Cleared	Check	Balance
—	—	Original balance			$167.88	$2,300.00
8/13	233	Rent		50.00	133.44	
8/14	234	Utilities		101.00	51.22	
8/14	235	Telephone		31.22		
8/14	—	Salary check	$1200.77			
8/15	—	Sold radio	33.45	160.00	165.44	
8/15	236	Cash		102.33	87.88	
8/16	237	Food				

The bank records show the following:

```
Balance   We have added   We have subtracted                    Current Balance

Statement Number Deposits  Number  Checks  Service Charges
$2,300.00 3       $1,400.77 5       $676.86 $1.44               $3022.47
```

```
Checking Account Transactions
Date      Amount      Description

8/15    $1200.77        Deposit
8/16      33.45         Deposit
8/16     100.00         Deposit
```

```
Checks
Date    Amount

8/17    $167.88
8/17     133.44
8/18     165.44
8/18      87.88
8/18     122.22
```

At the beginning of the period, your balance and the bank's balance were the same. There were no outstanding transactions of any type.

In your database, start with your balance, add the not-cleared checks, subtract the unrecorded checks, subtract the not-cleared deposits, add the unrecorded deposits, make adjustments for errors in recording and service charges, and produce a final balance to be compared with the bank's. Compare the use of a database and spreadsheet to solve this problem.

CHAPTER 8

Image-driven Graphics

Goals

Upon completion of this chapter, you will be able to do the following:

- List the types of computer graphics.

- Review the differences between types of graphics programs.

- Identify where graphics can be used.

- Discuss the fundamental tasks of graphics.

- List some popular graphics programs.

- Identify the hardware needed for computer graphics.

Outline

A Retail Operation

Gleem Paint Center in Mobile, Alabama, is a retail paint store. In the late 1980s the store had about 10,000 square feet of space, seven employees, and a spectrometer paint-analyzing computer. It added a desktop microcomputer to handle its inventory and accounting needs, as well as perform some spreadsheet functions. It also required a laptop microcomputer and bar code reader for updating inventory records.

Entering the 1990s, Gleem found that changes necessitated the addition of two more desktop microcomputers. The store now has 25,000 square feet of paint and wallpaper showroom and warehouse space, along with an interior decorating department and 18 employees.

One of the new microcomputers was added to the accounting/bookkeeping department

and the second, to the interior decorating department. It was decided that the second would be a color system in order to take advantage of the graphics and architectural drawing capabilities. The interior designers could design interiors to scale and show customers the color schemes and alternate choices, different furniture styles and their suitability, wallpaper designs, and flooring or carpeting colors and designs. Quick, stylish, and complete floor plans can now be produced within an hour or less using computerized drawing and desktop publishing programs, and using their stored and scaled templates and symbols for doors, windows, and other interior elements.

An **image-driven graphics program** is a program that helps the user create/edit/capture/transfer images, save/retrieve, print, and integrate images with text. Sources of images (Figure 8–1) include image-driven graphics programs; graphic images screen capture programs for capturing and saving images created in spreadsheet or other programs; transfer from data-driven graphics programs; image, symbol, and **clip-art libraries;** specialized banner-drawing programs; engineering programs; and animation programs. An image-driven graphics program helps the user create/edit/capture/transfer images, save/retrieve, print, and integrate images with text. A clip-art library is a collection of images provided with image creation programs that can be recalled and used to create new illustrations. The Micros in Action "A Retail Operation" illustrates how a graphics design program was used to increase sales. The images in Figure 8–1 were obtained from both Lotus Freelance Plus and Harvard Graphics.

A scanner is used to scan any image printed or drawn on paper into a file that can be transferred into an image-creating and editing pro-

Image-driven graphics program
A program that helps the user create/edit/capture/transfer images, save/retrieve, print, and integrate images with text.

Clip art library
A collection of images provided with image creation programs that can be recalled and used to create new illustrations.

Figure 8–1

Sources of Images Using Lotus
Freelance Plus and Harvard
Graphics

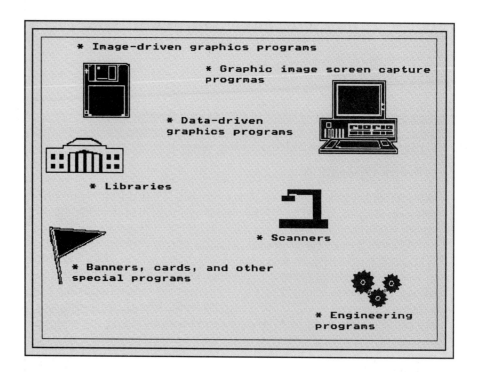

gram. Image-driven graphics programs can create images from scratch. In addition, programs such as Harvard Graphics, Lotus Freelance Plus, and PC Paintbrush either come with image libraries or have image libraries available for purchase.

Many image-driven and support programs exist. Specific image-driven program tasks are performed differently in each program. The image-driven programs used in this chapter are Animator, AutoCad, Auto-Sketch, Harvard Graphics, Lotus Freelance, PC Paintbrush IV, Publisher's Paintbrush, VP-Graphics, and Windows-Paint. Some of these programs are both data-driven and image-driven programs. The specialized image-driven programs used are ATLAS*GRAPHICS, Map-Master and PrintMaster. The support programs used are ComputerEyes, Frieze, HiJaak, and InSet. These programs are among the more popular ones available.

Why Image-driven Graphics?

Business, academic, personal, and other reports can be enhanced through the use of graphic images. An examination of almost any magazine illustrates how businesses use graphics to sell products and educate users about their potential use. The images are often used to attract the attention of readers.

Reports enhanced with both data-driven and image-driven graphics help sell more products, earn better grades, obtain jobs, and explain concepts and principles. They usually result in benefits greater in value than the effort used to produce the graphics. Graphics are a tool that you can use to improve your reports.

Image-driven Graphics Programs

The capabilities of image-driven graphics programs vary from single-screen drawing with simple tools to engineering drafting and architectural drawing. Generally, the costs of screen drawing programs are low and these programs produce limited-sized images while the costs of engineering and architectural programs are high and these programs are capable of producing large-sized drawings.

    The selection of an image-driven graphics program depends on the objective of using the display, the audience, and the method of presentation and reproduction. For example, images of beautiful young women, good-looking young men, movie stars, and so on have been added to illustrations to capture the attention of selective audiences. Image-driven graphics programs make it easy to combine images from several sources into a single display.

    Often, the medium used influences the selection of an image-driven graphics program. A graphic display can be used in publications (textbooks, newspapers, magazines, newsletters, and internal or business reports) and in presentations (using an overhead projector, photographic slides, and the computer screen). Each type of presentation may be the product of a different process. Computer output methods include the screen, cameras that photograph the display, direct transfer from computer memory to photographic media, a variety of printers, and a plotter printer.

Creating, Editing, Capturing, and Transferring Images

Image-creating and editing programs can be stand-alone programs or part of a data-driven graphics program. Image creating and editing includes drafting, drawing, freehand, and paint programs that help the user create, assemble, and enhance images. Image-driven programs often use **tool boxes,** which give the user power to manipulate and use arcs and circles, curves, lines and boxes, paint (color and crosshatching), points, text, area identification, move, copy, delete, enlarge-shrink, zoom, rotate, and invert.

    Most of these tasks can be performed by moving a screen **cursor,** using a **pointing device** such as a mouse, and using built-in menus or **function keys.** The cursor is the symbol on the monitor that indicates

Tool box
The set of capabilities that make it easy for the user to manipulate and use arcs and circles, curves, lines and boxes, paint (color and crosshatching), points, text, area identification, move, copy, delete, enlarge-shrink, zoom, rotate, and invert.

Cursor
A symbol on the monitor that indicates where an action will be started (such as drawing a line) or text will be typed. The cursor is often a dot (.), line (⎵), or box. It may be steady or blinking.

Pointing device
An input device that moves the screen cursor in a manner similar to the arrow keys. It usually includes keys that duplicate the function of the <Esc> and ↵ keys.

Function key
A computer keyboard key labeled F1, F2, and so on.

Icon
A symbol that represents choices in a screen menu.

where an action will be started (such as drawing a line) or text will be typed. The cursor is often a dot (.), line (—), or box. It may be steady or blinking. A pointing device is an input device that moves the screen cursor in a manner similar to the arrow keys. It usually includes keys that duplicate the function of the <Esc> and ↵ keys. The function keys are computer keyboard keys labeled F1, F2, and so on. Some capabilities of an image creating and editing program may be studied by examining the Publisher's Paintbrush tool box (Figure 8–2). Figure 8–2 was created in Publisher's Paintbrush by using their capture program (Frieze) to capture the screen and then adding text to the captured image (Figure 8–3).

Figures 8–2 and 8–3 show **icons** on the left. Icons are symbols that represent choices in a screen menu. In Figure 8–3, the icon pointer highlights the paintbrush, indicating that it is the active icon. Image-creating programs help users create, assemble, and edit pictures. They help users create original images and allow the use of image libraries. With these programs users can produce any image they can create in their imaginations.

Using a Mouse

The steps for drawing a line in PC Paintbrush IV Plus (using a mouse) follow:

> Select the pencil–line draw icon.
> Move the screen cursor to the starting position of the line. The cursor position is displayed in the screen's upper left.
> Press the left button.
> Move the cursor to the end of the line.
> Release the left button.

Figure 8–2
Publisher's Paintbrush Tool Box

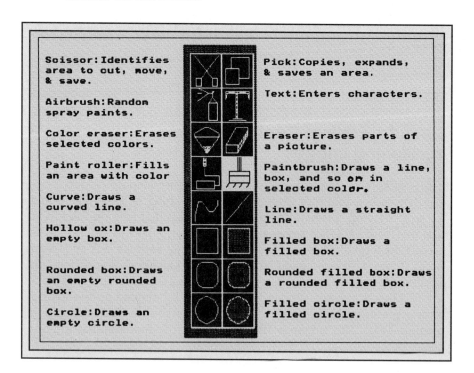

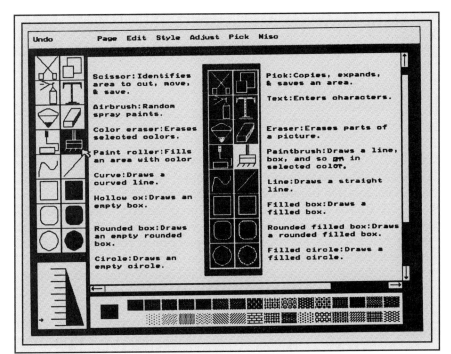

Figure 8–3
Using Publisher's Paintbrush

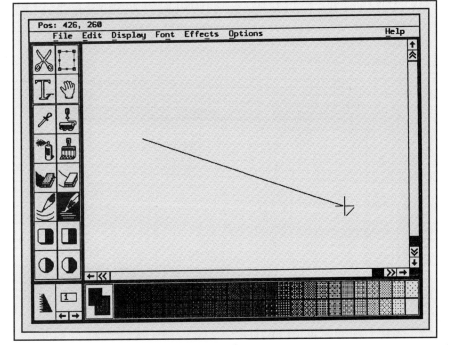

Figure 8–4
Drawing a Line in PC Paintbrush
IV Plus

The pencil–line draw icon is selected by moving the icon selector with the mouse to the desired icon and clicking the left button. Figure 8–4 illustrates a line being drawn from position column 96, row 150 to position column 426, row 260.

Draw and Paint

The following steps are used to draw an empty circle in PC Paintbrush IV Plus (using a mouse):

> Select the empty circle icon.
> Move the screen cursor to the center of the circle.
> Press the left button.
> Move the cursor to create the desired circle.
> Release the left button.

Figure 8–5 illustrates an empty circle (ellipse) being drawn from position column 96, row 150 to position column 80, row 287.

To fill the circle in Figure 8–5 with a pattern, activate the paint roller, select the pattern by moving the screen pointer to the desired pattern, and click the left button. Locate the paint roller within the circle, and click the left button. Figure 8–6 illustrates the results.

In Figure 8–7, using the PC Paintbrush IV Plus screen capture program, Frieze, the hand icon was captured and prepared for editing. Figure 8–7 illustrates the hand being covered by the gadget box icon with a second hand for moving. The gadget box is the top icon in the second column. Figure 8–8 illustrates the results after the hand has been moved to the middle of the screen.

One of the EDIT menu options is to invert the color within the gadget box. Figure 8–9 shows the results of the selection with the menu displayed. The other options in the EDIT menu include cut, copy, and paste. The cut and copy options allow the user to save a part of a picture for transfer to another picture.

Figure 8–5
Drawing a Circle in PC
Paintbrush IV Plus

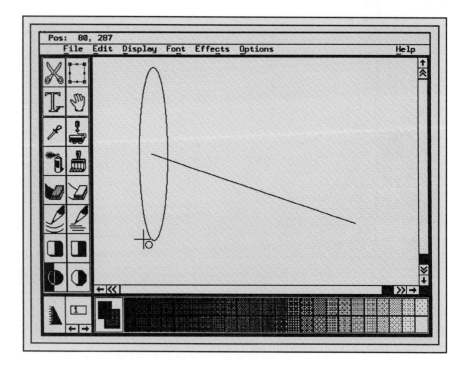

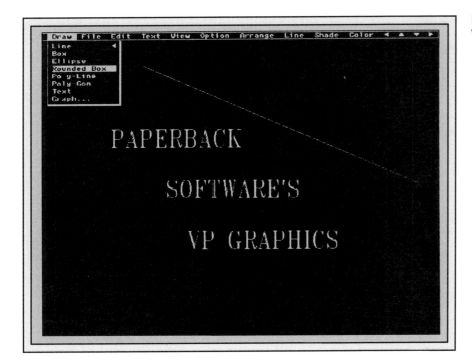

Figure 8–10
VP-Graphics Screen

Some programs allow users to control each and every pixel on the screen. Pixels can be turned on or off, or their colors can be changed.

Some programs, such as Publisher's Paintbrush, have the capability to manipulate images (shrink-grow, flip horizontally or vertically, tilt, and so on). Figure 8–11 illustrates the hand from PC Paintbrush IV Plus edited in Publisher's Paintbrush.

Zoom

The **zoom**-in and zoom-out capabilities of create and edit programs help the user visualize the final effect. Figure 8–12 illustrates the use of the zoom-in feature using the eagle file (provided with some copies of PC Paintbrush) in PC Paintbrush IV Plus.

Zoom
To move out for an overall view or move into a small portion of an image for an enlarged view of a small area.

Windows

The computer screen is too small to create large, high-quality images. One method programs use to increase the size of the working space available is to create a **virtual screen** and use the physical screen as a window into the virtual screen. A virtual screen is a large video display in the RAM of the computer. The physical screen is a display of a part of the virtual screen. Figure 8–13 illustrates a window on a large virtual screen.

Virtual screen
A large video display in the RAM of the computer. The physical screen is a display of a part of the virtual screen.

A part of an image can be created in part of the virtual screen. The cursor is moved to another part of the virtual screen, and then the image is completed. When the results are printed, the entire image is shown.

Figure 8–11
Editing Hand in Publisher's
Paintbrush

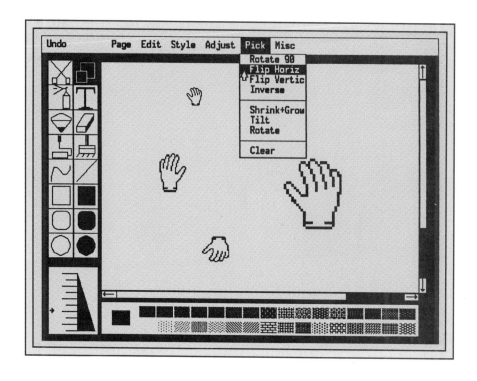

Figure 8–12
Use of Zoom-in for Editing in PC
Paintbrush IV Plus

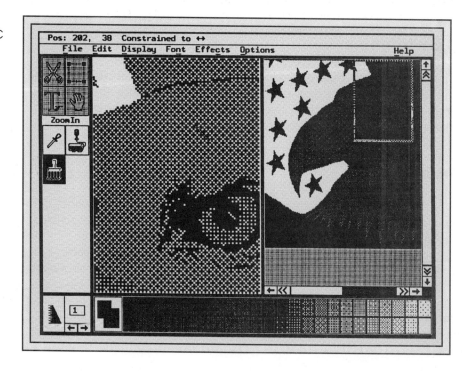

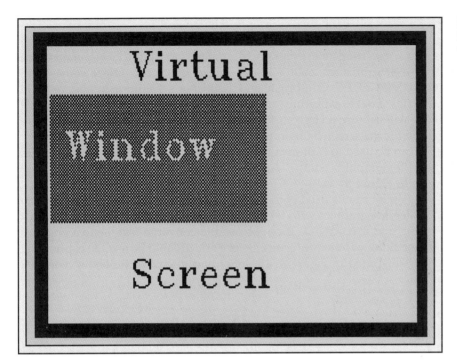

Figure 8–13
Physical Window to a Large
Virtual Screen

Screen Capture

The **graphics screen capture routine** can be used to capture a computer graphics screen display and then save it as a file. Usually, screen capture routines are part of a **terminate and stay resident (TSR) program** that can be called to the screen using **hot keys** and then used to capture a graphics (or text) computer screen display and save it as a file. TSR programs are loaded into memory and remain in memory while other programs are loaded and used. A TSR program once loaded may be recalled using a series of keys while some other program is running. Hot keys are combinations of keystrokes such as <Shift> + <Scroll Lock>. Often users can control the hot keys used for a particular TSR program.

When a computer displays a **text screen,** it uses a location in RAM to save ASCII code numbers to represent the screen display. When a computer displays a **graphics screen,** it uses a location in RAM to save the bit pattern displayed on the screen. A text screen displays characters controlled by ASCII code numbers saved in computer memory. A graphics screen is a bit image pattern on a screen controlled by a bit image pattern saved in the computer memory. Text screen capture programs only capture text screens. Some graphics screen capture programs capture both text and graphics screens while others only capture graphics screens.

Rather than being TSR, some graphics screen capture programs require that you use them to load the program from which the screen will be captured. For example, when using a capture program named CAP.COM and a drawing program named DRAW.EXE, the loading instruction CAP DRAW ↵ is required. As a result, the capture program CAP can be used to capture any screen created in DRAW. When an exit command is given to leave DRAW, CAP is terminated.

Graphics screen capture routine
A routine that can be used to capture a computer graphics screen display and then save it as a file. Most screen capture routines are part of TSR programs.

Terminate and stay resident (TSR) program
A program that is loaded into memory and remains in memory while other programs are loaded and used. Once loaded, a TSR program can be recalled using a series of keys while some other program is running.

Hot keys
The key combination that calls a TSR program to the screen.

Text screen
Characters on a screen controlled by ASCII code numbers saved in computer memory.

Graphics screen
A bit image pattern on a screen controlled by a bit image pattern saved in the computer memory.

Because of the many graphics files used by each individual program, screen capture programs have become a popular method of transferring a file from one program to another. Among the popular screen capture programs are ZSoft's Frieze and InSet's InSet. Frieze comes with most copies of PC Paintbrush and Publisher's Paintbrush. Figure 8–14 illustrates Frieze capturing an Aston-Tate Map-Master screen display. Frieze will capture a large variety of graphics screens, but it must be configured for the screen being captured. Frieze will not capture a text screen. InSet can be used to capture a text screen and then convert it to a graphics screen for graphics editing. InSet was used to capture the display with Frieze in Figure 8–14.

InSet can be used with many word processing packages to capture and integrate graphics with text output. InSet automatically captures most graphics and text screens. It can be used to convert a text file to a graphics file for editing or other purposes. Before Frieze could be used to capture the screen illustrated in Figure 8–15, InSet had to covert the text screen to a graphics screen.

Scanning

Scanner
A device for sensing printed material (text and graphics) or images and entering them into a computer system.

A **scanner** is a device for reading printed material into a computer system. Currently, scanners are most effective with line art and next most effective with black-and-white photographs. They have the most difficulty with color photographs.

Gray tone
One of a continuous series of colors from black to white.

Halftone
A picture made by a photographic process that uses dots of different sizes to simulate gray tones.

Black-and-white photographs use a continuous series of tones from black to white, referred to as **gray tones.** Gray tones are a continuous series of colors from black to white. **Halftones** are pictures made by a photographic process that use different sizes of dots to simulate gray tones. **Dithering** is the grouping of pixels on a computer screen to simulate the gray tones. Figure 8–16 illustrates the difference between these approaches. Hand scanners often have dithering controls built in as part of their hardware. Micros in Action "Preparing Reports" illustrates how to edit graphics for a retail application.

Micros in Action

Cut and Paste

The interior designer at Gleem Paint Center selected her colors from the color chart. She then located the symbols to represent a den with a couch, two armchairs, several tables, and lamps. She used the drawing program to lay out the walls and locate the symbol for each piece of furniture.

Using the color display, the interior designer illustrated the customer's room on the screen. The designer and customer discussed the colors selected, changes were made, and a final selection was agreed upon. The computer was then asked to print the paint-mixing instructions.

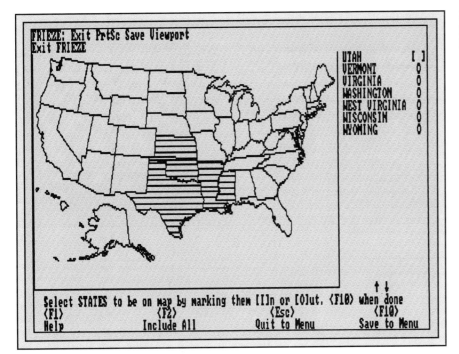

Figure 8–14
Frieze Capture of a
Map-Master Screen Display

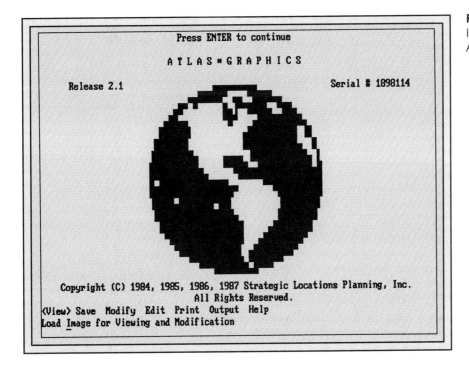

Figure 8–15
InSet Capture of
ATLAS*GRAPHICS

Figure 8–16
Halftones versus Dithering

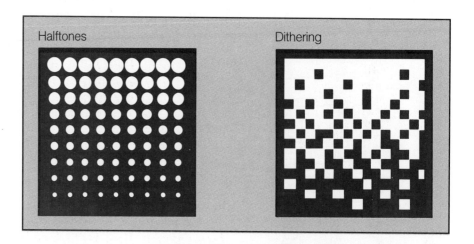

Figure 8–17
Dithered Video Image

Dithering
A method of representing gray tones through the use of areas of dots with varying densities.

Among the scanning devices available are PC boards that allow the user to connect a video device, such as a videocassette recorder (VCR) or video camera, to a microcomputer. Video scanner boards use software to control the dithering. Figure 8–17 illustrates a dithered image captured by a video camera picture of a black and white photograph. Figure 8–18 illustrates the controls available in the ComputerEyes program, and Figure 8–19 shows the same image shown in Figure 8–18 using halftones.

The best sequence of steps for capturing a video image, saving the image as a file, and printing the image depends on the source of the image, the size of the file saved, the type of files used to save the image, the program used to convert the gray scales to bits, the size of the picture printed, and the printer used. The original image in ComputerEyes and

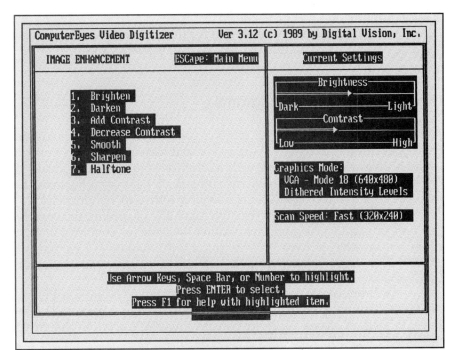

Figure 8–18
Enhancement Controls in
ComputerEyes

Figure 8–19
Halftone Image

many other scanners contains gray scale data. In ComputerEyes, when the original image is saved as a .RAW or .TIF file, the gray scale data are saved. A laser (and dot-matrix) printer might print a bit image file (300 dots per inch). The key step in obtaining high quality gray tone printed images seems to be the program that converts the gray scale data to bit image data for printing. In some gray scale to bit image conversion programs, the exact number of dots can be specified. If the dots converted are matched to the dots printed, good results can be obtained in many cases.

Libraries and Transfer Programs

Libraries of clip art, images, and symbols can be purchased or saved from earlier work. Many drawing programs are sold with libraries. It is easier to create a display using predesigned art from a library than to create an original display. Figure 8–20 illustrates the eagle (shown in Figure 8–12) that was a PC Paintbrush file being edited in Microsoft Windows-Paint.

A **file transfer program** has the capability of reading the code for one type of graphics file and then writing the code for another. An **algorithm** (set of rules) is used to make the transformation. No matter how good the transformation algorithm is, some data are lost when making the transformation.

The popular file transfer program HiJaak provides one way of moving the PC Paintbrush file to a Microsoft Windows file. Figure 8–21 illustrates the HiJaak screen ready to transfer EAGLE.PCX (a PC Paintbrush file) to EAGLE.MSP (a Microsoft Paint [Version 2]) file.

Table 8–1 lists the files that HiJaak can transfer and their extensions. HiJaak transfers files from one format to another, captures material as it is printed and saves it in a file, and handles data transmission through **facsimile (FAX) machines,** devices used to transmit images over telephone lines. HiJaak integrates the files produced by different programs.

File transfer program
A program with the capability of reading the code for one type of graphics file and then writing the code for another. An algorithm is used to make the transformation.

Algorithm
A set of rules to perform some mathematical operation.

Facsimile (FAX) machine
A machine used to transmit images over telephone lines.

Figure 8–20
PC Paintbrush Eagle in Windows-Paint

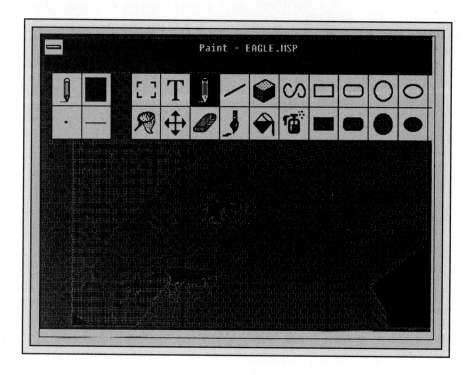

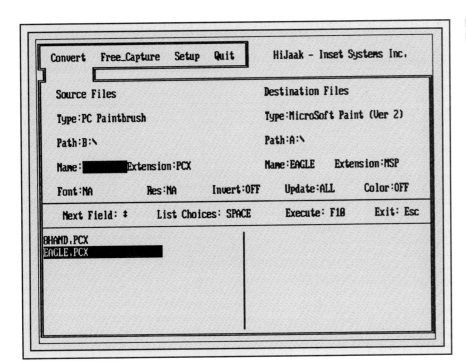

Figure 8–21
Using HiJaak

Many data-driven graphics programs include a symbol library. Symbol libraries provide graphics images that can be transferred to both image-driven and data-driven programs. Harvard Graphics and Lotus Freelance include many predrawn symbols that a user can add to charts. Figures 8–22 and 8–23 illustrates some of the symbols available.

Saving and Retrieving

The save and retrieve routines of image-driven graphics programs are menu driven. Figure 8–24 illustrates the RETRIEVE (LOAD) file menu in Publisher's Paintbrush.

Most graphics programs have their own data file storage methods. A few programs can read files created by other programs. Transfer programs can move files from one format to another. One reason for differences between program graphic files is the method of data representation. Some programs use **raster** (digital) information, whereas others use **vector** (starting location, direction, and distance) information.

Digitized data are what you see on the screen. A line consisting of 50 pixels in a row is saved as 50 lighted pixels. Macintosh users refer to raster graphics programs as paint programs.

A vector is defined by the x and y positions of its starting point, the distance (length of the line), and the angle in which the line goes from the

Raster
A program that saves images as a series of on-off dots.

Vector
A program that saves images using mathematical formulas, including the starting location, direction, and distance of each line.

Table 8–1
HiJaak File Transfer

File Extension	File
.CPF	Complete PC Files
.CPS	PostScript files with extensions for color bit-map printers
.CTF	GannaFax files
.CUT	Dr. Halo files
.ESP	Encapsulated PostScript files
.FAX	CCITT Group 3 (bits oriented right to left) for Gamma Fax, TEO . . . cards
.GAM	GammaFax file format
.GIF	CompuServe Graphic Image Format files
.HPC	LaserJet files
.IFF	Amiga files
.IMG	GEM Paint files
.JTF	JT Fax file format
.MAC	Macintosh files
.MCX	Intel Connection CoProcessor files
.MH	TeliFax "500" files
.MP1	Microsoft Windows-Paint (Version 1.0)
.MSP	Microsoft Windows-Paint (Version 2.0)
.PCC	PC Paintbrush cut files
.PCL	HP LaserJet files
.PCX	PC Paintbrush
.PGL	HPGL pen plotter—HP 7440 pen plotter
.PIC	Lotus 1-2-3 files
.PIX	Inset files
.PM	PrintMaster files
.RIC	Ricoh Fax file format (one-dimensional)
.SHP	NewsMaster files
.TIF	TIFF uncompressed files
.TXT	Text files
.WFG	WordPort files
.WPG	WordPerfect graphics files (raster data only)
.XFX	JetFax and EFax files

starting point. Images saved as digitized graphics may result in errors when the scale of a drawing is changed (expanded or contracted). A vector, in contrast, is independent of scale. The scale of graphics saved as vectors can be changed with no loss of quality. Macintosh users refer to vector programs as draw programs.

Programs using digitized graphics data allow you to enter data by moving the cursor to draw a line or figure. Programs using vector graphic data require the identification of the beginning of a line, its direction, and

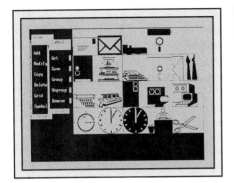
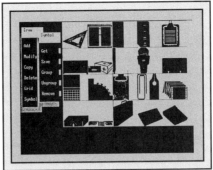

Figure 8–22
Harvard Graphics Symbols

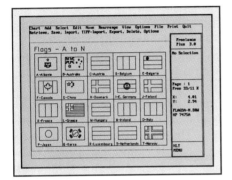
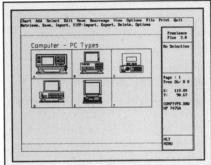

Figure 8–23
Lotus Freelance Symbols

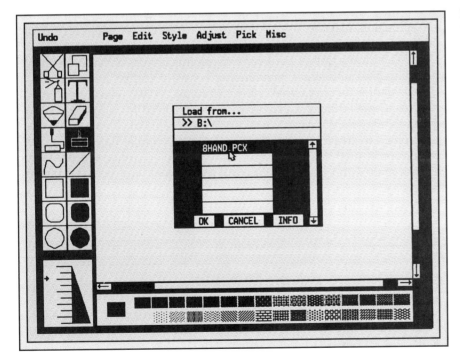

Figure 8–24
RETRIEVE File Menu in Publisher's
Paintbrush

its distance. Often on the screen you enter the beginning and end of a line, and the program calculates the information needed to store the line. Vector graphics are independent of the number of pixels on a screen.

Graphics save routines (raster and vector) are similar to routines for saving other types of data files. The data files are unique for each type of graphics.

Printing

The capability to print graphics is a function of both the printer-plotter hardware and the software. The software must send specific codes to the printer or plotter to make it perform in a particular manner. The user must make sure a software package supports the specific printer or plotter.

Graphics programs come with a number of printer-plotter drivers that are installed when the program is first used or are selected when the user gives the print command. Each printer-plotter driver is designed to handle a set of codes. Some coding systems are used on a variety of different printers. The Epson codes are popular with many printer manufacturers, but there is no standard for plotters. Thus, if a specific plotter is not listed in a program's printer selection, it probably cannot be used.

Laser printers can be designed to emulate (act like) a number of printers. When a laser printer is emulating a particular printer, the codes used for that printer will produce the same results on the laser printer as on the original printer. **Emulations** (hardware or software) allow the user to have the features of a number of machines available in one machine. One emulation may be used for text and another for graphics on the same page.

Emulation
Hardware or software that permits one device to act like another device.

The production of hard copy of graphic images is limited by hardware more than software. Obtaining hard copy of graphic images requires a printer-plotter that uses dots, ink jet, or lines. A daisy wheel printer that produces a solid character generally cannot be used for graphics. An exception to this rule is a daisy wheel printer with special characters that can be combined to create images. Among the more popular hard copy graphics production methods (black and white and color) are screen photography, dot-matrix and laser printers, ink-jet printers, and pens on plotter-printers.

Special Image-driven Graphics

There are a number of image-driven graphics programs designed for special-purpose applications, such as the creation of banners, cards, posters, engineering drawings, and animation.

Banners, Cards, and Posters

PrintMaster is an inexpensive program for producing banners, calendars, cards, posters, and stationary. Banners are useful for social events, professional meetings, and so on. Calendars with custom graphic symbols can help advertise meetings and groups. Cards are useful for greetings and meeting notices. The poster and stationary options can be used to create covers for effective reports.

The opening screen of PrintMaster Plus V2.0 has a menu pointer located at the selection Banner. Pressing ↵ begins the banner option. PrintMaster has a menu for creating a new banner, printing a banner, or editing a banner. After selecting new banner, PrintMaster displays its banner-creating menu (Figure 8–25).

PrintMaster allows you to use existing graphic symbols, edit existing symbols, or create your own symbols. These same symbols can be used in any of the PrintMaster options. Figure 8–26 illustrates the selection of a symbol.

Figure 8–27 illustrates the use of PrintMaster's preview function. The completed banner required eight sheets of paper once it was output. If the banner is produced on a dot-matrix printer using tractor feed paper, it is ready to hang up and use. The PrintMaster poster option can be used to produce a cover for a report and similarly previewed.

Engineering Applications

Engineers, architects, and some artists require drawing programs that provide accurate screen cursor location and dimensionally accurate drawings.

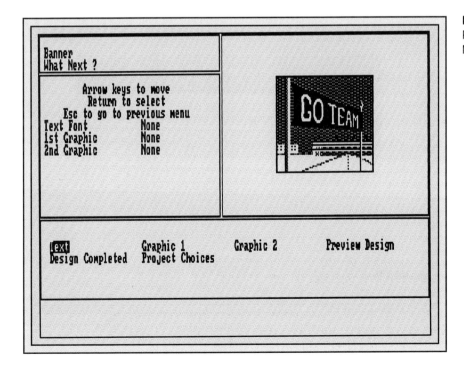

Figure 8–25
PrintMaster Plus V2.0 Banner Menu

Figure 8–26
PrintMaster Symbol Selection

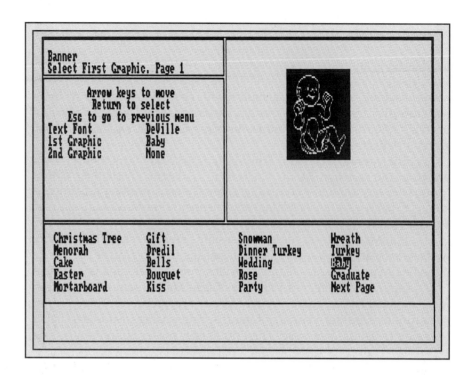

Figure 8–27
Preview of Banner in PrintMaster

Engineering drawing programs contain many of the same types of mouse controls, menus, and file-handling procedures as drawing programs.

Generally, engineering programs use vector graphics, and freehand drawing programs use raster graphics. Programs using bit image (raster) graphics are generally better for images that start as bit images, such as scanned material and screens captured from other programs. Programs that use vector graphics are better for images that must be expanded, shrunk, rotated in space, relocated on the screen, and drawn accurately on screen and paper. Table 8–2 illustrates some applications that are better performed using raster graphics, some that are better performed using vector graphics, and some that can be performed by either type of program.

The characteristics that separate engineering programs from drawing programs include capabilities such as accurate cursor location on the screen, accurate sizing on the screen and printer, unlimited zoom capabilities, and the use of vector graphics for scale control. Vector graphics programs include **computer-aided design (CAD)** and **computer-aided design and drafting (CADD).** CAD and CADD programs can be used to create drawings of products. Both types of programs often allow the user to locate the cursor on the screen by using a mouse or by entering in the cursor's new location. Usually, the programs use vector graphics and provide the user with unlimited zoom capabilities. Drawing programs using raster graphics are limited in their zoom capabilities by the number and size of pixels. Figure 8–28 illustrates the ZOOM menu in AutoDesk's AutoSketch using one of the package's sample drawings.

Computer-aided design (CAD)
Vector graphics programs with the capability to produce drawings for machine parts and other products. The design tools are the dominant feature.

Computer-aided design and drafting (CADD)
Vector graphics programs with the capability to produce drawings for machine parts and other products. There is a balance between design and drafting tools.

Table 8–2
Raster versus Vector Graphics

Raster Graphics Are Better for:	Either Can Be Used in:	Vector Graphics Are Better for:
Digitized photographs	Work-flow charts	Architectural drawings
Screen capture transfer	Organizational diagrams	Interior design
	Proposals	Facility layout, planning, and design
	Presentations	Animation
	Greeting cards	Topographic maps
	Clip art	Nautical charts
		Yacht design
		Technical illustrations
		Fine art
		Engineering drawing

Figure 8–28
Using the Zoom Menu in
AutoSketch

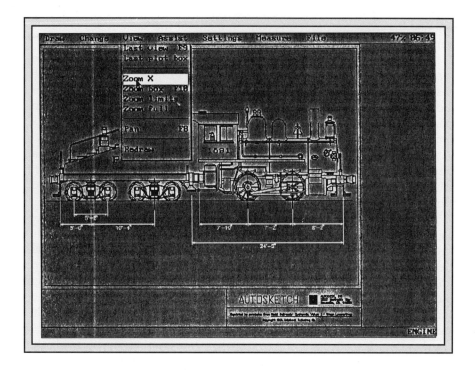

Engineering drawing programs, such as AutoDesk's AutoCAD, are found on a number of systems, including Macintosh OS, MS-DOS, OS/2, PC DOS, UNIX, and VMS (an operating system for mainframe computers). Any training received on AutoCAD in one system can be carried over to other systems. In addition, a number of support programs take the data file created in AutoCAD and automatically produce code ready for computer-aided manufacturing (CAM) or other purposes.

Figure 8–29 illustrates the opening menu in AutoCAD. An example data file, AIRPLANE, has been identified for loading. Figure 8–30 illustrates the initial view of an airplane. Using a mouse, the cursor can be moved to the top of the screen and the DISPLAY menu selected. Selection of the ∃D viewpoint (V point) option results in the display illustrated in Figure 8–31. Figure 8–32 illustrates another view of the airplane. When designing a product, the capability of viewing the object from a number of different angles helps eliminate errors.

Data- and Image-driven Graphics

Some data-driven graphics programs, such as Harvard Graphics, Lotus Freelance Plus, and VP-Graphics, and most image-driven graphics programs can be used to combine data-driven output and images. Figure 8–33 illustrates a Harvard Graphics bar chart with an image added. Figure 8–34 illustrates a Lotus 1-2-3 graph combined with the digitized image of a child using Publisher's Paintbrush.

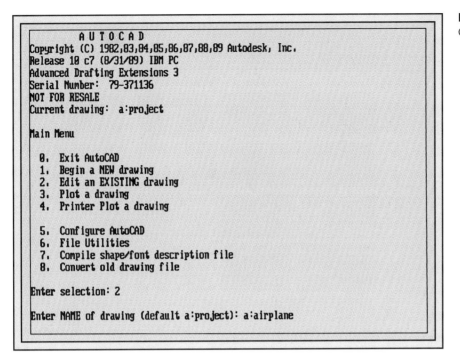

Figure 8–29
Opening Menu in AutoCAD

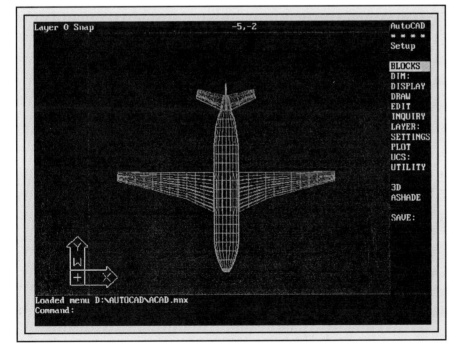

Figure 8–30
Initial View of an Airplane in AutoCAD

Figure 8–31
Selecting a New Viewing Angle
in AutoCAD

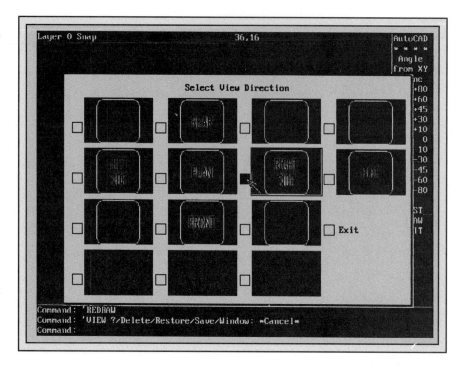

Figure 8–32
New Viewing Angle in AutoCAD

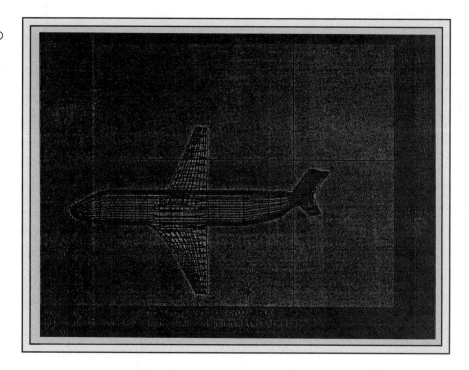

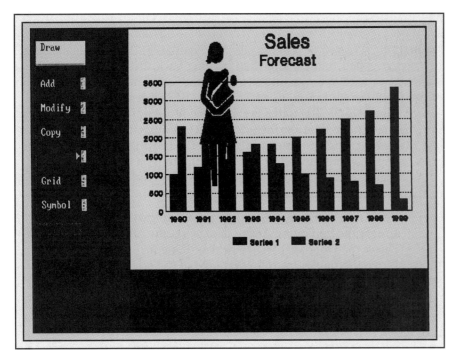

Figure 8–33
Harvard Graphics Using an
Image within a Bar Chart

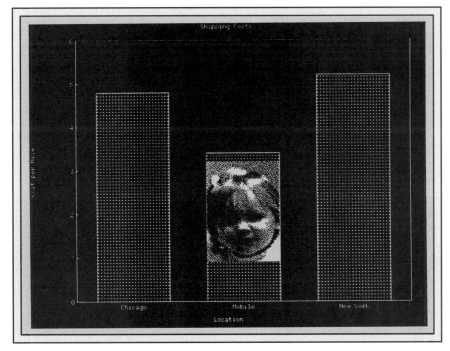

Figure 8–34
Child's Image Added to a Bar
Chart in Lotus 1-2-3

Animation

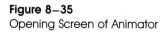

Animation
The creation of displays that look
like moving objects on the screen.

Animation is created by making selected changes in individual still images in a series (called frames) and then playing back these images at a speed sufficient to trick the eye into believing that the images are moving. To create the illusion of motion, a minimum of two frames is needed.

Figure 8–35 illustrates the opening screen of AutoDesk's Animator. The menus and controls include all the creating/editing, saving/retrieving, displaying, and printing capabilities of a drawing or engineering program, as well as the capability to control the motion of images.

Figure 8–36 illustrates two screens of an animation sequence. The following steps are required to create the animation:

Select the DEFINE STARTING IMAGE menu.
Create the beginning image (a star) on the left side of the screen.
Select the DEFINE ENDING IMAGE menu.
Move the points from the left side of the screen to the right one
    at a time to create the car on the right side of the screen.
Select the ANIMATION menu.
Select the animation characteristics, such as speed.
Instruct Animator to display the animation.

The animation procedure in Figure 8–36 is just one of a number of optional image motions available using Animator. Fixed images can be moved and shapes changed from one shape to another. The program has a large number of capabilities that take a little time and effort to master.

Figure 8–35
Opening Screen of Animator

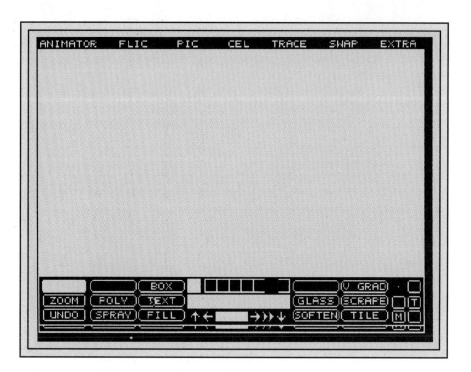

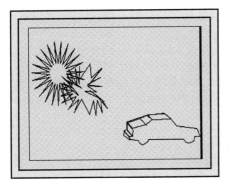 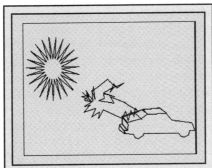

Figure 8—36
Animation Using Animator

Image-driven Graphics Hardware

The number of quality image-driven creating/editing programs has increased and the programs' costs have decreased as microcomputer capabilities have grown. Image-driven programs are available for many low-end MS-DOS/PC DOS systems. Generally, image-driven programs require a large amount of RAM, fast on-line data storage, good-quality monitors and video boards, math co-processors, scanners, video cameras, good-quality printers, and usually a mouse. MS-DOS/PC DOS computers can be configured for image-driven graphics applications. Most Macintosh models are ready for image-driven graphics without additions.

The RAM is needed to store the large amount of data for a graphic image. On-line storage is needed to store the images. Good-quality monitors and video boards are required to display the images. Math co-processors help reduce the amount of time needed to process and display an image. Scanners and video cameras reduce the complexity of the task of transferring images into the computer. Printers, plotters, and other high-resolution output devices produce the final result.

A mouse should be used with all graphics programs, even those that offer the option of using the keyboard arrow keys. With a mouse you can point (move the mouse on a surface to relocate the cursor on the screen), click (quickly press a button), and press (hold a button down). Each program controls the functions of the mouse buttons. A typical two-button mouse was used to create all the illustrations in this chapter. When a three-button mouse is used with programs designed for two-button devices, the middle button usually is disabled.

Summary

An image-driven graphics program is a program that helps the user create/edit/capture/transfer images, save/retrieve, print, and integrate images with text. Clip-art libraries are collections of images provided with image creation programs that can be recalled into image-driven graphics programs and used to create new illustrations.

Image-driven graphic programs use tool boxes. A tool box is a set of capabilities that make it easy for the user to manipulate and use arcs, circles, curves, lines, boxes, paint (color and cross-hatching), points, text, area identification, and to move, copy, delete, enlarge-shrink, zoom, rotate, and invert.

Image-driven graphic programs use a screen cursor for specifying the location on the monitor where the next action will be started. Actions include drawing a line, entering text, erasing a color, drawing a box, and so on. A pointing device such as a mouse is used to locate the cursor. Zoom-in for an enlarged view or Zoom-out for an overall view are often-used features of image-driven programs. To create large images, a virtual screen is used. A virtual screen is the creation of a (large) video display in the RAM of the computer. The physical screen is a display of a part of the virtual screen.

Terminate and stay resident (TSR) graphics screen capture programs are used to transfer graphics into image-driven programs. Scanners may be used to scan printed material, including gray tone photographs. The computer uses halftones (dots of different sizes) and dithering (varying patterns of dots) to create gray tones.

A file transfer program is another method of transferring images into an image-driven graphics program. A file transfer program is a program with the capability of reading the code for one type of graphics file and then writing the code for another. One reason why transferring graphics between programs may be difficult is that two different data storage methods are used: raster and vector. A raster program is a program that saves images as a series of on/off dots. A vector program is a program that saves images using mathematical formulas, including the starting location, direction, and distance of each line.

Key Terms

Algorithm
Animation
Clip art library
Computer-aided
    design (CAD)
Computer-aided
    design and drafting
    (CADD)
Cursor
Dithering
Emulation
Facsimile (FAX)
    machine

File transfer program
Function key
Graphics screen
Graphics screen
    capture routine
Gray tone
Halftone
Hot keys
Icon
Image-driven graphics
    program
Pointing device
Raster

Scanner
Terminate and stay
    resident (TSR)
    program
Text screen
Tool box
Vector
Virtual screen
Zoom

Review Questions

1. What is an image-driven graphics program? What would you use one for?
2. What is a clip art library? How is a clip art library useful?
3. What is a tool box? Give some examples of capabilities found in a graphics tool box.
4. What is a cursor? In an image-driven graphics program, what does one look like?
5. What pointing devices are used for editing graphics? What is the procedure for drawing a line with a pointing device?
6. How are function keys used in an image-driven graphics program?
7. What is an icon? What are icons used for?
8. Explain how the zoom feature works.
9. What is a virtual screen? What is a physical screen? How does a physical screen relate to a virtual screen?
10. What is a graphics screen capture routine?
11. What are the differences between graphics and text screen capture routines?
12. What is a TSR program? Why is one needed?
13. What are hot keys? How are they used?
14. What is the difference between a text and a graphics screen display?
15. What is a scanner? How is one used to capture images?
16. What are gray tones? What is a halftone? What is dithering? Why would you use it?
17. What does a file transfer program do? Why is one needed?
18. What is the importance of the algorithm used to transfer files?
19. What is raster graphics? What is vector graphics? Why are both types needed?
20. What is animation? How is it used?

Discussion and Application Questions

1. Using magazines and newspapers, find an article on computer graphics and report on its observations.
2. Find an article on the use of television cameras and computer graphics. What do you think the future developments in this area will be?
3. Find an article in either computer magazines or industrial publications on the use of computer-generated backgrounds for movies and television. What potential use do these capabilities have in business?
4. Discuss the value of computer-generated graphics in presentations and reports for your other courses.

Laboratory Assignments

1. Using an image-driven graphics program, create a box and draw a circle in it. Paint the area of the box that is not part of the circle. Add some text. The following is an example:

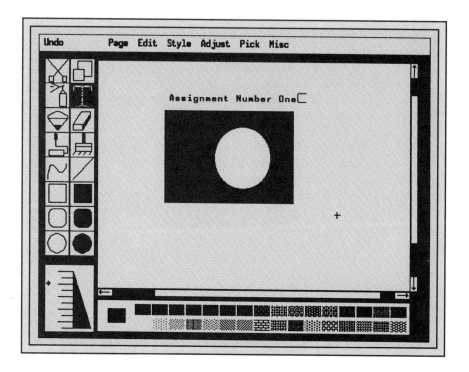

2. Using an image-driven graphics program, create a cover page for a school report.

3. Create a pie chart in your spreadsheet program, data-driven graphics program, on both. Read the manual on your image-driven graphics program, and then import the image into this program or show that it cannot be done. Enhance the chart.

CHAPTER 9

Desktop Publishing

Goals

Upon completion of this chapter, you will be able to do the following:

- Identify sources of text and graphics.

- Describe how fonts can be controlled and used in desktop publishing.

- List methods of combining text and graphics.

- Describe text and graphics merging routines.

- Review page layout programs.

Outline

Using Image-driven Graphics

Imagineering Concepts is a 23-year-old advertising and public relations agency that employs six professionals in various fields. There is a commercial artist, a photographer, a public relations specialist, an advertising specialist, a writer, and the owner, who specializes across all fields. The agency has prospered through the years and has recently become computerized.

Among the requirements for their computer system, Imagineering Concepts indicated a need for the following:

- Word processing for correspondence.
- Databases for client and marketing characteristics, advertising outlets, mailing lists, and label preparation.
- Spreadsheets for data-driven graphics and client reference, estimates, proposals, and so on.

- Graphics programs to edit scanned material; draw; produce full-color materials; create logos; and make finished artwork for catalogs, stockholders' reports, corporate annual reports, and so on.
- Desktop publishing to make typeset copy for advertising, brochures, newsletters, reports, catalogs, and so on.

The system the agency now owns contains five computers that are networked together, three laser printers, one ink-jet printer, one plotter, and two 24-pin dot-matrix printers. It also has installed a facsimile (FAX) machine to send clients preliminary artwork for approval.

Desktop publishing is the creation of a quality document using the microcomputer and specialized **page layout** (composition) software. A **page layout program** helps the user lay out (arrange) text and graphics on a page for printing. The objective of many desktop publishing activities is to produce a document that looks as if it were typeset. Micros in Action "Using Image-driven Graphics" indicates the advantages of using desktop publishing for business purposes.

Desktop publishing software refers to programs that help users create/edit/transfer, format/integrate text and graphics, save/retrieve, and print/typeset output on a good-quality output device. The original text and graphics creation can be performed in most desktop publishing programs; however, an alternate way is to use word processing, spreadsheet, data-driven graphics, database, and image-driven graphics programs for the original creation and then transfer the text or images into the desktop publishing program. A key task of the desktop publishing program is the formatting of text and graphics on each page, including the font selection. The final task is producing hard copy on a printer or creating a file that can be transferred to a typesetting device.

Desktop publishing
The creation of a quality document using the microcomputer and specialized page composition software.

Page layout
The arrangement of text and graphics on a page for printing.

Page layout program
A program that helps the user lay out a page for printing. Usually, text and graphics are imported from other programs and then combined in a page layout program.

Desktop publishing software
Programs that help users create/edit/transfer, format/integrate text and graphics, save/retrieve, and print/typeset output on a good-quality output device.

Many desktop publishing and support programs exist. Specific desktop publishing program tasks are performed differently in each program. The desktop programs used in this chapter are Aldus PageMaker and NewsMaster. The support programs used are Allways, FONTASTIC, Microsoft Works, Omnipage 386, Publisher's Type Foundry, Quattro Pro, ReadRight, UltraScript PC, and WordPerfect. These programs are among the more popular ones available.

Why Desktop Publishing?

Desktop publishing programs expand the capabilities of word processors, spreadsheet programs, and database programs and integrate the output of data-driven and image-creating programs with other programs. Desktop publishing programs help improve the output of written documents.

The quality of presentation influences a reader's perception of the value of a report. A better-looking report may get a better grade, get read by the boss first, and produce better results.

Desktop Publishing

Desktop publishing includes page layout, typesetting, pasteup, proofreading, production editing, and coordination. A number of microcomputer methods can help users produce documents that looks as if they have been typeset:

Cut and paste from word processing programs (text) and graphics programs (art).
Font creation and control programs.
Word processors combined with graphics-merging programs.
Page layout programs.

Desktop publishing programs—both high-end programs (powerful programs with many features), such as Aldus PageMaker, and low-end programs (those with fewer features and lower cost), such as NewsMaster—are built around the page layout activity. Figure 9–1 illustrates the page layout screen of Aldus PageMaker, and Figure 9–2 illustrates the page layout screen of NewsMaster.

Depending on your computer hardware and software, the process of creating a page may approach WYSIWYG (what you see is what you get). Complete WYSIWYG can be obtained by matching computer hardware (monitor and graphics display board), programs, and printers, or by performing all text displays and printing in graphics mode. The page layout program must have complete knowledge of what the printer can do in

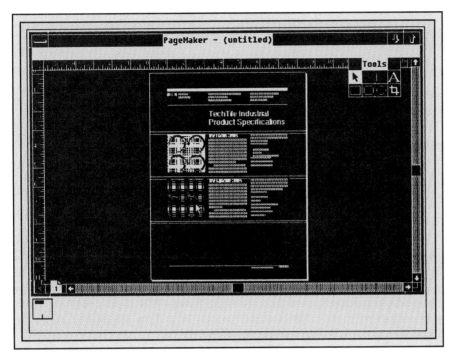

Figure 9–1
PageMaker Page Layout Screen

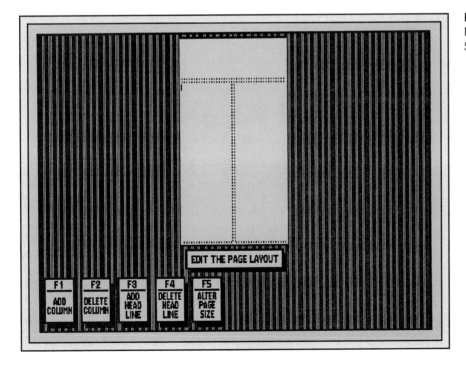

Figure 9–2
NewsMaster Page Layout
Screen

order to create and display matching fonts on the screen. Historically, the capabilities of the components have not been matched, and graphics has been used to obtain WYSIWYG.

Text

Text includes characters (letters and numbers), words, sentences, and paragraphs. Text is stored as numbers in the computer using a coding system such as American Standard Code for Information Interchange (ASCII). Generally, text files created by one program can be transferred to another program either directly or by first converting the file into an ASCII file that conforms exactly to the standard file and then transferring the new file to the second program.

Sources of text include computer data files (word processing, spreadsheet, database, and other files), keyboard entry, remote data collection devices, bar code readers, and the scanning of printed matter with an optical character recognition (OCR) routine (Figure 9–3). When bar code readers, remote data entry devices, and OCR procedures are used, the normal method is to save the results in a data file before importing them into a desktop publishing package.

Graphics

Graphics are often needed in written documents or as part of a publication. Sources of graphics include data-generated graphics program files, image-

Figure 9–3
Sources of Text

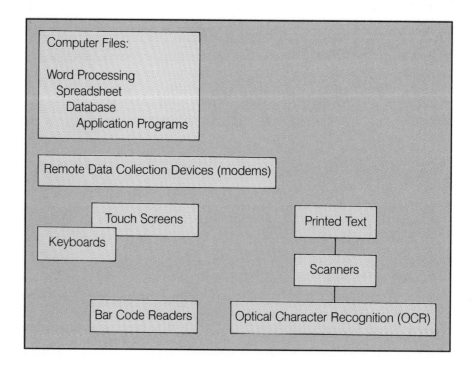

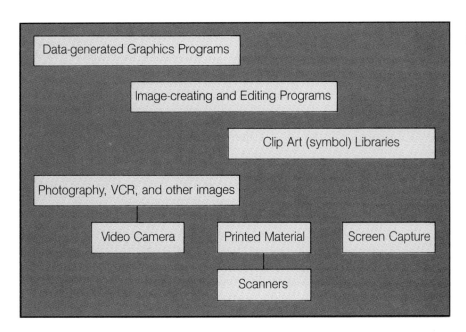

Figure 9–4
Sources of Graphic Files

creating and editing program (including engineering program) files, scanned images or real-life and printed material files, clip art library files, and screen capture files (Figure 9–4).

Good Practice

A document is usually created to communicate an idea or concept to a target audience. The creation of a page starts with the identification of the objective of the page. Examine a page from a newspaper, magazine, textbook, and children's book. Each has a different style. The style is controlled by the graphic artist to improve communications with the target audience.

The graphic artist considers many factors when creating a page. There are no absolute rules to follow. Think about the final design; visualization is the designer's tool. Beginners should consider the following guidelines:

Do not use more than two **typefaces** per page.
Be conservative in the use of unusual typefaces.
Integrate words and graphics—tie them together.
Use size and type variations within a typeface—headers should be in larger type than text.
Use **italics** rather than reverse video, bold, or underlining.
Limit the use of all capital letters to headings.
Use large-sized text for slides and overhead transparencies.
Make the length of a line approximately two times the width of an alphabet list (a, b, c, . . ., z).

Typeface
A set of similar characters that are available in a variety of sizes.

Italic
A font type that resembles handwriting (script); however, the characters are not joined.

Options

Sales of desktop publishing programs are increasing, but many users are turning their backs on these page layout programs in favor of updated versions of their favorite word processing programs. With the introduction of desktop publishing to the office environment, companies saw the need to put life and pizzazz into their documents. Desktop publishing enabled many companies to produce newsletters for employee and customer relations uses. However, problems arose when a company employed no people trained in the graphic arts. The time required to learn the operation of the new program restricted other company functions, and the added requirements of peripheral hardware strained company budgets.

What, then, are the advantages of desktop publishing programs over the word processor? Text and graphics can be integrated, and versatile type fonts are available. However, many of today's word processing programs contain text and graphics integration, page preview features, and support for laser printers that allow access to different type fonts. Users have found ways to enhance documents, add graphics to a proposal, and highlight special information. All this is available without the need to switch from word processing to another program.

If your needs require true WYSIWYG capabilities, support for more than three columns of type, importation of bit-mapped graphics, leading (the distance between lines of print), object orientation (direction a paragraph or picture faces), font and size changes, dropped capital letters (setting a capital letter below the line rather than above the line), or continuing columns of text, then possibly a desktop publishing program is your answer. Although word processing programs may offer some of these features, they cannot match the composition requirements for producing newsletters, magazines, or brochures. However, you also can find relatively inexpensive programs produced by different vendors that can interface with your word processor and that allow you to produce the documents you desire. Whether you choose a word processor or a desktop publishing program, features should be chosen to fit your needs.

Creating, Editing, and Transferring

The creation, edit, and transfer of text and graphics can be accomplished by using cut and paste techniques, fonts, optical character recognition, and page layout languages.

Cut and Paste

Cut and paste
Combining text and graphics from a number of sources.

Cut and paste, using a pair of scissor and glue, was the traditional method of combining text and graphics from a number of sources. The text can now be created and printed using your word processor. Graphics can be created and printed using a graphics program. The Micros in Action "Preparing Reports" illustrates how an advertising firm, Imagineering Concepts, created a final report.

Micros in Action

Preparing Reports

Imagineering Concepts uses photographs, line art, scanned images, and data-driven graphics to enhance the appearance of annual and stockholders' reports. These techniques also add emphasis, highlights, and dramatic impact and improve overall comprehension.

In a report, the desired perception of the corporate image and the overall goal of the report's publication should set the style for artwork and type. Imagineering Concepts personnel believe they should have complete control over the production of their output. They have found great savings in time and costs since they have become computerized.

Fonts

A **font** is a character set of a given size. The height of a font is measured in **points** from the lowest **descender** to the highest **ascender** (Figure 9–5). A point is a unit of measurement often used for font size. Seventy-two points equals one inch. The **x-height** is the height of a lowercase letter without descenders or ascenders. A descender is the part of a letter that extends below the **baseline** such as the bottom part of the letter y. The baseline is the line on which the x-height of a letter sits. An ascender is the part of a letter that extends above a lowercase letter such as the top of the letter k. The **cap height** is the height of a capital letter. The width of a font is measured in **pitch** (number of characters per inch). **Leading** is the distance between two lines of type, measured from baseline to baseline or from cap height to cap height.

Font
Size and shape of a character set.

Point
Unit of measurement often used for font size. Seventy-two points equals one inch.

Descender
The part of a letter that extends below the baseline such as the bottom part of the letter (y).

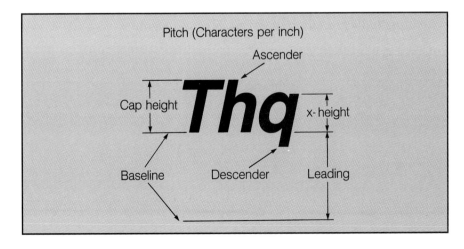

Figure 9–5
Measuring a Font

Ascender
The part of a letter that extends above a lowercase letter, such the top of the letter (t).

X-height
The height of a lowercase letter without descenders or ascenders.

Baseline
The line on which the x-height of a letter sits.

Cap height
The height of a capital letter.

Pitch
The number of characters per inch.

Leading
The distance between two lines of type, measured from baseline to baseline or from cap height to cap height.

Slant
The tilt or rotation of a character.

Serif
With lines embellishing the ends of a letter.

Sans serif
Without lines embellishing the ends of a letter.

Compressed print
A smaller-than-normal font.

Portrait mode
The normal way a sheet of paper is printed. The width is narrower than the height.

Landscape mode
Printing on paper with the width wider than the height.

Bitmapped font
A font created using dots such as those used in raster graphics.

A font may have a **slant** (tilt or rotation of characters). A font includes the complete set of characters (letters, numbers, and special symbols). Fonts are also classified as **serif** (having extenders) or **sans serif** (not having extenders). See Figure 9–6.

Printer fonts can be stored in printer and computer read-only memory (ROM), which is internal to the printer or an add-on PC board, can be downloaded from computer to printer random access memory (RAM), can be included in software in computer RAM, or can be on a physical device such as a daisy wheel. Dot-matrix, ink-jet, and laser printers often can be instructed to switch between a variety of fonts that are recorded in the printer's ROM or on a PC board internal to the computer. Special codes are sent to the printer to tell it to switch between fonts. For example, Epson printers print in **compressed print** after the binary number equal to the decimal number 15 is received. Methods of instructing programs and computers to send a binary 15 to the printer include typing \015 and pressing ^O (pressing the control key and the letter O). The letter O is the 15th letter of the alphabet. When ^O is pressed, the binary number 15 is sent to the printer. The code \015 also sends a binary 15 to the printer. The printer must receive the number 15 to change into compressed mode. The software determines how the user must give the instruction to send the code.

The code <27>[380;0;1s is used in a QMS KiSS laser printer to change the font from what it is to Epson compressed. This is the same font as is produced by most Epson printers when the number 15 is received. Fonts may be in **portrait mode** (normal orientation) or **landscape mode** (sideways orientation).

Figures 9–7 and 9–8 illustrate screen displays from two font creation programs. A font creation program allows the user to design the fonts used on the screen or by the printer. In Figure 9–8, the screen shows the font for ASCII code number 050, a 2. The font being developed is rotated 90 degrees to print sideways. The user can control each dot produced by the printer to obtain the effect needed. Custom characters can be created using this technique. Figure 9–8 shows the opening screen for ZSoft's Publisher's Type Foundry. This program allows the user to create a variety of custom characters and download them to a printer RAM. In Publisher's Type Foundry, the user can create both **bitmapped fonts** (raster graphics) and **outline fonts** (vector graphics) as shown in Figure 9–9.

Figure 9–6
Serif and Sans Serif Fonts

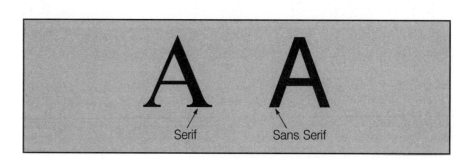

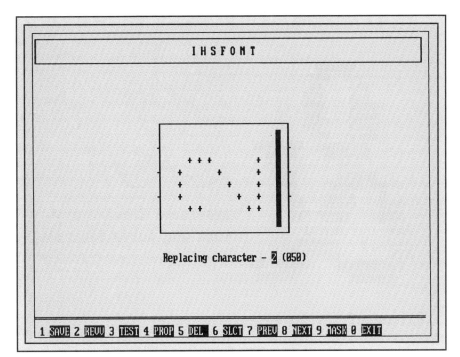

Figure 9–7
Font Design Using FONTASTIC

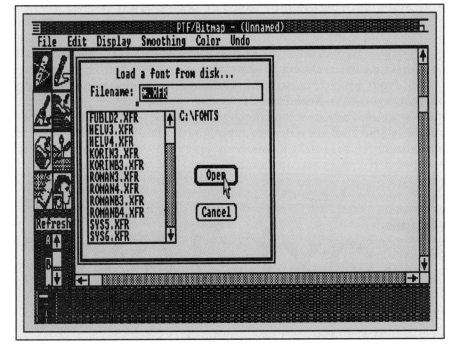

Figure 9–8
Publisher's Type Foundry
Opening Screen

Figure 9–9
Publisher's Type Foundry
Bitmapped versus Outline Fonts

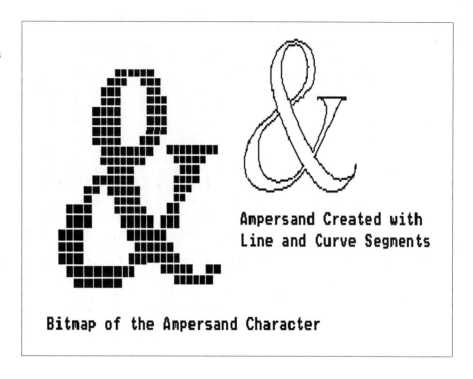

Outline font
A font created using point + direction + distance, as in vector graphics. It is easy to change the size of outline fonts.

Some custom font printing programs are RAM resident and work with the printer driver of word processors. Others are independent printing programs that must be used in place of the normal printer driver.

Daisy wheel printer fonts can be physically changed by changing the daisy wheel. Software, however, cannot control the change of a daisy wheel.

Among the leaders in desktop publishing has been the Apple Macintosh computer. Many of the original programs that contain desktop publishing capabilities were developed on the Macintosh. These capabilities include **kerning** (fitting letters closely, as shown in Figure 9–10), batch hyphenation, vertical depth justification, column grids to 48 columns, and alternating left/right pages. Batch hyphenation is hyphen control of the entire document with a single instruction. Vertical depth justification is the alignment of text so that the bottom lines of every page appear in the same location. An example of alternating left/right is the placement of page numbers on the upper left for even numbered pages and upper right for odd numbered pages.

Kerning
Fitting two letters together such that they look just as close together as other members of the character set.

Figure 9–10
Using Kerning

Optical Character Recognition

Scanners include **hand scanners, platform scanners** (flat bed scanners), and video camera scanners. Platform scanners provide the best-quality image file, because it is easier to line up a page on this type of scanner. Hand scanners can scan either down or across a page. When a hand scanner is used to scan across a page, the software must be able to turn the image sideways before conversion to a text file.

    Optical character recognition (OCR) programs are often configured to use selected scanners or they may read text from an image graphics file (.TIF). An OCR program is a program that can be used to input a graphics file and output the text code associated with the graphic images, if any. Figure 9–11 illustrates an OCR program called Omnipage.

    Optical character recognition programs output text files. Figure 9–12 illustrates the text file created by the program shown in Figure 9–16, along with a graphic scan of the document using Omnipage 386. Notice that the brackets—{ and }—were scanned as parentheses—(and), and other errors appeared. The current state of the art in optical character recognition is good, but still not perfect.

Hand scanner
A small device that can be held in the hand and moved across text or graphics.

Platform scanner
A device into which text or similar material can be placed and then scanned.

Optical character recognition (OCR) program
A program that can be used to input a graphics file and output the text code associated with the graphic images, if any.

Page Layout Languages

A **page layout language** defines an entire page and then sends the page to the printer, as compared with a dot-matrix or daisy wheel **line printer,**

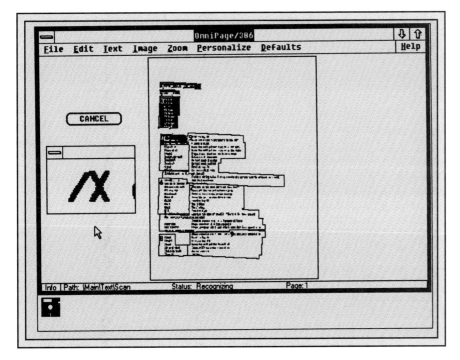

Figure 9–11
Scanning Using OmniPage, an OCR Program

Original text output

```
LOTUS AND VP PLANNER MACROS

/X commands

/XC Call
/XG Goto
/XI If
/XL Label
/XM Menu
/XN Number
/XQ Quit
/XR Return
/XW Wait


{Abs}                    Function key F4
{BackSpace n}            Moves the cursor n characters to the left
{Beep tone, duration}    Creates a sound
{Bigleft n}              Moves the cell pointer n pages to the left
{Bigright n}             Moves the cell pointer n pages to the right
{Blank}                  Erases the contents of cells in a range
{Branch address}         Option is IF statement
{Breakoff}               Control break disabled
{Breakon}                Control break enabled
```

Scanned output with errors

```
LOTUS 1/4ND VP PL1/4NNER UACROS

/X commands

/XC Call
/XG Goto
/XI If
/XL Label
/XU Uenu
/XN Numbor
/xa auit
/XR Return
/XW Wait


{Abs)                    Function Key F4
{BackSpaco n)            Uoves the cursor n characters to the left
{Beep tone, duration)    Creates a sound
{Bigleft n)              Uoves the cell pointer n pages to the left
{Bigright n)             Uoves the cell pointer n pages to the right
{Blank)                  Erases the contents of cells in a range
{Branch address)         Option is IF statement
{Breakoff)                Control break disabled
{Breakon)                Control break enabled
```

Figure 9–12
Text Output Using Omnipage 386

which receives a line of instructions and then prints the line. A page layout language locates each letter and graphic symbol and then sends the instructions to a laser printer to print the page.

Popular page layout languages include Adobe's PostScript **page description language (PDL)** and Hewlett-Packard's **page control language (PCL)**. Both languages produce quality results. Many manufacturers produce laser printers using a clone of the HP PCL control language. Until 1989, Adobe closely controlled the use of PostScript to limit the number of clones being produced.

For best results, the user should know what printer will be used to produce the final results. When some selected features are used, results will be different on different printers. For example, font scaling is easier on a PostScript printer than on a PCL printer.

Using special programs, it is possible to obtain PostScript results on non-PostScript printers. QMS's UltraScript PC program receives input in the form of PostScript code and produces output on HP PCL laser and dot-matrix printers. Figure 9–13 illustrates an Aldus PageMaker document, and Figure 9–14 shows the printer menu using UltraScript PC. Figure 9–15 illustrates the final product.

Page layout language
A language that defines the entire bit image of a page and then sends the code to a printer.

Line printer
A printer that receives a line of instructions and then prints the line.

Page description language (PDL)
Adobe's PostScript language for defining a page.

Page control language (PCL)
Hewlett-Packard's language for defining a page.

Formatting and Integrating

The creative talent of the user is a critical factor in the creation of a page that communicates an idea to a specific target audience. The graphic artist uses many tools to create a page, including fonts (character size and shape), graphics (location, size, and so on), shape of the text (for example, number of columns), size of the page, page layout, and color.

Quality text and graphics output can be produced using a pair of scissors, text from a typewriter or word processing file, and images from a variety of sources. A quality publication is the result of hard work by trained professionals who know what they want the final product to look like. New users should not expect to produce good publications simply by learning to use a page layout program.

Among the alternate methods of merging text and graphics are using a TSR program, word processing program, spreadsheet program, integrated program, and page layout program.

Merging Text and Graphics Using TSR Programs

Terminate and stay resident (TSR) programs are available to monitor the stream of code sent to the printer and to print a graphics file when instructed to do so with special codes. A code is placed in a word processing text file where the printing of a graphics file is wanted. The graphics file is printed under the control of the TSR program. Common print codes include {file} and [file2]. These codes instruct the TSR program to print the graphics file file1 or file2 (saved in a disk file) in the middle of a text printout.

Terminate and stay resident (TSR) program
A program that is loaded into memory and remains in memory while other programs are loaded and used. A TSR program, once loaded, can be recalled using a series of keys while some other program is running.

Figure 9–13
PageMaker Document

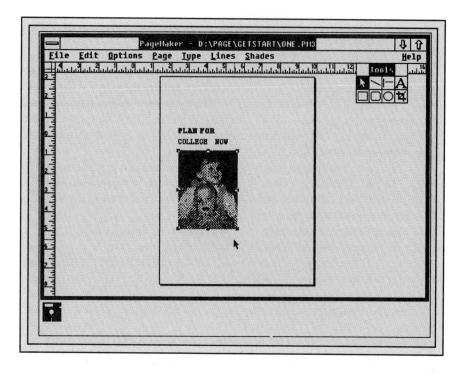

Figure 9–14
PageMaker Printer
Configuration

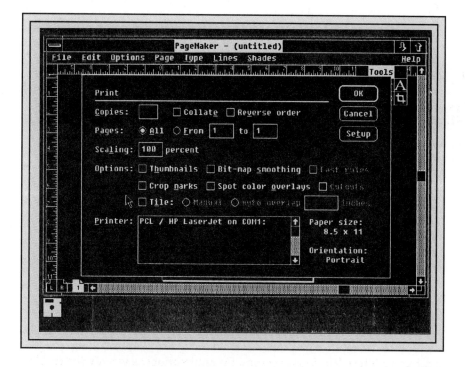

Figure 9–15
Output from UltraScript PC

TSR programs like InSet not only control the printing process but also provide a screen preview capability. When the file code {file 1} is on the screen and InSet is started, the size of the graphics image is displayed (Figure 9–16). InSet also can be used to preview the screen, including text and graphics (Figure 9–17). A graphics screen is required to display graphics.

Merging Text and Graphics Using Word Processing Programs

Current versions of word processors such as Microsoft Word, WordPerfect, and WordStar include many desktop publishing features, including merging graphics with text. The word processor graphics routines include the capability to capture a graphics screen and convert graphics files to the format required. Figure 9–18 illustrates WordPerfect being used to locate a graphic image. Figure 9–19 shows the page preview capability of WordPerfect.

Figure 9–16
Sizing Graphic Displays

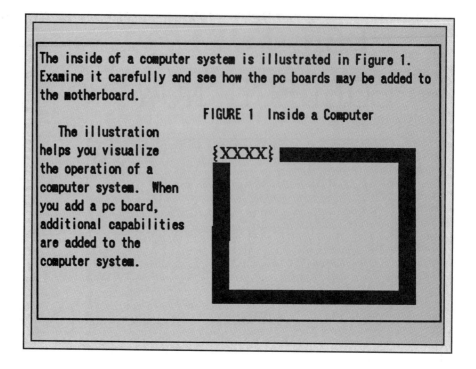

Figure 9–17
Graphic Displays

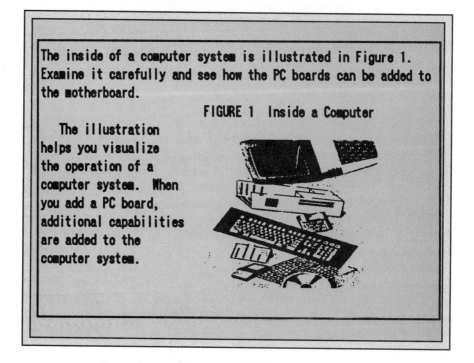

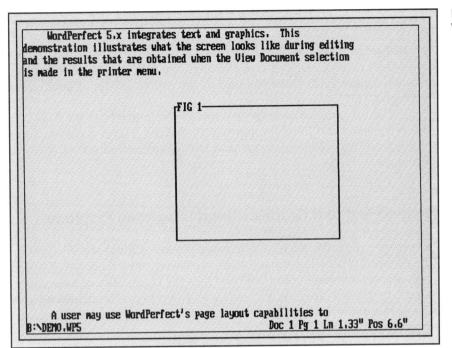

Figure 9–18
WordPerfect Editing Capabilities

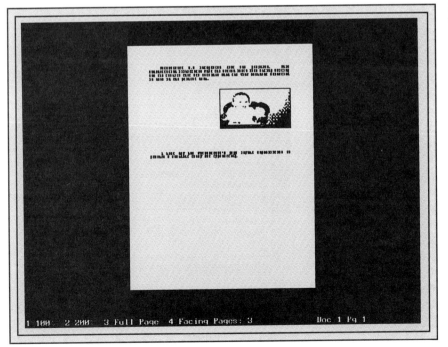

Figure 9–19
WordPerfect's View Document

Merging Text and Graphics Using Spreadsheet Programs

Spreadsheet programs such as Lotus 1-2-3 (Release 3.0), Excel, and Quattro Pro contain controls for printing shading, controlling fonts, and locating graphics. Figure 9–20 illustrates part of the printer control capabilities in Quattro Pro.

Add-in programs, such as Allways for Lotus 1-2-3 (Release 2.2), add font control and graphics-locating capabilities. Figure 9–21 illustrates the use of Allways to prepare a report with graphics and special fonts for printing.

Merging Text and Graphics Using Integrated Programs

Integrated program
A program that combines the capabilities of two or more general or specific application programs.

Integrated programs, such as Microsoft Works, Ability, and Symphony, contain word processing, spreadsheet, database, and data-driven graphics modules. An integrated program combines the capabilities of two or more general or specific application programs. Reports can be generated containing files from each module. Chapter 11 discusses the use of integrated programs.

The Microsoft Windows makes it possible to generate reports containing word processing, spreadsheets, databases, data-drive graphics, and image-driven graphics. Chapter 12 contains additional details on the use of Microsoft Windows for this purpose.

Figure 9–20
Printer Control Capabilities in Quattro Pro

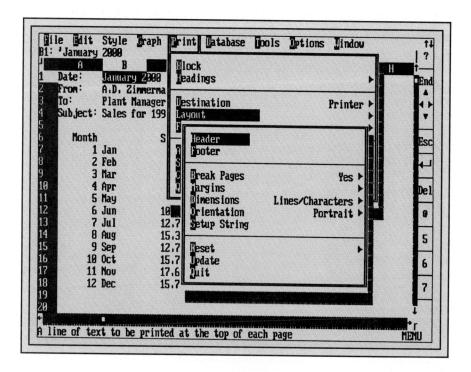

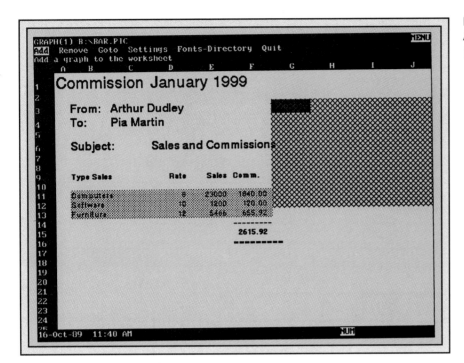

Figure 9–21
Allways in Lotus 1-2-3
(Release 2.2)

Merging Text and Graphics Using Page Layout Programs

Page layout programs import and/or use directly text from word processors and graphics files from graphics programs, combining them into a final product. Users can use page layout programs to create text and graphics. However, word processors, data-driven graphics programs, and image-creating programs are usually easier and faster to use for the initial creation process. Some desktop publishing programs are relatively expensive (for example, PageMaker), whereas others are lower in cost and have fewer features and capabilities (for example, NewsMaster).

The capability to use graphics is an important part of a page layout program. Figure 9–22 illustrates a close view of a scanned image in News-Master II.

The procedure for using a page layout program starts with a definition of the number of pages and the page size (Figure 9–23). Notice that Wide (landscape mode) was selected rather than Tall (portrait mode).

The next step is page layout. The user should have a good idea of the desired final product before this step. Figure 9–24 illustrates the Page-Maker display of the page in landscape mode. A page of PageMaker's clip art manual was scanned into the file CLIP.TIF. Figure 9–25 illustrates how the scanned clip art library file (CLIP.TIF) can be selected. Figure 9–26 illustrates the process of selecting a graphics image from a library.

Figure 9–22
Close View of the NewsMaster II
User's Manual Cover Scan

Saving and Retrieving

A desktop publishing program can retrieve and use files created in a number of different word processors, data- or image-driven graphics programs, and spreadsheet programs. It can also save/retrieve a desktop publishing file that includes all of the imported text and graphics.

Printing

Desktop publishing programs are able to send output to a number of different printers and typesetting machines. Laser and high-quality dot-matrix printers are the most popular devices used. The key to getting the most from the capabilities of a given printer is the capability to **configure** the printer with the desktop publishing software. To configure means to tell the printer all of the hardware capabilities available, including fonts, sizing, and other features of the printer, so the software user can control the printer using software commands.

Configure
To tell the software the exact
hardware capabilities available.

One of the reasons why the Macintosh was first used for desktop publishing was that two and only two printers were available for use with this microcomputer. Both printers could produce quality output when configured correctly, and configuration was relatively easy.

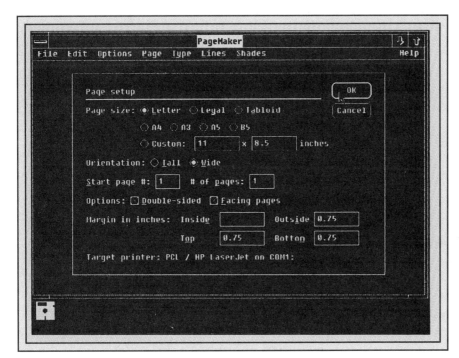

Figure 9–23
Defining the Page in
PageMaker

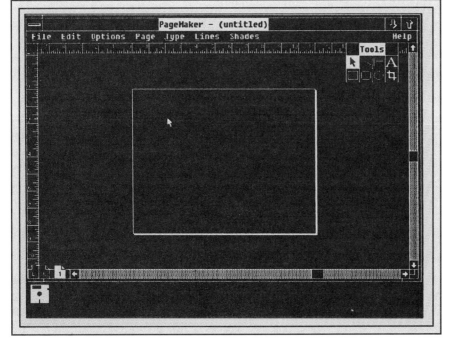

Figure 9–24
Page Layout in PageMaker's
Landscape Mode

Figure 9–25
Selecting a Scanned File in
PageMaker

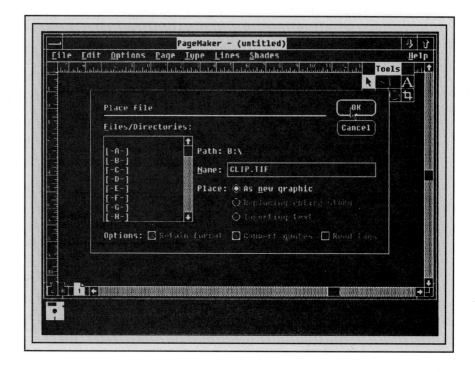

Figure 9–26
Locating Text and Graphics in
PageMaker

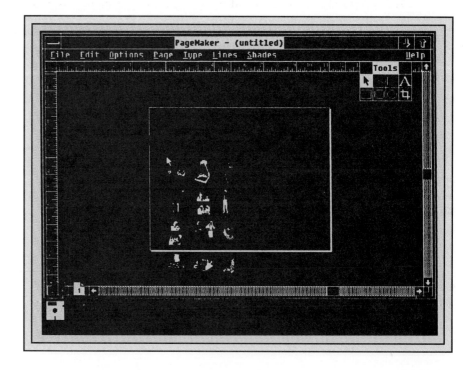

Communication and Local Area Networks

Financial Services

Dean Witter Reynolds is a large financial service brokerage firm owned and operated by Sears. It has offices in all major cities and in many smaller ones. In the local offices, the professionals who advise and place orders for the public are called account executives. The account executive's potential needs for microcomputers were identified as follows:

- Communication with the Financial Action Service Terminal (F.A.S.T.) system.
- Maintenance of the client's database.
- Special application programs and spreadsheet analysis of client's needs.
- Word processing.

The F.A.S.T. system is a dial-up service operated by Dean Witter for both the account executives and individual clients. Clients can access their own data files, enter into the company's research files, learn what is available, and obtain an up-to-date stock value at any time using their own microcomputers.

Because Dean Witter Reynolds allows its clients access to the database by telephone, it must be able to accommodate a wide variety of computers and communication peripherals.

Its system allows modems using 300-, 480-, 1,200-, and 9,600-baud rates equal access through the use of multiplexers that can automatically adjust to the baud rate of the customer's modem. Other communication conventions can be preset as well. Security systems make use of passwords, identification numbers, and a special access code that prevents access to data files, market quotations, and personal portfolios for anyone who cannot run the identification process completely.

An account executive at Dean Witter Reynolds found he could save time by getting a laptop computer and preparing memos and letters at home in his time off. After he completed a letter, however, he had the problem of transferring it to his desktop unit, since the disk drives were different sizes.

The account executive had the option of using either a modem or a null-modem to connect his laptop computer to the 80286 desktop system. Because both were at the same location, he purchased LapLink III and used a null-modem cable to transfer data from the laptop computer to the desktop.

Communication is the transfer of data, computer instructions, or both from one computer to another or to peripherals. **Communication software** is programs that, with the addition of communication hardware help users create/correct/edit, communicate/transfer between devices, and save/ retrieve files using special hardware. **Communication hardware** includes devices to connect the computer to a telephone (modems), cables, switches, use of the **serial** and **parallel** computer ports, emulation methods and interfaces, and devices to connect computers to networks. Many communication hardware devices include programs in read-only memory (ROM). Without communication hardware and the programs in ROM,

Communication
The transfer of data, computer instructions, or both from one computer to another or to peripherals.

Communication software
Programs (with the addition of communication hardware) that helps users create/correct/edit, communicate/transfer between devices, and save/retrieve files.

Communication hardware
Serial and parallel computer ports, devices that connect the computer to a telephone, special cables, and devices to connect computers to networks.

Serial
Communication method that transmits data one bite after another.

Parallel
Communication method that transmits data along a number of parallel paths (wires) at one time.

communication could not occur. Because of the importance of communication hardware, it will be discussed early in the chapter rather than near the end. Micros in Action "Financial Services" illustrates how Dean Witter used a database and communications to support customer decision making.

Computer communication within a computer system is similar to communication between different computer systems. Communication concerns the transfer of data and instructions between pairs of microcomputers, a microcomputer and a host system, a computer and a network, and a computer and its peripherals.

Many communication, network and support programs exist. Specific communication program tasks are performed differently in each program. The communication and network programs used in this chapter are LapLink III and PROCOMM. The network system used is Novell (merged with Lotus in 1990). These programs are among the more popular ones available.

Why Communication?

Knowledge of communication procedures helps the user get the most from each part of a computer system and select the best available system for a particular task. Often, a central computer system uses a host computer that has capabilities and data storage capacity that are not available on microcomputers. It is possible, however, to use any size computer for a host, from a small microcomputer to a minicomputer to a mainframe.

Communication considerations include internal communication between the parts of a system; speed for data transfer and computer operation; computer size (capacity) and costs; program availability; data management, including security; need for multiple users and networking; use of external data collection devices; and control of external devices.

Internal Controls

Transfers of data and instructions from a microcomputer to its printer, disk drives, monitor, and hard disk are the same as, or similar to, the data and instruction transfers between two microcomputers. For example, to be able to use all the capabilities of a printer, the user must know what instructions are needed to make the printer perform a task, as well as how to get the microcomputer to send these instructions.

Many printers can boldface, underline, make subscripts, and superscripts, produce extra-large type and small type, and change fonts. Some programs make it easy to perform the tasks, whereas others make it difficult or impossible. The user must know the need, what the device can do, and what the program can do.

The accomplishment of a result depends on the capability of the device and program. If the device can accomplish a desired result but the program cannot, the user must find new programs or ways to change the available program to get the job done. If the device cannot do the job, it must be replaced with a device that can.

Speed, Size, and Cost

Because the design of large computers is different from that of microcomputers, it is difficult to make a direct comparison of speed. The speed of a computer is a function of the speed of the central processor, the activities performed by the central processor, the operating system of the computer, the individual memory chip, and many other design aspects. No matter how speed is measured, larger computers are faster and can be used where such speed is needed. Microcomputers can be used to collect data and then transfer that data to the central computer for the routine that requires the extra speed.

The amount of random access memory (RAM) available in microcomputers has increased from 64K to 4GB and is still growing. Operating systems limit the uses that can be made of memory in some microcomputer systems. The size of on-line storage devices has increased from 50K to 6GB and is still growing. The only limit to on-line storage seems to be budget and need.

It often does not pay to install large amounts of RAM and on-line memory in devices used by a single individual. When it is necessary to justify large storage capacities with multiusers, communication to a central system is required.

A telephone call from one microcomputer to another may be the most economical method of transferring data and instructions. Data and instructions sent this way are usually in the form needed for printing or use by the second microcomputer.

Programs

The rule "Find the software and then select the computer" still applies when selecting a host computer service. Many programs are developed only for specific central computers that may be needed by the microcomputer user. When one of these programs is needed, the purchase of time on a host computer is a logical choice. Programs for analyzing large data sets may be limited to a particular computer due to program size, data set size, and computer speed.

The Need for Networks

It is difficult to separate the need for many users to access a database from speed, size, and cost factors. The large central host computer system of a network with a **central file server** is required for this task. A central file server system is the hardware and software system that controls the access to files by individuals using a network.

Central file server
Hardware and software system that controls the access to files by individuals using a network.

Networks mean cost savings in equipment, better control of data files, and the sharing of expensive programs. Networks are needed in situations in which sharing must occur. Small organizations may need only personal computers that work alone. As an organization grows, however, and more individuals use microcomputers, sharing may be the best alternative for company growth.

Large organizations need both stand-alone workstations and coordination between individual microcomputer users. Data management and security are important where a number of users need to use and update the same data file constantly. In organizations where cash is short, the sharing of peripherals may be the most important reason for a network. In larger organizations, the sharing of data and programs, as well as the use of the specialized capabilities of some computers, may be more important.

Hardware

Port

A plug on a computer that allows the user to connect cables for communication to peripherals and other computers.

Computers communicate with peripherals and other computers using input/output **ports.** Ports are plugs on a computer that allows the user to connect cables for communication to peripherals and other computers. Most ports, including those listed as input or output only, perform two-way communication. For example, printers are output devices; however, because printers are usually much slower than computers, they must be able to send a code to the computer telling it to hold up data communication when necessary and then to start again when the printer is ready. The next time you use a printer, notice how the computer waits for the printer. Table 10–1 lists some microcomputer ports.

Table 10–1
Communication Ports

Input Ports	Output Ports	Input/Output Ports
Keyboard	Monitor	RS-232C
Bar code reader	Printer (parallel)	Communication
Joystick	IEEE 488 (lab equipment)	Printer
Voice recognition	Voice synthesis	Plotter
Mouse		Device control
Pad		Disk drives
Scanner		Fax communication

The RS-232C port is commonly used for communication between computers. Figure 10–1 illustrates the ports commonly found on a desktop microcomputer, and Figure 10–2 illustrates the ports found on a laptop computer. Communication hardware devices are available for using the telephone, connecting to a host computer, and connecting two microcomputers. Communication devices either fit into an expansion slot or use the serial or parallel ports found on both laptop and desktop computers.

Modems

The built-in or add-on RS-232C serial port can be used to connect the microcomputer to a **modem.** A modem is a device that changes the binary code generated by the microcomputer into a signal that can be sent over telephone lines to a second modem, which changes the signal back to binary code. The word *modem* comes from the tasks it performs: MOdulate and DEModulate.

Modem
A device to connect the microcomputer to the telephone. It changes binary codes to signals for telephone transmission, and then back again.

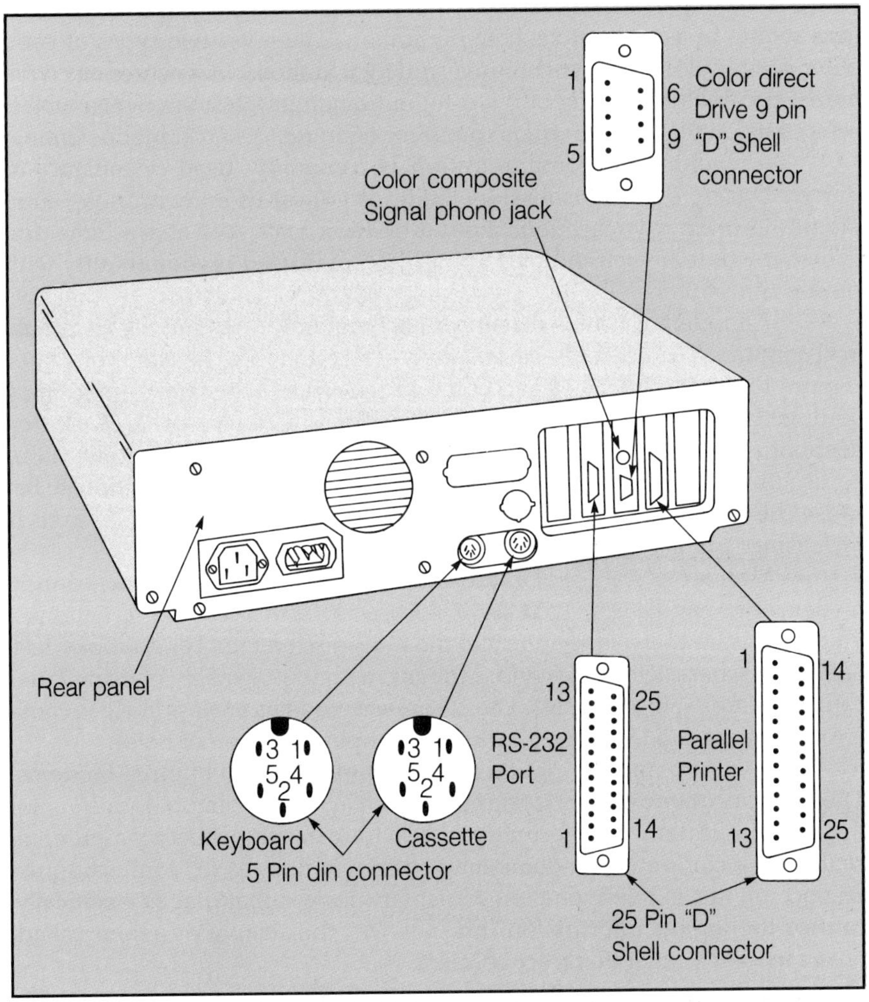

Figure 10–1
Outlet Ports on a Microcomputer

Figure 10–2
Outlet Ports on a COMPAQ LTE

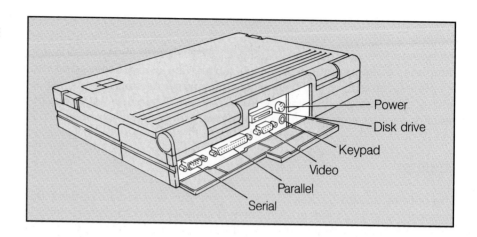

Power
Disk drive
Keypad
Video
Parallel
Serial

Answer
A modem setting in asynchronous communication. One partner must answer and the other originate.

Originate
A modem setting in asynchronous communication. One partner must originate and the other answer.

Asynchronous communication
Communication that requires timing only when a bit is being transmitted.

Synchronous communication
Communicating that requires continuous timing.

Direct connect modem
A modem that is connected into the telephone lines.

Acoustical coupler
A device that cradles the telephone receiver and connects the computer to a telephone system.

Baud
A unit of measure that usually refers to the transmission rate. For example, 1200 baud is 120 characters per second.

Answering microcomputer modems send their code on one frequency, while the originating microcomputer uses another. This is why one microcomputer must be the originator and the other, the answerer. **Answer** is a modem setting in asynchronous communication. **Originate** is a second modem setting in asynchronous communication. There are two types of computer communication: **asynchronous** and **synchronous.** Asynchronous communication requires timing of the communication process only when a bit is being transmitted. Synchronous communication requires continuous timing.

Asynchronous communication is commonly used on microcomputers. During data transmission timing is critical in asynchronous communication. An asynchronous communication may start at any time and end at any time. Synchronous communication is used predominantly with central computers.

A modem can be a **direct connect modem,** or it can use an **acoustical coupler.** A direct connect modem is connected into the telephone lines (Figure 10–3). It works well in a home and in offices where telephones may be directly connected. An acoustical coupler is a device that cradles the telephone receiver and connects the computer to a telephone system. It can be used anywhere: an office, hotel room, telephone booth, or home. Because the number of places where a direct connect system can be used is increasing, the use of acoustical couplers is decreasing.

Most acoustical couplers are limited to 300 **baud,** while direct connect modems can handle 300, 1200, 2400, 4800, 9600, and 19200 baud. Baud is a unit of measure that usually refers to the transmission rate. For example, 1200 baud is 120 characters per second. Modems with the capability of using faster baud rates are more expensive. Direct connect modems are less likely to cause errors than are modems using acoustical couplers because of noise.

In laptop microcomputers, it is common to find internal modems. These microcomputers are designed to be carried to remote locations for the communication of information back to a desktop microcomputer or central host computer. Modems may be simple devices for connecting the microcomputer to telephone lines or smart devices that dial automatically, control the log-on information, and answer the telephone when called. Smart modems must be direct connect.

One advantage of the smart modem is that the user can use the microcomputer to call other microcomputers automatically in the middle of

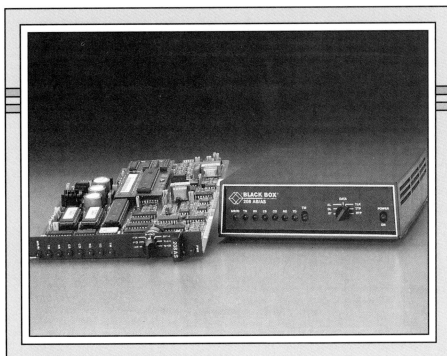

Figure 10-3
A Direct Connect Modem, Black Box Model 208 AB/AS with Interior (for 4800-baud communication)

the night, when long-distance telephone costs are at their lowest. The microcomputer can be instructed to send a series of prepared files for processing the next day, and then break the connection. The smart modem also allows the microcomputer to answer incoming calls and receive and store messages, as well as send automatic messages.

Both the automatic send and automatic receive functions require special programs. These features open the microcomputer to the security problems of the national database operator. Users of autoanswer modems may have unwelcome users break into their systems and damage files or obtain confidential information. Some users think it is fun to create programs and introduce them into computer systems without the knowledge of the system operators. These programs **(computer viruses)** may be designed to display funny messages, destroy programs and system operation, or destroy data. Systems that allow users to call up must protect themselves from computer viruses.

Computer virus
A program introduced into a computer as a joke or to damage the operation of the computer.

Cables and Null-modems

The growth of laptop computers using two 3½-inch disk drives has resulted in the need to transfer data and programs to and from desktop computers with 5¼-inch drives using cables. A **null-modem** is a method of wiring an RS-232C cable to connect the communication ports of two microcomputers. The computers are made to behave as if they were connected to a modem. Baud rates of over 115,200 are possible using null-modems. Some communication packages include both software and

Null-modem
A method of wiring serial communication cables to allow two computers to communicate as if they were connected to modems and a telephone.

Figure 10–4
Laplink III

cables. One product, Laplink III (Figure 10–4), comes with a cable for connecting two microcomputers using their parallel ports as well as their serial ports. The parallel communication rate is over twice the fastest serial communication rate because of the capability to transmit data over a number of (often eight) parallel lines at one time rather than over a single line in series (one after the other). As indicated in Micros in Action "Data Transfer," a common use of Laplink is the transfer of data from a laptop to a desktop with different-sized disk drives.

Micros in Action

Data Transfer

An account executive at Dean Witter found he could save time by getting a laptop computer and preparing memos and letters at home in his time off. After he completed a letter, however, he had the problem of transferring it to his desktop unit, since the disk drives were different sizes.

The account executive had the option of using either a modem or a null-modem to connect his laptop computer to the 80286 desktop system. Because both were at the same location, he purchased LapLink III and used a null-modem cable to transfer data from the laptop computer to the desktop.

Table 10–2
American Standard Code for Information Interchange (ASCII)

Binary Number	Decimal Number	Character
0 0 0 0 0 0 0	0	Control
0 0 0 0 0 0 1	1	Control
0 0 0 0 0 1 0	2	Control
0 0 0 0 0 1 1	3	Control
0 0 0 0 1 0 0	4	Control
0 0 0 0 1 0 1	5	Control
0 0 0 0 1 1 0	6	Control
0 0 0 0 1 1 1	7	Bell
0 0 0 1 0 0 0	8	Backspace
0 0 0 1 0 0 1	9	Tab
0 0 0 1 0 1 0	10	Line feed
0 0 0 1 0 1 1	11	Control
0 0 0 1 1 0 0	12	Form feed
0 0 0 1 1 0 1	13	Carriage return
0 0 0 1 1 1 0	14	Control
0 0 0 1 1 1 1	15	Control
0 0 1 0 0 0 0	16	Control
0 0 1 0 0 0 1	17	Control
0 0 1 0 0 1 0	18	Control
0 0 1 0 0 1 1	19	Control
0 0 1 0 1 0 0	20	Control
0 0 1 0 1 0 1	21	Control
0 0 1 0 1 1 0	22	Control
0 0 1 0 1 1 1	23	Control
0 0 1 1 0 0 0	24	Control
0 0 1 1 0 0 1	25	Control
0 0 1 1 0 1 0	26	Control
0 0 1 1 0 1 1	27	Esc
0 0 1 1 1 0 0	28	Control
0 0 1 1 1 0 1	29	Control
0 0 1 1 1 1 0	30	Control
0 0 1 1 1 1 1	31	Control
0 1 0 0 0 0 0	32	Blank
0 1 0 0 0 0 1	33	!
0 1 0 0 0 1 0	34	"
0 1 0 0 0 1 1	35	#
0 1 0 0 1 0 0	36	$
0 1 0 0 1 0 1	37	%
0 1 0 0 1 1 0	38	&
0 1 0 0 1 1 1	39	'
0 1 0 1 0 0 0	40	(
0 1 0 1 0 0 1	41	)

Table 10–2
American Standard Code for Information
Interchange (ASCII), continued

Binary Number	Decimal Number	Character
0 1 0 1 0 1 0	42	*
0 1 0 1 0 1 1	43	+
0 1 0 1 1 0 0	44	,
0 1 0 1 1 0 1	45	–
0 1 0 1 1 1 0	46	.
0 1 0 1 1 1 1	47	/
0 1 1 0 0 0 0	48	0
0 1 1 0 0 0 1	49	1
0 1 1 0 0 1 0	50	2
0 1 1 0 0 1 1	51	3
0 1 1 0 1 0 0	52	4
0 1 1 0 1 0 1	53	5
0 1 1 0 1 1 0	54	6
0 1 1 0 1 1 1	55	7
0 1 1 1 0 0 0	56	8
0 1 1 1 0 0 1	57	9
0 1 1 1 0 1 0	58	:
0 1 1 1 0 1 1	59	;
0 1 1 1 1 0 0	60	<
0 1 1 1 1 0 1	61	=
0 1 1 1 1 1 0	62	>
0 1 1 1 1 1 1	63	?
1 0 0 0 0 0 0	64	@
1 0 0 0 0 0 1	65	A
1 0 0 0 0 1 0	66	B
1 0 0 0 0 1 1	67	C
1 0 0 0 1 0 0	68	D
1 0 0 0 1 0 1	69	E
1 0 0 0 1 1 0	70	F
1 0 0 0 1 1 1	71	G
1 0 0 1 0 0 0	72	H
1 0 0 1 0 0 1	73	I
1 0 0 1 0 1 0	74	J
1 0 0 1 0 1 1	75	K
1 0 0 1 1 0 0	76	L
1 0 0 1 1 0 1	77	M
1 0 0 1 1 1 0	78	N
1 0 0 1 1 1 1	79	O
1 0 1 0 0 0 0	80	P
1 0 1 0 0 0 1	81	Q
1 0 1 0 0 1 0	82	R
1 0 1 0 0 1 1	83	S
1 0 1 0 1 0 0	84	T

Table 10–2
American Standard Code for Information
Interchange (ASCII), continued

Binary Number	Decimal Number	Character
1 0 1 0 1 0 1	85	U
1 0 1 0 1 1 0	86	V
1 0 1 0 1 1 1	87	W
1 0 1 1 0 0 0	88	X
1 0 1 1 0 0 1	89	Y
1 0 1 1 0 1 0	90	Z
1 0 1 1 0 1 1	91	[
1 0 1 1 1 0 0	92	\
1 0 1 1 1 0 1	93	]
1 0 1 1 1 1 0	94	^
1 0 1 1 1 1 1	95	_
1 1 0 0 0 0 0	96	'
1 1 0 0 0 0 1	97	a
1 1 0 0 0 1 0	98	b
1 1 0 0 0 1 1	99	c
1 1 0 0 1 0 0	100	d
1 1 0 0 1 0 1	101	e
1 1 0 0 1 1 0	102	f
1 1 0 0 1 1 1	103	g
1 1 0 1 0 0 0	104	h
1 1 0 1 0 0 1	105	i
1 1 0 1 0 1 0	106	j
1 1 0 1 0 1 1	107	k
1 1 0 1 1 0 0	108	l
1 1 0 1 1 0 1	109	m
1 1 0 1 1 1 0	110	n
1 1 0 1 1 1 1	111	o
1 1 1 0 0 0 0	112	p
1 1 1 0 0 0 1	113	q
1 1 1 0 0 1 0	114	r
1 1 1 0 0 1 1	115	s
1 1 1 0 1 0 0	116	t
1 1 1 0 1 0 1	117	u
1 1 1 0 1 1 0	118	v
1 1 1 0 1 1 1	119	w
1 1 1 1 0 0 0	120	x
1 1 1 1 0 0 1	121	y
1 1 1 1 0 1 0	122	z
1 1 1 1 0 1 1	123	{
1 1 1 1 1 0 0	124		
1 1 1 1 1 0 1	125	}
1 1 1 1 1 1 0	126	~
1 1 1 1 1 1 1	127	▓

to 255. There are a number of different standards for the numbers over 126. Screens and printers often use the **high-bit** (8th bit) numbers for line draw, control, and other purposes.

Two commonly used methods can help a device using ASCII communicate with a device using EBCDIC. Emulators in the ASCII computer can change the code to EBCDIC before sending it. Hardware-software translators can input and output ASCII to one device and EBCDIC to another.

Communication Parameters

Combinations of hardware and software are used to set the **communication parameters.** These parameters must be agreed upon before two computers can communicate using ASCII asynchronous communication. They include who will originate and who will answer, the baud rate, the **character size** (bits per character), parity, the number of stop bits, and the use of different types of **duplex** (the communication protocol). Duplex may be full or half. In **full duplex,** both communication partners can send and receive at the same time (similar to telephone communication). In **half duplex,** one partner can send and the other receive (similar to citizen's band [CB] radio communication).

In communication between a central computer and a microcomputer, the usual convention is for the central computer to answer and the microcomputer to originate. The computer that answers is sometimes referred to as the host, and the originator is called a terminal. Some programs limit the hardware they are used on to one role, but many programs allow the computer to answer or originate. In communication between microcomputers, one microcomputer must answer and one must originate. Communications will not occur otherwise. However, either microcomputer can take either role.

Setting Up Communication Parameters

Parameter setup procedures depend on the communication program.PROCOMM enters its communication screen when it exits the opening screen. The brief menu at the bottom of the communication screen indicates that `<Alt>` + `F10` starts the help screen. Figure 10–11 illustrates the help screen. PROCOMM refers to the parameters—baud rate, parity, character size, and stop bits—as line settings. Duplex is controlled by pressing `<Alt>` + `E`. PROCOMM requires that you return to the communication screen and then press `<Alt>` + `P` to start the line settings screen (Figure 10–12).

When using a communication program, the user should read the information on the screen carefully. Communication programs tend to have more differences than some other program groups, such as word processors and spreadsheet programs.

Using an Electronic Library

Electronic libraries (national electronic databases) are available that can be called to research many different topics. Table 10–3 lists some of the avail-

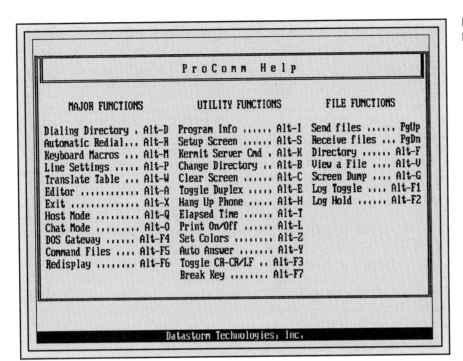

Figure 10–11
PROCOMM Help Screen

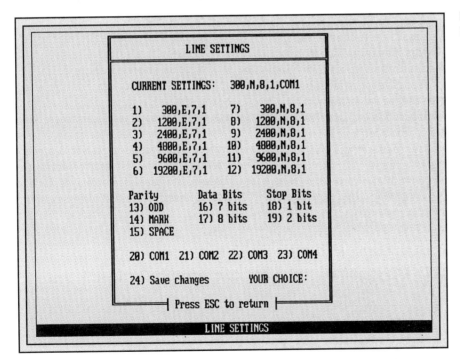

Figure 10–12
PROCOMM Line Settings Screen

able databases. Electronic libraries allow researchers to complete projects in minutes, transfer the results, and generate reports without the production of hard copy until the final report.

An **electronic library** is a collection of computer-stored data that is similar to that maintained by a manual library and that can be searched

Electronic library
Computer-stored data that are similar to that maintained by a manual library and that can be searched electronically for information.

Table 10–3
Selected National Databases

Database	Notes
Accountant's Index	Corresponds to hard copy of the *Accountant's Index*
Commerce Business Daily	Corresponds to U.S. Department of Commerce's printed *Commerce Business Daily*
CompuServe	Has general features including electronic mail
Dow Jones News	Provides searcher access to *Wall Street Journal* stories; Dow Jones News records data
Financial Action Service Terminal (F.A.S.T.)	Provides financial and stock quotation services
WESTLAW	Provides a database for lawyers and legal researchers to research court cases and laws

Most databases charge fees for joining and usage.

electronically for information. Figure 10–13 illustrates the initial screen obtained when calling the University of South Alabama (USA) library in Mobile, Alabama. The library can communicate with a number of different terminal types. USA's terminal type is VT100, as shown in Figure 10–13.

After a welcome message appears in the next screen, the user presses the ⏎ key, and the Library User Information Service (LUIS) information screen appears with instructions on how to use the libraries' services (Figure 10–14).

When NEWS ⏎ is typed on the information screen, the news screen appears. Figure 10–15 illustrates this screen (with the university telephone numbers blanked out). When A ⏎ is typed, the display shown in Figure 10–16 appears. Here the system instructs the user in the use of the system. Even a user who has never used the system before will find it easy to search the database for an author or title.

Data Management, Transfer, and Analog Devices

Data are a valuable asset, and the security and use of data must be controlled. The protection schemes available for some microcomputer databases are limited. In many situations, using a central host computer as a central file server provides the tools needed to ensure data security. The host system requires and justifies a staff of technically trained personnel that are specifically responsible for data security, backup, and system operation. Chapter 1 discussed the problem of computer viruses, which exist on all sizes of computers. The technically trained staff of a central computer system is better able to handle viruses than is an individual user.

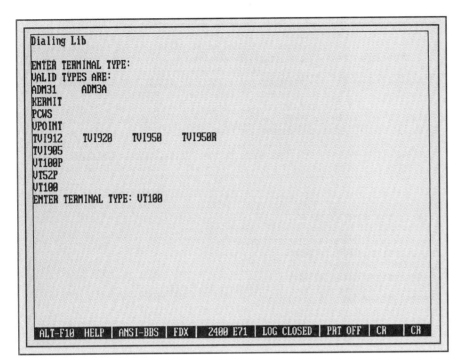

Figure 10–13
Initial Library Screen

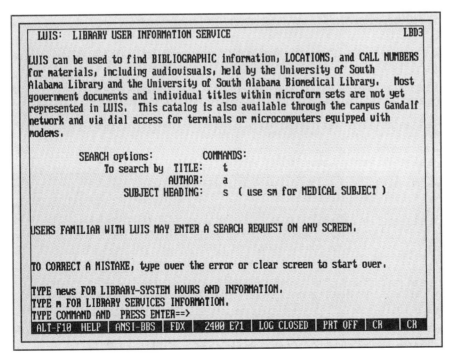

Figure 10–14
Library Information Screen

Figure 10–15
News Screen

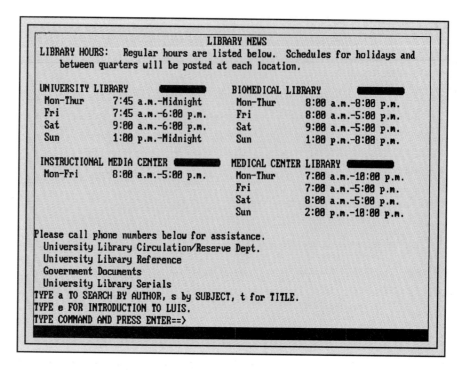

```
                              LIBRARY NEWS
     LIBRARY HOURS:   Regular hours are listed below.  Schedules for holidays and
        between quarters will be posted at each location.

     UNIVERSITY LIBRARY         ▬▬▬▬▬     BIOMEDICAL LIBRARY         ▬▬▬▬▬
       Mon-Thur    7:45 a.m.-Midnight       Mon-Thur    8:00 a.m.-8:00 p.m.
       Fri         7:45 a.m.-6:00 p.m.      Fri         8:00 a.m.-5:00 p.m.
       Sat         9:00 a.m.-6:00 p.m.      Sat         9:00 a.m.-5:00 p.m.
       Sun         1:00 p.m.-Midnight       Sun         1:00 p.m.-8:00 p.m.

     INSTRUCTIONAL MEDIA CENTER ▬▬▬▬▬     MEDICAL CENTER LIBRARY     ▬▬▬▬▬
       Mon-Fri     8:00 a.m.-5:00 p.m.      Mon-Thur    7:00 a.m.-10:00 p.m.
                                            Fri         7:00 a.m.-5:00 p.m.
                                            Sat         8:00 a.m.-5:00 p.m.
                                            Sun         2:00 p.m.-10:00 p.m.


     Please call phone numbers below for assistance.
       University Library Circulation/Reserve Dept.
       University Library Reference
       Government Documents
       University Library Serials
     TYPE a TO SEARCH BY AUTHOR, s by SUBJECT, t for TITLE.
     TYPE e FOR INTRODUCTION TO LUIS.
     TYPE COMMAND AND PRESS ENTER==>
```

Figure 10–16
Searching for an Author

```
     TO SEARCH BY AUTHOR:                       EXAMPLES:

     Type a= followed by author's last name or    a=bellow
     first part of last name.  Omit accent marks.  a=shakespea

     When last name is common, type complete last  a=johnson s
     name followed by author's first initial.      a=clarke a

     Organizations or institutions may be authors. a=american hospital sup

     If correct form of name is not known, try
     alternate forms.  Common variants are:
        - Use of prefix (varies by language)       a=de la mare  a=calderon de la
        - Pseudonyms                               a=twain m
        - Spelling variations                      a=organization  a=organisation

     IMPORTANT: If unsure of correct name or if search results in "no entries
     found", try shortening name or search by TITLE, or SUBJECT.

     IF YOU NEED ASSISTANCE, ask at the service desk.

     TYPE t FOR INTRODUCTION TO TITLE SEARCHES,  s FOR SUBJECT.
     TYPE e FOR INTRODUCTION TO LUIS.
     TYPE COMMAND AND PRESS ENTER==>
     ALT-F10  HELP | ANSI-BBS | FDX | 2400 E71 | LOG CLOSED | PRT OFF | CR |  CR
```

Because of their size and portability, laptop computers are often used to collect data for later transfer to a bigger computer. Because laptop and desktop computers are often equipped with different sizes of disk drives, communication procedures are used to transfer data between these machines. Figure 10–17 illustrates the opening screen of Laplink III on/a desktop computer with a 5¼-inch disk drive, after connecting the cables and establishing communications with a laptop computer which uses 3½-inch disk drives.

GRAPHICS.COM on the laptop is to be transferred to the desktop. The remaining steps required (using the desktop's keyboard) to transfer the file to a disk in drive B of the desktop follow:

1. Press L to select Log
2. Type B: ↵
3. Press the right arrow key to change to the laptop's directory
4. Press up or down arrows to highlight GRAPHICS.COM
5. Press C for copy

Figure 10–18 illustrates the desktop's screen when the transfer is complete.

Analog Devices

An **analog device** uses a continuous voltage rather than binary codes. These devices are often used to monitor real-world conditions such as temperature, sound, and movement. Microcomputers can communicate with analog devices that measure continuous changes in voltage. A special interface, such as the IEEE 488, is required to allow a computer that is a binary device to understand an analog device. Laboratory equipment, machine monitors, and other data collection devices are often designed to operate as analog devices.

With external devices, the microcomputer can control the temperature in a room, the lights in a house, the flow of liquid in an experiment, and many other things in offices, hotels, and industrial plants. In many cases, the microcomputer must first be able to determine facts about the process being controlled in order to make feedback adjustments needed to control the process.

Analog device
A device that uses continuous voltage rather than binary codes. These devices are often used to monitor real-world conditions such as temperature, sound, and movement.

Communication Programs

Communication capability depends on both hardware and software. As with all other capabilities of a microcomputer, a program is needed to make things happen. Many communication programs are available. They are sold as individual programs or can be purchased as part of a database, spreadsheet, or integrated program package.

The types of communication programs are **dumb terminal** programs, **smart terminal** programs, and **automatic originate and answer** programs. A dumb terminal program allows the microcomputer to communicate only under the supervision of a human being. When information is typed, it is sent. The information returning is displayed on the screen. A smart terminal program allows the opening of a disk file and

Dumb terminal
A terminal that can communicate only under the control of an individual.

Smart terminal
A terminal that can transfer files between computers.

Automatic originate and answer system
A combination of software and hardware that makes it possible to answer telephone calls and automatically make calls without a human operator.

Figure 10–17
Communication between
Laptop and Desktop
Computers

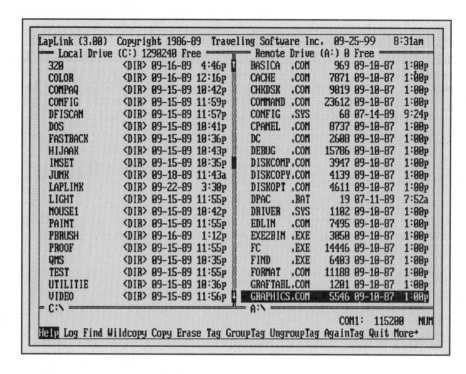

Figure 10–18
File Transfer

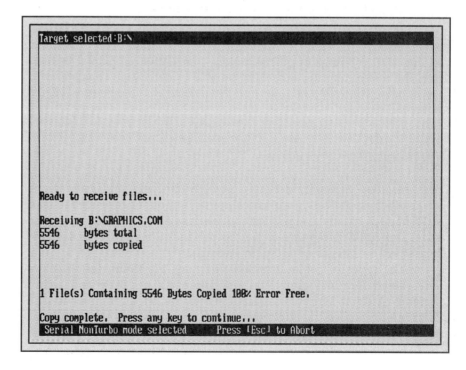

the transfer of a file out (uploading). It also allows the capture and storage of data received (downloading) and can control a printer to obtain hard copy. Automatic originate and answer systems are combinations of software and hardware that make it possible to answer telephone calls and automatically make calls without a human operator. Automatic operation helps take advantage of off-time telephone rates to reduce costs.

Communication and Transferring

Communication includes the selection of a communication partner, the use of national databases, and the use of networks.

Selecting a Communication Partner

The cost-conscious user should determine what is best done by a microcomputer as a stand-alone unit and what is best done by a central computer. Time-sharing started with the use of large mainframe computers in the mid-1960s. The idea was to allow the user access to the central computer by way of terminals. This service allows individuals to perform **real-time** processing of data instead of **batch runs.** A batch run is a scheduling system in which computer tasks are collected and given to a controller, which then runs them as a single job. The original terminals were capable of operating only when connected to a host computer.

> Batch run
> A scheduling system that requires that computer tasks be collected and given to a controller, who then runs them as a single job batched together.

  The dial-up terminal (via telephone) was developed for the time-sharing computer. Users quickly realized that microcomputers could act as terminals for central computers.

  The economic problem was to balance the costs of on-line processing with off-line processing. The original business computers in the late 1950s and early 1960s were so expensive that great efforts were made to create and use off-line machines for sorting, printing, and other services.

  The on-line/off-line problem still exists. Today, however, off-line equipment is a low-cost smart microcomputer. The microcomputer can do many of the tasks of a central computer at lower cost. As a user, you will have to answer the question, What is the best way to do the job: microcomputer or central computer? You answers will vary as the capabilities and costs of the two alternate approaches continue to change. In addition to performing many of the tasks of the central computer and acting as a terminal for the central computer, the microcomputer may be the central computer.

National Databases

Institutions can maintain their own databases, use those established as commercial services (Table 10–4), or both. The procedure for logging on all

Table 10-4
On-Line Subscription Databases

Type of Service	CompuServe Information Services	Dow Jones News/Retrieval	EasyNet
Electronic mail	Yes	Yes	No
Paper copy delivery	No	Yes	No
Stock quotations	Yes	Yes	Yes
Public access	No	No	Yes
Number of			
Databases	400	38	65
Subject areas	1,000+	11	Unlimited
Subscribers	400,000	235,000	NA
On-line publications	Yes	Yes	Yes
Access type			
Datapac	Yes	No	No
Direct 800	No	No	Yes
iNet	No	No	Yes
Telenet	Yes	Yes	Yes
Tymnet	Yes	Yes	Yes
Uninet	Yes	Yes	No

Note: Rates vary during the day and at night.

large host systems is similar. Usually, you must identify yourself with some codes before you can get started.

Dow Jones News/Retrieval System is a news and financial database service for up-to-the-minute information on stocks and bonds. You may research a company in depth and maintain a stock portfolio for automatic update.

Specialized databases exist in law, advertising, aviation, medicine, engineering, and many other fields. You will find books listing these databases in your library or at your local bookstore.

Electronic Mail

Electronic mail uses a computer to send messages through a computer network. Today users have the choice of electronic messaging (computer-to-computer transmission) or computer-generated mail (computer input and terminal output). Mail can be sent using an internal company system or through one of the commercial electronic mail carriers such as MCI, ITT, Western Union, Telex, or one of the electronic bulletin board systems. Internal company networks may consist of a microcomputer with an auto-answer telephone modem and a communication program that can save any message received. The system is turned on after business hours, and all messages received are printed the next morning and forwarded as needed.

CompuServ and The Source, which are now combined, were early suppliers of the electronic mail (E-mail) service. To use this service, both senders and receivers must be members of the service, and receivers must check their own mailboxes with their own microcomputers. Any brand of microcomputer can be used, because the communication uses standard asynchronous ASCII. One feature of the electronic mail service is the capability to send up to 200 messages at one time, to be forwarded at specific times.

CompuServe has electronic mail, a bulletin board, news, weather, magazines, wire services, a directory, and more. News services, such as the one for commodities, are updated every 20 minutes. The cost of use during business hours is much greater than during off-hours.

Some commercial electronic mail services provide a local toll-free telephone number. The user is expected to compose the letter off-line and upload it to the electronic mail service. There is usually an on-line charge to discourage on-line composition. The commercial service will save a message for downloading to the receiver's microcomputer, forward it by first-class or overnight mail, or hand deliver a printed copy of the message for various charges. Electronic mail is not seen as a substitution for a personal letter. Instead, it is a way to reach someone who is not available by telephone, to send out mass mailings, or to get a document delivered rapidly.

Setting up a system to use electronic mail requires knowledge of the communication parameters and of how to set up the program available on a microcomputer to match the settings with the electronic mail service.

If a company has a central computer or a microcomputer with a modem that will automatically answer the telephone, it can set up its own electronic mail service. The ability to standardize the parameters and software used internally in an organization makes the creation of an internal electronic mail service easier than the use of a commercial service in many circumstances.

Computer Conferencing

Computer conferencing is similar to telephone conferencing except that microcomputers, terminals, or central computers are on both ends of the communication partnership. Many systems accept text, graphics, and voice. Using your own resources or a database service, you can set up a `Participate` communication network. This allows individuals in different physical locations to "meet" using microcomputers. The advantage of this type of meeting over the telephone is that text, graphics, and voice can be transferred. If you have a microcomputer with a communication program that can capture and save what is received, you may transfer the material to your disks for future use.

Bulletin Boards

Electronic bulletin board
A computer with software that acts as a host to a variety of computers. The system allows users to call up (using telephone lines and modems) and use libraries, mail, and other services on an ad hoc basis.

Specialized computer databases service almost every industry and community. Many local retail microcomputer stores will run **electronic bulletin boards** for their customers and potential customers. These computer software systems allow the computer to act as a host to a variety of computers. Users can call up the bulletin board using their computer-modem system and can access a variety of services. Many bulletin boards are multiuser. Most have charges for their services.

Forum80 is a bulletin board found in many communities. It was originally set up by TRS-80 microcomputer owners, but it usually serves all users. This bulletin board includes some business information, but mainly hobby information.

Network Concepts and Background

A network system is controlled by a central human manager or management team. Each computer or other device connected to the network must operate within the limitations set by the system manager. Management controls are needed to eliminate or reduce problems from bad plugs (connections), bad routing, blown PC boards, broadcast storms, buffer overflow, data collision, incompatible software, misdirected output or data, piggish users, protocol errors, traffic jams, and unsecured terminals.

One task of the system management is to make sure that disk storage devices are backed up in a timely manner. When working alone, microcomputer users often fail to make backup copies of disks until they have a major loss and learn what can happen. When a management team is responsible for operating the system, proper backups are made. For example, power failures can result in days or weeks of redoing work. A professional system management team can reduce this work to mere hours.

A network may allow users to share peripherals such as laser printers and plotters. In common practice, a peripheral is connected to a control device, and then the computers on the network send codes to the control device that controls the peripheral. The codes are sent to the peripheral in the order received or according to some other priority rule.

The most basic network uses a mechanical or electronic switching device to connect microcomputers and peripherals. The connection of microcomputers to peripherals forms networks that can be considered low-end limited case networks.

Several individuals often must use the same file. In a network, all users can get to the file. The latest version or update is always available, and there is no need to transfer disks among individuals. The network accomplishes the communication objective of making data available to several users at different locations.

Networks also allow many individuals to use a single copy of a program. The program may be stored in a central area along with the common data files. When needed, the program is called up.

Networks are needed when many computer users with communication capabilities need to share peripherals, files, programs, and computer capabilities. **Multitasking,** the capability of performing more than one task at the same time, is often needed to share capabilities. A central host computer may share capabilities or simply perform as a file server.

A special type of network can be created by using **multiusing.** In a multiusing environment, all users share the same central processing unit (a microprocessor if the central unit is a microcomputer). This means the system need only have dumb terminals, but many use both smart and dumb terminals. Standard RS-232C, asynchronous serial communication, can be used in this type of network.

The capability for multiusing is part of the hardware and operating system. It is not found in all computers. The user can purchase software that adds this capability in some computers. Multiusing is not a solution to all problems. If only one person uses a microcomputer, or if the microcomputer used does not have to share databases, multiusing may not be needed.

The cost of multiusing relative to the cost of operating two stand-alone microcomputers is changing. For small offices, a central computer with a limited number of terminals may be an economical solution to computer use in the future. The terminals often will not have all the capabilities of the stand-alone microcomputer. The operation of a terminal in a network is similar to the operation of a microcomputer, except data and instructions can be sent and received from other workstations in the network.

A **central file server program** makes a microcomputer a central file server. It is often used in a network to control the access of individual workstations to the files stored in the "large" central storage device (hard disk). The central file server handles problems that occur when several users are trying to update a file at the same time. It is often designed to handle the problem of file security, keeping selected users from using specified files.

The control, such as limiting users, that management can exercise with central file servers approaches that of a large central computer. Data management of central data files is critical in many business situations.

The network's central data storage device may be a hard disk with 100MB of memory or more. Generally, LANs are designed for computers to communicate within an organization, using direct-wire connections with special interface devices for communication across telephone lines. When a LAN uses telephone lines, the operator will encounter many of the security problems of the time-sharing minicomputer and mainframe computer operators.

The sharing of commercial programs has led to some unresolved copyright problems. The technical developments in LANs have progressed faster than the legal and moral solutions to the use of software on more than one microcomputer.

Multitasking
The capability of performing more than one task at the same time.

Multiusing
The capability of microcomputers and programs that allow more than one user to share the same microprocessor.

Central file server program
A program that controls the access to files by individual workstations in a network.

Physical Transmission Media

The microcomputer is connected to a LAN through a port. This port may be built-in or created with the addition of a special-purpose PC board to the microcomputer. Among the cables used for computer networks are standard serial cables, standard parallel cables, single twisted pair, multiple twisted pair (up to 8), optical fiber, and coaxial for **baseband** and **broadband** transmissions (Figure 10–19). The standard serial and parallel cables usually use standard ports. The other cables always require custom PC boards. Baseband is the channel used for direct transmission of pulses over short distances (less than 10 miles) without the use of special cables. Broadband is a channel with a wide bandwidth (greater than voice-grade width) using special cables. The coaxial cables come with a variety of insulations. Cost limitations, performance, and speed determine the best selection.

Baseband
A channel used for direct transmission of pulses over short distances (less than 10 miles) without the use of special cables.

Broadband
A channel with a wide bandwidth (greater than voice-grade width) using special cables.

Twisted-pairs are the lines used to connect telephones. Networks using this type of wire are often designed around a central switching station. Generally, this type of network is the least expensive, has the slowest speed (approximately 1 million bytes per second), and is limited in the distance data can be sent to approximately 500 feet.

The current interest in networks is due to the drop in the cost of network PC boards, programs, terminals, wiring, and all other aspects of networks. Technical improvements and cost reductions are making networks a solution for many more problems.

Often, a single network combines many different types of cables, telephone lines, and satellites. For example, the type of cable used varies from twisted wire pairs, like those in telephone lines, to optical-fiber cables.

Baseband coaxial cable networks are medium speed (between 1 million and 10 million bytes per second), depending on the physical type of cable. This type of cable is used by PC Net and Ethernet (two popular commercial networks). A baseband coaxial cable is similar to cable television wiring. The baseband allows only one terminal or microcomputer to transmit at a time. The single **bus** can handle only a single user at a time. A bus is the pathway or channel for data and instructions to move between hardware devices. Distances are limited to a few thousand feet without the use of repeaters. A repeater is a device similar to an amplifier that inputs a weak electrical impulse and then forwards a stronger impulse. The installation cost of baseband coaxial cable is generally higher than that of twisted-pair wires or broadband cables.

Bus
A pathway or channel for data and instructions to move between hardware devices.

Broadband coaxial cable can handle many transmissions at one time, even different kinds of transmissions. Speeds from 1 million to 10 million bytes per second in each of up to 30 channel pairs are common. (For communication, a channel pair is needed to transmit information in both directions.) Optical-fiber cable is becoming more popular for broadband applications. Broadband cable can extend for miles with the use of inexpensive amplifiers.

A system built around one type of cable is easy to control and understand. Hybrid systems requiring a mixture of cables, interfaces, collectors, and telephone lines can become complex and technical.

Figure 10–19
Types of Cable Construction

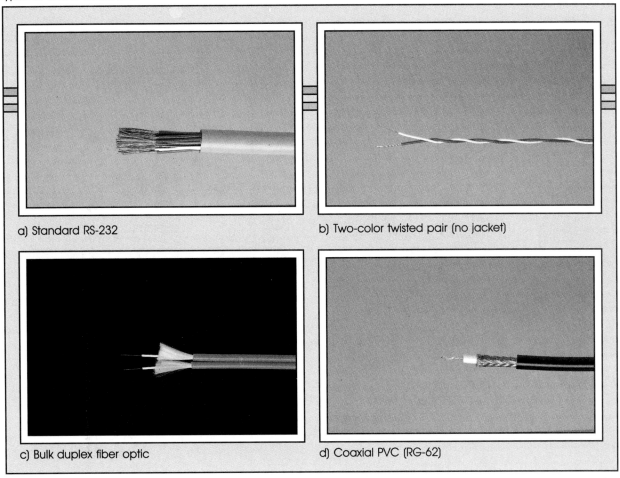

a) Standard RS-232

b) Two-color twisted pair (no jacket)

c) Bulk duplex fiber optic

d) Coaxial PVC (RG-62)

LAN Topology

The arrangements of stations relative to one another and relative to a central file server fall into some simple classifications. A LAN is often perceived to be a central communication network among individuals and machines in a local office. LANs require flexibility in adding and changing hardware devices to keep themselves current as technological changes occur. A LAN may need to be interfaced with mainframes or other LANs. Some popular **LAN topology** configurations include **central switching stations** (star), **communication buses, communication rings** or **communication circles,** and **point-to-point communication** (Figure 10–20). LAN topology is the relative physical and logical arrangement of stations in the network. A central switching station uses a central microcomputer connected to a series of stations in a LAN. This type of topology is often called a star. A communication bus is a LAN layout around a bus that serves as a

LAN topology
The relative physical and logical arrangement of stations in a network.

Central switching station
The central microcomputer connected to a series of stations in a LAN. This type of topology is often called a star.

Communication bus
A LAN layout around a bus that serves as a channel of communication.

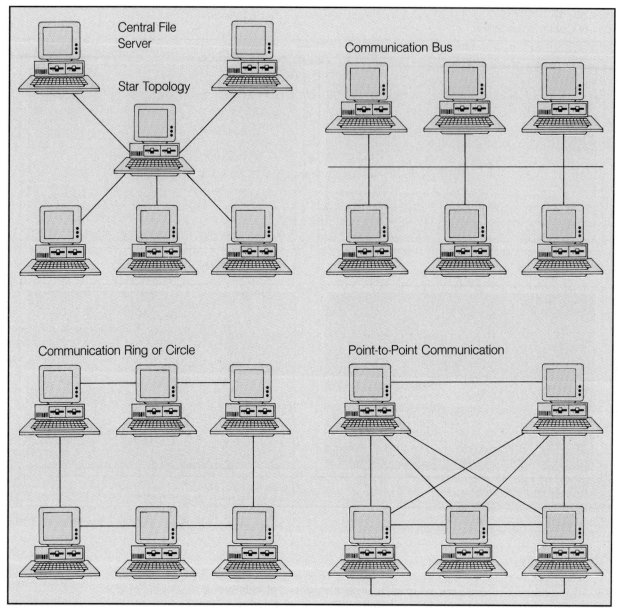

Figure 10–20
LAN Topology

Communication ring, or communication circle
LAN topology where the stations are connected in a ring or circle.

Point-to-point LAN
LAN topology where each station is connected directly to other stations.

channel of communication. A communication ring or circle is a LAN layout where the stations are connected in a ring or circle. A point-to-point LAN is a LAN layout where each station is connected directly to other stations.

Access Methods

Access methods determine how stations communicate with the other physical parts of the network. The access method is the scheme used by the

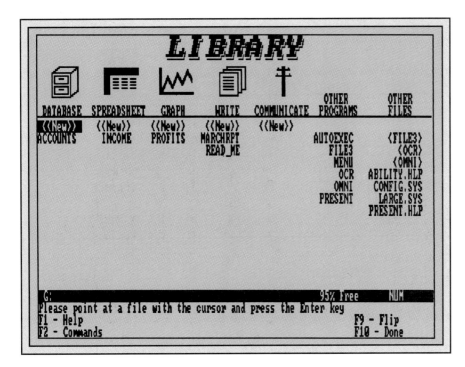

Figure 11-5
Ability Main Menu

Figure 11-6 shows the word processing screen of an integrated program, Microsoft Works. Microsoft Works can display text, spreadsheet output, database output, and graphs. If the value under the cursor in any application is changed, it is changed in all applications.

Including a spreadsheet (Figure 11-7) or graph in the Microsoft Works word processor document is simple, and the cost of an integrated program is usually less than the cost of all of its modules. For new computer users, the reduced cost and training needs make an integrated program a good selection. In some instances, users who need only two or three modules of an integrated program will find that it still costs less to purchase the integrated package.

Some of the disadvantages of integrated programs include the need for large amounts of RAM. For example, Microsoft Works requires less RAM than some stand-alone programs, needs greater speed than individual programs, and does not have the power of many stand-alone programs. The cost of RAM has decreased in recent years, so most users should purchase RAM in the quantity needed by integrated programs. With a few exceptions, the speed of today's microcomputers is adequate to support an integrated program. Some integrated programs require turbo boards and math co-processors to bring their performance up to acceptable levels. The need to display a combination of text and graphics often requires the greater speed.

Originally, individual modules of some integrated programs did not have the power of stand-alone programs. Some of the newer versions of integrated programs contain modules that utilize features competitive with today's stand-alone programs. For example, the power of peripherals (specifically, printers) has increased. Word processors need extensive con-

Figure 11-6
Microsoft Works—Letter

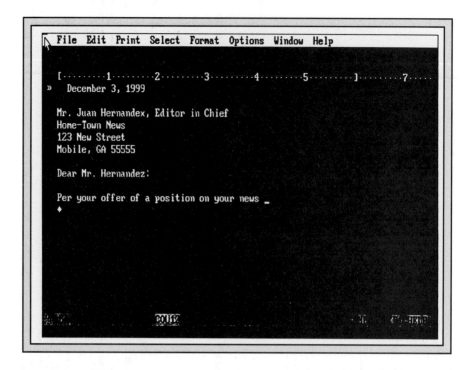

Figure 11-7
Microsoft Works—Spreadsheet

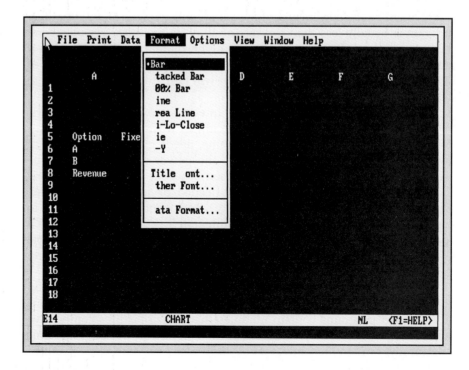

trols to obtain the features available in these printers. Often the controls are available in stand-alone word processors and not in integrated programs. When selecting an integrated program, the user should carefully examine the features of each part of the package.

Integrated and modular software packages are available for such special applications as general ledger, job costing, project control, time management, billing/accounts receivable, accounts payable, school administration, and banking applications. Some packages combine both general and special applications. Many software producers use general application programs as their base. Accounting, real estate, and statistical templates can be purchased for popular spreadsheet programs, making them ready to solve specific applications and giving the user a starting point for custom applications.

Add-in Programs

Add-in programs can be attached to an application program to add special capabilities such as screen display control (increasing and decreasing the number of columns and rows displayed), integration of text and graphics display, and desktop publishing (fonts and integrated graphics printed at the same time). Add-ins are most commonly found for spreadsheet programs.

Most add-in programs are created for a specific vendor's software. Figure 11–8 illustrates the use of SeeMORE and Lotus 1-2-3 (Release 2.2) to integrate the display of text and graphics. Figure 11–9 illustrates the use of Allways, a desktop publishing add-in that is sold with Lotus 1-2-3 (Release 2.2). Add-ins are available from both the original producer and third parties.

Operating System Shells

Operating system shells are integrating programs that have been created to hide the complexities of the disk operating system and to add features. The early shells were aimed at making the operating system user friendly rather than trying to integrate operations or data files between applications.

Operating system shells include **text shells** and **graphical user interface (GUI)** shells. A text shell is a user interface that uses the text display capabilities of a computer. A GUI is a user interface that uses the graphic display capabilities of a computer. Text shells reduce the complexity of system operations and text transfer but do not facilitate graphic image transfer. Microsoft Windows (a GUI shell for MS-DOS/PC DOS) and the Macintosh GUI make cutting and pasting text and graphics between applications easy. Figure 11–10 illustrates a Microsoft Windows screen in the process of cutting part of a picture in Paint.

Text shell
A user interface that uses the text display capabilities of a computer.

Graphical user interface (GUI)
A user interface that uses the graphic display capabilities of a computer.

Figure 11-8
SeeMORE Graphics Window
and Lotus 1-2-3 (Release 2.2)

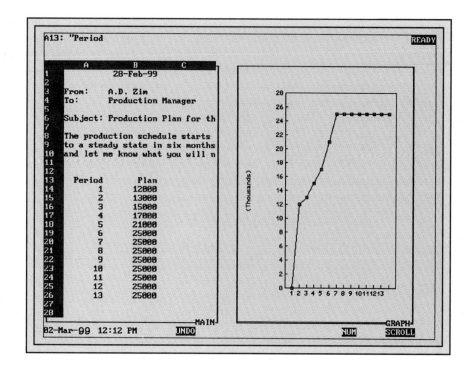

Figure 11-9
Allways and Lotus 1-2-3
(Release 2.2)

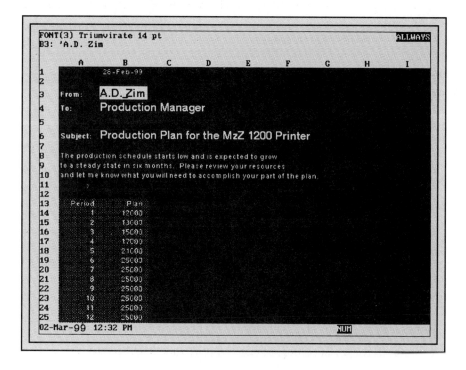

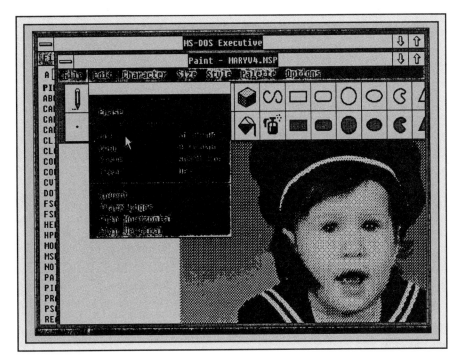

Figure 11–10
Cut in to Microsoft Windows
Using Paint

In general, text-based shells are faster and do not require special programming, while graphical shells provide the advantage of combining text and graphics at the cost of speed and the need for special programming. One advantage of a GUI is that the same user interface is used for most of the programs that use the shell. In general, a common interface makes it easy for a user to learn a new application.

The shells available today not only control the capabilities of the operating system but also add some of their own capabilities in a manner similar to the overlay utility programs, as well as allow the transfer of data between applications. Often, a utility program cannot be operated at the same time as an operating system overlay program because they fight with each other for control of the microcomputer.

Among the features added by many operating system overlay programs are multitasking and windows. Concurrent operation of word processing, database, and graphics is possible in some shells. Some shells use windows, allowing the user to view the operation of more than one program at a time. Text can be transferred between windows in a manner similar to moving blocks of text in word processing.

Data File Transfer Software

Data file transfer programs change one program's file format to match the file format used by a second program. Among the files used are ASCII files,

Data Interchange Format (DIF) files, near-ASCII files, special custom files (some using all 8 bits), symbolic link (SYLK) files, and graphics data files. Micros in Action "Transferring Output to Word Processors" indicates why some file transfer is required.

Micros in Action

Transferring Output to Word Processors

Bethco Mobile, Inc., has found that its clients often need to use the output of accounting and spreadsheet programs in word processing programs for report generation. Many clients also have a number of word processing programs and must be able to transfer files between them. Bethco tries to limit a client's selection of programs so that transfer is easy.

With the exception of some special custom files and graphics data files, the standard code used in each file is available from manuals or user groups. You can purchase programs that transfer material between these files. Some application programs include routines to transfer files between formats. Some graphics files that contain text can be transferred to text files by using optical character recognition programs.

It is often easier to transfer data into a word processor text file than into a spreadsheet, database, or graphics program file. Spreadsheet and database files contain labels, formulas, and numbers, whereas text files contain text and numbers. Transferring formulas into a spreadsheet, database, or graphics file is difficult unless you are using a DIF or SYLK type of format or you have a transfer utility.

Graphics file transfer is important in desktop publishing. This topic was covered in Chapters 6, 8, and 9. Many programs come with their own conversion software. Figure 11–11 illustrates the Lotus TRANS.COM program for converting files between spreadsheet formats and database formats. The number of such transfer utilities is increasing. In addition, programs such as SuperCalc5, VP-Planner PLUS, Quattro Pro, and so on are able to read many of the files that use the Lotus 1-2-3 format.

TSR Software

TSR software can add a variety of capabilities that are readily available to the user. With TSR programs, users can stop what they are doing and call up a second program to perform some necessary function without leaving the first program. Figure 11–12 illustrates the use of Lightning, a TSR spelling program.

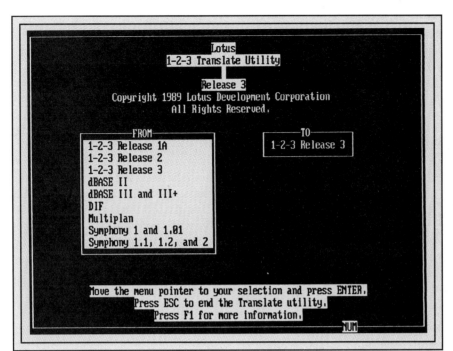

Figure 11–11
Lotus 1-2-3 (Release 3.0)
Transfer Program

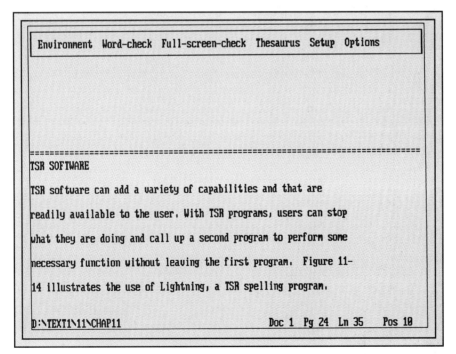

Figure 11–12
Lightning Spelling Checker in
WordPerfect

Checking the time or date, making calculations, looking up a telephone number, and writing a note are examples of the types of utilities that TSR software can add. Table 11–3 lists some TSR programs and their characteristics.

A common method of transferring graphics between applications is to capture a screen display. A TSR program is needed to perform this task. Many programs, such as InSet and Fancy-Fonts, stand between an application program and your printer. InSet merges graphics, and Fancy-Fonts produces special fonts.

TSR programs may conflict with one another and with application programs. For example, when InSet or Fancy-Fonts is loaded, certain codes cannot be sent to the printer. The codes have special meanings to the TSR programs and are captured rather than being passed through to the printer.

It is possible to jam a computer with combinations of TSR programs. You will learn which programs work with each other and which do not. If you have more than two TSR programs, it is difficult to forecast how they will work together without trying them.

Table 11–3
TSR Programs

Feature	Fancy-Fonts	Frieze	Home-Base	InSet	MYDESK	SideKick
ASCII table						x
Autodialer			x		x	x
Calculator			x		x	x
Calendar						x
Cut/paste		x		x		x
Database			x		x	x
Data transfer			x			
DOS control			x			x
Merge Graphics						
Into text				x		
Into editor		x		x		
Notepad			x		x	x
Printer control	x			x		
Rolodex			x			x
Screen capture						
Graphics		x		x		
Text				x		x

Summary

Among the methods of integrating operations are using integrated programs, modular programs, add-in programs, operating system shells, and TSR programs. An integrated program is a program that combines several different types of programs such as word processing, spreadsheet, data-driven graphics, and database. Modular programs are a series of programs designed to work together that may be purchased separately. An add-in program is a program that is attached to an applications program to add capabilities. An operating system shell is a program that takes over the disk operating system, adds capabilities (multitasking and file transfer between two programs operating concurrently) and controls the operation of applications programs. Data file transfer software are programs designed to read data in the format produced by one program and change them to a format needed by a second program. A TSR program is a program that is loaded into memory and remains in memory while other programs are loaded and used. A TSR program, once loaded, can be recalled using a series of keys while some other program is running.

There are two types of operating system shells: text and graphical user interface (GUI). A text shell is an interface that uses the text display capabilities of a computer. A GUI is a user interface that uses the graphics display capabilities of a computer.

Key Terms

Add-in program

Data file transfer software

File linkage

Graphical user interface (GUI)

Integrated program

Modular program

Operating system shell

Productivity

Terminate and stay resident (TSR) program

Text shell

Review Questions

1. What is an integrated program?
2. What features would you expect to find in an integrated program?
3. What is a modular program? What is the difference between an integrated and a modular program?
4. What is an add-in program?
5. Identify what an add-in program does.
6. What is an operating system shell?
7. Why would you want to use an operating system shell?
8. Identify what a data file transfer program does.

9. Why would you want to use a data file transfer program?
10. What is a TSR program?
11. How does a TSR program help integrate operations and data?
12. What is productivity?
13. What is the difference between personal productivity and organizational productivity?
14. What is a text shell?
15. What is a GUI?
16. Why would you select a text shell over a GUI? Why would you select a GUI over a text shell?
17. Give an example of a GUI.
18. Identify some of the capabilities added by an operating system shell.
19. Identify the techniques available for integrating operations and data files.
20. Identify some of the reasons for selecting one technique over another in integrating operations and data files.

Discussion and Application Questions

1. Examine microcomputer magazine advertisements for data file transfer software between programs. What programs are available, how much do they cost, and what features do they have?
2. Examine microcomputer magazine advertisements for modular software. What programs are available, how much do they cost, and what features do they have?
3. Examine microcomputer magazine advertisements for integrated software. What programs are available, how much do they cost, and what features do they have?
4. Examine microcomputer magazine advertisements for overlay utility software. What programs are available, how much do they cost, and what features do they have?
5. Examine microcomputer magazine advertisements for system overlay software. What programs are available, how much do they cost, and what features do they have?

Laboratory Assignments

1. Determine the number of ways you can transfer data files between the programs available in your laboratory. Use as many of these methods as possible to move data files. Report on the results.

2. If available in your laboratory, use a modular program and an integrated program to solve the problems outlined in the earlier chapters of this text, and report on the differences among these programs.

3. If available, use a utility program, and report on its features.

PART IV

Microcomputer Software and Hardware Selection

CHAPTER 12

Software and Hardware Selection

Goals

Upon completion of this chapter, you will be able to do the following:

- Outline a method for selecting a program.
- Describe a method for selecting a computer.
- Detail a procedure for justifying the choice of a microcomputer system.

Outline

Why Know Your Needs?

Sources of Programs

Planning and Analysis

Idea

Objective

Plan

Analysis

Implementation

Summary

Key Terms

Review Questions

Discussion and Application Questions

Laboratory Assignment

Decision Making

Hospitality Investor Services, Inc., of Memphis, Tennessee, is a large motel/restaurant investment and management firm. It owns and manages properties in the southeastern part of the United States between Florida and Texas. Over the years, Hospitality Investor Services has developed a number of evaluation procedures for the selection and evaluation of properties. It specializes in purchasing properties that have the potential for growth under the firm's special management style.

Hospitality Investor Services decided to use microcomputers in a number of different evaluation and analysis methods, including breakeven analysis, determinations of gross multipliers, and calculations of average daily rates combined with occupancy ratios in motel and hotel investments. These simpler techniques are used in the initial pass to determine if additional time and effort should be spent making a detailed period-by-period income and expense analysis. The analysis procedures apply to the purchase of investment properties; the bidding on management service contracts; and the investment in equipment, including trucks and microcomputers.

Hospitality Investor Services uses its microcomputer system to help in decision making processes by making use of financial models, calculating the sensitivity of each decision to market conditions, and graphing the results of the analysis.

The microcomputer is a low-cost method of solving problems. It can solve problems and save money when it is fitted for, and accepted into, an overall system. You must learn how to identify which of your needs might be solved with microcomputers. You have computer options in addition to microcomputers, and some of these options may better satisfy specific needs. Micros in Action "Decision Making" illustrates how a real estate management company, Hospitality Investor Services, selected equipment, including a microcomputer system.

Why Know Your Needs?

You must analyze your situation to determine your needs before purchasing a microcomputer to fill them. You are in the best position to determine your current and potential needs and to identify where a microcomputer system might be used to meet these needs. To prepare yourself to perform a microcomputer analysis, your background should combine microcomputer training, business and professional training, and experience in an organization. A microcomputer purchase requires a detailed plan and analysis, and it is your job to make it.

Selecting a microcomputer system for home use involves the same considerations as selecting one for professional use. The key issues include the current and future needs of all family members for compatibility with school and with work.

An organization may employ a microcomputer manager who can help organize and evaluate the needs of the institution. You may be the **micromanager,** the manager in charge of purchasing and controlling microcomputer equipment in an organization. At home, you must perform the job of the micromanager and identify the entire family's needs for microcomputer equipment.

Home resources are limited in the amount of available software, the level of computer training of each family member, and the money available for the investment.

Micromanager
A manager in charge of purchasing and controlling microcomputer equipment in an organization.

Sources of Programs

Finding the exact program to perform a task often requires research. General purpose programs, such as word processor, spreadsheet, database, etc., are easy to find. Programs to perform surveying calculations or engineering bridge construction analysis, for example, may be more difficult. Common sources of programs are professional sources, computer suppliers, shareware resellers, and educational publishers. Professional organizations, magazines, suppliers, and competitors of existing software are good places to start looking.

One low-cost method to obtain software is to use **public domain programs** and **shareware.** Public domain and shareware programs are available through computer clubs, your public library, computer communication networks, friends, and commercial firms that distribute the software for the value of the distribution charge (between $2 and $5 per disk). The new owners of shareware programs are asked to send a purchase fee of between $25 and $100 to the holder of copyright if they find the program useful. In essence, the user has a moral and legal obligation to pay for the use of the shareware. Users of public domain software are not expected to pay any fees.

Some shareware programs are limited-capability demonstration parts of commercial programs, and some are more powerful than commercial programs. Generally, if you have unregistered shareware or public domain software problems, you are on your own. Only if you become a registered shareware program owner (that is, pay the purchase fee) can you expect any support.

Included among shareware programs are word processors; font generators; and spreadsheet, database, graphics (business and drawing), communication, games, training, mathematical, and statistics programs. You can operate a system using shareware programs only. Programs ob-

Public domain program
A program available for use without cost except for distribution and copying costs. Usually, no support or updates are available for public domain programs.

Shareware
A program available for review at no cost except for distribution and copying costs. If the user decides to keep and use the program, a small registration fee paid directly to the programmer is expected. The user is often provided with support and updates when the registration fee is paid.

tained from shareware suppliers include complete working programs, partially-disabled demonstration programs, and free public domain programs. It usually costs more in time to examine a program and understand it enough to determine its value, than what is paid for the disk. Shareware suppliers advertise in professional and computer magazines.

Educational versions of software are often included with textbooks or sold with reduced capabilities to the educational market. These programs are designed for educational purposes, and are excellent within that field.

Planning and Analysis

A microcomputer system consists of both software and hardware. Usually, the selection of software comes before the selection of hardware. The steps in analyzing the needs for both software and hardware include the idea, objective, plan, analysis, and implementation.

Idea

A human being evaluates any and all facts available and comes up with an **idea,** a recognition that there may be a problem or opportunity in need of study. The idea precedes all other actions, because it is the recognition of need.

Idea
The recognition of a need or opportunity.

Brainstorming sessions, a good night's sleep, a passing sight, or the occurrence of a problem might trigger an idea. Only people can create ideas or dreams. One of these ideas might be using a program and microcomputers to solve problems.

Objective

An **objective** is a goal. To transform an idea into an objective, it needs to have several characteristics. It must be feasible, it must be measurable, it must have a time limit, its limitations must be recognized, and it must have a plan for completion.

Objective
A goal that is feasible, is measurable, has a time limit, has recognized limitations, and has a plan for its accomplishment.

Feasible Objective

A **feasible** objective is one that can be accomplished. For example, it is meaningless to dream of earning $10 million this year if you are starting at

Feasible
Able to be accomplished.

a base of $1,000. It is better to set realistic objectives and then modify the goals as capabilities grow.

No software-computer combination can do everything. Some of the considerations when selecting software are needs, capabilities (being simple to learn and use, having the power to produce results), compatibility with a specified user group, availability of national and local support, market penetration, look and feel of the operation, and price.

Often, a package that is easy to learn and use does not have the power to perform the complex tasks needed for a particular application. The new user must decide whether to purchase either the ease of learning or the capability to obtain the results needed.

There is a lower limit to the price of any software-hardware system. For example, your organization might require a new word processor and microcomputer system with 640K of random access memory (RAM), a 20MB hard disk, a 360K floppy disk, the MS-DOS/PC DOS operating system, a high-resolution card and color graphics, and a color monitor. With a budget of $300, purchasing this equipment would not be a feasible objective. No matter how hard and long you worked, the objective could not be realized unless you purchased a stolen microcomputer system or the current price level dropped.

Measurable Objective

Measurable
Able to be quantified.

A **measurable** objective is one that can be quantified. If you cannot measure the completion of a goal, you cannot tell if you have achieved it. For example, to be rich is a meaningless goal. To earn a million dollars is a measurable objective that can be accomplished.

The goal "To improve the operation of this office" does not mean anything and cannot be measured, because the word *improve* does not have a precise meaning. If there were a 2 percent increase in the output of the office, would this be an improvement? If the lighting were replaced and the employees found the office an easier place to work, would this be an improvement? If a microcomputer with a word processing program were purchased to replace a typewriter, would this be an improvement? A restatement of the objective as "To increase the output of letters by 20 percent with no increase in personnel" gives the manager a goal that can be measured.

Time Limit

Time limit
A specified date by which an event must occur.

A **time limit** is a specified date by which a task must be completed or an event must occur. If an objective does not have a time limit, you can never fail to reach it. For example, "To computerize my organization someday" is a dream, whereas "To replace 90 percent of the typewriters being used with microcomputers in the next 12 months" is an objective, if it is feasible.

You may wish to purchase a software-microcomputer system, but if you do not have the cash or credit to make the purchase, you will have to delay your purchase until this limitation can be eliminated. The time limit is what makes limits real in any given decision-making situation.

Table 12–1
Milestones of the Plan

Microcomputer Needs	Start	6 Months	12 Months	24 Months	36 Months
Microcomputer	x				
Furniture	x				
Single disk drive	x				
Second disk drive	x				
Daisy wheel printer	x				
Cables	x				
Word processor program	x				
Dot-matrix printer		x (80 column)			
Printer switch/cables		x			
Graphics program		x			
Dot-matrix printer			x (132 or 200+ column)		
Spreadsheet program		x			
Database program		x			
Hard disk				x	

Once all the data are stored in the spooler, the microcomputer is free to be used for another purpose. The printer continues to produce output from the data in the spooler as the microcomputer is used.

Spreadsheet, database, graphics, and integrated programs tend to use the most RAM. Programs designed for CP/M, TRS-DOS, Apple-DOS, and other 8-bit systems are designed to operate within the limitations of these systems, that is, usually 64K of RAM. MS-DOS/PC DOS programs often use from 400 to 640K of RAM or more because of added program features.

To estimate the needed RAM requires that you identify specific programs that perform each of the capabilities you need. Because RAM cost is low, buy a little more than the maximum you need initially. As your skill in using the microcomputer grows, you will find that you need more memory. New program upgrades often require more RAM.

A hard disk drive adds speed and storage capacity to a microcomputer system Speed is convenient for many different program applications. Storage capacity allows flexibility when many applications are needed on short notice and when a database system is established. Databases for inventory control, personnel, customer identification, credit, club membership, and data analysis may require large amounts of memory. There are ways you can estimate the amount of storage needed. The database discussion in Chapter 8 described a field, record, and file. Capacity planning starts with determining the size of a record and then estimating the number of records needed. Growth estimates are added, and the size is rounded off to the next largest hard disk system available. It is usually more cost effective to purchase more storage than you need initially than to add additional storage by replacing one hard disk drive system with another at some future time.

Another factor that will affect the selection of a hard disk drive is how it is organized. There are ways to partition the hard disk between different applications and different operating systems used on the same microcomputer. Figure 12–4 shows two checklists to use as starting points.

Figure 12–4
Starting Point Checklists: Factors to Be Analyzed

RAM
On-line storage
Printer or printers
Monitor type
   Color
   Monochrome
Printer type
   Dot-matrix
   Daisy wheel
   Laser
   Ink-jet
   Plotter
Special boards
   Graphics
   Communication
   Speech recognition
   Speech synthesis
   Special interfaces
   Additional memory
   Network
Other devices
   Mouse
   Joystick
   Koala pad
   Bar code reader
   Digitizer pad
   Touch-sensitive screen
   Scanner
   Optical character recognition
   Voice mail

Vendor Selection

The price of a microcomputer is only one of the factors upon which to base the selection of a microcomputer. A business selling in a local market should make some of its purchases in the local market. You cannot expect business professionals to buy from you unless you give them the opportunity to sell to you.

You may elect to purchase from companies that either sell you a computer-in-a-box or provide you with a computer and support. Generally, you will pay less for a computer-in-a-box than you will for a computer and support. However, unless you are trained in hardware and software installation, you may end up spending many costly hours getting your system started and supporting it once started. Some mail order firms give good long-distance support. Some local firms provide no support, and others provide good support. Support and service are critical parts of the purchasing decision.

A microcomputer, once installed, rapidly becomes an important part of your operational needs. The ability of your vendor to train your personnel and repair, service, and upgrade your microcomputer is important. A loss of several days' work for equipment repair may be costly in terms of lost time and effort, as well as inconvenience. You can purchase different types of service plans from many vendors. You can have on-site service, have carry-in service, or risk just paying for service as needed. Remember, a microcomputer is like any other piece of equipment; when used by a large number of individuals, it will require more maintenance than the same unit operated by a single user.

Training takes time and costs money. Training needs include start-up expenses and personnel replacement and retraining. When additional capabilities are added, you will again need more training. You must evaluate the ability of a vendor to provide such training and determine the expected costs. A retail store may provide introductory-level training for new programs but little more. Further training from an additional source or a hired consultant is often necessary.

Many individuals learn how to use a program by reading the documentation. If you do not have the time or background to understand the documentation, you should consider hiring someone to help. Some firms with centralized purchasing procedures often prepare a bid request form when purchasing equipment as part of the computer use and purchase plan. You must know what your microcomputer is to do before its configuration can be determined. Whether you prepare a formal bid request or not, you should identify the required capabilities of your system.

If you have a problem and do not wish to spend the time finding out how to solve it, it is often advisable to hire a consultant to do the job for you. Developing microcomputer specifications is a time-consuming task. You or an associate must spend the time to learn your microcomputer needs, or you must spend you money hiring an outsider to do the job. If you spend neither the time nor money needed to do the job right, you are likely to make costly errors by purchasing the wrong equipment. A good, reputable vendor may also be able to help.

Analysis

Analysis
A comparison of alternate management actions.

Productivity
Output divided by input.

The **analysis,** or comparison, of alternative methods for solving a user's microcomputer dilemma is based on the productivity of an organization, office, or individual. **Productivity** is output divided by input:

$$\text{Productivity} = \frac{output}{input}$$

You must identify and measure the input and output as part of your analysis.

Input

Input includes all the factors of production:

> Land (raw materials).
> Labor (the people who do the work).
> Capital (the money and the equipment that the money can purchase; software and hardware).
> The enterprise (management and other aspects of the organization).

The substitution principle of the factors of production says that if one factor becomes expensive, it should be replaced by another factor so that the lowest cost balance is maintained. In a like manner, if one factor becomes less expensive, it should replace the other, more expensive factors.

Microcomputers with application programs are a part of the capital factor. The capital factor as applied to microcomputers is decreasing. As the capabilities of microcomputers and the effectiveness of their programs improve, the cost of using this equipment decreases. You have learned what a microcomputer can do.

Output

Output is the goods and services produced by a company. The output of each company, office, or individual is a function of the job that must be done. You are in a good position to determine what this output is.

Each person or work station in an organization adds to the overall objective by producing some contribution. Table 12–2 shows the possible priority of some objectives in a local car dealership. Simply writing down the objectives and output of specific positions brings to light some possible uses for microcomputers.

Measuring Input and Output

Money and time are the most common measurements of input (factors of production). Each of the input factors must be identified and then measured.

Table 12–2
Hierarchy of Some Objectives

Level	Objective
Business enterprise	To make a profit
Sales department	To sell vehicles
Individual salesperson	To sell vehicles To set up and maintain a database of all contacts
Secretary	To produce contracts, letters, and other documents To set up and maintain a database of all buyers
Repair and maintenance	To make a profit

In general, for a specific output you must count the amount of material or power used, the number of hours of labor used, the number of capital dollars or the amount of hours of capital equipment used, and the dollar and time costs of management input. The key word is *count.* There is no substitute for hard work and counting. After counting you must record the results. Table 12–3 shows a work-sampling report used to measure the labor activities (input) in a typing group.

Once the input has been measured, the output must also be measured. The output of a typing group might be documents. If the mix of

Table 12–3
Work-sampling Report on a Typing Group

Activity	Percent Observations
Talking on phone	20
Typing	60
Talking to individuals	10
Being out of area	7
Other	3
	$\overline{100}$

large documents (contracts) and small documents (letters) is constant, just counting documents may be satisfactory. If the mix changes, a more detailed measure of output is needed. When the study is complete, you will have a productivity equation:

$$\text{Productivity} = \frac{\text{documents}}{\text{power and supplies} + \text{labor hours} + \text{equipment cost} + \text{management costs}}$$

Finding a combined measure of input is difficult and often not necessary. If the costs of power, supplies (including land), and management does not change, you need not be concerned about measuring them. When replacing a typist/typewriter with a typist/word processor, you need to be concerned with labor hours input, equipment costs, and document output. The objective is to compare the productivity of the old method with the productivity of the new method to determine if the investment in the microcomputer system is justified.

Justifying a Microcomputer

There are a number of investment justification techniques. Among them are breakeven analysis, payback period analysis, and present worth analysis. All techniques depend on the measurements made in determining productivity. The breakeven and payback period analyses are simple and will be covered in this chapter. An ideal method of solving breakeven, payback, and present worth problems is with the use of an electronic spreadsheet and microcomputer graphics.

Breakeven Analysis

The objective of breakeven analysis is to determine the number of units of output when the total cost of one method is equal to the total cost of another method.

Assume one method is using a typist with a typewriter and the other, a typist with word processor. Assume also that the cost and time data are as shown in Table 12–4.

The increased output of the word processor is often due to its editing capability, especially when correcting second and third drafts. It is assumed that the document would be typed once and two additional edited copies produced. The breakeven equation follows:

$$\text{Breakeven} = \frac{\text{capital cost (new method)} - \text{capital cost (old method)}}{\text{old cost per unit} - \text{new cost per unit}}$$

$$= \frac{3,000 - 0.00}{1.9512 - 0.9639}$$

$$= 3,038.39 \text{ documents}$$

The calculations tell us that it is more economical to use the typewriter until 3,039 documents are produced. Above 3,039 documents, the word processor becomes more economical.

Table 12–4
Breakeven Analysis

Alternative	Typist with Typewriter	Typist with Word Processor
New investment	None	$3,000.00
Pages per hour	4.1	8.3
Cost at $8/hour per page	$1.9512	$0.9639

Note: Estimates for the typist are based on 45-character-per-minute average, including the time required to load and unload the typewriter, 10 characters per line, and 66 lines per page. The result is 14.7 minutes per page, or 4.1 pages per hour.

   The word processing cost per page assumes one original and two copies. The time to correct and print a copy is 25 percent of the time to create an original. The result is 7.252 minutes per page, or 8.3 pages per hour.

The breakeven equation can be used to compare any two alternatives. The equation can also be used to compare a revenue with a total cost. The revenue is considered an alternative with no capital cost in the formula.

Payback Period Analysis

A payback period analysis is a breakeven analysis with the scale in terms of time rather than pieces. Assuming that enough work exists to keep the typist/word processing system operating at full speed, the output per day would be 8.3 × 8, or 66.4 pages per day. Dividing 3,039 by 66.4 yields a result of approximately 46 days for the payback period. Figure 12–5 illustrates the results on a spreadsheet. The total cost at breakeven for the two alternatives should be equal. The spreadsheet shows the values to be typewriter = 5928.57 and word processor = 5928.57.

   The mathematical results tell us that if full output is maintained for 46 days, it pays to purchase the microcomputer with a word processor.

   The breakeven and payback period analysis can also be performed using a spreadsheet and graphics program. Figure 12–6 shows a Quattro Pro spreadsheet with the formulas displayed for the breakeven problem. Figures 12–7 and 12–8 are graphical analyses of the problem produced on Quattro Pro. Figure 12–7 illustrates a completed graph with a cost and piece scale; the point where the lines cross is labeled *breakeven*. Figure 12–8 illustrates the payback graph in the menu selection mode of Quattro Pro. The differences between these two graphs are the labels and the scale.

   Both graphs tell the same story. The total cost of the old method (use of typewriters) is less than the total cost of word processors until the breakeven point (3,039 documents) or the end of the payback period (46 days).

Figure 12–5
Spreadsheet Analysis Using
Quattro Pro

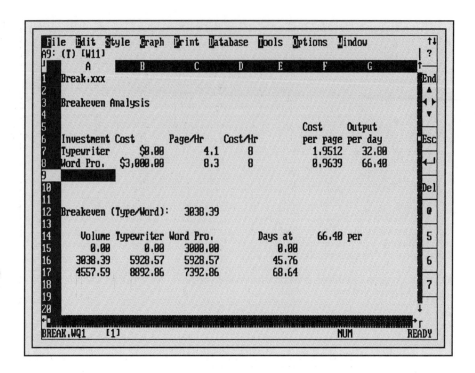

Figure 12–6
Spreadsheet Showing Formulas
in Quattro Pro

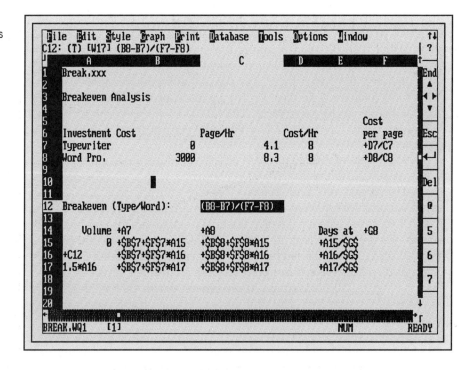

Decision Support Systems

A decision support system (DSS) is a set of computer-based aids used to assist in decision making. DSS programs are available for accounting, statistical analysis, billing and invoicing, business and engineering evaluation, customer records, elementary education, the entertainment industry, government, inventory control, medicine, political science, social science, employee training, management science, quality control, and many other applications. In some areas the number of programs is so great that it is difficult to select the best program from the many good ones available. As microcomputer capabilities increase, costs decrease, and computer skills are developed by more individuals so that new DSS applications are constantly being developed.

In general, a DSS is oriented towards decision making rather than towards information processing. A DSS is designed to solve semi-structured problems and combines many disciplines such as management science, statistics, engineering, management, computer science, operations research, and others. A DSS uses custom, spreadsheet, database, and any other programs that can help solve a particular problem or produce forecasts or estimates. Statistical, management science, and accounting programs are among the programs used in DSS.

Statistical Programs

Table 1A lists some popular statistical programs and some of the procedures they perform. Students often have the opportunity to purchase or use student versions of popular professional packages. MINITAB-Student Edition and SPSS/PC+ Studentware programs are included in Table 1A to illustrate reduced capacity, capabilities, and priced programs. Often, student packages may be operated using floppy disk systems, while full version programs require hard disks.

In addition to software, spreadsheet templates are available for solving many statistical problems. When you use a template prepared by a second party, it is similar to using a software package. Spreadsheet programs, however, are simple enough that many users learn to develop their

Table 3A
Statistical Programs—Data Files

	GB Stat	MINITAB Student Edition	Stat-Graphics	SPSS/PC+ V3.0	SPSS/PC+ Studentware	Structuring and Solving Operations Management Problems Using Lotus 1-2-3
ASCII	x	Data	x			x
Custom	x	Instruc.	x			
dBASE			x			
DIF	x		x			x
Map				*		
SYLK				**		
Lotus 1-2-3 WK?			x			x

* Produces files for direct export to Ashton-Tate Map-Master.
** Produces SYLK for use by Microsoft Chart.

Because SPSS was originally created when computer graphics were poorly developed, graphical analysis was added to SPSS data through the use of programs such as Harvard Graphics and Graph-in-a-Box. Provisions for using these graphic programs are built into SPSS. GB-Stat and Stat-Graphics come with graphics routines integrated into their operation. In GB-Stat, the selection of graphics is menu-driven (Figure 3A).

Management Science Programs

Programs are available for most management science models used in decision support systems, including economic, inventory, and simulation. As students, you may use some of the management science educational software. In addition to management science programs, texts and software which also contain spreadsheet templates for solving operations management and management science problems are available, such as *Structuring and Solving Operations Management Problems Using Lotus 1–2–3*, 2d edition, by Zimmerman and Zimmerman (St. Paul, MN: West Publishing Company, 1991); *Microcomputer Models for Management Decision-Making*, 2d edition, by Dennis and Dennis (St. Paul, MN: West Publishing Company, 1988); *The Management Scientist and Quantitative Methods for Business*, 4th edition, by Anderson, Sweeney, and Williams (St. Paul, MN: West Publishing

Figure 3A
Graphics Menu GB–Stat

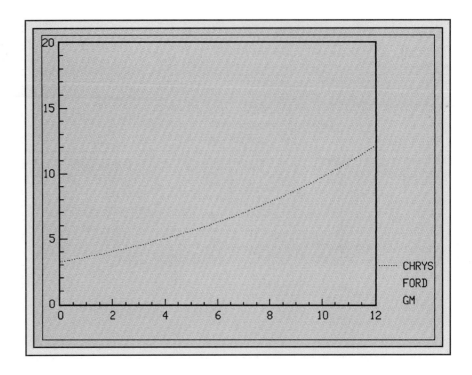

Company, 1989); and *Storm: Quantitative Modeling for Decision Support (Personal Version 2.0)* by Emmons, Flowers, Khot, and Mathur (Oakland, CA: Holden-Day, 1989).

Figure 4A illustrates the opening menu for Microcomputer Models for Management Decision Making, and Figure 5A illustrates the opening menu of Storm. Table 4A is a comparison of the three software packages and the spreadsheet collection. An advantage of using the spreadsheet approach over programs is that you can rewrite the spreadsheets to accomplish a more specific objective. When using programs, you are limited to the imagination of the programmer.

Accounting Programs

In both profit-making and non-profit organizations, accounting records provide most of the data for managerial decision making. An accounting system includes procedures for processing data and for generating reports.

Figure 6A illustrates the opening menu of an accounting program. Figure 7A illustrates the transaction data entry screen. No matter what accounting program selected you need to select the task to be performed and to enter transaction data. In many point-of-sale systems, the data entry is performed automatically when a transaction is entered into the cash register. A computer may be combined with a cash register for data entry into an accounting system and at the point-of-sale.

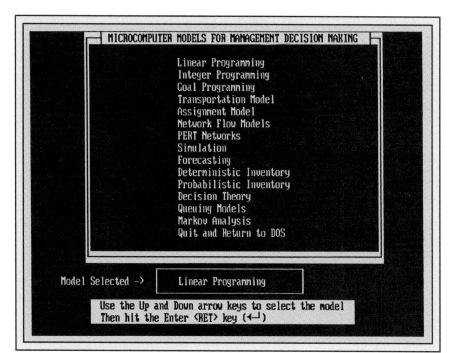

Figure 4A
Microcomputer Models for
Management Decision Making,
Opening Menu

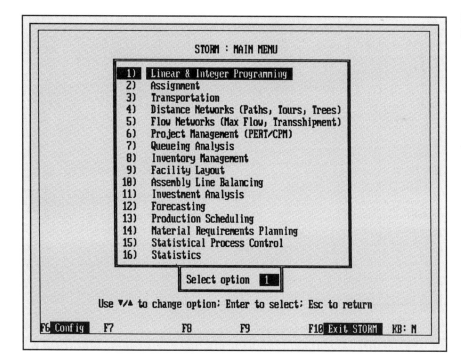

Figure 5A
Storm Opening Menu

Table 4A
Management Science Coverage—Comparison of Software

	DPac	Microcomputer Models for Management Decision Making	Storm	Structuring and Solving Operations Management Problems Using Lotus 1-2-3
Assembly Line Balancing	x			
Assignment		x	x	
Average Outgoing Quality	x			
Decision Theory		x		
Distance Networks	x	x	x	
Facility Layout	x		x	x
Flow Networks	x	x	x	
Forecasting	x	x	x	x
Graphical Method	x			x
Goal Programming		x		
Integer Programming		x	x	
Inventory Management	x	x	x	x
Investment Analysis	x		x	x
Linear Programming	x	x	x	
Material Requirements Planning	x		x	x
Markov Analysis		x		
Operating Characteristics	x			x
Production Scheduling	x		x	x
Project Management PERT/CPM	x	x	x	x
Queuing Analysis	x	x	x	x
Statistical Process Control	x		x	x
Statistics	x		x	x
Simulation	x	x		x
Transportation	x	x	x	x

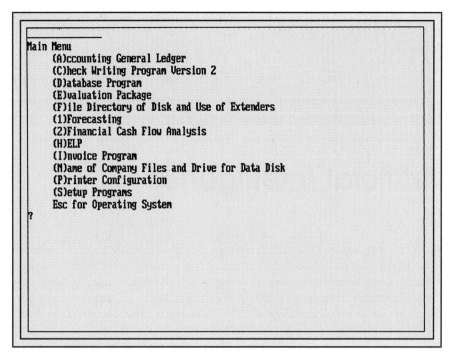

Figure 6A
Accounting Program Opening
Menu

```
Main Menu
    (A)ccounting General Ledger
    (C)heck Writing Program Version 2
    (D)atabase Program
    (E)valuation Package
    (F)ile Directory of Disk and Use of Extenders
    (1)Forecasting
    (2)Financial Cash Flow Analysis
    (H)ELP
    (I)nvoice Program
    (N)ame of Company Files and Drive for Data Disk
    (P)rinter Configuration
    (S)etup Programs
    Esc for Operating System
?
```

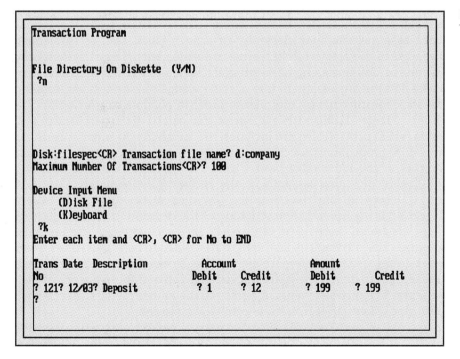

Figure 7A
Transaction Data Entry

```
Transaction Program

File Directory On Diskette  (Y/N)
 ?n




Disk:filespec<CR> Transaction file name? d:company
Maximum Number Of Transactions<CR>? 100

Device Input Menu
    (D)isk File
    (K)eyboard
 ?k
Enter each item and <CR>, <CR> for No to END

Trans Date  Description      Account          Amount
No                        Debit    Credit    Debit       Credit
? 121? 12/03? Deposit      ? 1      ? 12      ? 199    ? 199
?
```

Artificial Intelligence

Artificial intelligence (AI) includes all computer operations that resemble human intelligence. Among AI applications are robots with sensory capabilities, knowledge-based expert systems with decision making rules, and natural-foreign language translation applications. A robot is a device equipped with sensing equipment for identifying input signals or environmental conditions, a guidance mechanism which can react to the input data, or a stored program which determines a desired response.

Expert systems are one of the most developed areas of AI. An expert system is application software with the capability to recommend solutions to problems and trace the logic applied to the decision. Expert systems require a knowledge base (a set of decision making rules stored in a database for a situation or application, usually within a DSS). A knowledge base includes four elements: an actions block, clauses (sometimes included in the action block), rules, and statements. Expert systems also include an inference engine (a program which derives conclusions from facts). It is the processing portion of a knowledge base system and contains the logic for interpreting the rules in order to obtain a conclusion.

Figure 1B illustrates the opening screen of the expert system program VP-Expert. VP-Expert includes the capability to enter a series of IF-THEN propositions (decision rules) that represent the knowledge (expertise) of the knowledge base. Figure 2B illustrates the execution of a VP-Expert consulting session with the decision rules showing.

Figure 3B illustrates how decision rules can be edited in VP-Expert. Figure 4B is a graphical representation of the decision rules. The decision rules illustrated are part of VP-Expert's inference engine. The inference engine is the mechanism that uses the knowledge base and solves problems during use. The inference engine uses blocks that include key words and clauses to define the goals of a consultation and the sequence of their solution. The three elements of a rule are the name, premise (*if/condition*), and conclusion (*then* can include confidence factors).

VP-Expert provides the user with a method of entering decision making rules into the computer, using data stored in databases and spreadsheets, entering additional data from the keyboard and producing a conclusion.

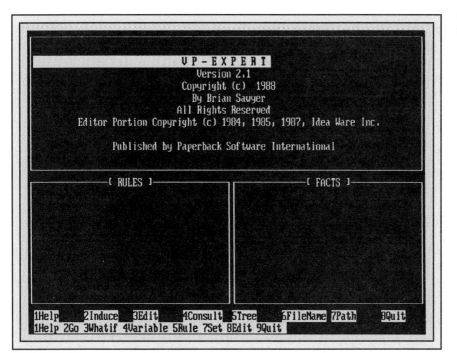

Figure 1B
VP-Expert

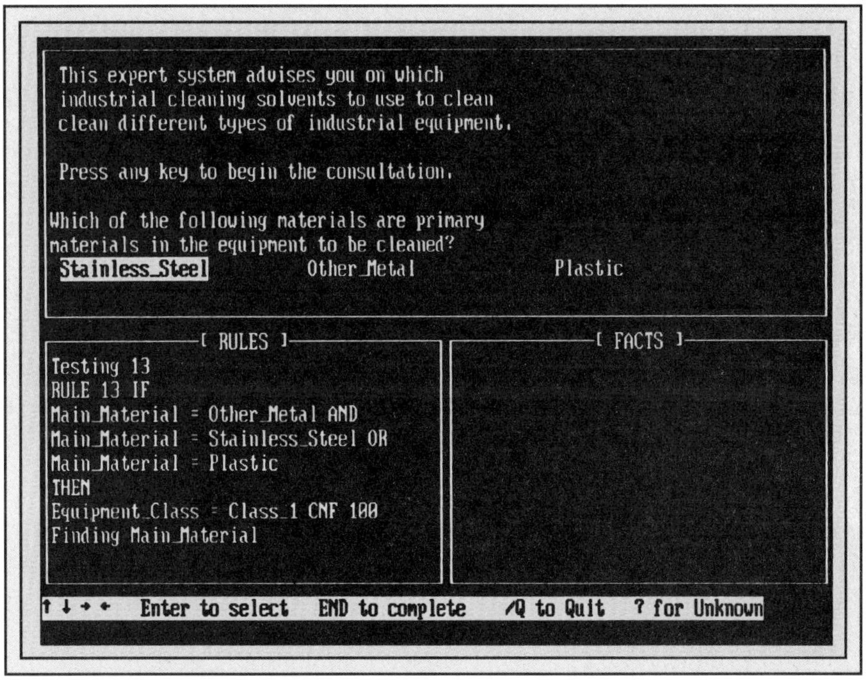

Figure 2B
VP-Expert Decision Rules

Figure 3B
Editing Decision Rules in
VP-Expert

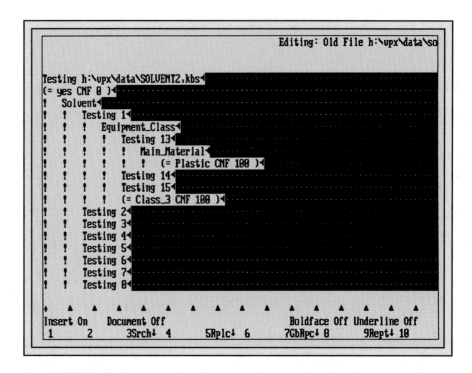

Figure 4B
Graphical Representation of
VP-Expert Decision Rules

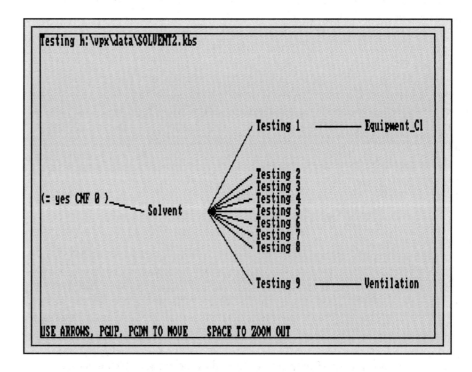

Types of Index Organization

An index is a directory of where records, files, programs, and so on are stored on a disk. The index contains a key to the record and a pointer to either the physical location on the disk or another index. The schemes used for creating an index include binary search methods, hashing, index entry, inverted (keyed) file, sequential (ordered) file, index sequential access method (ISAM), key words, and pointer.

The binary search technique works only on data that is in sequence. It is a technique for locating an item by continuously dividing the file into groups by two. This is a simple but effective method for making a rapid search for data in a file. The B-Tree, inverted B-Tree, and modified B-Tree are variations of the binary search concept.

Hashing is used in multiuser database systems. Hashing is a nonlinear rather than linear algorithm for storing data in and retrieving it quickly from a database. Linear refers to a straight line. Nonlinear is a mathematical relationship that is not a straight line. An algorithm is a sequence of mathematical rules used to obtain a desired result. A nonlinear algorithm is a sequence of mathematical rules based on nonlinear mathematical relationships for obtaining a desired result, the rapid storing and retrieving of data in a multiuser database.

An index entry is an individual line or item of data contained in an index. It is similar to an entry in a dictionary.

An inverted file is a file indexed on characteristics. For example, all individuals on a scout master's list who are trained are given a code to indicate their level of training. Key numbers are maintained to tell the system the meanings of the codes.

A sequential or ordered file is one where the data has been ordered (sorted). Such sorting is slow but necessary for binary searching. When it is necessary to sort on more than one field, individual indexes for each field are often more effective. This is referred to as ISAM, the index sequential access method.

Key words are used to retrieve data from libraries and other databases. A set of key words for searching is entered. The key word list of each record is searched. When a complete match is made, the record is flagged. Key word search is often combined with one of the other indexing schemes above.

The pointer method is a table look-up technique that permits each data set to be stored with an indicator pointing to a list of associated data.

Using BASIC and Other Programs

Program types are often identified by their extensions. Files with the extensions .BAS (BASIC), .COM (command), and .EXE (execute) are programs.

BASIC Programs

Operation of a program file with the .BAS extension requires the use of a BASIC interpreter. Files with .COM and .EXE extensions may be started from the DOS prompt by typing the name of the file (without the extension) and pressing ↵. (.COM files are limited to 64K; .EXE files have no such limit to their size.)

BASIC interpreters are programs which have either a .COM or .EXE extension (Figure 1D). Depending on the brand of computer and operating system used, BASIC interpreters may be named BASIC, BASICA, or GWBASIC.

Usually BASIC is smaller and more limited than BASICA. BASICA's additional features include graphics display and use. In a dual-disk-drive system, the steps required to use a BASIC program are:

1. Start the computer system
2. Make sure you are logged into drive A
3. Locate the disk with BASIC
4. Place the disk in drive A
5. Type and name of the BASIC program and press ↵
6. Locate the disk with the .BAS program on it
7. Place the disk in drive A
8. Type RUN name ↵

Figure 2D illustrates the screen after BASICA.EXE was started by typing BASICA ↵ in a COMPAQ microcomputer. Notice that the program is identified as being specific for COMPAQ equipment. Usually, a BASIC interpreter will only operate on a designated system. Most BASIC programs will operate under many different interpreters without change. However, the

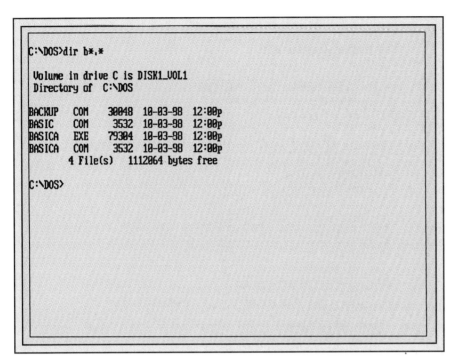

correct hardware to support the program must be present. BASIC programs that use graphics must have a graphic card and BASIC programs that use a printer must have a printer available. In addition, BASIC programs that use new features must have interpreters that support them.

The BASIC instruction files"*.bas ↵ tells the computer to list all files on a disk or in a subdirectory with the .BAS extension. Figure 3D illustrates the use of the files"*.bas ↵ instruction. The command RUN"filename' ↵ is needed to start any of the listed programs.

Figure 4D illustrates the EVALPAC.BAS instruction used to start the program. Notice that the extension is not included in the RUN instruction, and that the second quotation mark is not required. Figure 5D illustrates the screen after pressing ↵. Once the BASIC program is started, the program takes over. The procedure for operating a given program is under the control of the user.

After you have completed a BASIC program and the system is under the control of the BASIC interpreter, typing SYSTEM ↵ terminates BASIC and returns the computer to DOS. Some users will instruct their programs to automatically return the system to DOS.

Other Programs

Any program with the extension .COM or .EXE will execute by typing the file name at the DOS prompt. Figure 6D illustrates a screen after a system with a hard disk has been logged into the disk in disk drive A and the instruction DIR *.COM ↵ was entered. Figure 7D illustrates the screen

Figure 2D
Starting BASICA

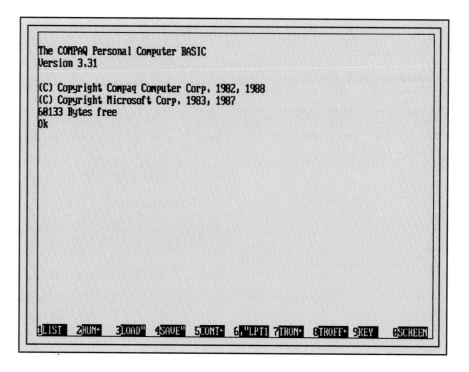

Figure 3D
Listing .BAS Files

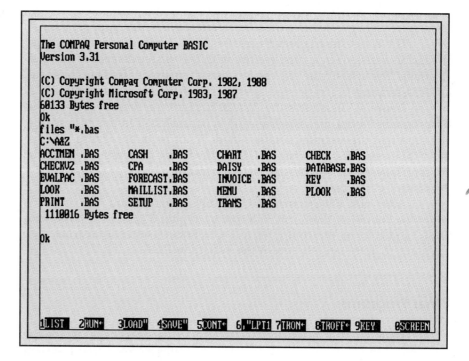

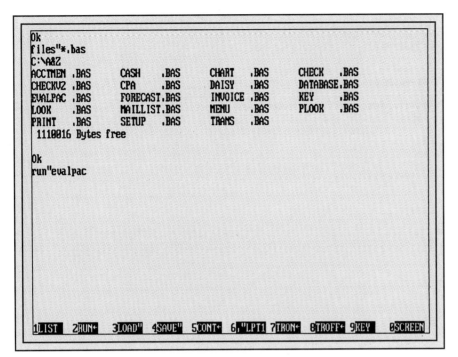

Figure 4D
Starting a BASIC Program

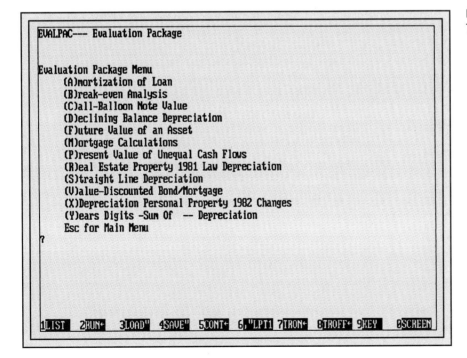

Figure 5D
The Opening Screen

Figure 6D
Directory

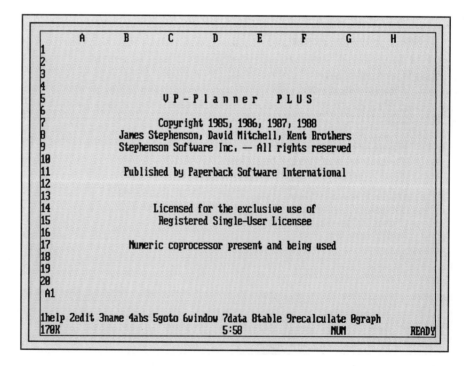

```
A:\>dir *.com

 Volume in drive A has no label
 Directory of  A:\

UPP      COM    63474  5-19-88   2:00a
README   COM      958  5-19-88   2:00a
         2 File(s)    610304 bytes free

A:\>
```

Figure 7D
Starting VP-Planner PLUS

```
       A        B        C        D        E        F        G        H
1
2
3
4
5                      U P - P l a n n e r    P L U S
6
7                   Copyright 1985, 1986, 1987, 1988
8            James Stephenson, David Mitchell, Kent Brothers
9            Stephenson Software Inc. — All rights reserved
10
11               Published by Paperback Software International
12
13
14                  Licensed for the exclusive use of
15                  Registered Single-User Licensee
16
17             Numeric coprocessor present and being used
18
19
20
A1


1help 2edit 3name 4abs 5goto 6window 7data 8table 9recalculate 0graph
170K                             5:58                 NUM          READY
```

after VPP ↵ was typed. The system is under the control of the program after it is started.

README.NOW

On almost all program disk there is a file called READ.ME, README, README.NOW, or something similar. These files contain information about the program(s) on the disk that should be read before using the program. Often, README files contain last minute corrections or changes to documentation or operation. Sometimes they contain warnings to keep the user from making errors. Some software companies also include a program such as README.COM listed on the screen as illustrated in Figure 7D.

Common practice is to create README files as standard ASCII files by typing TYPE README ↵ the contents of the README file may be displayed on the screen. If the size of the README file is greater than a single screen, pressing ∧S (the control key and S at the same time) stops the display. Pressing any key restarts it. Pressing ∧C breaks the action. By typing TYPE README >prn ↵ the output of the README file may be sent to the printer rather than the screen. README files should be examined before using a new program.

.ARC FILES

To save space on a disk, programmers often store their files in a compressed, achieved, format. The extension .ARC is usually used for files in this format. A special program is required to convert the achieved file to programs, documentation files, or data files. Often the required program is provided on the disk with the .ARC files. A README file normally includes instructions on how to convert the .ARC files into a form where they may be used.

Glossary

Absolute referencing (absolute addressing)   In a spreadsheet, the use of a cell or range reference that always refers to the same cell when copied or moved. A dollar sign ($) placed before the column letter and row number, such as A2, is often used to indicate absolute referencing. The term *addressing* is often used in place of *referencing*.

Access method   The scheme used by the operating system to control the communication between workstations in a LAN.

Acoustical coupler   A device that cradles the telephone receiver and connects the computer to a telephone system.

Active cell   The cell into which characters can be entered.

Active window   The window where editing can be performed and where the cursor is located.

Add-in program   A program that is attached to an application program to add capabilities.

Ad hoc   Formed or created as needed, with little or no preplanning.

Algorithm   A set of rules to perform a mathematical operation.

Alphanumeric   Including both characters and numbers.

American Standard Code for Information Interchange (ASCII)   A 7-bit binary code. Numbers from 00 to 127 can be produced with a 7-bit number. The decimal number 90 is 1011010. Each number in ASCII stands for a character or symbol.

Analog device   A device that uses continuous voltage rather than binary codes. These devices are often used to monitor real-world conditions such as temperature, sound, and movement.

Analysis   A comparison of alternate management actions.

Animation   The creation of displays that look like moving objects on the screen.

Answer   A modem setting in asynchronous communication. One partner must answer, and the other must originate.

Area chart   A line graph in which the area under the horizontal line represents a quantity.

Ascender   The part of a letter that extends above a lowercase letter, such as the top of the letter *t*.

Asynchronous communication   Communication that requires timing only when a bit is being transmitted.

Attribute   An inherent characteristic.

AUTOEXEC.BAT   A computer program file that is executed when the system is started.

Automatic originate and answer system   A combination of software and hardware that makes it possible to answer telephone calls and automatically make calls without a human operator.

Backup   A copy of a disk or file.

BACKUP.COM   A MS-DOS/PC DOS utility for making a complete backup of a hard disk.

.BAK   An extension of a backup file. This file contains the duplicate of an original file.

Bar chart   A chart that compares parts of the whole using bars. Bar charts may be horizontal, vertical, stacked, grouped, or three-dimensional.

Bar code reader   A device that reads the codes associated with bars.

Bar-line (combination) chart   A bar and line chart using a common x scale.

Baseband   A channel used for direct transmission of pulses over short distances (less than 10 miles) without the use of special cables.

Baseline   The line on which the main body of a letter sits.

.BAT   An extension of a batch program file. The file contains disk operating system instructions. This file can be executed by typing its name and pressing ⏎.

Batch run   A scheduling system requiring that computer tasks be collected and given to a controller, which then runs them batched together as a single job.

Baud   A unit of measure that usually refers to the transmission rate. For example, 1,200 baud is 120 characters per second.

Binary file   Programs stored in machine language form using 0s and 1s. A binary file can be directly executed by the microcomputer.

Binary number   A number consisting of 0 and 1. Each 0 or 1 is a bit. The decimal numbers 0 to 126 require 7 bits. Adding the decimal numbers 127 to 255 requires the eighth bit.

Bit   The smallest component in binary code. A bit is a single binary digit (0 or 1). The microcomputer uses a binary number system consisting of 0 and 1.

Bitmapped font   A font created using dots like those used in raster graphics.

Block   A collection of text defined by a marker at the beginning and end.

Bold   A term that describes letters printed in a darker font and often displayed on the screen in a special shade or color.

Bootstrap program   A program (set of instructions) used to load the operating system from disk to RAM when the system is started.

Box draw   The capability to draw, display, and print boxes.

Bridge   Hardware and software used to match circuits to one another to minimize transmission problems (impairments) between networks.

Broadband   A channel with a wide bandwidth (greater than voice-grade width) using special cables.

Bus   A pathway or channel for data and instructions between hardware devices.

Byte   A sequence of 8 binary digits (bits) taken as a unit.

Cap height   The height of a capital letter.

Carrier sense multiple access/collision detect (CSMA/CD)   A protocol that operates a LAN in a way similar to a party line telephone system. The line is checked by the workstation's program to see if it is being used. If it is not, transmission proceeds.

Cathode ray tube (CRT)   A computer monitor.

Cell   The column and row intersection of a spreadsheet screen.

Cell copying Replicating (copying) the contents of cells from one range to another.

Cell counting The capability to define a group of cells and count (in a range) the number of data points that fall into each cell.

Cell pointer The display that indicates which cell is the active cell.

Central file server A hardware and software system that controls the access to files by individuals using a network.

Central file server program A program that controls the access to files by individual workstations in a network.

Central processing unit (CPU) A silicon chip that includes the arithmetic, logic, control, and memory units.

Central switching station The central microcomputer connected to a series of stations in a LAN. This type of topology is often called a *star*.

Character size The number of bits per character.

Clip art library A collection of images that is provided with image creation programs that can be recalled and used to create new illustrations.

Code The use of symbols or numbers to represent letters, numbers, or special meanings.

Cold boot The starting of a microcomputer operating system by turning the microcomputer on.

Collector An interface that collects messages from a number of devices, organizes the messages, and then forwards them to the central computer.

Column A vertical division of a screen and spreadsheet.

.COM An extension for a command program file. This file can be executed by typing its name and pressing ⏎.

Communication The transfer of data, computer instructions, or both from one computer to another or to peripherals.

Communication bus A LAN layout around a bus that serves as a channel of communication.

Communication circle, communication ring A layout of LAN topology where the stations are connected in a circle or ring.

Communication hardware Serial and parallel computer ports, devices that connect the computer to a telephone, special cables, and devices to connect computers to networks.

Communication parameters   A setting that must be agreed upon in order to establish communication.

Communication software   Programs (with the addition of communication hardware) that help users create/correct/edit, communicate/transfer between devices, and save/retrieve files.

Compatibility   The capability of microcomputers to work together as a system and to exchange physical parts.

Compressed print   Printing with approximately 17 characters per inch rather than the standard 10 or 12.

Computer-aided design (CAD)   Vector draw programs with the capability to produce drawings for machine parts and other products. The design tools are the dominate feature.

Computer-aided design and drafting (CADD)   Vector draw programs with the capability to produce drawings for machine parts and other products. There is a balance between design and drafting tools.

Computer graphics metrafile (CGM)   A graphics file used for the transfer of graphics to some word processing programs.

Computer network   A number of connected computers that can share the devices connected to them.

Computer virus   A program introduced into a computer as a joke or to damage the operation of the computer.

Configuration   The matching of hardware, software, and operating system settings so that all the parts work with, and communicate with, all the other parts of a system.

CONFIG.SYS   A MS-DOS/PC DOS file that contains data used by the operating system to set up the system environment.

Configure   To tell the software the exact hardware capabilities available.

Controller board   A PC board that controls specific devices.

Copy   To duplicate an image of a block at a new location.

COPY   A MS-DOS/PC DOS function for copying the files on one disk another or for copying one file to a second file using a new name.

Copy protected (program)   A term used to describe a program sold with a limit placed on the number of copies a user may produce.

<CR>   An instruction telling the user to press the Return or Enter key.

Creating   The initial entry of characters into a text or word processing program file using a word processing program.

Cursor   A symbol on the monitor that indicates where an action (such as drawing a line) will be started or where text will be typed. The cursor is often a dot (.), a line (—), or a box. It may be steady or blinking.

Cut and paste   The combining of text and graphics from a number of sources.

Data   Facts stored in a database.

Data analysis   Techniques for the evaluation of ranges of data.

Database   A collection of data saved in microcomputer memory and used for one or more purposes. A database usually consists of a number of data files.

Database management program   A program to create/edit (update) input format data structure, data, and output format; to process data; to save/retrieve data saved in one or more files; and to print reports.

Data-driven graphics program   A program to create/edit/format area, bar, high-low, line, and similar types of graphs; to save/retrieve data; and to print results on a printer or plotter.

Data file   A collection of related data.

Data file transfer software   A program designed to read data in the format produced by one program and change them to a format needed by a second program.

Data handling   The use of the database functions included in many spreadsheet programs.

Data Interchange Format (DIF)   A standard ASCII file format for transferring data between spreadsheet programs.

Data structure   The number of fields in a record, the size of each field, and the number of records in a file. The number of records per file may or may not have a limit.

Default   The original settings for line spacing, formatting, and so on.

Default drive   The disk drive from which data and programs are read unless the microcomputer is instructed otherwise. The default drive is the logged drive if no additional instructions are given.

Delete   An instruction to remove a character, a collection of characters, or a file. When characters are removed, the text closes up.

Descender   The part of a letter that extends below the baseline, such as the bottom part of the letter *y*.

Design architecture   The design philosophy used to create a specific microcomputer.

Desktop microcomputer   A microcomputer that has the greatest capabilities and most expansion room; it requires a part of a desk for its work.

Desktop publishing   The creation of a quality document using the microcomputer and specialized page composition software.

Desktop publishing software   Programs that help users create/edit/transfer, format/integrate text and graphics, save/retrieve, and print/typeset output on a quality output device.

DIP switch   A series of toggle switches mounted on a dual in-line package (DIP), which is in turn mounted on a PC board. The switches are used for system configuration.

DIR   The MS-DOS/PC DOS instruction that tells the operating system display a listing of the files on a disk.

Direct connect modem   A modem that is connected into the telephone lines.

DISKCOPY.COM   A MS-DOS/PC DOS utility used to make a copy of a disk.

Dithering   A method of representing gray tones through the use of areas of dots with varying densities.

Documentation   Narrative supplied with programs to help the user operate the software.

Dot-matrix printer   A printer that uses small pins to make marks on paper to form text and graphics.

Downloading   Transferring data from another computer into the user's computer.

Downward compatible   For new hardware or software, having the capability of working with old hardware or software.

Dual in-line package (DIP)   A housing to hold a chip or other items to a PC board.

Dual scales chart   A line or bar chart with two y scales.

Dumb terminal   A terminal that can communicate only under the control of an individual.

Duplex   A communication protocol.

Editing   Changing the characters in a text or word processing program file using the capabilities of a word processing program.

Electronic bulletin board   A computer with software that acts as a host to a variety of computers. The system allows users to call up (using telephone lines and modems) and use libraries, mail, and other services on an ad hoc basis.

Electronic library   Computer-stored data that are similar to those maintained by a manual library and that can be searched electronically for information.

Emulate   To act like.

Emulation   For hardware or software, the capability to permit one device to act like another device.

Emulator   Software and hardware that give the computer the capability to act like a special-purpose terminal.

Encapsulated PostScript (EPS)   A graphics file using the PostScript language format.

Endnote   Text placed at the end of a document.

Entity   Something that has a separate and distinct existence.

Erase (delete)   To remove a marked block or character.

.EXE   An extension for an execute program file. This file can be executed by typing its name and pressing ↵.

Extended Binary Coded Decimal Interchange Code (EBCDIC)   The standard code developed and used by IBM for its mainframe computers. It is a binary code made up of 8 bits that allows 256 characters.

Extended Industry Standard Architecture (EISA)   A design architecture built around an internal communication system that speeds operation and reduces the problems associated with communication with host computers. EISA motherboards accept expansion boards used in Industrial Standard Architecture (ISA) motherboards.

Extension   In MS-DOS/PC DOS, a three-character addition to a file name to indicate the file type.

Facsimile (FAX) machine   A machine that transmits a copy of a document from one location to another, usually over telephone lines. There are PC boards available that allow a computer to act as a FAX machine.

Fact   Something having real, demonstrable existence.

Feasible   Able to be accomplished.

Field   A unit of data about an attribute of an entity.

File   A collection of related data or program code.

File linkage   The dynamic joining (linkage) of two files. Whenever the second file is used, the latest version of the sending file is transferred.

File management program   A program to create/edit (update), save/retrieve, process data saved in a single file, and print reports.

File management report generator program   A program to create/edit (update), save/retrieve, process data saved in a single file, and to print reports.

File transfer   The movement of a computer file from one application to another. Changing the text in the original program after a transfer has no effect on the second program.

File transfer program   A program with the capability of reading the code for one type of graphics file and then writing the code for another. An algorithm is used to make the transformation.

5¼-inch floppy disk drive   A disk drive that reads and writes computer data on a 5¼-inch disk covered with a paperlike cover.

Floppy disk   A plastic circle with a coating of magnetic material that rotates within an outer sleeve.

Font   The size and shape of a character set.

Footer   Text placed at the bottom of a printed page in a document.

Format   To control the display and printer output.

FORMAT.COM   A program that tells the microcomputer to prepare a disk for use. Magnetic marks are made on the media to identify tracks and sectors where data are to be stored.

Formatting code   A code placed in a word processing file to instruct the printer to change fonts, spacing, and so on.

Formed-character printer   A printer that uses a thimble, ball, or daisy wheel to produce characters.

Formula   A rule defining the relationship between numbers to achieve a numerical value (outcome). Spreadsheet program formulas use cell references as their source of numbers.

Free-format database A database that combines different types of data structures, such as text, lists, tables, charts, and graphs.

Full duplex A term used to describe communication where both partners can send or receive.

Full-screen editing The capability to move the cursor anyplace on the computer screen and make changes.

Function key A computer keyboard key labeled `F1`, `F2`, and so on.

Function (operating system) A routine that is part of the operating system. These routines provide the user with the capability to perform often-needed tasks. Functions are loaded into RAM with the operating system and remain there.

Gateway Hardware and software that connect networks using different protocols.

Graphical user interface (GUI) A user interface that uses the graphics display capabilities of a computer.

Graphic metrafile (GMF) A graphics file used for the transfer of graphics to some word processing programs.

Graphics integrating routine A routine that integrates the output of graphics with text.

Graphics screen A bit image pattern on a screen that is controlled by a bit image pattern saved in the computer memory.

Graphics screen capture routine A routine that can be used to capture a computer graphics screen display and then save it as a file. Most screen capture routines are part of TSR programs.

Gray tone One of a continuous series of colors from black to white.

Half duplex A term used to describe communication where one partner can send and the other, receive.

Half height The space available for a disk drive that is equal to half the height of the original IBM PC disk drives.

Halftone A display that uses dots of different sizes to simulate gray tones.

Hand scanner A small device that can be held in the hand and moved across text or graphics.

Hard copy Printed copy on paper of a file.

Hard disk   A high-capacity data storage device that may be fixed or removable.

Hard hyphen   A dash that is always used by the word processor wherever one is placed.

Hard space   A space that does not allow two words to be separated at the end of a line.

Hardware   The part of a microcomputer that can be seen and felt.

Header   Text placed on the top of a printed page in a document.

Hewlett-Packard Graphic Language (HPGL)   A graphics language file used for printing to plotters, CAD drawing, and desktop publishing.

Hierarchical database   A database organized from the top down.

Hierarchical file structure   A file structure consisting of a top-down organization. Files are organized in what is often referred to as a tree structure. Some operating systems allow sophisticated security to be established for hierarchical files.

Hierarchy   The classification or grading of a group or set from high to low.

High bit   The eighth bit in a binary number. High-bit numbers are the decimal numbers from 127 to 255.

High-low chart   A line graph showing the high, low, open, and closing values of a stock over time.

High-low volume chart   A high-low chart and a bar chart using the same time scale.

Hot keys   The key combination that calls a TSR program.

Icon   A symbol that represents choices in a screen menu.

Idea   The recognition of a need or opportunity.

Image-driven graphics program   A program that helps the user create/edit/capture/transfer images, save/retrieve, print, and integrate images with text.

Implementation   Putting a method or microcomputer to work.

Index generator   A routine that creates an index with page numbers.

Indexing scheme   A method of creating a directory of where records and files can be found.

Industrial Standard Architecture (ISA)   The original open architecture design of the IBM PC.

Information   Data that have been processed and recalled from a database in an organized manner.

Ink-jet printer   A printer that uses dots of ink to produce text and graphics.

Input device   A device connected to the microcomputer through which data and instructions are entered.

Input/output (I/O)   Input and output devices or methods for transferring data or network communication.

Input/output (I/O) port   A connection found on most computers that connects the computer to printers, plotters, and communication devices.

Insert   The mode in which a character typed into existing text causes the following text to move right to make room.

Instruction set   Instructions built into the computer. The instruction set is contained in the microprocessor.

Integrated program   A program that combines several different types of programs, such as word processing, spreadsheet, data-driven graphics, and database programs.

Italic   A font type that resembles handwriting (script); however, the characters are not joined.

Justification   A text-formatting control of the right margin. The margin may be ragged (not lined up), even (right justified), or centered (words located evenly between margins).

Justified   Lined up. *Left justified* means lined up evenly on the left side, and *right justified* means lined up evenly on the right.

Kerning   Fitting two letters together such that they look just as close together as other members of the character set.

<Key> + <key>   A computer instruction telling the user to hold down the first key (usually the `<Alt>`, `<Ctrl>`, or `<Shift>` key) and then press the second key. The instruction `<key> − <key>` is an alternate method of giving the instruction.

Knowledge   The assignment of meaning to information by a human being.

Label   A word that identifies columns, rows, or overall titles in a spreadsheet.

Landscape mode   Printing (on paper) with the width wider than the height.

Laptop microcomputer   A computer that fits easily on a lap or inside a briefcase; has its own power supply (battery); and offers full functions, including a hard disk drive. Most laptop microcomputers have AC adapters that can run the unit and that can be used to recharge the battery.

Laser printer   A printer that uses light and an electrostatically controlled toner (ink) to produce characters and graphics on paper.

Leading   The distance between two lines of type, measured from baseline to baseline or from cap height to cap height.

Level   A division or part of a plan.

Limitation   A restriction that inhibits the ability to make decisions.

Line draw   The capability to display and print lines.

Line printer   A printer that receives a line of instructions and then prints the line.

Line/xy chart   A chart that shows the behavior between two variables. A line chart requires even divisions of the x scale, whereas the xy chart performs scaling.

Load   To transfer a program from disk to RAM.

Local area network (LAN)   A series of computers in a local area that are connected and share peripherals, files, programs, and computer capabilities.

Local area network (LAN) topology   The relative physical and logical arrangement of stations in a network.

Logged drive   The disk drive from which data and programs are read.

Logical function   A conditional statement that evaluates a condition in the form of an equation.

Macro   A set of commands and keystrokes to perform a task. Macros can be created by the user and stored for future use.

Math co-processor   A chip that reduces the amount of time required to perform mathematical operations.

Mathematical operator   A symbol that indicates a mathematical process such as power ($\wedge$), multiplication (*), division (/), addition ($+$), and subtraction ($-$).

Mathematical precedence   The order in which mathematical operations are executed. The standard order is parentheses, power, multiplication and division, and addition and subtraction.

Measurable   Able to be quantified.

Menu   A list of microcomputer actions displayed on the screen from which the user selects the one wanted.

Metropolitan area network (MAN)   A series of computers in a fairly small geographical area that are connected and share peripherals, files, programs, and computer capabilities.

Microchannel architecture (MCA)   A design architecture built around an internal communication system that speeds operation and reduces the problems associated with communication with host computers.

Micromanager   A manager in charge of purchasing and controlling microcomputer equipment in an organization.

Microprocessor   An integrated circuit on a silicon chip that is the central processing unit (CPU).

Milestone   An event that can be easily identified. It completes a part of a plan.

Mode   Manner of operations. The mode determines the optional actions available to the spreadsheet program user.

MODE.COM   A MS-DOS/PC DOS utility to change printer ports, serial communication parameters, screen displays, and printer time-out duration.

Modem   A device to connect a microcomputer to a telephone. Modems change binary code to a signal that can be sent over the telephone lines.

Modular programs   Programs designed to work together and that can be purchased separately.

Monitor   A television-like device for displaying the output of computers.

Motherboard   A PC board containing the microprocessor, computer memory, and selected controller circuits to direct the signals that are received from external connectors.

Move   To relocate a block.

Multitasking   The capability to instruct the microcomputer to perform more than one task at a time.

Multiuser database   A database that allows more than a single user access to the database at the same time.

Multiusing The capability of microcomputers and programs to allow more than one user to share the same microprocessor.

Network Telecommunication pathways between computers, terminals, and the host computer. A network may contain a mixture of forms of communication channels.

Network database A hierarchical database with the additional capability of allowing multiple relationships at different levels.

Nonprocedural language A programming language that does not require programming techniques to be used. It allows the user to send instructions to the computer in English-like statements.

Null-modem A method of wiring serial communication cables to allow two computers to communicate as if they were connected to modems and a telephone.

Number A mathematical value.

Objective A goal that is feasible, is measurable, has a time limit, has recognized limitations, and has a plan for its accomplishment.

Off-line Independent from the microcomputer operation of a device.

On-line Operated at the same time as other equipment under the control of the microprocessor.

On-line storage device A device containing memory available to the microcomputer through communication cables.

On-line storage media Material used to store microcomputer files.

Operating system The program that controls the printers, monitors, disk drives, and hard disk drives connected to a central processing unit so that they work together.

Operating system convention A standard and accepted abbreviation or symbol with its meaning, for users of microcomputer operating systems.

Operating system shell A program that takes over the disk operating system, adds capabilities (multitasking and file transfer between two programs operating concurrently), and controls the operation of application programs.

Operating system windows The operating system capability to divide the screen into parts.

Operational compatibility The capability of microcomputers to work together as a system.

Optical character recognition (OCR) The ability of a program to read the characters represented by graphic images.

Optical character recognition (OCR) program A program that can be used to input a graphics file and output the text code associated with the graphic images, if any.

Option A choice.

Originate A modem setting in asynchronous communication. One partner must originate, and the other must answer.

Outline font A font created using point + direction + distance, as in vector graphics. It is easy to change the size of outline fonts.

Outline program A program that allows the user to enter information in any order and then helps in the organization of the concepts and text.

Output device A device connected to the microcomputer through which data and instructions are communicated to users or to other devices.

Overwrite The mode in which a character typed replaces the character formerly at the location of the cursor. Some word processors use the term *typeover* rather than *overwrite*.

Page break A code entered into a word processing file to tell the printer to feed a sheet of paper. Often a line will be drawn across the screen to indicate the page break location to the user.

Page control language (PCL) Hewlett-Packard's language for defining a page.

Page description language (PDL) Adobe's PostScript language for defining a page.

Page layout The arrangement of text and graphics on a page for printing.

Page layout language A language that defines the entire bit image of a page and then sends the code to a printer.

Page layout program A program that helps the user lay out a page for printing. Usually text and graphics are imported from other programs and then combined in a page layout program.

Page preview A display on the screen of exactly what is sent to the printer, including unusual fonts and graphics.

Parallel A communication method that transmits data along a number of parallel paths (wires) at one time.

Parameter A variable value. Parameters are values that must be set before communications can occur.

Parity bit An error-checking bit.

Peripheral A device such as a printer, bar code reader, or modem connected to a microcomputer to give it special capabilities.

Physical compatibility The capability to exchange physical parts between computer systems.

.PIC A graphics file created in Lotus 1-2-3 and some other spreadsheet programs. The .PIC extension is used by some image-driven graphics programs and is not usually compatible with other Lotus files.

Pie chart A chart that compares parts to the whole using a circle; it may be exploded and three-dimensional.

Pie-column (combination) chart A pie and column chart showing parts of a whole and parts of a part in a single bar.

Pitch The number of type font characters per inch.

Pixel A picture element; screen dots used to create letters and graphics.

Plan A series of steps detailing what must be done to move from where one is to where one wants to go.

Platform scanner A device into which a text or similar material can be placed and then scanned.

Plotter A device that uses pens to produce text and graphics on paper.

Pocket computer A computer that fits in a pocket.

Point A unit of measurement often used for fonts; 72 points equals 1 inch.

Pointing device An input device that moves the screen cursor in a manner similar to the arrow keys. It usually includes keys that duplicate the function of the arrow, <Esc>, and ↵ keys.

Point-to-point local area network (LAN) A layout of LAN topology where each station is connected directly to other stations.

Port A plug on a computer that allows the user to connect cables for communication to peripherals and other computers.

Portrait mode The normal way a sheet of paper is printed. The width is narrower than the height.

Printed circuit (PC) board   A flat piece of material with circuits (electronic connections) printed on it plus electronic components to add special capabilities to a microcomputer.

Printer   A device for producing text and graphics on paper.

Printer driver   Software that allows a given program to send output to a specified printer.

Productivity   Output divided by input.

Program   A set of instructions telling the computer how to perform a task.

Programming language   A language used by programmers to create/edit and save/retrieve instructions to computers.

Proportional spacing   Characters spaced according to the form and size of each individual letter.

Protected cell   A cell that has been protected from change by the spreadsheet designer. It is good practice to protect the cells with labels when a standard form is created.

Protocol   The relationship between equivalent parts of a network.

Public domain program   A program available for use without cost except for distribution and copying costs. Usually no support or updates are available for public domain programs.

Radar chart   A 360-degree-axis chart that displays data in polar coordinates (angle versus radius).

Random access memory (RAM)   Memory used for data and program storage by the user. The user can write and read data in RAM.

Range (of cells)   Cells in a spreadsheet identified by the specification of the cells in the upper left and lower right positions. For example, the range A5..C7 identifies the cells A5, A6, A7, B5, B6, B7, C5, C6, and C7.

Range name   The name given to a range of cells.

Raster   A program that saves images as a series of on/off dots.

Read-only memory (ROM)   Memory with instructions (programs) needed when operating the microcomputer. The user cannot write data into ROM.

Real time   Computer execution as an event occurs; the transmission of text as it is typed.

Record   A collection of data about an entity.

Reformatting   The re-display of the screen text around the characters that were changed or deleted.

Regression analysis   A procedure for fitting a line or curve to a data set and calculating statistical information about the relationship between the line and the data set.

Relational database   A database that organizes data into files as arrays of rows (records) and columns (fields) and that includes at least one field that is keyed into at least one other file.

Relative referencing   A cell or range reference that refers to a cell that is a set number of columns and rows away in a specified direction. When the formula in a cell is moved or copied, the relative references are changed to maintain their relative positions.

Report generator   A program that creates a formatted report to output information from a database.

↵   A computer instruction telling the user to press the return or enter key.

Retrieving   The loading or recalling of a file from disk or other storage media into computer memory.

Routine   A part of a computer program that performs a specific task.

Row   A horizontal division of screen and spreadsheet.

Ruler   A line on the screen with marks to indicate locations.

Sans serif   Without lines embellishing the ends of a letter.

Save   To record a data or program file on disk or other recording media.

Scan   The use of a device for sensing printed material (text and graphics) or images and entering them into a computer system.

Scanner   A device for sensing printed material (text and graphics) or images and entering them into a computer system.

Scatter diagram   A line chart with only points plotted; may be two- or three-dimensional.

Screen data capture   The capability to capture data from a screen display and transfer them into a second program or save them as a file.

Scroll To display different parts of a word processing program file on the screen. Generally, text is moved up or down to display text that cannot be shown on the monitor at one time.

Search To locate a specific group of characters.

Search and replace To locate a specific group of characters and replace it with another group.

Sector A division of a track on a disk.

Sensitivity analysis The determination of how fast an output variable changes for a given change in an input variable.

Serial A communication method that transmits data one bit after another.

Serif Any of the lines embellishing the ends of a letter.

Shareware A program available for review at no cost except for distribution and copying costs. If the user decides to keep and use the program, a small registration fee paid directly to the programmer is expected. The user is often provided with support and updates when the registration fee is paid.

Slant The tilt or rotation of a character.

Smart terminal A terminal that can transfer files between computers.

Soft hyphen A dash that is used by the word processor only when needed at the end of a line for a word break.

Software Programs.

SORT.EXE A MS-DOS/PC DOS utility to sort lists.

Spelling checker A routine that helps the user correct the spelling of text in a file.

Spreadsheet A method for organizing, calculating, and presenting numeric data for decision making.

Spreadsheet (electronic) A model form or template consisting of labels and values; sometimes called a *worksheet*.

Spreadsheet program A program that helps users enter/edit, save/retrieve, calculate, and present results of numeric operations.

Start bit The bit that tells a computer that a character is being sent from another computer.

Step chart   A chart that shows the behavior between two variables as a series of incremental changes.

Stop bit   The bit that tells a computer that the character being sent from another computer is complete.

Storing   Saving a file.

String   A contiguous set of characters treated as a unit. It is a series of characters, including blanks.

Style checker   A program that helps correct grammar and style problems.

Symbol   A saved image; may be used to represent a menu selection on the screen.

Symbolic Link (SYLK)   A standard file format for transferring data between spreadsheet programs.

Synchronous communication   Communicating that requires continuous timing.

Syntax   The manner in which a code must be put together for the computer to understand, including spelling.

Tab   A mark on the ruler line to indicate cursor movement when the <Tab> key is pressed.

Table of contents routine   A routine that automatically adds page numbers to a table of contents.

Tagged image file format (TIFF)   A graphics file carrying gray scale information.

Template   A complete spreadsheet or other model saved on disk to be recalled into a spreadsheet or other program as a pattern for future applications. Templates can be created by a user, purchased on disk, or copied out of books for many applications.

Terminal   A computer input/output device. It may consist of a keyboard and a monitor or may be a microcomputer.

Terminate and stay resident (TSR)   A term describing a program that is loaded into memory and remains in memory while other programs are loaded and used. A TSR program, once loaded, can be recalled using a series of keys while some other program is run.

Text   Characters found on paper or the screen, or stored in a microcomputer text file. Text may be a letter or a manuscript-length book.

Text chart   A display using words rather than images.

Text editor   Software that makes creating, editing, formatting, saving, and retrieving of text in a file possible.

Text file   A computer file that contains words and characters. Such files are commonly created during word processing.

Text screen   Characters on a screen controlled by ASCII code numbers saved in computer memory.

Text shell   A user interface that uses the text display capabilities of the computer.

Thermal printer   A printer that uses a heating element and either heat-sensitive paper or heat-sensitive ribbons to produce text and graphics on paper.

Thesaurus program   A program that helps the user find alternative words.

3½-inch disk drive   A disk drive that reads and writes computer data on a 3½-inch disk covered with a hard plastic shell.

Time limit   A specified date by which an event must occur.

Time-sharing   The capability of having more than one terminal connected to, and operated at one time by, the same computer.

Token passing   A transmission method used in circle networks. Each station checks to see if a given transmission is for itself, and if it is not, the station passes the message along to the next station.

Tool box   The set of capabilities that make it easy for the user to manipulate and use arcs and circles, curves, lines and boxes, paint (color and cross-hatching), points, text, area identification, move, copy, delete, enlarge-shrink, zoom, rotate, and invert.

Track   A magnetic circle on a disk for storing data.

Transportable microcomputer   A portable microcomputer that is packaged with most of the features of a desktop (including a monitor) and that requires the use of electrical power.

TYPE   MS-DOS/PC DOS instruction to display a file on the screen.

Typeface   A set of similar characters that are available in a variety of sizes.

Underlined   A term used to describe letters printed with a line under them and often displayed on the screen in a special shade or color.

Undo   The capability to back up a step and eliminate a change, returning to the old version of the spreadsheet.

Uploading   Transferring data from the user's computer to another computer.

Upward compatible   For old hardware or software, capable of working with new hardware or software.

Utility   An external program available on the disk with the operating system. Utilities often include programs that support the operation of the operating system by adding capabilities.

Value   The number appearing in a cell as the result of entering a formula or a number.

Vector   A program that saves images using mathematical formulas, including the starting location, direction, and distance of each line.

Video display tube (VDT)   A computer monitor.

Virtual screen   The creation of a large video display in the RAM of the computer. The physical screen is a display of a part of the virtual screen.

Voice recognition device   A device that can understand human speech.

Warm boot   The restarting of the microcomputer operating system while the microcomputer is running.

Warning message   A warning displayed on the screen to tell users about a potential problem.

"What if?" investigation   The study of the changes in the values of an important output variable or variables as the values of a selected input or inputs are changed.

Wide area network (WAN)   A series of computers in a large geographical area that are connected and share peripherals, files, programs, and computer capabilities.

Window   A division of a screen into parts so that different documents or different parts of the same document can be displayed at once.

.WK*   An extension for Lotus 1-2-3 spreadsheet files. The * is a wild card, meaning that a number of different characters will appear in this position.

Word processing program   A program used to create, edit, and format text; save and retrieve files to and from a disk; display results on the screen; and print results on a printer.

Word processing program file   A file that contains text, text and graphics, or text and references to graphics files.

Word size   The number of bits a microprocessor can handle at a time. In communications, word size is the number of bits per character.

Word wrap   The moving of the last word in a line to the next line below when there is no room between margins.

WYSIWYG   The screen formatting in which what you see (on the screen) is what you get (out of your printer).

X-height   The height of a lowercase letter without descenders or ascenders.

Zoom   To move out for an overall view or move into a small portion of an image for an enlarged view of a small area.

Index